T0210112

Married 2 Destiny

A Memoir

KENDRA JOHNSON

authorHOUSE

AuthorHouse™
1663 Liberty Drive
Bloomington, IN 47403
www.authorhouse.com
Phone: 1 (800) 839-8640

Published by AuthorHouse 03/31/2020

ISBN: 978-1-7283-4539-0 (sc)
ISBN: 978-1-7283-4537-6 (hc)
ISBN: 978-1-7283-4538-3 (e)

Library of Congress Control Number: 2020902635

Print information available on the last page.

This book is printed on acid-free paper.

Dedication

As I sit here with the tough task of finishing the book alone that we started together, I want to cry but refuse to. Instead, I choose to focus on the time we had. We were goofy. We had fun. We laughed so hard. We had random dance parties with just me and you. We didn't need an audience to be ourselves. We cried together. We worked hard together. We played even harder together.

I'm the risk-taker, the thrill seeker, the live out loud type-A personality. You were the usually calm, still voice; the calm to my storm. You were my balance. You were my biggest encourager, and I was yours. You adored me and made sure that I and everyone else knew it daily. You wanted the best for me. You never betrayed my trust. You, my guy, were special.

We had some of the dumbest arguments, dumb enough to make me giggle. There was a song that came out some years ago that talked about not worrying because as long as we're together, we're cool. I Googled the lyrics to the song and read them out loud to you while we were on our way home from a date night. I told you that I thought the song sounded nice, but some of the lyrics were crazy. The lyrics were saying that we don't have to worry about food, we can get full off of love and we can be broke, as long as we've got each other. I told you that I get what he's saying but let's not take this too far. You actually got mad at me because you said I was too focused on money. I got offended and told you that we're not going to be cool if we're broke because security means a lot to me. We argued for two days off this foolery, all to come to an agreement at the end that money and security is important in a relationship. Really? In my mind, I was thinking that if you had just heard me out the first time, we would've had a great ending to our date night.

Another time was when we got into an argument about Dana having a boyfriend at sixteen. I thought that she would be able to handle herself as a young lady because we did a decent job instilling in her what she needed to do so. You, on the other hand, was all about remembering the boy you were at sixteen. You were firm on the fact that you didn't want her to date anyone until she was an adult. Although I understood your plight, how realistic was that Mr. Johnson? You actually raised your voice at me because I felt that you were being a bit over-protective, but I'm sure the look on my face told you that you were going too far. After arguing for about an hour on this same subject, I had to walk away because we were doing too much. The next day, you told Dana that you were O.K. with her having a boyfriend at sixteen as if you had never disagreed with the notion. I looked at you as the two of you were talking and wanted to punch you. How are you sitting here talking to her all calm about it when you just yelled at me about it yesterday? Then, once she walked away after your talk, you looked at me and broke out in laughter. I couldn't do anything but laugh at you. Ugh! You got on my nerves sometimes.

My biggest pet peeve was when I'd tell you something and you'd brush it off. Then, someone else would tell you exactly what I said, and you'd act like it was the biggest and best idea ever. I remember giving you a business idea. I sat there and broke it down to the details for you. You told me it was a good idea in the most casual way and never spoke of it again. About three months later, someone told you the same thing I told you. You came home and regurgitated what they said, which was exactly what I said and acted like it was the next best thing to shoestrings. That junk irked me to my core. The look on my face said it all and you caught on quick, causing you to laugh hysterically while I was sitting there staring at you in pure disgust. Again, once it was all over, I couldn't do anything but laugh with you.

Growing up together was great. We made plans of how we were going to travel in the RV with our future grandkids. We talked about home improvement projects. We were going to start taking overseas vacations. You were supposed to take me to the beach with jet black sand, remember? We witnessed each other mature in ways unimaginable. People wouldn't believe some of the things we've been through. No one knows everything except you and me. And that's why it was just you and me.

Twenty-three years together weren't enough. Eighteen years, six months, two weeks and three days married weren't enough either. Never in a lifetime did I ever think that at this age, I'd have to face this world without my life partner. I love and miss everything about us. I love and miss everything about you. This is dedicated to you Tyrone D. Johnson, Sr. As this book closes and another is opened in my life, I just want you to know that I'll never, in a million years, forget you, nor will I ever "drop my end". See you later my best friend, lover, and life partner.

I'll always love you,
Kendra

In the Beginning

E very year at W.H. Kirk Junior High School, the promoted eighth grade class would go to Cedar Point for the end of the year trip. Ever heard of Cedar Point? It's the roller capital of the world! It was one of Ty's and my favorite places to go and have fun, even as we got older. Anyway, I was hugged up in a corner with a boy who was on the trip. We were waiting to board the Disaster Transport ride when I felt someone staring at me. Out the corner of my eye, I noticed him. He was a skinny, dark skinned kid with a big head, big pretty eyes, and a nice smile. But why is he staring at me all creepily? Me and the boy I was "being fast" with boarded the ride and left the creepy staring guy behind. But I noticed after the ride that everywhere I went, it seemed as if he would randomly show up. It was so weird.

After the Cedar Point trip was our promotion to high school. We were all looking forward to becoming high school freshmen. The interesting thing about East Cleveland [where we both grew up] is that it's a 3.10 square mile city with [at the time] six elementary schools that funnel into one middle school, which funnels into one high school, the distinguished Shaw High School, home of the Cardinals. As freshmen, Tyrone and I had little to no contact at all. However, he did let me know later in our marriage that he was still creepily watching me from a distance.

Once we hit 10th grade, Tyrone and I had become really good friends. I was an honor student. I was involved in plenty of academic programs that the school had to offer and traveled a lot during my high school years with these programs. Tyrone was just the opposite. He wasn't involved in any extra high school programs. He was the cool guy that got along with everyone in our class and beyond. He wasn't a troublemaker of any kind. He was a kind-hearted guy with decent grades who just loved to have fun with his friends.

He and I laughed so much together because he was also a complete clown. We had chemistry class together. The class was located on the 3rd floor of the Tech building, down a side hallway. He would walk to the hallway and wait on me to get to the 3rd floor before walking with me the rest of the way to class. Honestly, I have no idea how we even passed that class. Although I was the nerd, I used to cry laughing while he and a brother-sister duo would hump the floor, dance, and clown in class as soon as the teacher's back was turned. No, I mean they'd get up out of their seats and literally hump the floor! How did the teacher not hear all of the noise and commotion behind her back is beyond me. I can remember a few times when I couldn't contain myself and would burst out in laughter. When she'd turn around, we'd act like nothing was happening and would look confused like we had no idea who was making the noise. All I know is that the four of us passed the class in the midst of pure foolishness and chaos while being the only distracted clowns in the back of the class. I also know that I looked forward to seeing Tyrone's face when I got to the top of the Tech stairs, because I knew chemistry class was about to be lit. Throughout our 10th grade year, we became even better friends. But I have to admit, from the time I noticed Tyrone staring at me at Cedar Point up until the end of 10th, I never looked at him in the way he looked at me. I saw him as a homie but the way he looked at me definitely said far more than a homie status.

In 11th grade, I started working at Randall Park Mall at a personalized gift store kiosk inside of a large department store. My best friend who also went to Shaw as a senior also worked at Randall Park Mall. After school, she and I would meet in the school's courtyard and walk to the bus stop, where we would catch the number 41 bus to work together. Once there, we would go our separate ways, seeing each other occasionally throughout the evening, maybe even taking our lunch breaks together. One day, while walking back from my break, I noticed someone standing at the kiosk counter. I picked up the pace thinking it was a legit customer. When I got closer, I noticed that the person standing there looked familiar. It was Tyrone. "Dude, why are you here?" He responded, "I wanted to see you". Now I knew he didn't have a car, but never did I put two-and-two together to think that he was catching the bus all the way from East Cleveland to Warrensville Heights to see me at the job for less than an hour. Then having to catch the bus back to East Cleveland after the hour (or less) visit. This one-time visit turned into an (at least) once a week occurrence. Somewhere during those frequent visits, I began to like him. His consistency was wearing on me. I don't know if at this point, I started liking his persistence and determination, or if it was the fact that he thought the almost forty-five-minute ride on the bus was worth it to see me. And I can't put my finger on the exact time and date I started liking him, but it happened. One day, he came to the job and bought a keychain. He wanted me to engrave the keychain with our names on it. Of course, I did it because by this time, I was really feeling him. His charm was undeniable, but I wasn't sure if he liked me the way he claimed to and I'd always been determined to not be anybody's fool.

Our senior year really set off our relationship. I used to walk to and from school daily with my sister-friend, Dott, who lived across the street from me. One day in October, while walking home with my girl, I heard the loudest version of "Pistol Grip Pump" I had ever heard in my life. As the song got closer, I was so curious, but I was determined not to turn around and give whoever it was any of my attention. The car got closer and pulled up on us. It was Tyrone. He had gotten himself a car and apparently, some quality speakers. He turned the music down and asked, "Want a ride home?" After I refused the ride, trying to play hard to get, he rode next to me trying to convince me to get in. A car pulled up behind him, which was my saving grace. After he pulled off, I blushed so hard trying not to let Dott see me, but she did. We laughed from Huron Road Hospital all the way home at Tyrone's antics and my response. This same drive-by action continued for eight straight school days. Some days, he would pull up and have some of his boys in the car with him. I definitely wasn't getting in with all of them; although, I was cool with every last one of them.

By this time, Tyrone had a clue that I liked him, he just didn't know how much, and neither did I. Although I tried to hide it, I knew that there were certain things I did, said, and ways I looked at him that gave him all the hints he needed to move forward with pursuing me. The only issue with his pursuit was that by now, I had a boyfriend and he had a girlfriend. There was a part of the hallway that me and some of my classmates called "The Block". It was the tucked away part of the hallway where our lockers were and where we would hang out in-between classes. Tyrone started showing up on The Block daily. We shared laughs, flirty words, and googly eyes at my locker before going our separate ways heading off to our 4th period classes. However, we were extra careful about displaying any feelings toward each other because we both were in relationships, just not with each other.

One day, Tyrone finally got his nerves up to ask me out on a date. It was our first official date as a non-couple, and I said yes. He took me to the Spaghetti Warehouse, a pasta restaurant in The Flats of downtown Cleveland. That was the night. Over lasagna and Pepsi, we fell in love with each other. His sense of humor was goofy but cute and he had the perfect amount of confidence without being a jerk. He was so nervous that night. Every time he'd move, his hands would shake. I felt so bad because I wanted him to relax but I didn't want to seem easy. It was obvious that he was head over heels in love with me, but I still wouldn't show too much interest. This was that night that he stood out from everyone else.

We went from a date to rides home, to more frequent job visits, and sincere hugs. We had gotten to the point of not really caring about my boyfriend and his girlfriend seeing us, although we still tried to stay incognito because my mom worked at the school. Tyrone had gotten so bold that he would drive up my street with his music blasting while I was sitting on the porch with my boyfriend. He'd just stare at me while riding past as if I was on the porch alone. I was just as petty. He and his boys had a three-period long class in the Vocational building. They would stand outside the classroom in-between periods, lean against the lockers, laugh, and people watch. His girlfriend would also stand outside the class with the fellas. I'd walk past them and stare at him while his girlfriend was standing in front of him, staring at me, staring at him. All his boys would laugh out loud and bump elbows because they knew what was happening. Between my pettiness and their obnoxious laughter at my pettiness, I'm sure his girlfriend felt completely uncomfortable.

Now that I think back on it, he and I did a lot of things that were totally disrespectful to the people we were in our high school relationships with at the time. I had a home economics class that required me to carry a baby doll around for a week. In my childish efforts to test Tyrone and how he really felt about me, I took my baby to him and asked him to babysit her for me during school. He didn't think twice about carrying my little chocolate baby doll around. I'd walk past him, and he'd be cradling it like a real life infant. He took a lot of heat from his girlfriend. She knew it was my baby and couldn't believe that he was as bold as to carry it around. I was also a part of the Mock Trial team. We were headed to Columbus one morning for a mock trial competition and Ty and I knew we weren't going to talk to each other for days. After boarding the bus and waiting on the final count prior to pull off, I saw Tyrone running up to the bus window trying to hand me something. I stood on the seat and leaned out the window to get whatever was in his hand. It was a pager. He had bought the two of us matching pagers so that we could randomly let each other know that we're thinking about each other while apart. Oh my goodness! I was shocked. Who thinks like that? This dude was in love and I knew it. This had to be the absolute sweetest thing for a young man his age to do! We used them often while I was gone and after I returned home. He was too young to be thinking about love and commitment like he did when we were kids.

Wednesday, February 14, 1996 was the day of our school group pictures. The photoshoot was set up in the Korb Lounge. You preordered your photoshoot and you and your friends could dress up and take pictures together. This was also a day that we could dress down from our normal school dress code which consisted of black or dark blue pants, white or light blue shirts, and any shoes with the exception of gym shoes. Everybody was excited to wear something other than what we were used to. Somehow, Tyrone had gotten word to me for me to meet him in the basement of the Tech building during 2nd period. This was the basement of the school. When we were freshmen, the Tech cafeteria was where everyone wanted to be. However, by now, they had closed the cafeteria and there was really no traffic, unless you were down there doing something you shouldn't be doing. I went down there not knowing what to expect. As I walked toward him, I could see the nervous smile on his face which prompted a nervous smile to pop up on mine. I knew we only had a few minutes to be down there before security did their rounds, so I began the conversation with an extra cool "What's up?" He reached in his pockets and pulled out a box. He looked at me and said, "I know we're young. And I know this is probably crazy. We're about to go our separate ways after we graduate. But this is a promise ring because I want to marry you." He opened the box and a beautiful ring was staring back at me. "What?! Are you serious? We're kids." I was blown away! Within about 5 seconds, I had a flurry of emotions. I was thinking:

- We're way too young to be thinking about this… right?
- What about our boy/ girlfriend?
- My Momma and Daddy are going to kill me if I get caught in this basement with Tyrone…
- I'm leaving for college, who says I'm coming back?
- How in the world am I going to hide this ring from everyone?

And with all of those thoughts, I looked in his eyes, said ok, and extended my left hand for him to slide the ring on my ring finger. He was shaking so bad. He reached out to hug me, I wrapped my arms around him and somehow our lips locked. It was the very first time we kissed. We commemorated that moment over dinner at Spaghetti Warehouse on March 16, 1996, where our first date took place not too long ago. After that, it was no coincidence that he went to prom with his girlfriend and I went with my boyfriend, but we all wore the same colors; cream and gold.

Miles Apart

I got accepted to several colleges. However, I decided to attend Alabama State University in Montgomery, AL. Why did I decide to go all the way to Alabama from East Cleveland? There were so many things going on at home. The drug use, manipulation, and the physical and emotional abuse in the home was enough to run anybody away. Plus, if someone wanted to come visit, I wanted it to be planned, not a pop-up. Alabama was my escape from my East Cleveland reality. In spite of my attempt to escape, when I went to Alabama, an escape was the last thing I got. It seemed that the unhappiness and drama that I tried to escape followed me 800 miles away. I thoroughly enjoyed my freshman year at ASU. I had a cool roommate, we lived in a cool dorm, and we had a cool dorm family. The HBCU experience was line none other. My first week was like a family reunion. There were several people from Cleveland and East Cleveland that attended the school, one of them was also a Shaw High graduate from the class of 96. We had a ball. We met up often to talk all things East Cleveland and Cleveland. I met girls and guys from all over the nation, and plenty of boys on the baseball and baseball teams from the Virgin Islands.

Living on campus was enjoyable, but the summer going into my sophomore year was when my roommate and I decided to move into our own apartment. We also invited one of our other dormmates to live with us. We didn't really think through moving off campus as neither of us had transportation or income when we made the decision. We had already told the housing office that we were moving off campus, so we had to be out by a certain date. At the time, I was dating a guy from New York. He had an apartment and invited me and my roommates to live with him until our apartment was done. We stayed with him for about three weeks until our apartment was move-in ready.

Once we moved and got settled, the three of us got jobs working at a buffet restaurant about five miles from our apartment yet, we had no transportation; another not-so-well-thought-out plan. We had a few good friends that would pick us up from home and take us to and from work at times. Sometimes we had to catch the cab, as there was no such thing as Uber back then.

Our apartment was the kick-it spot. We had friends come over often. There were two guys who worked with us at the restaurant. They both worked as cooks. One night we invited them to the house to play spades and have a few drinks. These two were supposed to be cool with us as we've shared so many laughs at the job together. At some point during our card game I got up to use the bathroom. When I came back, I sat down and continued the game. I picked my drink up, took a sip, and that was the last thing I remembered. The next morning, I woke up in my room with the door locked and one of the guys on top of me. I woke up to being raped. It was the most disgusting feeling ever. I prided myself on the fact that not just any guy deserved what I had and who I was. Once this happened, something flipped inside. That rape did something to me. I turned into a monster. I became the nastiest person ever. I literally became the type of person I could barely stomach. It was this experience that broke me. The walls that were already built around me from my home experiences became triple thick and triple high. I told no one. My roommates didn't know. My parents didn't know. No one knew with the exception of me and the creep that took it upon himself to drug and take advantage of me. I never returned to work at that restaurant and never saw him again. Shortly after that, some things happened between me and my roommates and I had to return to East Cleveland. It was either that or possibly end up in jail.

While I was going through what I was going through in Alabama, Tyrone was at home working and going to school. One late night, on his way home, he fell asleep at the wheel and ended up pinned underneath a truck. He was taken to the hospital where they had to perform surgery and wire his mouth shut. That was the week I came home from Alabama with zero plans of going back. Leaving Alabama was the best thing for me, at that moment, because staying while in the mind frame, I was currently in would've caused me to destroy my future. I had no idea about Tyrone's accident when I got home. A close friend of mine found out that I was home and told me about what happened to him. She gave me his hospital contact info and said that she was sure that he'd be happy to hear from me. When I called, a female answered the phone. It was his high school girlfriend who was still his current girlfriend. I asked to speak to him. She knew exactly who I was and [reluctantly] passed him the phone. He answered with an almost incoherent "hello". I said, "Hey, how are you?" and could hear him smile over the phone. He mumbled that he was ok but that his mouth was wired shut. Although I was sad that he was in this situation, I was so happy to hear his voice. It didn't matter that I could barely understand what he was saying. It was a voice that I hadn't heard since I left for college in 96. His voice brought so much peace to the anger and hate I had growing inside. His voice was the calm to the storm that had brewed inside me after the rape, although he had no idea any of that even happened to me at this time. At the sound of his weak voice through the wires, those high school feelings began to resurface.

Where Is This Going?

*T*ime had gone by and Ty was out of the hospital, fully recovered, and in a new relationship with his fiancé that I had no idea even existed. However, our on-again-off-again relationship was in play, yet again. Once he told me about her, I had to have a serious conversation with him. We drove to Euclid Creek where he parked the truck so that we could have a conversation about our current situation undisturbed. He told me her name. "Congratulations!" I said with an obnoxious amount of disguised sarcasm. "But I hope that you don't think that I'll be with you while you're with her. How is that fair to her? And I'm second to no one. You already know this." He looked at me with the saddest eyes as if he thought I would agree to be his side chick. But the seriousness in my eyes told him "I'm not playing and this is no joke". "I'm not trying, nor do I want to break up your engagement Tyrone. We can be friends." His eyes filled with tears, "I don't want to be your friend" he told me. "I told you that you were going to be my wife when we were in school and I meant that". "Then why would you go and proposed to someone else? If you were so sure, why did you make the same offer to someone else?" I responded. He told me it was because he was "willing to settle" since he didn't know if I was ever coming back from Alabama. He told me he knew that he would never be happy, but it was a chance he was willing to take not knowing if I would ever return. I was so smitten by the sincerity in his eyes ans his words. He had me. I told him that if he and I were going to be together, he had to end the relationship he had with his current fiancé. He was clear that he was willing to do it. We rode back to my house in silence. Not one word was spoken until I was getting out the car. "We'll talk later." I said as I was exiting the truck. "Can I have a kiss?" he asked me as I opened the door. "No sir, you've got a fiancé." I responded. I looked at him and said, "We'll talk later." as I closed the door and walked away.

Deep in my heart, I felt bad for whoever she was because I knew he was going to do exactly what he said he was going to do and end the relationship. It wasn't my goal to break up what they had. I had no idea that he and I would rekindle anything we had already had. But I knew what he felt about me and I knew what I felt about him.

I refused to call Tyrone. Yet, four days later, he called me. He asked if he could come see me and I agreed. I heard in his voice that he needed to talk to me immediately. He came to my mom's house where we sat outside on the porch. He looked me in my eyes and told me that his relationship was over, but he felt bad because she was pregnant. She told him when he ended the relationship that she was getting an abortion. My heart was broken for her and for him. I tried to get him to go back and talk to her about the abortion factor, but he was hurt at the fact that she was willing to abort a baby just because they weren't in a relationship anymore. I asked him was he sure that this is what he wanted to do because an abortion was the last thing I wanted for his [now] ex-fiancé and the unborn baby. He said that he was hurt about the baby but was no longer willing to settle when he knows he's not going to be happy. At this point, he and I knew how he felt about me. He and I also knew how I felt about him. Because of the things I had already experienced as a child, I was scared to be in a real relationship. I trusted no one, but he made me feel safe. I figured that if I was going to risk it with anyone, it would be with Tyrone. I was willing to risk it all with him.

Our Little Family

When Dana was born, he was the second man to hold her, my dad being the first since he was at the hospital already. Within the fifty-three hours of labor I experienced with her, I had been to the hospital twice and sent home both times. Although he told me to call him as soon as I go into labor, I wasn't willing to waste his time--- like I felt my time was being wasted with all of the back-and-forth trips to the hospital. When she finally came that night, he was in class, I was exhausted, and I couldn't take another minute without rest. I called him to tell him that she was here and was so tired that I didn't even remember hanging the phone up. I have no idea what our conversation even consisted of that night, I was that exhausted. The next morning, he was at the hospital bright and early. I woke up to him coming in the room. He held her in his arms and stared at her for about 20 minutes in silence. I wanted to say something but didn't want to ruin the moment he was having with the baby girl in his arms. He looked up at me and told me, "I'll never leave her, regardless of what happens between me and you. I love her.".

Tyrone talked to me about moving into an apartment shortly after Dana was born. Although I was a little skeptical with a new baby and no experience being a mom, I agreed. We moved in together when Dana was three months old. We lived in a small one-bedroom apartment on Lakeshore called The Shorewood. We loved our little intimate home for just the three of us. Literally, It was so small that only the three of us could fit. We were a young family. We'd get up each morning, get ready for work and go about our separate ways. I'd take Dana to the babysitter then go to work. He'd head straight to work. We'd handle our workday then come back together like the perfect little family. Dana loved to go underneath the kitchen sink, get pots and bang on them while I cooked dinner and Tyrone would watch T.V. He loved my cooking. He was so appreciative of the fact that I was a cooking woman and couldn't wait till dinner was done every evening. After I would finish cooking in our tiny kitchen, the three of us would sit at our tiny dining table, in our tiny home and eat dinner. The love was apparent around that table. While in our apartment, we established that we would always sit and eat dinner together as a family for as long as we were together, regardless of any situation that may arise.

Dana turned one year old and we had planned a birthday party at my mom and dad's house. While getting dressed for the party, we got into a disagreement about spending money. The disagreement turned into a yelling match between the two of us with Dana standing there looking up at us and yelling in her baby language. I don't remember the end of the argument. All I remember is walking away, getting Dana, and leaving. The party went well but our relationship seemed to fold that day. We didn't talk for the next three days. We didn't greet each other with our normal good morning when we woke up next to each other, we didn't kiss and wish each other a good day when we separated, and we didn't speak when we both arrived home from work. On the third day, I arrived to my mom's house to pick Dana up from the next door neighbor, who was also her babysitter, to Tyrone parked in my parents' driveway with all of our things packed in the truck. He had taken it upon himself to "put me out" of the apartment that we were paying for together. I was pissed, but I'm the one that would never let anyone know that they've gotten to me. I walked past him with Dana in tow, went into my mom's house, and fed my child as he brought mine and Dana's things in the house. After he was done, he got in the truck and started backing out the driveway. As soon as he got to the street, a car coming down the street crashed into the rear passenger side of his truck. He was disgusted; he loved that truck.

When I heard the crash, I ran to the door to see him with a disgusted look on his face and with what looked like tears in his eyes. I locked eyes with him, stared at him from the door for about thirty seconds, then turned around and walked away. I didn't care that his truck was smashed. As long as he was O.K. physically, I didn't care what happened to his truck. I felt like what he done by packing our things and bringing them to my parents' house while I was at work was rude and extremely passive aggressive. In a way, I was glad that his truck was messed up. I knew that he loved that truck and I felt disrespected. Call it wrong but I was glad he was hurting over his truck. My eyes pierced through his soul with the "God don't like ugly" stare.

A few months passed with him living in our apartment and me and Dana living in my parents' house. He was over everyday visiting and somewhere in there we went back to talking. In that process, we decided to move to a townhouse further out Euclid. We loved every part of life at this point. We were proud of ourselves for progressing in our relationship as well as our living arrangements. While lying in the bed one night, I told him that I loved him. He rolled over and just stared at me. He laid there so long staring at me without blinking until I thought he had fallen asleep with his eyes open. After staring at me in silence for about three minutes and me feeling completely awkward, he rolled back over and pulled a ring from under the mattress. He rolled back over to me, sat up and opened the box. "Kendra, now that we're old enough, will you marry me for real this time?" "Of course!" I responded. About two weeks later, we started making plans without telling anyone. We had decided to marry on August 12, 2000.

Things between Ty and me had been really good, but after that new ring hit my finger things started shifting in our relationship, and not in the right direction. The conversations between the two of us became shorter and fewer. We stopped wanting to do things or go places together. I'd come in from work and cook, but we wouldn't eat dinner together like we vowed to do when we lived in our tiny apartment. Tyrone would sit at the computer and play games all evening. I would go to the room and play with Dana until it was time to go to bed. Dana would go get him from the computer, "Daddy, come play with me and mommy". Sometimes he would stop what he was doing on the computer and we'd play "nice" for Dana's sake. Sometimes, he'd stop, but I would walk away when he'd come in the room. Then other times, he would refuse and either play with her in the living room or just tell her "no". Because she has always been a sharp girl, she knew then that there was something wrong. Any time we were in separate parts of the town house, she'd try her hardest to do something to bring us together in the same room. One day, I heard her yelling "MOMMY! DADDY!" in what sounded [to me] like a panic. We both came running, me from the kitchen and him from the living room. We busted through the bathroom door around the same time only to find her sitting on the potty with the biggest smile and brown stuff all over her face. Afraid to touch her because we were skeptical about what was on her face, we looked at each other with the "you do it" look. She started clapping and yelling "yay!" When I looked up, I noticed that there was a chocolate pudding cup on the sink which answered the question of what was on her face. I told her to stand up. When she did, we saw that she had successfully went into the bathroom, took her pamper off, sat on the potty and used it all alone. We made a big deal out of her independent accomplishment. Just as Tyrone was leaving out and I was about to clean her up, she said, "No daddy, stay right here" as she pointed to the tub in her normal bossy baby tone. He sat on the edge of the tub while I did what I needed to do to get her cleaned up. She then took both of our hands and lead us into the living room and told us to sit next to each other while she sat on the floor on my right foot and his left foot. I guess that was to keep us from moving. We laughed and watched T.V. together for about two hours until it was time for bed. That was the most time we had spent together over the past three weeks. She saw the divide and thought that she could fix it. Her sweet innocence wasn't even enough to keep us together.

I had become fed up with Tyrone and I'm sure the feeling was mutual. One day I had decided to leave and go back home until I was ready to move out into my own place. After packing our things, I gave him his ring back, put my baby in her car seat and rolled out. He acted as if he was unconcerned. I acted as if I was happy to be leaving. The truth was that we were both heartbroken, but weren't allowing ourselves to see the true emotions behind the separation. After about four months of being apart and only seeing each other when he would come to see Dana, Tyrone called me and told me that he was moving to Florida. "Florida? Why Florida?" I asked. He had been sent to Jacksonville by his job, loved it, and decided to move. He told me that he couldn't stomach being without me and then seeing me with anyone else since we were now broken up. He said he'd rather move from the state than to see me happy with someone else knowing I'm supposed to be with him. We played the blame game on the phone for almost an hour before I told him to do what he felt would make him happy, then hung up on him. A week later, he asked could we go out one last time before he left. I reluctantly agreed. We went to dinner and to the hotel. Two days later, he was headed to Florida with Moe, his baby brother, in the passenger seat to make a home and life for them there while Dana and I were still in East. Cleveland with me planning our new life in Virginia Beach, VA.

Duval? What's That?

fter they got to Jacksonville and was settled, Tyrone called me every day. We'd talk about his new job and coworkers. I'd tell him about Dana's progress and the drama on my job. Never did I mention to him that I had my eyes on Virginia Beach. Eventually, I would've told him, but I didn't feel like talking about it with him when I had no solid plans set yet.

Ty wasn't in Jacksonville for a good month before he called me and told me that he was planning to come back to Cleveland to see me and Dana. Although I was still upset about him moving, I was happy that he was coming home to see Dana. She was missing him and would ask about him every single day, multiple times a day. He told me his itinerary and I assured him I'd be there to meet him at the airport. The night of his flight, I sat at the airport waiting and anticipating his arrival. I didn't know how much I missed him until the moment I was sitting there staring at the board waiting to see his flight status update to "Arrived". When he saw me, he ran and grabbed me like we hadn't seen each other in years. "Damn sweetheart, you lookin' thick" he said in a slick tone. Thinking he was trying to call me fat, I whipped my head around looking him up and down, "You trying to say I'm fat?". "No, it looks great. Look at your butt." He had me blushing all the way to the car. We got to his mom's house where he dropped Moe off then headed to my parents' house to spend time with Dana. After Dana was all tired out and fell asleep, he asked if I thought my mom would keep her while we go spend time together. I asked and she agreed, and just like that, we were out. He told me to pack an overnight bag and I did. We got in the car and headed east. I had no idea where we were going, and apparently Ty didn't either, but we decided we would ride to a destination where no one could find us. We ended up in Erie, Pennsylvania. We spent the weekend there before heading back to East Cleveland. When we got back to my parents' house, Dana was eagerly awaiting. He spent more time with Dana, laughing and wrestling before it was time for him to pick his brother up and get to the airport for their flight back to Jacksonville. We stood and hugged for about ten minutes in silence. At that moment, no words were required. Shortly after releasing each other, he left. We had no idea when we would see each other again.

One day, I woke up in severe pain in my appendix. I waited until I couldn't take it anymore and went to the hospital thinking my appendix was about to burst. I checked in and waited for them to call me back, which literally took over two hours. In any other case I would've left. But the pain I was in would barely let me stand up and walk. While sitting in the waiting room in excruciating pain, I witnessed a lady die in her wheelchair and an infant have a seizure in the arms of a panicking mom. Finally, the admissions nurse called my name. I stood slowly and made my way over to her, where I barely was able to walk to the room she was putting me in. The nurse took my vitals, had me take a routine urine test, and told me to relax before she shut the door to room number eleven. I laid back on the bed, curled up in the fetal position, and fell asleep. I had no idea how long I had been asleep having no idea how long I had been asleep before the doctor entered the room. What I do know however, is that it was freezing in that room. I remember pulling my arms inside my shirt to keep warm prior to falling asleep. I heard someone enter the room. Before I could open my eyes, she called my name "Hi Kendra". It was the doctor and the same nurse who had walked me to the room. I sat up and felt that the pain had eased up a bit. "What brings you in honey?" the doctor asked in the calmest tone. I told her that according to my self-diagnosis, I felt like my appendix was about to burst. I pointed to the area where I had been experiencing the most pain. She felt around, pressed a bit and asked the nurse who was now standing behind her how were my vitals and the result of my urine test. The nurse told her that all vitals were good, I had no fever, and that the urine turned up nothing. The doctor looked at her and told her to run my urine again. After mustering up another sample, I went back into the cold room, tucked my arms and curled back up in the same fetal position. I hadn't even been curled up for two minutes before the doctor came back in and said, "Kendra, it's not your appendix dear. You're pregnant." You know that feeling you get when it feels like you just swallowed a bread lump and it won't go down? Yeah, that was my throat. I instantly got cold sweats. I started shaking nervously. I had a sudden headache and could feel my heartbeat in my eyes. I felt like my heart was about to stop, restart, then stop again. Every single anxiety response my body could give me, it did, at that very moment. I had an urge to cry. I wanted to laugh out loud of disbelief. I was completely sick to my stomach. "How in the world do I tell this man that I'm pregnant? He's in Florida and I'm in Ohio making plans to move to Virginia Beach. I'm not moving to Florida, that's out of the question! As a matter of fact, it's not even an option. But I didn't even want kids to begin with. What is this? What's going on? Why in the hell is this happening to me? I knew I shouldn't have gone on that last date with him, especially not to the hotel! Wait! Which date was it? Was it before he left or when he came back? He trapped me! Damn Kendra! You did this to yourself! You knew better! UGH!"

I walked in the house from the hospital feeling both numb and dumb. My eyes were swollen from crying hysterically in the hospital room for about twenty minutes, while walking to the car which took about five minutes, and while riding back home, which took about fifteen minutes. Yes, I cried for about forty-five minutes straight before I got home. I tried to get myself together before walking in the house to face my mom and daughter because I wanted to answer no questions. When I opened the front door, I just remember silence. I'm not sure where my mom was at the time. I don't remember seeing my daughter or little brother either. It was later in the evening and I was mentally and emotionally spent. I went to my room and laid down thinking about my approach to this crazy situation. I waited for hours until I got up enough energy to pick up the phone and call Tyrone. He answered on the first ring, as if he was waiting for me to call, "What's up sweetheart?" I snatched the phone away from my ear because the sound of his voice brought tears to my eyes. I was so close to hanging up on him but in a brief second thought to myself, "Girl! He knows it's you! Get yourself together! You're a grown ass woman!"

Me:	Hey (softly)
Tyrone:	What's goin on? Everything good with you and Dana?
Me:	Yes, we're good. You? Moe?
Tyrone:	We're good. I got Moe registered in school finally. We're settled and everything is good.
Me:	That's good. So, I've got something to tell you.
Tyrone:	What? You O.K. (sounding nervous)?
Me:	I'm pregnant (as the tears begin to fall).
Tyrone:	For real?
Me:	Yep (crying hysterically).
Tyrone:	Why are you crying?
Me:	Because I didn't want any kids and now, I'm about to have two!
Tyrone:	Baby, it's ok! (crying)
Me:	NO IT'S NOT!
Tyrone:	Let's get married. I'll come get you and baby girl. Y'all can move down here with us. We'll be good. I'll get another job if I have to. Everything will be O.K.

Me:	[still crying hysterically]
Tyrone:	Sweetheart, stop crying please? You're going to stress my baby out. Where's Dana? Is she in there with you? Stop crying. You know how she gets. It's gonna be O.K.
Me:	I can't do this. I'm not moving to Florida! Jacksonville? I've never even seen Jacksonville on the map! We'll be good. I'm not moving to Jacksonville. I'm tired. I need to go to sleep. Can we talk tomorrow?
Tyrone:	Yes, but promise me you'll think about it? And stop the crying! Please!
Me:	We'll talk tomorrow. (hangs up the phone)

The next morning, the phone rang at exactly 8:23 a.m. I answered, knowing it was Tyrone. "Good morning sweetheart. How are you feeling?" he greeted me in his usual calm voice. I sat up in my bed and saw my reflection in the mirror. "Besides looking like a bug from crying all day and night, I feel O.K." I said. He chuckled and asked me about my decision on moving down to Florida. I was silent because I was still wavering on the inside. He said, "I'm picking up this second job. I'm going to set everything up so that I could come get you and Dana in February. We're going to be good. We'll talk about the details later. I'm on my way to work. O.K.?" I responded with an unsure but calm "O.K." He told me that he loved me and that he would call me after he got off work. I told him that I loved him and disconnected the call. When I did, I asked myself "What just happened?" I had already told myself that I wasn't moving to Florida. I was determined to not change my mind either. I found myself questioning why is he so convincing. All day my head was pounding thinking about the possibility of moving to Jacksonville, the huge life change of having two children, and being married. The stress was making my stomach hurt. I had no appetite and I felt weak. Thankfully, Dana was her normal independent self, so she required a very little of me that day. Usually we'd play, read books and talk each other's ears off, but not this day. It was almost like she sensed that I wasn't my normal self. That evening, Tyrone called me. We solidified the plans of him coming to E. Cleveland on February 10th, us getting married on February 12th, and leaving for Duval county the next day.

February 10th arrived. I was at work sitting at my desk when Tyrone called me and and said he was in Cleveland and on his way to my job. Once he got there, he called me back and told me to come downstairs for a few minutes. The elevator doors opened, and he was standing there with the biggest smile on his face watching me and my pregnant belly walk toward him. He left looking like E. Cleveland and came back looking like a straight up Duval resident. He had these braids in his head that made me do a double-take. I guess the look on my face said it all, as I had never seen him with braids, let alone some where it looked like he had a side bang hanging on the side of his face. Nonetheless, I walked out and gave him a huge hug to match the smile he was wearing. When we connected, I melted in his arms. I didn't realize how much I wanted and needed to be in them at that very minute. Once we released each other, he got down on one knee in front of my job and asked me for the third time to marry him. Although the plan was to get married already, the fact that he proposed for a third time with a new ring was so sweet. "Of course!" I responded with a goofy giggle. We walked three minutes away to the courthouse on Lakeside Avenue to get our marriage license, giggling like two little mischievous kids, cracking jokes and staring at each other the entire way. Once done, we walked back to my job just in time for the end of my lunch break. Ty promised me he'd be there to pick me up at five. On my way back to my desk I was in a state of disbelief. The reality of what was about to happen was setting in. Not only am I getting married (which I never planned on doing, at least not so soon), but I'm about to move all the way to Florida (which had never even been a thought, ever), raise 2 children (which I never even intended to have), and settle down as a wife and mother at the age of 23. I sat at my desk for the rest of the day contemplating life. I didn't get an ounce of anything else done that day. The thought of what was about to happen was nuts and overwhelming. My coworkers noticed that I was off because after lunch, they had each come up to me asking if everything was alright. I was telling them I was good, but on the inside, I wasn't. I remember thinking that none of this was a part of how I planned my life. But when five o'clock came, I walked out the building, and he was sitting right there waiting for me as promised, I thought, "But I can get through anything with this guy in it with me." And it was at that point that I accepted this new life that I had never dreamt of but was about to become my reality.

It's February 12th, yikes! with a nervous excitement. I, Kendra Richardson, was about to become Kendra Johnson. This day was special for a couple reasons. Not only was I about to get married, but for the first time that Tyrone could remember, his dad had just gotten out of prison where he had been for almost all of Ty's life and was coming to our wedding. Well, it wasn't really a "wedding" that people were coming to, it was more like coming to our "vow exchange". Tyrone and I were surrounded by our immediate family and our closest friends when we committed ourselves to each other in the office of Mayor Emmanuel Onunwor of East Cleveland, OH. We often joked with each other when we would make up from an argument that we needed to check our marriage certificate because we might not even be married. Knowing Mayor Onunwor's history would bring light to our inside joke.

The next day I woke up as Kendra Richardson-Johnson. Although it didn't feel different, I knew that it was going to be all kinds of different from this day forward, I just had no idea how different it was going to be. All our things were packed in the red Ford Taurus he drove up to Ohio from Florida. We said our goodbyes to the family and off we drove, on our way to a different life with one baby in the car seat and one in the belly. We had so much stuff packed in the trunk and the back seat behind Tyrone. Dana sat in her car seat behind me. We also had a twin-sized baby bed tied to the top of the car, both frame and mattress. How we thought we would make a nine hundred plus miles trip from East Cleveland to Jacksonville with a bed frame and mattress tied to the top of a Ford Taurus was beyond me. We didn't get a full hour into the trip before the base of the baby bed flew off the top of the car. After almost causing an accident on the freeway, we knew this was a terrible idea. There was no way the rest of the bed would make it to Jacksonville. We pulled over and ended up throwing what was left of the bed in the dumpster behind a gas station then continued on our way to palm trees and sunshine.

That ride was rough for a seven months pregnant woman. My back was hurting. I had a constant headache from riding through the mountains. My legs and feet were swollen. I tried not to complain the entire ride but couldn't avoid the frequent restroom requests. They turned what would normally be a 14-hour trip into an almost 18-hour trip. When we pulled up to our apartment, I had zero thoughts or emotions. I was exhausted and really didn't have time to process anything. We unpacked everything from the car, called our parents to let them know we had arrived safely, took showers and went straight to bed. It was a new chapter. Time to adjust and adapt accordingly.

Coming from East Cleveland where it snowed in May, I'm still struggling to get used to Florida's heat. With that said, imagine being pregnant and having to adjust. The Ford Taurus that Tyrone drove to Cleveland was just a rental. The real car that we had, as our primary transportation, was a four-door Ford Tempo with no air condition. It was already warm in Florida and it was only going to get warmer. We had a three-bedroom, two-bathroom apartment. My brother-in-law and I were already close, and now that we were all living together under the same roof, we would become even closer. I loved our little family and our little apartment. Tyrone was working two jobs to make ends meet and to my knowledge, he was doing a good job at that time.

After finally finding a doctor to attend to this ever-growing belly I was wagging around, I began going twice a month since I was a new patient. Our doctor loved me, and I loved her. We cliqued immediately. She also loved Tyrone. She loved that we were two young married kids with a growing family. Every time we'd go to the doctor, she would tell us how much she was proud of our young family. She was nurturing and encouraging. I loved going to see her, but I absolutely hated the rides to and from the downtown hospital. I was already big, frustrated, and pregnant. Add the heat to this combination and it made for a bad situation almost every visit. By March, the heat was obnoxious. I tried to make my appointments as early in the mornings as possible to at least avoid the heat during the trips to and from the doctor's office. Coming back home after the appointments was the biggest problem. I'd have to turn my big pregnant belly around and fan my two-year-old baby with an envelope or a piece of paper while I drip sweat. Tyrone would be driving as fast as legally possible to get us home while he was drenched in sweat. Getting home and never leaving the house was always the goal when we had to go out for whatever reason, but not having to leave the house was the main goal the entire time I was pregnant and living here.

I was now nine months pregnant and miserable. It was only April, but it was hot as hades and I hated it. I wasn't used to the heat and humidity that Jacksonville had to offer, add a nine-month pregnant belly and sixty-two extra pounds gained during the pregnancy. I was getting close to my due date of April 23rd and was feeling every bit of anxiety possible. I didn't have my mom here with me like I did when I had Dana. In my mind, I was about to be all alone, although Tyrone was right there with me every single day.

Monday, April 23rd, I began having contractions. I was home alone with Dana but didn't want to call Tyrone just yet. His vacation time was skimp, and he needed all of it after I had the baby. I laid around a bit while still trying to entertain Dana. She sensed that something was going on with me and asked, "Is my brother hurting your belly mommy?" "Yes, he is" I replied while wincing and breathing through the pain. Those words kicked Dana into caretaker mode. She wanted to do everything for me, although she wasn't even three years old yet and couldn't do much. Tyrone walked in from work around six o'clock, not having to go to his second job this day. Moe came in shortly after. When Ty saw me laying on the couch and no dinner prepared, he knew something was going on. "You O.K. baby?" he asked. I told him that I had been having pains all day and felt like I needed to go walking. With a sense of urgency, he went to the room to get my shoes and ask Moe if he would watch Dana while we walked the neighborhood.

After making it down the twelve stairs moving like molasses, we began our slow walk around the apartment complex. Anytime I'd feel a contraction and would double over in pain, he'd bend over and hold his knees so that I could lean over his back for support. He was so patient with me during our walk. I couldn't take 10 steps without pain. Once we got outside the apartment gates, I told Tyrone that I think we should head toward the hospital. The pains were coming back to back. After getting back to the apartment and struggling to make it back up those twelve stairs (only to be coming right back down them), I grabbed my bag while Ty talked to Moe about keeping Dana while we're at the hospital. I also decided to drink some castor oil. I remember being told that this was a remedy to keep the contractions coming, which, in turn, will cause me to dilate. Ty heard me grunting in the bathroom, not knowing that I was in there doing squats. I was determined that they weren't going to send me home from the hospital without a baby in arms. He knocked on the door and asked, "Baby? You good in there?" before opening the door and finding me in mid-squat position and unable to stand back up because the pain was just too overwhelming. He helped me up and back down we went to get to the hospital.

After getting admitted and hooked up to all the machines used to monitor the baby and me, Ty picked a chair to pull next to my bed and sit in. He dose in-between each contraction, which I understood because he had worked a long day and came home to all action. I'd giggle at him as his head droop while his eyes were still partially open (he always slept with his eyes open). However, any time he heard me in any pain he'd wake up immediately trying to see how he could help me through it. After about two hours of constant contractions with no active labor progress, the nurse came in and told me the doctor instructed her to give me an injection to help me relax and get some rest. Within minutes of getting the injection, the contractions stopped, and I started dozing with Tyrone.

Hours later they released us to go home, which was bittersweet to me. I was ready to go home but was even more ready to have this baby already. You mean to tell me I drank that castor oil for nothing? The next day we had an appointment to see the doctor.

When I walked in, she looked at me and said, "Oh Kendra, you look miserable!" "I AM!" I exclaimed. She knew me well, so she knew I was completely fed up with this pregnancy. Since the day before was my due date and there had been no true labor progress, she said she would be willing to induce labor on April 27th if the baby hadn't come yet. I agreed but was hoping she would've sent me back to the hospital at that very moment.

On Friday, April 27th, we were headed to the hospital to have a baby. I was excited and nervous at the same time. Ty, Dana, Moe, and a hugely pregnant me all loaded up in the car. We had been told that we needed to be at the hospital at 7 a.m. to get checked in. Ty dropped me, Moe, and Dana off at the door and parked the car. We were taken to a huge birthing suite at the end of the hall where I was hooked up to the same machines I had been hooked up to during my last visit. Moe settled in on the couch and Ty set Dana's toys up on the table and settled in on the opposite end of the couch. We all expected it to be a long day ahead. The doctor walked in and explained that she was about to have the nurse begin the medicine that would start my contractions. She told me that once we got to a certain point of active labor, the medicine would stop, and it would be game time. I agreed, I was ready to have this baby. I was exhausted.

Dana was my little counter. She'd count me through each contraction. It was the cutest thing, "… eleven, twelve, thirteen, bainteen, bainteen, bainteen, bainteen…". Basically, anything after thirteen was "bainteen" until she hit twenty. We giggled every time she'd count my contractions through. I knew the labor pains were getting serious when I could no longer laugh at her counting, but it didn't stop her from doing it. After about five hours, the pains w out of control. I called the nurse for an epidural. Tyrone was right there talking me through the process but I could see the nervousness in his eyes. He didn't know what to expect and just wanted me to be alright.

The epidural worked like a charm. I was able to get a little rest before the doctor came in to check to see if I was fully dilated. "Kendra and Tyrone, it's time to have a baby!" my doctor said. After three pushes, Moe almost passing out while filming from behind, Dana asking every question she could've thought of in her two-year-old mind, and Tyrone being both grossed out and amazed at the same time, Tyrone Jr. was born at 5:14 p.m. He was a tiny nineteen inches long baby boy, weighing only six pounds and three ounces.

After giving birth to Ty Jr. and returning home, I sat on the bed thinking about the fact that I'm now the mother of two babies. Tyrone had gone back to work, and I was home alone with an independent almost three-year-old baby girl and an infant baby boy. My days were filled with changing diapers, playing whatever Dana wanted to play, and missing Tyrone. I had zero adult interaction throughout the day and although I had two babies, I felt so alone. At times, I would sit in the middle of the bed and cry while holding one baby with the other one staring at me trying to figure out what was going on. The sound of Ty's keys opening the door each night, after coming home from his second job, would revive me from the depressing day I had, night-after-night. My brother-in-law was home, but a lot of times, he had his friends over. They'd be in the room making beats and rapping. I loved having him around though because I couldn't imagine how it would be if I was completely alone with two babies. He was a big help to me after he got out of school each day. He would come and get Lil Ty and take him in the room with him and the boys. Or he would come and get Dana and they would go play whatever she dictated. Sometimes, I would peek in the room where he and Dana were to see her having not only him but his friends playing whatever she wanted. She was definitely a little bossy baby girl.

Ty Jr. was 5 days old and I was in so much pain from lactating. I told Ty that I needed a breast pump and asked him to get it for me as soon as he could. Without hesitation, he jumped up and went to the nearest store to see what he could find. He came back with a twenty-five-dollar manual pump that I was so grateful for. The next day, on Ty's way out, I asked him to leave some money for some groceries, diapers, and baby wipes. He looked at me as if he wanted to say something but was afraid. It took me to ask what was wrong for him to tell me he didn't have any. "Any what?" I asked, looking at him apparently confused. "Any money." he responded. He told me he had spent the last twenty-five dollars on the breast pump that he got for me the night before. "So what do we do now? Are you saying it's my fault? There are no groceries. How do we eat?" I asked. Tyrone looked at me and shrugged his shoulders. "That's all you got for me? A damn shoulder shrug?" I asked before walking off crying from frustration. I was always the one to retreat when I was mad. It was the best thing to keep me from saying what I really wanted to say in the moment. When I stayed, it was all out war. Controlling what came out of my mouth was a challenge at times. I knew that he went out and bought the breast pump knowing it was something I needed so I couldn't be mad at him for that. On the other hand, why wasn't he communicating with me? Why didn't I know that we were down to our last $25? Aren't we supposed to be in this together? It was Tuesday. Tyrone didn't get paid until Friday. This was a problem. I know he didn't want me to stress, but here I am stressing. I know he heard me crying but what could he say? I heard the door close and when I came out of the room, he was gone. Both kids were still asleep, and my brother-in-law was gone to school. I went to the kitchen and looked in the cabinet. The only things we had in there were two packs of noodles and some cereal. I was praying that when I opened the refrigerator, we had milk. I pulled the door open slowly and saw a carton with a few eggs and a little milk. I was getting WIC at the time, so the baby was the only one who had plenty of formula to drink. I fixed Dana a scrambled egg and a piece of toast, fed the baby and decided not to eat that morning. I wanted to save the noodles just in case Moe and Ty were hungry when they came in from school and work.

Moe came in that afternoon with some fast food burgers. He asked me if I wanted some and I said no, knowing I was starving from not eating all day, with the sounds coming from my stomach as evidence. Tyrone came in and was followed by his Vice President and his supervisor from work. They had boxes in their arms, but I had no idea what was in them. Turns out they had gone to the wholesale club and bought groceries and diapers for us. Apparently, Tyrone had gone to work and told his V.P., who also his close friend, what was going on financially. I was grateful for the help but knew that something needed to be done and that there was a conversation needing to be had between the two of us. I fixed spaghetti that night, knowing it'll last for a few days until Ty's payday from both jobs came.

The next day, I woke up to a ringing phone. Tyrone had already left for work. When I answered, a male's voice asked to speak to "Mr. Tyrone Johnson". I told him that Tyrone wasn't home and identified myself as his wife. It was a bill collector. He told me that he was from a payday loan collection agency. Payday loan? This is how I found out how and why we didn't have any money. Tyrone had been getting payday loans to make ends meet from the time he came to East Cleveland to get me and Dana. I also found out that they had withdrawn money from our account a few days before, which is why we had no money for groceries. I knew things were hard, but I had no idea they were this hard. Ty refused to tell me just how hard they were because he knew that it was him who convinced me to move from home to Jacksonville and told me that everything was going to be good. He admitted that he thought if he told me just how bad things were, I'd leave, and he thought right. The thought of me being in a foreign place with two children and no means of supporting myself in this unfamiliarity was both uncomfortable and a threat to my desire of stability. I understood why he was doing what he was doing, but I hated that he didn't tell me what was going on. That day, I told him that things needed to change, and he agreed. We had to be on the same page, or at least in the same book going forward.

God, Is That You?

*M*oe and his friends would get out of school and go play basketball at a nearby church. Every time he'd come in, he would talk about how nice the youth pastors were and how much fun he had. One day, he came in with church service times and suggested that I go. He was adamant and wouldn't let up about me going so I told him I would, eventually. I didn't that week, but the following week I decided I would give it a shot. I got the kids dressed and tried to get Ty to go with me, but he was making a huge fuss about getting up so early. I grabbed the keys and kissed him on my way out with my two babies in tow.

When I pulled up to the church, the parking lot was packed from front to back. I tried to park as close as possible because although I had a walking now three-year-old, I also had an infant in a heavy car seat. Before I could get to the doors, they swung open and I was met with a gang of pleasant smiling faces. I'll never forget the first and most impactful face I saw. She was a light-skinned woman with long beautiful hair. Her eyes were tender and sincere. Her loving heart showed on her face. Her "Welcome" was warm and heart-felt. Out of everything that happened that day, she was the one that left an impression on me. She walked me to the children's nursery and invited me to drop my son off. I refused. I had no idea who any of these people were. This could've been a cult. They could've been selling babies on the black market for all I knew. You know we think the worse as parents, right? I needed to know where I was before I just release my kids in the care of strangers. I mean, let's not act like crazy stuff don't happen in church. She also told me that there was a separate area for my toddler, which I also refused with a smile on my face. She then walked me to the next set of doors. When they opened, I saw a sanctuary full of people of different nationalities. Although black people were the majority, I saw white people, Native

Americans, Africans dressed in traditional garb, Asians; the mix of nationalities was almost unbelievable. There was a group of people on the stage praising God like nothing I had ever seen before. They too were mixed with different nationalities and was led by a young African American man. It was intense in there. I scanned the crowd and saw people, jumping, weeping, singing, and dancing. Some were laying on the floor. There were some who were running full speed around the sanctuary. I wasn't used to this behavior in a church. I had grown up in a traditional black Baptist church where you sang hymns and washed feet at communion, where you were told that wearing red fingernail polish was inappropriate. And Lord forbid you wear lipstick! According to the "mother" of the church, you're headed to hell on a one-way ticket. But I looked around this colorful congregation and saw people in jeans, skirts, shorts, tank tops, blouses, suits, tennis shoes, wearing red lipstick and tank tops. There seemed to be no rules. This was strange to me.

After the praise team sat down, a white woman walked to the podium. "Surely this was not the pastor nor the wife of the pastor, not with all of these black folks in here" I thought. She stood before everyone and welcomed all newcomers then sat down. After the praise team stood and sang another song, an energetic tall white man came to the podium, opened his Bible and began speaking. By the end of the service, I realized that he was the pastor and the woman who welcomed everyone was his wife. I was shocked, as this was completely unexpected. Coming from East Cleveland, I didn't know how I felt about attending a church with some white pastors standing in front of a predominately black congregation. I couldn't wait to get home to tell Ty what I had experienced. I was sure he would be just as shocked as I was, and he was. "You going back?" he asked after I told him about my experience. I looked at him and said, "I think I am."

My next visit was the visit that reeled me in. That morning, Ty and I got into a serious argument about money, or the lack thereof. I didn't even plan on going to church that day but if I didn't leave his presence, something bad would've happened between the two of us that day. Since I was new to the city, it wasn't like I had a friend's house to go to, or an escape route, so to church it was. I got my children ready and left him lying in bed, pissed. He wanted to talk it through. I wasn't that girl. I was always the one who needed to leave and cool off before having a conversation. That was always the safest for the situations we had.

When I walked in, praise and worship was in full swing. I sat down with my two babies as I still wasn't comfortable dropping them off with the nursery ministers. These people were still strangers to me. After sitting down, I closed my eyes and was totally immersed in the words that were coming from the stage. Tears of frustration mixed with regret started flowing down my face as the praise team was softly singing. For some time while they were singing, I felt like I was all alone with no one surrounding me. Although I closed my eyes with a sense of disgust from the morning's happenings, when I opened them I felt a peace. The pastor stood and spoke on the power of agreement. His message was so on-time because that morning, Ty and I were arguing about what needed to happen financially in the home. We couldn't agree and that non-agreement is what started a fight between us. In the midst of the fight, I knew that if I didn't leave for church, it could've resulted in me leaving him and taking our children with me. Where was I going to go? I had no idea, but it wasn't going to be anywhere that he was. I didn't want to talk to him when I got home, and it felt like his feelings were mutual. I was good at holding grudges, but he wasn't, so I was surprised to see that he didn't want to talk to me about anything. Trying be the adult in the situation, although I didn't want to, I shared with him what the pastor spoke on. My tone was dry and uninviting. I told him that according to the pastor, it was important that he and I agreed because we were more powerful together than we were apart. Although I was a baby at this "relationship with GOD" thing and Ty hadn't even given it a shot just yet in his grownup life, the message of togetherness made complete sense to the both of us. I mean, we were two married people with a whole family. How could it not make sense, right?

Within the next few months, Ty joined me in attending the church. We went through new members class and decided to become full time members. I was finally comfortable with my children going to the nurseries during church services and was convinced that these people were not going to sell my children or harvest their organs. Ty and I became active members, serving in multiple ministries. We were over the step team and had a hand in the youth ministry. I joined the praise and worship team. Ty began ushering and eventually became the right-hand man to the pastor. We were one hundred percent dedicated to our ministries and GOD, unfortunately in that order.

A Felony My Guy?

Shortly after Moe moved out, we moved into a two-bedroom apartment in the same complex. We did so to save money to catch up on bills. Since I still had a baby and a child too young for school, I started selling dinners out of our apartment. There were days that I would make five hundred dollars in a day from fried chicken wings and Cleveland-style polish boys. We had a little money stashed in an emergency fund and things were starting to look up. One day, Tyrone and a close friend of his went to lunch. When he came home, he had a sense of excitement but didn't want to give me any details as to why, despite my attempts to pry it out of him. Two days later, he and his friend had me and his friend's wife sitting in our living room for a business presentation. They pitched this idea for them to put their sales and creative skills together to start a marketing business. They presented the details that they had come up with during their lunch two days prior. Their excitement was undeniable, but so were the bills. We could see in their eyes that they were praying that we'd agree with them about quitting their jobs and going full time with this idea. These were two grinding young men with a vision, a wife, and two children each. They were going to do everything they needed to do in order to make money from the vision they presented to us. They knew that in front of them were two women who would be their loudest cheerleaders but would also hold them accountable for what they were presenting to us. After some consideration, the four of us agreed on this business venture. I was making good money with the dinners and we had a small stash saved so why not, right?

The guys went all in for the next two weeks developing their ideas and their sales pitch. After those two weeks were over, they hit the streets running hard in their hard-bottom dress shoes. Ty would come home with stories about how his day went. He rarely came home with any type of success stories. I was encouraging him to keep going. I was also monitoring his attitude about what he was doing. At the moment his energy shifted or doubt set in, I knew that it was my responsibility to encourage him to either crank it up a few notches or shift tracks. After two months, the guys hadn't brought in one green dollar, nor one red penny. They were spending much but making nothing. I could tell that Ty's mood was changing about the decision we agreed on. He wasn't engaged anymore, and although business takes time to make money, his mood told me that he wasn't willing to wait any longer. I'm sure that seeing the monthly bills didn't help. I told Tyrone that we had some money, but it would run out quick if this continued. He agreed and after month three, the guys decided to go back to work. They agreed that they needed more time than their current money situations would allow. Thankfully, Tyrone's Corporate America job was still available and waiting for him, he just needed to go through the full hiring process again which shouldn't be a problem. Tyrone started the process, completed his background check and drug testing and came home with the expectation of getting a call a few days later.

After waiting four days and not receiving a call, Tyrone called Dee, the same Dee that brought us groceries, to get a status on his application. Dee told him that his application was denied because of a felony that showed up on his background check. I was confused, but Tyrone knew exactly what the problem was. When he hung up, he told me that he didn't get his job back because of a felony he got before he moved to Florida. I'm sure my face was saying, "WELL, WHAT THE HELL HAPPENED?! WHAT FELONY?!" He told me that when he was in college, he created counterfeit checks worth thousands of dollars from a company that he was working for and deposited them into his account. Four days after depositing the checks, they cleared, and he thought everything was good. That is until his supervisor came to him and told him that she knew what he had done. He was busted and he just knew everything was about to go downhill at that point. The entire time he's telling me this story, I'm thinking about the bills getting paid. We've known each other for what seems like forever, why didn't I know about this? When did all of this go down and where was I when it was? As his details were flowing about the felony, I totally blocked him out. My mind was going a thousand miles a minute. In my mind I'm thinking, "So are you gonna keep these kids while I get a job, or what? And what other secrets are you keeping from me? First payday loans and now this?" Nothing else mattered to me if the bills weren't being paid and Tyrone knew this. Tyrone said that he tried to keep everything a secret from his family, but it was too hard to hide because of the things he had to get his life back on track. "So this is what you call back on track? So, you're telling me that you can't go back to the job you just quit because of a felony? A felony my guy? Why didn't it come up before you even started at the job in the beginning? Before you came to Jacksonville? Why didn't you tell me this before I came to Florida?" I had so many questions, but Ty didn't have the answers I was looking for. I don't think anyone could've given me the answers I was looking for.

As we sat there trying to figure out life and our next moves, the phone rang again. It was Dee with a suggestion. He asked Tyrone if had the money to try to get his record expunged. We did have our small savings that could cover the cost. He told Tyrone to work on it immediately. Dee told Ty that once he has spoken to a lawyer and the paperwork had been completed, to give him a call back so that he could see if there was anything he could do to push the hire through. Tyrone went out that same day to find a lawyer. Once he returned home, he called Dee and told him that it had been done. Miraculously, eight days later he was back to work.

Back to life as usual. Tyrone would get up and go to work, I would take Dana to school, and me and baby boy would come back home to fry chicken wings, make Polish Boys, deliver food and get paid. One day, several people from Ty's job placed orders for me to deliver. I told Ty that I would prepare everything and be on my way. I cooked everything fresh, packed it up, grabbed Lil Ty, and was on my way to drop off the food. After making the delivery, we went to pick Dana up from school and stopped at the corner store to get the kids a bag of chips and a juice. When we pulled into the apartment complex, I saw smoke billowing in the sky but didn't think much about it. As I pulled around the corner to the parking lot near our apartment, there were several fire trucks and a ladder extended from one of the trucks to our apartment living room window. I panicked! Being homeless had never been an option, until now as it flashed before my eyes in an instant. WHAT THE HECK?? Is our apartment scorched? What in the world are we going to do? What happened? All I knew---at that very moment was fear. How was I supposed to tell Ty that I burnt down everything we owned and now we're homeless and in major debt? We had just gotten back to work! After identifying myself as the person who lives in the apartment, one of the firemen had me go upstairs and open the door. This gave me the indication that apparently the apartment wasn't still on fire. If it was, why would he tell me to open the door? I walked up the stairs and had the kids stand further away. As soon as I opened the door, the smoke took my breath away. After the smoke cleared (literally), I walked in and noticed that everything was still intact but smelled charred. I was standing on the living room wondering what happened. The firefighter told me that they received a call about the smoke from the downstairs neighbor who was worried about their own apartment. I'd never met our downstairs neighbor but was grateful that they were home that day. The firefighter went on to say that when they got to the apartment the smoke was oozing from underneath the door. He said they had to force the window open in order to get in and that it was immediately obvious that the kitchen was the source of the smoke. He told me that there was a pot of oil on the stovetop that was cooking with nothing in it. That's when it hit me, I fried the chicken and never turned off the pan with oil in it. We were almost homeless over some chicken wings and fries?! What kind of story would that have been to tell?! Thank GOD it was only smoke! After airing the apartment out, the firemen left me and the kids standing in the living room looking around. Dana looked up at me and said, "Mommy, you need to slow down. We need our bunkbeds to sleep in." She was only four years old. That was a lesson from a baby that I didn't take for granted. Lil Ty looked up at me with his big brown eyes but didn't say a word because he was still snacking on his barbeque chips. His innocence and cluelessness made the anxiety disappear and a smile appear on my face. Again, I was grateful. From that day, I was extra careful to double, triple, and quadruple check to make sure I turned the stove and oven off before I walked out the kitchen. GOD knows we couldn't afford to be homeless, especially not over some chicken wings.

The Power Of Agreement... The Lack Of Knowledge

was in need of a job, not just for the money, but also for the purpose of getting out the house and interacting with other adults. I was tired of baby talk with one and what seemed like grown lady talk to the other. I had been asking around about legit babysitters. A lady I knew from church told me about one that she had trusted for years with her children, so I decided to go and meet her. I wanted to see her home and how she dealt with the other children. She was like an older auntie. The kids loved and respected her, and she was very attentive to them. She had a minute-to-minute schedule for them that included lunch, nap, and dance times. She followed this scheduled by the book every single day. I liked her. When Tyrone got home from work that evening, I told him about her and we made the decision to start taking the kids to her the following week so that I could look for a job.

It didn't take long for me to find a good job making decent money. Coincidentally, I ended up working at the same company as Tyrone, right upstairs from him. We'd ride together in the mornings to drop the kids off to school and to the babysitter. Then we'd make our way to the job, sometimes stopping to get a cup of coffee. Once we walked into the building, we'd kiss each other and head our separate ways. Sometimes we would meet on our breaks to go to the on-site store to get a snack. Every now-and-then we'd meet for lunch to go get a bite together. However, we made sure not to see each other too much at the job as to not get tired of seeing each other's face. We would've hated to get home and not want to talk because we've seen each other too much throughout the day. After work we would meet downstairs in the lobby, go get the kids and be on our way home while discussing our day. This was probably the most peaceful, yet routine point in our lives. We expected nothing worse nor greater to happen. We were at peace having two incomes and a regular life like we saw others having. We were still active in church and were committed to four ministries each, which turned out to almost be the demise of our marriage and our family.

One sunny afternoon we figured we'd take the kids out for a while. It was beautiful outside, hot too hot and not cold at all. The plan was to go to the park and let them run until they looked like they'd had enough. We'd bring them home, bathe them both, then put the to bed. While riding, we spotted a subdivision and wanted to go check out model homes. We weren't in the market for a house, we just wanted to stop in and dream for a minute. Ty pulled into the parking lot, we got the kids out and walked in. A black woman walked up to us and introducer herself to us. We started walking through the house, looking at the decorations in each room, seeing what we liked and what we didn't. The house was beach themed. There were seashells and sailboats in every room. The majority of the colors were cool tones, like sea green, soft yellow, and turquoise. The house was beautiful. She asked us were we interested in buying. We both looked at each other with excited eyes but gave her a solid "No". After the tour, we strapped the kids in and sat in the parking lot for a few seconds. The kids started talking about the model home bedrooms as if they owned them. Tyrone looked at me and asked, "So what you think? Wanna buy a house?" I smiled, "You really think we're ready?" I responded. He said, "Let's do it." In this same season, every one of our married couple friends were buying houses. Seemed like each week we'd get together, someone else was telling us that they had just been approved for a house. Well, it was now our turn. We walked back into the model home and told the sales representative that we wanted to move forward with buying a house. She didn't hesitate to pull out the paperwork and get our commitment. We were so excited! We were about to be young homeowners!

After processing our commitment letter and obtaining every piece of information they needed to begin the loan approval process, they told us that our home would be ready on September 1, 2003. We were so excited! By now, we were in the second week of July with a new lease to sign for our apartment in September. We discussed it with each other and agreed that we'd write a letter to the leasing office to let them know that we were terminating our lease at the end of August. The goal was to pay our last month's rent then move straight into our new home on September 1st. Now, because we were young and inexperienced, we had no idea how the homebuying process worked. We didn't know that houses are never finished when they tell you it's going to be finished. And even if the house is finished, the loan approval process is a beast and could be extended and take weeks, or even months. Fueled by excitement, we started packing small stuff in boxes and putting it in a rented storage unit. We didn't have much to pack since we had already downsized, but what we did have we were packing with pride. When August rolled around, we called the builders to make sure that the house would be ready, and they assured us that it would. Still not knowing the process, we just knew that September 1st would be our move-in date. We went on family rides to the house weekly to see the progress. By the second week in August they had all the sinks, toilets, and countertops in. The four of us were so anxious to move in.

On August 14th, we had gone to pick the kids up and had made it home when the phone rang. It was the loan officer who was working on our home loan. I put him on speaker and called Ty to the room. The loan officer basically told us that he knows we were told we only needed fifteen hundred dollars for a down payment but after pulling our credit, running some figures, and consulting with multiple banks, the least we could come to the table with if we wanted to buy the house was twenty thousand dollars. "Excuse me? How do you go from fifteen hundred to twenty thousand dollars?" I asked. He went on to explain in so many words that because our credit scores were garbage and we never owned anything in our young lives, no bank would trust us with so much house and a fifteen hundred dollar down payment. After going back and forth with the loan officer about false promises, deadlines, blah, blah, blah, I hung up. I was so hurt. I looked up at Ty and his face was blank. After sitting there with nothing to say, knowing full well that we didn't have twenty thousand dollars, I'm sure we both were thinking "Now where in the hell are we gonna get twenty thousand dollars from?" If we're keeping it one hundred, we barely had the fifteen hundred that we were originally told was required; proof that we really weren't ready to be homeowners, but it was too late now. After snapping out of that lucid phase of thought, I said, "Oh crap Ty! Our lease is about to end." Ty's eyes stretched so big. Not only were we not able to move into our new house, but we were about to be on the street with two babies. In an effort to keep me calm (which he always did when he knew I was on edge), Ty told me that he would go to the leasing office in the morning to see if we could extend the lease. He told me not to worry, everything was going to work out. I trusted his word and was determined not to worry, but my determination wasn't working in this instance. We ate dinner, settled down and went to bed. I didn't sleep an ounce that night, and by the tossing and turning he did all night--- neither did Ty.

The next morning, as promised, Tyrone woke up, got dressed for work and drove over to the leasing office. He was gone for about twenty minutes before I heard the horn outside. I got both kids out the door, locked up, and headed downstairs, trying to lock eyes with Ty before I got in the car. I figured if I did, his eyes would reveal the conversation he had with the leasing office representative. For some reason, he wouldn't look up at me; he stared straight ahead until I got downstairs to the back-passenger door to let Dana in. He got out and strapped Lil Ty in while I made sure Dana was secured in her seatbelt, never even looking in my direction. We got in the car, buckled our seatbelts and began our daily routine. He waited until we got out of our apartment complex before he said, "Babe, it's too late. We can't sign another lease. They've already leased our apartment out." without even looking at me. My stomach dropped. "What are we supposed to do now? Where are we supposed to go?" I asked. He just stared straight ahead in silence. We drove all the way to Dana's school, Lil Ty's babysitter, and work in silence. I wanted direction and he was giving me nothing. Once the car was parked, we got out and went to our designated departments. We didn't even kiss each other before separating, which was a part of our daily routine. We didn't call each other for a break. We didn't plan to go to lunch together that day. We didn't even send each other an email like we'd do at some point during the day telling each other "I love you" or asking how the day was going. We were both numb. That evening, we met in the lobby and walked to the car, again in silence. We didn't ask each other about our day. We got in, picked up the kids, went home and did our normal, just without words to each other. We weren't angry with each other, just disappointed that we allowed ourselves to get in a situation like this one, with two children and no family to fall back on.

Saturday morning when we woke up, Tyrone told me that we were going to get our house one way or the other. In my mind, I'm thinking we're about to have a "Set It Off" situation. I'm not sure how it was going to work out, but it was better than sleeping in the storage unit that we were storing our boxed up belongings. "I mean, I'm down for whatever." I told him. He started laughing, "No woman! GOD is going to do it." he said with confidence. "Oh. That'll work too." He said he would reach out to two of our closest friends, Carlton and Carmen, to see if we could stay there for a week or two if needed until GOD manifested the twenty thousand. They attended the same church that we went to and by this time, had become like family. "O.K. babe. So, we're agreeing that this house is what we want right?" I said to Ty. "Yep!" he responded. In my mind I was thinking, "If GOD manifests twenty thousand dollars, I might be able to think of something else we can do with that money my guy," but I checked my thoughts and was all in with the manifestation. I'll admit that I was hesitant about moving in with our friends. Living together has the tendency of ruining relationships. I had already experienced this with my college roommates and didn't want to kill the great relationship we had with these two. They were special to us. But on the other hand, what was the option? Live in a hotel with two babies? Live in the storage unit? Go to another apartment with the fifteen hundred we had saved and forget the possibility of owning our home? To be honest, there were about three other possibilities but none of them would've really worked. Ty went in the bedroom and made the call to our friends, who opened the doors to their home for us with zero expectations or hesitation after consulting with each other.

We moved in with Carlton and Carmen on September 2nd. We would go pick up the kids after work daily and ride out to the house to pray. We were so radical about GOD manifesting that twenty thousand dollars until we would march around the outside of the house quoting scriptures and praising GOD at the top of our voices, kids and all. I'm sure the people who had already moved into their homes were looking at us like we were completely nuts. We didn't care. We knew what we wanted and was believing that it was going to happen. The kids would ask about the house every single day, wanting to know when we were moving in and if they could they paint their rooms as soon as we did. We had no idea when we would be moving in, or even if we would be moving in. We all believed! We had friends praying and agreeing with us. We had family praying and believing with us. We were set on having that specific house, no exceptions.

Week two of us living with our friends rolled around and still no call from the loan officer. Ty and I encouraged each other to keep from doubting what we felt we knew GOD was going to do for us. We were still going out to the house, marching, praising, quoting, and scaring the neighbors. We were still living with our friends and enjoying family dinners with them and their daughter. We were still going to work and keeping up with our new normal routine. Saturday, September 13th, we had gone out to the house, took the kids to the park, went to get something to eat, and walked the mall. Essentially, we spent some family time with just the four of us before we went back to the house with Carlton and Carmen. We were careful to give them their space, so as to not wear out our welcome too quickly since we didn't know how long we were going to be in this situation. That evening, we had just pulled up to the house when the phone rang. It was Tyrone's mom. She shared with him that his grandmother had just passed away. Tyrone was distraught. This loss rocked him to his core. This was the woman partially raised him. She spoiled Tyrone. The love he had for his grandma was special. She was the first one in his family that I actually felt welcomed by when I met everyone, with the exception of Moe. This was a deep wound as she was the matriarch of his family. We sat outside and cried together for about twenty minutes. Once I got it out of my system, I gathered myself so that I could be some sort of comfort and support for him. We sat there for about an hour before he asked me to go inside so that he could have a moment alone. As I was walking away, I heard him break down into audible sobs. My heart broke for him because I knew the importance of this woman in his life. I also knew what it felt like because I lost my grandmother, my rock, in May of 1998. It hurt me to see him so hurt, especially because I knew this hurt well.

On Monday, September 15th, we got up and went about our normal routine. While eating dinner that evening the phone rang. It was the loan officer. He told us to be at the closing table on Thursday September 18th at 1:15 with the fifteen hundred dollars we had initially committed to. I wasn't about to ask one question. All I knew is that we were showing up with our little fifteen-hundred-dollar cashier's check to sign closing documents for our new home. We were in total shock. What did GOD do? Where's the twenty thousand dollars requirement? We told the loan officer that we'd be there at 1:15 p.m. and not a minute later. Jobs? What jobs? Whatever! We hung up and started screaming. HE didn't do it how we expected it to be done but HE did it! We showed up at the closing table with our money order and the biggest smiles ever. Once we signed the paperwork, the loan officer put the keys in our hands and said, "Congratulations on your new home Mr. and Mrs. Johnson." Unbelievable. We were still the same young kids with bad credit, and barely two nickels to rub together. Yet, we were about to move into a three-thousand square foot home. How?

We immediately went to pick up the kids and went to the house. We didn't tell them that the house was ours until we pulled into the garage for the first time that evening. We opened the door with our new key and smelled the new-home smell. Technically, we were still kids with a young family. We didn't know what we were doing, we just know that we had accomplished something together. We acted like complete fools running up and down the stairs yelling and screaming from excitement. That night, we went and bought blankets and slept on the floor with no curtains, furniture, anything. We were just excited to be in our home. We were homeowners! The next day, we went to work and took that Wednesday off to move in. We got up Wednesday, took the kids to school and the babysitter, rented a moving truck and moved in everything we had, just the two of us. He pulled his weight and I pulled mine. After getting everything inside the house and in its proper place, we sat in the middle of the floor full of energy, still in shock, but not disbelief. Ty looked me in my eyes and said, "Thank you for being that "grab your end" type of woman. You never drop your end and I appreciate that about you". Those words meant so much to me. He had no idea how many times I wanted to give up because I hated being uncomfortable. But his acknowledgement that I never did was what I needed to know that he appreciated that I didn't. It was at this moment that we got the revelation of how powerful we were when we agreed on something.

A few months later, we were finally completely settled in. We had one of Jacksonville's best painters to paint each room in the house. I was in love with the kitchen because it was open, spacious, and red. We had furniture in every room but one. It was a two-story, three-bedroom, two-and-a-half-bathrooms home, and it belonged to us. We entertained family and friends often. The kids were loving their new space and new school. We had gotten into a new routine and by now because I had a new job. We were living our best lives! Now that we've got two cars, we would go our separate ways in the morning. We'd trade off weeks for taking the kids to school and picking them up. We would meet up at home in the evenings, eat dinner together as a family as usual, and enjoy each other's stories about how our day went, all to wake up and repeat it again the next day. We felt like we were progressing in life as a family. Our two-income situation was causing us to thrive and we were in a good place.

One day, while sitting eating dinner, Tyrone told me that he had been hearing talks about a massive layoff at his job. Hoping that he wasn't telling me that he was about to get laid off, I asked did it have anything to do with his department? He said Dee told him that they wouldn't be affected and that they were safe. "Thank GOD" I said, then changed the subject. This was not what I wanted to be thinking about right now. I was grateful that he was confident that his department was exempt from the office-gossip layoff talks. Our conversation shifted to telling the kids how when we were younger, we'd use cardboard and clothes baskets and slide down the stairs in our houses in East Cleveland. They doubted us, I'm assuming because it was too far-fetched for them to see us at our age flying down the stairs as kids. So of course, we had to prove it. I went and got a random box that we still had in the garage from the move and Ty went and got a clothes basket. We taught the kids the joys of simple, yet daring fun. Dana grabbed the cardboard and Lil Ty grabbed the basket and they were on their way. About twenty minutes in, I heard a loud tumble. I panicked as I ran to the stairs to see what was happening. Lil Ty had flipped down the stairs in the basket and ended up with the basket on top of him. "Son! Are you hurt?" I yelled, as I was running toward him. Before I could get close to him, he popped up, giggled and ran back up the stairs with the basket in hand ready to do it again. He had so much of what's considered "boy energy". I looked back and Ty was still sitting in the exact same place, unbothered as usual. "Baby, why didn't you come check on my son?" I asked. "Because you were doing it. What was I supposed to do when you were already right there? There would've been two of us staring at him while he jumped up giggling." Once Dana saw her brother flip down the stairs in the basket, she decided that it may be best for her to sit back and cheer him on. After seeing his tumble, she was not with the possibility of experiencing the same. She was having no parts of it. Every time he'd make it to the bottom, she would encourage him to do it again, and he would.

Two months later, what was just dinner time layoff talk became reality. Tyrone called me from work to tell me that he had just left a meeting where he found out that he was being laid off. Trying not to panic, I told him that we would talk about it when we got home. I hung up and my heart dropped to my stomach. I knew the income from my new job couldn't support our brand-new home and all of the expenses that came along with it. Once Ty got home, he told me that a part of his layoff was a not-so-big severance package. That severance package was enough to keep us afloat for two, maybe three months along with my income. This meant that I would have to take on everything alone. We wondered how things were going to work out since we were used to making it work with two full-time incomes. He immediately began thinking about remedies to replace his soon-to-be missing income.

In the months to come after the layoff, we faced tough times. Although we always had food in the refrigerator and lights, we had started getting behind on other household bills. Our mortgage payments fell behind. We had a car repossessed. Then, right after the repossession, the other car broke down. We had to get a two-seater stick shift truck from a friend for transportation, which I had no idea how to drive, but eventually learned. Something important to remember is that there were 4 of us; 2 adults and 2 not-so-babies anymore. We'd have to ride with Dana in the middle sharing the seat with me and Lil Ty sitting on my lap. If by chance a police officer was to ride by or pull up next to us at a red light, I'd quickly tuck Tyrone's head so that he wasn't seen by the police. At times, my baby would end up on the floor of the truck between my legs because we would be trying to hide so fast. We couldn't afford a ticket. We were "riding dirty" for months, as we had no insurance and no room in that two-seater truck for the four of us. Everything about those rides was both illegal and uncomfortable.

After hitting the 90-days delinquent mark on our mortgage, we knew that we were sinking. Ty walked to the mailbox and pulled the delinquency notice the mailbox. Because I worked for a mortgage company, I knew how the delinquency and foreclosure process worked. I knew that it took approximately 6 months to foreclose in the state of Florida. I knew that we had some time to make some money and bring our loan current. What I didn't know is where we were going to get the money from within 90 days. Tyrone started asking questions about bankruptcy to stall the process until we got the money. I answered with the knowledge I had gained from working at the mortgage company, but told him that we needed to speak to an attorney about the details. Within two days, we were sitting in a bankruptcy attorney's office. He educated us on the process and our options. Immediately after leaving the attorney's office, Tyrone suggested that we file Chapter 13. "O.K. but how will we get the money to pay for the debt that will remain, including the house?" I asked. He didn't know, but said that we would buy ourselves time to get things in order and try to figure it out. I didn't understand the plan and wasn't willing to budge until he helped me understand. In my mind, we were postponing the inevitable. Ty figured that we would file and give him time to find a job. I questioned what happens if he doesn't find a job but he was one hundred percent sure that he would. He had planned to follow Dee, his former V.P. to his new job. I told him he had two months to make it happen if we were going to go this route. He agreed with the two-month plan and I agreed with the bankruptcy. We filed nine days after speaking with the attorney.

Prolificreations

*T*yrone's job search was going terrible. Two months turned into 4 months. A Chapter 13 bankruptcy turned into another Chapter 13, then a Chapter 7. We went from trying to complete a repayment plan to keep our home to trying to find a buyer to sell the house that we believed so hard for. I was disgusted on so many levels. I was mad at him because I trusted his "plan". I was mad at myself because I trusted his plan. Since when did I trust anyone? Especially with my well-being? Kendra, you're falling off baby girl, get it together.

One day he sat me down and asked me about starting his own business. "Doing what?" I asked. Because he had been designing flyers and posters for the job, he thought that he would be great at graphic design. I jokingly brought up the fraud felony he had on his record, "I mean, if you can fool the bank and have them cash a check that isn't even theirs, I don't see why not. Then again, you got caught so…" After we laughed and made several jokes about it, he got excited about the possibilities. "How can you design anything without a computer? You need a computer babe." I reminded him. He knew he did, but knew we had no money to get one. It just so happened that I was scheduled to get my quarterly bonus from my job the next week. We took some of that money and bought him a new laptop with all the bells and whistles. We came home and set everything up with his office being in the upstairs loft. After the set-up, he thanked me for believing in him. "Babe, I got us. You go do what needs to be done to grow this. I'll hold down anything I need to hold down so that we could move forward. O.K.? You've got this." Tyrone was speechless and in tears, but I meant what I said when I looked him in his eyes. I believed in him. His talent and his humility was like none other I'd ever experienced in any man in my life. He named the business Prolificreations. He was ready to make some things shake; and I was willing and ready to hold him down. The stipulations to this "hold us down" agreement was as long as he was doing what he had to do to build the business and keep us first, I'm all in. He understood, and so did I. We shook on it the way married people shake on it. And just like that, we were business owners.

Although I was still going to work, there was no way for me to handle all the bills alone. The stress of it all had begun to push us both to the edge. He was concerned about what people would think once we sold our house and moved, because so many people were rejoicing with us when we closed on it. I couldn't care any less about what people thought, my concern was linked to the fact that I wanted stability for my babies. I hated the thought of moving my children from house to house, and from school to school, but I knew that at this point, we didn't have an option. After sitting down and coming to grips with the fact that we're about to lose our house, I dried my tears, opened the door to the closet that I was laying in crying my eyes out, and walked out with a new outlook. If we got it once, we'll get it again. At that point, it was whatever.

On the day we signed the paperwork to sell the house, Tyrone was distraught. It was no longer our home. We signed the paperwork with the agreement of staying in the property and renting from the new owners. We had no idea that we had signed our home over to a straw buyer who was a part of a scheme to commit bank, mail, and wire fraud. We paid rent for three months until we realized what we'd gotten ourselves into. By this time, we were being forced out by the new owner. We now had 31 days to find a new home. Tyrone wanted to rent a house in the hood. I refused to move to that area knowing the crime and activity that happens over there. "Are you crazy? I'm not putting my babies in that atmosphere when we can afford not to!" He was thinking about saving money. I was thinking about saving my kids. We argued for three days about this. I didn't care, I wasn't budging on this one, ever. All I could see was me beating up someone's child for messing with my children. Their mother could've gotten it too. I didn't want the drama that came along with moving in that area. After searching for about a week, I was able to find a new home to rent within the allotted time frame in the same area where we already lived. This was great because it saved us from having to find a new school for the kids. That meant that they wouldn't have to be stuck with being the new kids and having to make new friends, which allowed us to keep some stability for them. It was so hard to say goodbye to our home. Separating from it took a toll on our marriage.

Living in the new house that we had called home for 23 months was an emotional roller coaster. It was a nice 4-bed/ 2-bath house in a nice subdivision. It was affordable and had plenty of room for friends and family to visit. Tyrone had turned one of the bedrooms into an office for the two of us. I would wake up Monday through Friday, make sure the kids are ready for school, and head out to work. He would wake up, walk the kids to the bus stop, return home and get to work on Prolificreations. Over time, he began to get clients. People were paying Tyrone and Tyrone was pumping projects out left and right. His talent and creativity were second to none. He was doing work for churches, corporate America, financial institutions, charter and public schools, and non-profit businesses, while mentoring young men on how to do what he had been naturally blessed to do. The problem lied in the fact that he had never ran a business before and it was apparent. He would do work for people without receiving any form of payment up front. He was the honest and trustworthy guy and assumed that people were the same; they weren't. Because of his big heart, he would do things for people and it would end up being done for free. Free wasn't paying the bills. He was driving to deliver projects much further than the amount the project was worth. He did work for popular sports figures who never paid him during big events. He did work for a business man who was also a pastor and prominent figure in the city who not only refused to pay him, but who also ended up bad-mouthing me in a profanity laced email because I told Tyrone not to work with him in the beginning. I knew he was a crook and apparently, I wasn't wrong.

"O.K. baby, we've got to have a talk." I had to step up. Ty had done this alone long enough. I was there to help but was wondering if he would open up for the help. Oh well, whether he was or not, in my mind he didn't have much of a choice. If I'm the one supporting this, I'm going to say what I've got to say whether he liked it or not. But I had to be strategic about the approach. Ty was like the average man when it came to pride so I knew I had to set the mood for him to listen. Everyone thought of him as an easy-going guy all the time. As great as he was, he was also stubborn at times. I had to be wise, because my stubborn and his stubborn clashed when pride was involved. I invited him out to dinner one evening to a restaurant on the water. We sat down over dinner and wine and discussed current business practices and soon-to-be (which he didn't know yet) business practices. I "proposed" that he start taking 60% up front and collect the 40% upon completion of the print project. Tyrone push back on this idea at first. In his mind, he had done so much work for so many people and they may not agree with the new payment structure. I didn't care what they thought. I told him because of the work he had done, they should be more than willing to pay for it. He had already had a proven track record of excellence and a great relationship with most of his clients. After talking through it and another glass of wine, he agreed. I also placed on the table the execution of a contract for website development with a 70% deposit, a schedule of deliverables, and the collection of the last 30% upon proofing, right before the site went live with a solid "go-live" date. There was no going live if the remaining balance wasn't paid. He agreed but wanted to keep it at a 60% deposit with a 40% remaining balance, the same as print projects. I agreed because dealing with him, compromise was important in this situation. There were several other recommendations I came up with, most of which he agreed to. I made sure to express to Tyrone that this was OUR business, not just his. This meant that we both shared in the successes as well as the failures. He hesitantly agreed. I don't know if it was the 3rd glass of wine that had him so willing to change or if he was just fed up with losing money. Either way, I knew things were about to change. The next day, Ty immediately started to draft contracts. He went online to find accounting programs and did his research to figure out which one would be best for the type of business we were running. He began sending emails to current clients letting them know about the new policies that he had come up with. Yes, he made it seem like it was his idea, but I wasn't mad. I didn't care as long as that money was coming into our house, in our bank account. But trust me, I made it known that I heard him take credit for the ideas I gave him We laughed about it and kept moving. He was armed with some new artillery and was ready to do business. I was so proud listening to him handle business in the office with clients. His confidence radiated throughout the house, and I'm sure through the phone to his clients as well.

The business had started doing well and money was being made. It wasn't a huge amount but it was nice. It was also pretty awesome for enough money to come in to cover the business expenses with money left over for gas money and the extra activities that we loved to do. At times, the business would bring in some huge lump sums of money. At times, it would bring in absolutely nothing, [consequently,] and we had to take from the house's budget to cover its expenses. Being business owners, spouses, and parents of two active children was full of ups and downs, but we were all in together. However, somewhere along the line, there was a shift. Tyrone began ignoring home as if the only thing that mattered was the business. I know this was important to him, but he had a whole family that he wasn't attending to. His attitude also changed. He began to carry a sense of arrogance. I'd bring it up to him regularly, but he seemed to be uninterested in what I had to say about it. We argued about it often. What's the problem? It had gotten to a point that I would come home and sit in the garage for about 20 minutes prior to coming in the house to deal with him. Once I got my mind right enough to walk in the house, I'd greet the kids, go straight to the kitchen, and begin cooking before I even went in the office to speak to him. He wasn't enthused about coming to speak to me either. It had gotten so bad that we wouldn't even acknowledge each other on some days. I'd eat dinner with the kids and some days he would show up at the table.

We had become emotionally disconnected. There was no intimacy at all. We weren't talking at all. I had started going out and having conversation with random people, mainly men. I'm a sapiosexual. I love great conversation. I thrive off of adult conversation and interaction, and Tyrone wasn't giving it to me at all. Although this was something that I had become accustomed to, we had zero communication unless it was about the kids. Dana was a part of her school's news crew and both she and Lil Ty had Pop Warner football and cheer schedules to keep up with. These were the types of things we mentioned to each other in passing; nothing more and nothing less. I became extra petty. I'd do things like wash clothes, fold all but his clothes, and leave them in the basket on his side of the bed. I didn't care because he didn't. I figured, at least they were clean. After going out and getting conversation and attention from others for months, I had become fed up. I was tired of dreading my ride home from work every day. I was frustrated with coming in the house and only talking with my children about their day. I was tired of being ignored by Tyrone and being replaced by the business and his arrogance surrounding it. I was over it. One night, I sat in the bathtub and concocted the perfect plan to pack my children up and leave. The craziness in it was that I wondered if we left, would he have even notice. The next day I was ready to carry out my plan. I would leave work and get the kids out of school early. I'd then go home and get the already packed bags, put them in the car and leave before he even notices I'm gone. I had the money. I had a car. I had the ability to leave. Well, why is it that on that day I was unable to bring myself to leave? As much as my flesh wanted to, my heart wouldn't let me do it because I was so concerned that if I left, how would he take care of himself with no constant income. I came home that day and told him we needed to talk.

"What's up?"

"No, I need you to come away from the phone and computer."

"O.K." (visibly frustrated but I didn't care)

We sat down in the living room on the couch, him on one end and me on the other.

"What's the problem? I know you see that we aren't the same anymore. What is this arrogant vibe I'm getting from you?"

"I don't know what you're talking about."

I started pointing out how everything had changed since he started the business. I told him it's as if we no longer exist as a married couple and that he and I are like roommates who hate each other. I told him that the absence of his presence was so loud that it drowned out the peace in the house. I told him that it had gotten so bad that his children overlooked him. I exploded while telling him about the past several months of our coexistence. My words weren't sweet. I know that my tone was cutting and nasty as I was saying what I said. I was pissed and didn't care about his feelings. He sat in silence with a blank look on his face. Once I was done, he asked was I finished. "Who you talkin' to?" I asked with all physical restraint. I literally wanted to punch Ty in his face at that very moment. He said, "I'm just asking is that all you had to say." I looked at him with disgust, "Yeah." He got up and went back to the office. "No this clown didn't just get up and walk away from me without addressing anything I just told him. So, this is the game we're playing? O.K." Now I felt justified to leave him right there with nothing, zero. "Tomorrow, we're out." The kids were already in bed. I went to our bedroom, threw a pillow and blanket on the couch in the living room, and locked the door. I took my shower while thinking my plan through and went to bed. Hours later, I heard Tyrone trying to open the bedroom door. I completely ignored him. He eventually unlocked the door and walked over to my side of the bed. I turned over because I didn't want to see his face. I was heated from the inside out and knew that seeing his face would only ignite the rage I was feeling inside. He begged me to turn around and talk to him face-to-face but I couldn't. I was both disgusted and done.

"Baby, I'm sorry. I've been so caught up til I lost track of what I was supposed to be focused on."

"I don't know who got you feeling yourself in a whole new way, but you're not even yourself right now. Everybody's telling you you're that dude, because they think they know what's going on in this house. They have no idea my guy!"

"Can you please just turn around and look at me?"

"That's not what you want. Trust me."

"Please?"

I refused. I felt disrespected. I knew if I turned around, he'd be staring down at me with those big puppy dog eyes and I wasn't falling for it. I wasn't turning around. I wanted to stay mad because I wanted to leave. Nope. Bye. This was not the Tyrone I knew, ever. I felt like I wanted to fight. "Please leave?" I asked and demanded at the same time. Tyrone stood up from the edge of the bed and walked away. How was I supposed to take his apology seriously when for so long he had been acting like a jerk? I fell asleep thinking about my plan to leave. I woke up the next morning to him staring me in the face. I got out of bed and went to the bathroom to get ready for work until I realized that it was Saturday. I needed to get out of the house and away from him as quickly as possible. I showered and got dressed and pondered where could me and the kids go for some hours. When I came out of the bathroom, he was dressed too. "Where you going?" he asked me. "Out" I responded. Remember, I was good at holding grudges. "I'm going too" he responded. I was fuming inside because now I felt like he was trying to antagonize me. "Oh, so all of a sudden you wanna kick it?" The truth is that he really wasn't trying to antagonize me. He was sincerely trying to show me that he was making an effort to be there and involved. But at that moment, I didn't care. He grabbed my hand and in so many words told me that he was sorry and that he was feeling himself a bit. He admitted that his pride had gotten in the way. He also admitted that he felt like he was in competition with me and that he had to prove himself. I told him that I had been going out and was glad that he was coming around, because I could see the open door that I could've walked through had this unhappy home-life continued. (It's important to know that not only men are tempted.) I forgave him. He forgave me. We ended up going to the park in our subdivision with the kids, attempting to play tennis. None of us knew what we were doing, but it was family time.

It was something we hadn't had in a long time. It was what we needed in this moment. Laughing with the kids brought us back together, but I was still on guard.

Things were going much better at home. We were back to our normal, and life was flowing. At one point, we got the brilliant idea that we wanted to have another baby while trying to build a business and while I was still working a full-time job. Because we had previously taken actions to never have more children, we decided to go through the in vitro fertilization process. Over a period of three months my body went through so much. After the initial consultation we drove to the kids' school, parked in the parking lot to wait on them, and confirmed with each other that this is what we wanted to do before moving forward with the process. I went from having to give myself shots to Ty having to give them to me. I was walking around looking like I was four months pregnant for at least two of those three months. If you're black, you know that when your family hasn't seen you in a while, when they finally do, they think that talking about how fat or skinny you are is appropriate, and my family is no different. "Oh girl, look at your hips!" or "Oh Kendra, you sure ain't missing no meals!" was the typical greeting I'd receive when visiting my family in South Carolina during this time. They had no idea what my body was going through and I didn't I feel the need or desire to share with them what was going on either. Tyrone and I agreed that we would keep this process a secret until we had a bun in the oven.

Egg retrieval day arrived! Ty and I had to be at the hospital bright and early that morning. Because we both had to be sedated, we asked Moe to take us and pick us up from the hospital, which he did. He was the one family member who knew what was going on at this time, because we knew we could trust him to keep it a secret. My supervisor was the only other person who knew what was happening because she too had gone through this process. When he came to get us, he brought us these two little shell turtles that he had bought. They were out mommy and daddy gifts. He had always been like our oldest child, even when we were living in Cleveland together. After the retrieval, we were heavily sedated. Moe took us both home and made sure that we were good before leaving. Now, we just had to wait for days to see if the joining of the eggs and sperm was successful.

A few days later, we got the call saying that everything was looking great and that an appointment was set for us to come in for embryo transfer. We were excited. Although I was happy about bringing a new baby in the world, having no idea what the pregnancy would do to my body made me so nervous. I had fairly decent pregnancies with my other two, but the weight gain was excessive. I had already felt like I was huge due to the process, and that was with no baby. I feared what baby weight would do to me.

I had already taken off work for fertilization day. We took the babies to school together and headed to the hospital for the doctor to "knock me up" with three fertilized eggs. After it was done, which only took every bit of 10 minutes from laying on the table to the doctor saying everything was done, we went out to breakfast. We sat at the table wondering what we would do if all three babies were born. For the first time since making the decision to have another baby we both got scared. Apparently, we didn't think that part through. We went from enjoying breakfast to giggling nervously thinking about the possibility of having five children. What in the entire hell were we thinking? Nonetheless, we didn't regret our decision.

My body started responding to the fertilization with pregnant behaviors. My nose became sensitive to everything. The nausea kicked in. Certain parts of my body became super sensitive. I started craving ketchup. My supervisor would make fun of me. One day I stopped and got breakfast on my way to the office. I got to my desk, opened the to-go container and squirted 5-packs of ketchup on some home fries. She walked past and noticed the amount of ketchup, "Dang KJ! Let the babies grow first before you start craving!" I knew at that point that I was pregnant. All we needed was confirmation and the positive pregnancy test, which we had to wait for two weeks post-transfer to get. We still hadn't told anyone what was happening. It was the holiday season and we were planning to share the news with the family on Thanksgiving Day.

It was Sunday, two days from the pregnancy test day and four days from Thanksgiving. I woke up feeling nauseous. I went to the bathroom and sat on the toilet. Immediately large blood clots started falling in the toilet. I looked down to see chunks of blood the size of my palm. I yelled for Tyrone. When he walked in and saw the tears streaming down my face, he sunk to the floor at my feet. We cried together for about 30 minutes, just sitting there listening to the blood clots fall in the water. Although we didn't have confirmation that the pregnancy was over, we both felt it. After sitting there for about thirty minutes, I got up and showered as he sat on the sink watching me to make sure that I was ok. When I got out the shower, I called the on-call emergency nurse to let her know what happened and to get some sort of guidance. She told me what we already knew, that it was probably a miscarriage but not to be discouraged because it may not be a full miscarriage. She told me to have Tyrone get a pregnancy test to see what it says and to give her a call once we got the result from the test. In the meantime, she advised me to lay down with my feet elevated to ensure that the bleeding stopped. Ty went out to get the pregnancy test and came back. The negative pregnancy test further confirmed our thoughts. We were heartbroken. I cried more than I had ever cried before. I was hurt. Tyrone tried to comfort me in the best way he could, but it was taking a toll on him too. We went back for the blood test. At that moment, we conceded and didn't want to try again. We couldn't go through the physical and emotional toll again. This experience was too heavy on my body and our hearts.

The days after the miscarriage were rough. I had moments where I would sit and cry. I'm sure the hormone meds that were required during the process contributed to the emotional roller coaster I was having. There were times that I felt empty and hollow. My cravings instantly left. The weight that I had gained was still there, except the babies I had prepared my body for weren't. My husband was so supportive during this time. He would go out of his way to make sure I was O.K. in any way he humanly could. He could see me struggling. He heard me go in the bathroom and cry on many days. I knew this also took a toll on him. I would call him in the bedroom and have him lay his head on my chest and we'd cry together. Sometimes we'd lay there in silence; holding hands with tears streaming, speaking no words. It took weeks for us to bounce back from this one----still, the family had no idea.

You're Not My God!

Our lease had come to an end and we needed to make a decision on our next moves. Did we want to try purchasing again? Did we want to stay here another year? Did we want to try finding a house with cheaper rent so that we could save more money? Because I had the only stable income in the house at the time, we decided to look for a place with cheaper rent. Doing this would allow us to save more money to purchase another home in the near future. Ty and I began our search. We found a cute 3 bed/ 2 bath house on the southside of Jacksonville. The timing was perfect because it was time for Dana to go to middle school and Lil Ty was able to move to another magnet school with no problems. We moved into the home and quickly got accustomed to living back on the southside. One of the perks of living back on this side was we were closer to our church and my job. But by this time, business wasn't doing the best. It was costing more to run it, than it was making but we were still committed. I was still working full-time, and Ty was still working the business bringing in fresh ideas to grow it. We'd been doing this for 8 years now. By now, I was making really good money, was in management, travelling, taking Tyrone along with me on some trips, and in board rooms, so money wasn't a thing. What was a thing, was Ty running on what seemed like a hamster wheel with no progress in the business. I talked to him about shutting down and getting a job, but he was completely against that notion. "I don't think it's a good idea" he would tell me often. When asked why, he never had a real reason.

We were the perfect "show couple". What's a show couple? We went to church and smiled at everyone. We were still active in a bunch of ministries and people looked up to us. We had a following. We were what everyone thought was the perfect couple with the perfect little family. We were young with young well-behaved, well-spoken children. We had money, cars and clothes. We went on vacations regularly. We looked good apart and together. And even with all of this, we were miserable together. We'd get home after our super busy daily schedules and barely speak to each other. We were putting on a believable front on the outside of the house, but inside, we had fallen apart. We had hit another rough patch, but this one was super bumpy.

We had come home from church one Sunday afternoon. I went in the room to put my things down so that I could start dinner. I noticed Ty had already sat his stuff on the bed and was in the bathroom. Sitting with his notepad and Bible was a book titled Your Wife Is Not Your Mother. Wide-eyed, I walked out the room thinking the exact same thing and thanking GOD for whoever gave him that book. I had already made my thoughts known several times to Tyrone on this topic during our "shut the business down and get a job" talks. I was getting closer and closer to fed up. The business wasn't making money, it had been taking from the house for far too long, and Tyrone wasn't hearing it because he was in love with the notion of calling himself a business owner. Shutting the business down was something he didn't want to hear from me, but I was wondering if he was receiving it from anyone else, maybe even the person who gave him that book.

Pride had caught a hold of Tyrone and disgust had gotten a hold of me. I was done. I'd get up and go to work with the worse attitude. All I could think about was the fact that I'm up every day making money to babysit a business that has dried up and this dude didn't care. I started questioning his decision making. There was nothing he could tell me without me bringing up the business, and how it was sucking the house dry. He could mention something totally non-related, but I'd turn it into talk about shutting the business down. I was tired of it and I'm sure he was tired of me bringing it up. One day,

I came in from work and started dinner. He wasn't home but the kids were. After talking about our day with each other, he walked in the house and kissed me. I asked him where he had been, and he told me making a delivery. "Oh? Where?" I asked. He said he had to ride out to St. Augustine to deliver some business cards. "Why weren't they just shipped? You would've saved plenty of gas money." I asked with an intentional sharp tone. He went from calm to pissed immediately. "Because I didn't want to! Why you always got something to say?" he shouted at me. "Oh, this is what we're doing today?" I asked myself. I was ready. I had been waiting on this moment. I was tired of feeling like I was taking care of three children. I had been tired of coming home from work seeing him look busy, but not seeing progress. We had been in this self-employment thing for close to ten years now. I was fed up with his arrogance. Oh, I was ready and had zero intentions of watching what was about to come out of my mouth. I was once told by a wise woman to make my words sweet because I never knew when I would have to eat them. Well, that day wasn't the day for sweet words. They were about to come out as bitter as I had been feeling for months. "I know I told you I would hold us down while you build this thing but be for real my guy?!" Even his mom and my mom had already talked to him about getting a job since the season of self-employment seemed to be coming to an end. He got an attitude with every person who mentioned the word "job" to him.

"So you mad?" I asked. Yep, I was ready. I had this built up for a while and was ready to be the pettiest ever to get it off my chest.

"I'm tired of y'all telling me I need to get a job!" he yelled.

"Nobody should have to tell you if you get one! You think this is O.K.? You think where the business is at is O.K.? You think having to take from the house for years to cover the business is O.K.? You think me having to go to work every single day while you're here doing nothing is O.K. with me? Nah bruh! It ain't! At all!" Yes, I went there.

"Doing nothing? That's what you think I'm doing?"

"Whether it is or not, it's amounting to nothing! You ain't making nothing! No money, no good decisions, nothing! This crap is old! The business is broke!"

We went back and forth, loud-talking each-other and yelling over each other. The children were in their rooms. And although they had never heard us go at each other like we were in this moment, neither of us cared. We were going in on each other!

"You think you're better than me because you make the money!" he yelled at me. "You're not GOD! You're not my provider! You get on my nerves with that shit!"

"You still on this competition mess? We're supposed to be in this together! And I may not be GOD, but I've been your provider for the past how many years my guy?" I yelled back. "GOD has been using the hell outta me to provide for your grown man ass! Has He not?"

We were both totally invested in this argument and weren't letting up. In this moment, I didn't care about the outcome. He was throwing jabs at me and I was passing them right back. This was the most heated argument we'd ever had.

"I'm out!" he yelled at me. "I'm not dealing with this bullshit!"

"Good, you ain't no help here anyway! One less mouth to feed!" I yelled back on my way to the garage to pull out the boxes and bags we still had from when we had first moved in. I walked back in with the boxes and packing tape, started building boxes and started putting his stuff in them. He's looking at me like "Did she have those waiting on me?" I was done. He got on the phone and called Carlton to come get him. The same Carlton that we lived with while our house was being built. By the time he arrived I had everything packed up and ready to go. Tyrone hugged the children and walked out the front door with Carlton. I was pissed to the point of trembles. My son was in his room with a confused look on his face. It was a look that I'd never seen before. Dana was hiding under her bed crying hysterically. Because she was such a "daddy's girl", I knew she would be the one that would handle this the hardest. I tried getting her to come out, but she wouldn't budge. I went in my room where the true disgust set in. "You mean to tell me that this dude would rather leave his family than get a job?" I thought to myself. After that thought sunk in, I was done. I didn't want him to come back, ever. I didn't want to see his face ever again. I didn't even want to hear his voice ever again.

The next day, I got up, got the kids ready for school and went on about our regular routine. I was at work with the worse headache when my phone rang. It was the assistant principal at Dana's school. Her tone sounded concerning. She told me that Dana was in the bathroom and was refusing to come out. I told her that the night before we had some family drama and that I was on my way. I fussed out loud the whole way to the school alone as if Tyrone was sitting right next to me. "See! You don't even consider this type of crap when you're only thinking about yourself! Now, what if my V.P. wasn't as cool? What if I was to lose my job because I've gotta go deal with crap like this because of your selfishness? Then who's gonna make the money? Cuz you sure ain't!" I was still on it and wasn't letting up any time soon. It was a fifteen-minute ride of fussing and cursing. I walked in the school where the assistant principal was waiting for me in the front office. As we got closer to the bathroom, I could hear Dana whimpering. I walked to the stall where she was and had to beg her to open the door. The only other option was for me to kick the door in because I definitely wasn't about to crawl underneath it on the nasty floor. After about five minutes, she opened the door.

Her eyes were swollen shut from crying. I embraced her and walked her to the car, thanking the assistant principal for calling me on our way out. Dana blamed me for this, not knowing what had really been happening over the years. All she knew was that here daddy was gone and I was still there, so I had to have run him away. I could feel her bitterness toward me for days.

When I got home with Dana, Tyrone was there. He told me that he was leaving to go to Cleveland. He said he'd stay up there with his mom until he got on his feet. Once he did, he'd be back down to get him a place for the kids to come to. "You're going to stay with your momma? Instead of getting a job and staying with your family? You're going to leave your kids and go to a whole different state to keep from getting a job? Until you get on your feet? That's your plan? Bet." He bought his ticket that evening and the next morning he was at the airport. That day, I made myself a to-do list. At the top of it was to call a divorce lawyer. I didn't care if he had made it to Cleveland or not. I didn't care if he had made it to his mom's house from the airport or not. I had so many emotions and thoughts running through my mind. None of them resembled anything related to love or positivity.

When my mom got wind of the separation, she called me and in a gentle way, tried to soften my hardened heart. I wasn't having it, it was as solid as a rock. This wasn't something that had been happening just for a month, or even six months. This was something that we had been dealing with for years now. His friends, his mom, my mom, our spiritual parents, everybody tried to talk to us about this situation in hopes of bringing us to a happy medium about where to go next, with no success. "Mom, I'm done" I told her in the most definitive voice. I'm sure she heard the stern tone of my voice and knew that I was at the end.

Tyrone had been gone for two weeks. We weren't talking at all and I was good with it. The kids were back in the swing of things. Life was back to normal, or at least as normal as possible without him being there. On my way home from work one day, I heard a commercial on the gospel radio station about a service that was happening at a church on the Westside that evening and decided I would go. After eating dinner, I got the kids together and we headed to the service. The speaker was a world-renowned pastor who had a special way of getting the point through. His message was about faith and GOD's will for my life. It was so potent that it hit me in the pit of my stomach. At the end of the message, he began talking about how GOD is able to soften hearts. As he spoke, I felt like he was talking directly to me. He talked about being merciful and forgiving. Ever had the feeling while sitting in church that the pastor was talking directly to you? Well, I promise this man was not only talking to me, he was looking directly in my face. I was hearing him but didn't care about the heart-softening part. I was thinking to myself "Thank GOD I'm not GOD cuz I'm over it." I was refusing to receive anything he was saying about my heart being softened, although every time he talked about it, he'd turn my way and look me in the face. After so long of him dwelling on it though, I started feeling convicted. I felt like I was being bullied at this point, "O.K., get off of it already! Sheesh!" During that service, I decided to sew a seed of faith to mend my heart, but not my marriage because I was seriously done with that part. I just didn't want to be walking around with bitterness in my heart. I was totally aware of how hard my heart was at this point and was asking GOD to fix it. Things happened as I was growing up that made me build walls around myself. I had always had a zero-tolerance attitude about men and the drama they could bring due to what I witnessed as a child. Somehow though, throughout this relationship, I had become more tolerant to things that I felt like I shouldn't have been, although I probably should've. When I sewed that seed, it was in faith for GOD to tear down those walls but to keep me aware and protected. Although I still wasn't willing to put up with nonsense from anyone, I knew that these walls had a lot to do with my hardened heart. That night, I felt a shift.

The next day, was a Friday. It was also Tyrone's birthday. The kids and I started and ended our day as usual. My phone alarmed me of a text. When I picked it up, it was a message from Ty. It read, "Hey, look at what momma fixed me for my birthday". It was a picture of a steak and a baked potato. "That's cute. Happy birthday." I replied with a petty undertone. Some time passed before he sent me another message "Thank you. Send me some pics?" I said out loud, "We aren't even talking and this dude asking me for nudes?" So, me being me, I figured I'd be ignorant and extra petty. I started taking random stupid pictures of the sink, the backyard, the dog, etc. and sent them all to him at once. He responded "REALLY?" "Well, what do you want?" I asked. After going back and forth with him and starting to giggle a little, I decided to give him exactly what he wanted. He was pleased to say the least. Those pictures prompted a phone call from him, which was crazy because we hadn't talked in weeks. That phone call lead to at least one call each day, which lead to multiple calls per day.

Eventually we were talking about his return and the plans going forward, which included him getting a job. Part of these talks was the topic of competition. I asked Tyrone was there something that I had done to make him feel like he had to compete with me. If there was something, I was willing to apologize for making him feel this way. He admitted that it was something that had been brewing in his mind as the business started going down. He said that he started to feel dependent and not a partner. I did everything to ensure him that this wasn't how I felt until his refusal to get a job surfaced, which he understood. "We're life partners. We do life together. There is no competition as long as both of our names are on the bank accounts." I assured him. Ty grabbed my chin, looked at me and said, "Remember when I told you that you were a "grab your end" type of woman? I meant that. Thank you for never dropping your end baby." I assured him that I never would and the smile on his face said everything.

The Shift

On Saturday, November 24th, I packed the kids, some snacks, and some blankets and we headed to Orlando. It was completely random, so my babies had no idea why we were going to Orlando. I told them that we had to pick up my friend who was coming to spend Thanksgiving with us. We laughed all the way to the airport. Once there, while waiting for my friend's arrival, we walked around the Disney store and had lunch. When time got closer, we walked to the arrival terminal to wait. I looked up at the screen to see that the plane had arrived. Trying to keep the kids' attentive, I started a game that they quickly caught on to. Watching the gate in anticipation I kept the kids occupied. Tyrone came walking around the corner and my face lit up. He walked up behind the kids and freaked them out. We all cried. It was the perfect reunion. Dana embraced him so hard and wouldn't let go. He was excited to see the kids and we were excited to see each other. We grabbed his bags, packed the car, and was on our way back to Jacksonville with a plan to be even greater, together.

That Monday, Tyrone was online looking for jobs, but was still doing some odd graphic design jobs here and there trying to bring in some money. When I came in from work, he told me that he had put in several applications. I encouraged him that although he hadn't worked a job in ten years, he'd get something soon. However, because that was Thanksgiving week, I knew that he probably wouldn't hear anything too soon. I was just happy that he was back, and we were on the same page again.

Whispers on my job of a layoff had started brewing. The layoff was supposed to affect those in another location and the Jacksonville employees were supposed to be secure. Because this was the talk, everyone in our office moved as usual. I personally felt bad for our counterparts in the other location because I had traveled there so many times during the years with my job and they had become like family to me. I can't lie though, deep down inside, I was thinking that it was better them there than us here. I took a two-week-long vacation from work for Christmas that year and Ty suggested that we spend the holiday in Columbia, SC with my family. While there, I received a call from my AVP telling me that they had just left a meeting confirming that our office was going to be shutting down due to the layoffs. "But I thought we were secure?" I asked. She replied telling me that she thought the same thing. Mind spinning out of control, I hung the phone up and told Tyrone about the call. We were on vacation and enjoying ourselves, so he suggested that we talk about it when we got back home to Jacksonville. I know what he said but it was the only thing on my mind the entire time.

The New Year had come and gone, we were back from South Carolina, and I was back in the office. The atmosphere was thick because we had no idea what to expect next. We didn't know how long we had to work. We didn't know if we were getting any severance. We knew nothing. The next week a meeting was called to give us some details of the layoff. At this meeting we found out that we were getting a severance package that would be based on the number of years we'd been with the company; ten years for me and some of the other senior management. We found out that the department I was in was going to be the last department to be dismantled in July. My head was spinning all over again. All I knew was coming to an end in approximately six months. I called Tyrone that day from work and told him what I had just found out. Although I sensed a bit of concern in his voice, I could tell that he was trying to maintain his cool to keep me cool. He was always good at that, always the calm to my storm.

The next day, Tyrone got a call regarding a job. It was the manager from Harris Teeter, a grocery store located in Amelia Island. They offered him a position as a meat cutter in the deli. After talking to the manager for about 10 minutes, he hung up and told me that they offered him the position at ten dollars per hour. "Baby, that's an hour away. You'll be working for gas money driving back and forth from here to Amelia Island. It doesn't make sense." I said to Ty. He agreed but didn't want to call the manager back to yet turn down the job. About two hours later, he got another call. This call was from a local commercial real estate company. The owner was the person calling Tyrone to offer him a job as a web developer and graphic designer, however, he was only offering a salary of $25,000 per year. "A web developer getting paid $25,000 per year? Really?" Tyrone was slightly offended at the offer but had already agreed to meet with the owner in a few days to discuss. $25,000 was a slight portion of the salary I was about to be without after the layoff. Even with the severance package, that $25,000 wasn't going to cut it. Ty went in to meet with the owner a few days later and came home to discuss the meeting with me. He was wavering about taking the job because of the amount of money being offered, and so was I. What I did know, was that Tyrone was a hard-working, loyal man, and that he would get on that job and show just how amazing of a person he was. I looked him in his eyes with his face in my hands and said, "Babe, they're going to be blessed just to have you working for them. Go there, show them your worth, and they'll have no choice but to pay you for it. GOD will provide." Immediately I saw the stress leave him. I could only imagine the pressure on his shoulders thinking about what I would think of him only making $25,000 when I had been making so much more. Those words were all he needed to hear. Ty called the owner and accepted the web developer position. Then he called Harris Teeter to let them know that he wasn't going to accept their offer.

Thank GOD Tyrone had started working for the real estate company because the severance package money was leaving quickly. I was ready to go back to work and had a few job offers from people I had worked so long with at the prior company. After weighing the offers, I decided to go back to work with my former V.P and AVP who were both good friends of mine and were working together again. I went in for an interview, which went well. During the interview, I agreed to take the drug test so that I could start working immediately. When I got home, I called Tyrone to let him know that the interview went great and that I could start working as soon as the drug test came back clean. There was a brief pause, then he said, "Let's talk about it when I get home from work". "O.K. I love you." I said before hanging up the phone. When he got home, he told me to sit down. As I walked to the couch, I was completely confused. I had no idea what he was about to say to me. "Had he been fired already?"

"Baby, I don't believe you're supposed to go back to work. You've held everything down for the past ten years. Let me take this now. Go do what you know GOD has been telling you to do. I've got it from here."

"What do you mean? You're making $25,000 a year. How are we going to make it?"

"Remember when you told me GOD will provide. Didn't you mean it? GOD got us. I'll do what I've gotta do to make it work."

"Let me pray about this one."

"I already have."

"And that's fine, but I feel the need to do so too."

Being one hundred percent transparent, I was so used to having everything under control. If anyone called me needing anything, I always had it. When our family was in need, we were able to give it because of the money I was making. When we wanted to go on trips, the money was there. Tyrone suggesting that I not work meant that I no longer had control. This was hard for me. I didn't have to pray about it because I knew years ago that I was supposed to be switching gears. My "Let me pray about it" was my way of rebelling, because I knew the control was being relinquished and it was uncomfortable. Again, those walls that had been built up when I was younger were manifesting. Although I had gotten better, they weren't all the way down. We went back and forth for almost an hour talking about this new-found revelation Tyrone had received. Days later, I came back to Tyrone and told him that after praying, I was in agreement with him. After the initial shock wore off, he asked me what did GOD say I was supposed to be doing instead of working. I painted the big picture of a mentoring group for girls. He agreed and said that he already knew that was the route because he had seen the same in his prayer time. On this day, Epitome of Class Sorority, Inc. was birthed. He made sure that I had everything I needed to give birth to the vision before a launch date was even decided on.

Divine Order

*T*hings were going better than good. It was only God that we were making it off of a salary of twenty-five thousand dollars. Tyrone would go to work and put in a full day, then come home and do some jobs that were still trickling in through the business. I was busy building the non-profit and dealing with the very first group of girls who had come into the program. Trying to balance our busy schedules and family was a challenge, but we made it look easy. By now, we not only loved each other, but we actually liked each other again. We had put on the table that leaving or divorcing was no longer an option and that we would work through anything, with a couple of exceptions.

We were on a good path. Tyrone was getting frequent raises of substantial amounts at his job. Every time he would, he'd tell me remind me of what I said to him right before he accepted the job. And I'd remind him of how talented he is and how his talent and loyalty can't be denied. He was starting to see and feel his importance in the company and was happy in the position he was in. For the first time in our marriage, it seemed like we were in divine order. It had nothing to do with him working and me not. It had everything to do with the position that he had stepped into and the position that I had stepped out of. He was now the leader and protector for his family. Whether he made twenty-five thousand or twenty-five million, his attitude was different. His demeanor changed. His mindset changed to the mode of taking care of his family and being a well-rounded man. He was now a mentor for young men. They gravitated to him more now than ever. They actually listened to him when he spoke. They hung on his words and he was careful with them because he knew that he had a following. The pride and arrogance were both things of the past. Tyrone had flipped the switch. We were no longer in the "show couple" phase. What we displayed was true. By this time, we had left the church, but our spiritual relationship was growing. Our marriage was on track like never before.

We had both matured together. The kids that we were when we got married at twenty-two and twenty-three were not the people who we were today. I hadn't known this Kendra, but I loved who I was becoming. I saw my own spiritual growth. I supported compromise. I wasn't holding grudges like I was so used to doing. I hadn't known this Tyrone, but I loved him. He was confident and his swag was on full blast. He was supportive of the non-profit organization I had started and that he encouraged me to create. Our tithe went toward feeding the girls during our weekly meetings, providing personal hygiene supplies for the girls, transportation for some of the girls, and supplies that were required for our weekly meetings. We were sowing into the lives of these girls and we felt great about it. We knew who we were and where we headed. The kids were doing great in school and we had no worries

Usually, we'd take turns planning our anniversary, and although I had done it the year prior, I wanted this year to be memorable for Tyrone. I asked him if I could take the helm for this anniversary and he gladly obliged. I wonder if he did because he had nothing good planned. Either way, I had a few tricks up my sleeve. He was always Mr. Romance, where I was always the creative one. He liked to wine and dine. I liked to shock and awe. This year, I sent him on a scavenger hunt that started with a family dinner and ended with him walking into a fully decked out suite. He was definitely shocked and awed. Without putting the details out there, just know that he talked about this anniversary for years.

The Diagnosis

yrone would come home from work and I'd meet him at the door with a kiss inquiring about how his day went. He'd come in with a different story about what happened in the office every single day. Some days the stories were funny; some days, not so much. Often, he'd come home stressed after dealing with the owner and his wife not being on the same page. He'd sometimes feel caught in the middle, like a child. Sometimes he felt as if she had something against him because the owner favored him in a way. I found myself trying harder than normal to get his mind off the job. Because the demand on him was so high, he started the terrible habit of bringing work home with him. He'd sit at the table or in the bed working after we've sat down and eaten dinner. When I told him that I didn't want him stressing and working at home, he'd get frustrated. He felt that there weren't enough hours in a day to keep up with the demand that was put on him. I didn't want him stressing about that job, but he felt he had a point to prove.

Trying to help him de-stress, I started taking him fishing with me. Fishing had become my favorite hobby; and I felt that it would help take his mind off work. Although in the beginning fishing wasn't his thing, he loved the water. Eventually he began to like fishing and the peace it gave him. I tried getting him out on the pier or the bridge at least two to three times a month. Some weekends he'd refuse because he had work to do. It frustrated me that he had no outlet. There were even men in the office who tried to get him to go golfing with them on a regular basis. He went a few times and enjoyed himself but wouldn't make it a habit because he was usually at the job working on the weekends.

As the years went on, Tyrone's talents, loyalty, and leadership proved his greatness. The owner began to give him higher raises and bigger Christmas bonus each year. He had worked his way up the ranks to become the Vice President of Marketing and I.T. There were many perks that came with his brief advancement. We went to NFL football games regularly, at times watching the game from the owner's suite and being on the sidelines during team warmups. We attended concerts and comedy shows for free with either front row or box seats. We had free dinners and sat at the table across from influential people around the city. Because of the previous business, his job, and what I was doing with young ladies in the community, we had become well-known around Jacksonville and was influential in our own right. We had moved into our new home and were living the good life as we knew it, still smashing his thing called marriage.

One day, Ty came home complaining about heartburn. I had him take three Tums and drink some warm water. This remedy helped temporarily. The complaint started becoming more and more frequent. Tums and Prilosec weren't working anymore. I made an appointment for him to see the doctor, but he missed it because he had an impromptu budget meeting to attend with the company's owner. I was upset about him missing this appointment because I was the one who made sure that everyone in the house had their annual physicals and saw the doctor when something wasn't quite as right. Tyrone had never missed an appointment I set it for him. I was also upset because I knew they were going to charge us $35 for a missed appointment fee, no exceptions.

Without me knowing, Tyrone's breathing began to get shorter and harder. Friday, May 25th, my mom, aunt, and cousins were on their way down to Jacksonville from Columbia, SC to spend the Memorial Day weekend with us. Tyrone came home from work and went upstairs to install a ceiling fan in Dana's room prior to everyone arriving. He seemed pretty tired, but was pushing through. After taking everything out of the ceiling fan box, he asked me to go downstairs to get the screwdriver he left on the counter. When I came back upstairs, he was laying in the middle of the floor. I asked what was wrong. He responded, "need to go to the hospital because I feel like I'm about to die". I immediately slipped on my shoes and rushed him out. The hospital is only 6-minutes away from the house. When we pulled up, I asked him did he need a wheelchair or was he able to make it on his own. He assured me that he was good enough to make it. But when we got inside the double doors, he looked like he was about to pass out. The medic rushed to get a wheelchair for him. There was no one else waiting so we went to the back immediately. The doctor came in and asked about the symptoms he was having. After telling her about the shortness of breath, heartburn and dark stool, she decided to run a panel of tests to see what was going on. She was especially concerned about the dark stool which was a sign of internal bleeding.

They had to do an anal exam to see if he still had blood in his stool. Tyrone embarrassed me so bad. He was already skeptical about being there. After the doctor told him she had to stick her finger in his anus to examine him, he freaked out. I literally had to hold his hand and talk him through it. You would've thought that he was giving birth the way he was yelling. After doing the exam and finding blood in his stool and taking his blood, the results showed that his hemoglobin count was a 4. The average hemoglobin for a man is 13.5 – 17.5. The doctor told us that he was bleeding internally and needed to be admitted. Right as they were transporting us to a room, my mom was calling to tell me they had pulled up to the house. I told her that Lil Ty was home and that he would be able to open the door. She tried ringing the doorbell, calling his phone, and even banging on the door with no success. Thank GOD the hospital was so close. I left Ty after they got him settled in to go open the door for them. When I got home, I found my son on the toilet with his headphones on. I told them to make themselves at home because I was going back to the hospital to spend the night with Ty. That night, a blood transfusion was required to get his count back up to a functioning hemoglobin. They gave him two bags of blood.

The next morning, they ran more tests as he recouped from the night before. The results showed that his hemoglobin was rebounding on its own. This was a good sign because it gave hope that the internal bleeding had stopped. They decided they'd need to do an endoscopy and colonoscopy to make sure that there was nothing serious going on that couldn't be fixed with some medicines. That afternoon, I left the hospital to go home, take a shower, eat with the family that was here visiting and headed back to the hospital. Tyrone sent me home that night against my will. He told me that he was good and wanted me to go get some rest. I knew that the endoscopy and colonoscopy was scheduled for the next morning so I told him that I would be there at 8 a.m. the next morning.

Like clockwork, I walked in the room at 7:58 a.m. My mom and aunt joined me shortly after. They took us down for Ty's test. My mom and aunt made me walk down to the cafeteria with them, hoping to get me out of worry mode. Once we were done eating, we went back to Tyrone's room to wait on his return. We were talking when the doctor walked in and asked me to come to the consultation room with him. My mom and aunt followed for support. I sat down, my mom sat to my right side, and my aunt sat directly across from me. The doctor was sitting at the head of the table. He told me that when they did the colonoscopy, everything looked good. However, when they did the endoscopy, they found a mass that looked cancerous. This was insane. Tyrone rarely even had a cold, so where did cancer come from? My heart dropped. I felt faint. My eyes filled with tears.

My mom's face said worry. I could see her from my peripheral. But when I looked straight ahead, my aunt's face was stoic. I could tell that she was in prayer mode. The tears that were in my eyes dried up immediately and I felt a sense of strength. I looked at the doctor and asked what was next. He said that he would get with the surgeon to see what steps needed to be taken and that I should be expecting a call from the surgeon's office to set up an appointment. We walked back to the room where they eventually brought Tyrone. I sat on the edge of the bed and told him what the doctor said as well as the next steps. He didn't flinch. I don't know what was going on in his head, but his face remained calm and peaceful. He didn't say much. I asked if he had questions that we needed to ask the doctor. He told me that he was good and that all we could do was trust God.

My Insurance?

T yrone was released from the hospital the next day. By this time, the family had already gone back home. We went home and told the kids the diagnosis. We didn't know the next steps but were open and honest with them telling them that as soon as we found out, they would know. They were optimistic and so were we. Tyrone got a call that Wednesday to set up an appointment to consult with the surgeon that Friday. When we arrived at the doctor's office, Ty signed in and sat next to me. We waited for about 20 minutes before being called back. Once in the room, we waited another 15 minutes. The surgeon came in and introduced himself to us. After getting the formalities out, he told us that he wasn't going to be able to see Tyrone in this office because of the type of insurance he had. Confused, we looked at each other with a stare that only the two of us understood. The look between the two of us said, "I'm about to blow". The problem with this was usually I'm the only one giving the look while he's looking at me to calm me down, but this wasn't the case. We both had the exact same look. Before I could open my mouth, Tyrone went off. "Y'all play these types of games with people's lives? Really? This is my fuckin like we're talking about! And you're telling me the type of insurance I got won't allow you to see me in this office? Are you serious right now? Come on man!" I was sitting in the corner crying by this time. For the first time, I heard fear in Ty's voice. That fear in his voice matched the same fear in my gut. The surgeon calmed Ty down. He looked at me with tears in his eyes. He called his assistant in the office and told her to clear his schedule for Monday at 10 a.m. she gave him pushback because of something that she claimed she wasn't able to move. In a stern voice, he repeated himself for her to clear the schedule for Monday morning. He shook Tyrone's hand and told him not to worry, "We'll take care of you man". He shook my hand, "we're going to do what we need to do to get him right, O.K.?" The CNA walked us out to the elevator. She stopped and asked us could she pray with us. Of course, we accepted. Her prayer was direct and powerful. We got on the elevator with tears in our eyes, walked to the car, and drove home in silence. When we got home, both children were gone. We sat on the couch and prayed that GOD heal Tyrone completely. I don't know what he was thinking at that moment, but I know my fear turned into pure anger. I was upset that Satan felt that he could attack my husband, the best man that I know, like this. I was enraged.

The surgeon recommended chemotherapy to Tyrone to shrink the tumor before performing surgery to remove it. I asked Tyrone if this was what he wanted to do or if he wanted to take the natural approach. I presented a natural approach plan for him to consider before he made his decision. He told me that we could try chemo first and see how he responded. This required them to surgically insert a power port into his jugular vein in an outpatient surgery. Our first trip to the chemotherapy treatment center was surreal. His treatment consisted of the nurse sticking a needle through his chest into the port, drawing bloodwork for some pre-treatment tests, and upon favorable results, starting an IV drip cocktail of medicines into his body. The treatment took 4 to 5 hours every time. Once the meds were pumped into his body, he had to have a self-administering patch placed on the back of his arm filled with medicine to keep his immune system strong. He would be sent home with a fanny pack that held a battery-operated machine which pumped the same chemo medicines in him for two more days. On the third day, we would go back for them to remove the machine. Before we could exit the doors on the first day of treatment, Tyrone was throwing up uncontrollably. We were in for a wild ride.

Just The Two Of Us

𝓔very other week, our routine consisted of on-site chemo treatment on Monday, sleeping with a chemo pump in the middle of us like an infant for the next two nights, toilet hugging accompanied by back rubs, prayer, and bleach cleaning for the next three days, then back to the oncologist to get disconnected from the pump, inject sleepless nights. For the next five months, this was our lives together. There weren't many breaks during this five-month timeframe. During the weeks off chemo, Ty would try to recoup from the prior week, but it was hard knowing that once he gets a little strength back, we'd be right back at the oncologist that Monday. Tyrone was still working, and I was going to school. He'd be in the chemo chair getting treatment while carrying out his responsibilities for the job until the nausea set in. Even through that, he'd throw up in the little blue vomit bag, I'd clean him up, he'd rinse his mouth, and get back to work. I'd be sitting right next to him in another chair doing homework, praying for him, and encouraging him to eat the lunch that I had packed for our long days there. During this process, it was just the two of us. I tried my hardest to make sure that life for my children continued to go smoothly. I didn't want their lives to stop because we were battling this.

After those five months, the surgeon wanted Ty to stop chemotherapy. He told us that there was a specific medicine in the chemo cocktail that he was taking that would make him bleed out during surgery. To avoid any risks of hemorrhaging, he discontinued the chemo at the end of November and set the surgery for Monday, December 31st, New Year's Eve morning. We were readying ourselves for surgery physically, spiritually, and mentally. We were told that this surgery would be equivalent to a gastric bypass and that the recovery would be extensive. We were both in a decent place, knowing that this was going to be a challenge, but that we were going to come out on the other side of it. Tyrone was expecting to allow his body to heal and to push himself so that he would be able to get back to work as soon as possible, which changed on December 2, 2018, when he received an email from his former boss, the owner of the company at 12:24 a.m. The email read:

> As discussed previously you will be on disability as of the third week of December and off of our payroll.
>
> You do not work for our company anymore until and if I personally in writing ask you to work for my Company.
>
> I hope this is understood and I wish you luck and success. God bless you and your family.
>
> Thanks,

This was a game changer and a blow to Tyrone. He began to worry wondering how he would provide for me and the kids. I assured him that this was the least of his worries that I would hold us down while he's recovering by any means necessary. On top of the uncertainty, he was hurt because he was loyal to this man, his wife and his company, despite getting several job offers that were willing to pay him far more money than this man was. He also looked at this man as a business mentor and thought that the respect between the two of them was mutual. I used to tell Ty that he was loyal to a fault. He was the guy who would give everything to people who both didn't deserve it and didn't reciprocate it. I warned him about trusting people who could give you something then take it away without any hesitations, but he was just that type of guy. On this day, at 12:46 a.m. he found out that what I had warned him about was true.

The Second Half

December 31, 2018, everyone was there; our children, our mothers, Moe, and family friends. We sat in the waiting room expecting everything to go as planned. A call came through to the status phone and the surgical waiting room attendant told me it was for me. "Hello?" I answered. The O.R. nurse told me that they had Ty sleeping well, he was open on the table and the surgeon was looking around to ensure everything was O.K. with his organs. She told me not to worry and that the surgery was going as expected thus far. When I hung up, I felt a sigh of relief. I turned around to see the entire family looking at me with anticipation of what was said on the phone. I relayed the news to them, putting them all at ease.

While sitting there talking to one of our good friends, the surgeon walked in and asked to see me. He wrapped his arm around my shoulders as we walked to the consultation room. When I sat down, he looked at me with the look of despair. "What?" I asked. He told me what when he went in to remove the tumor, he found a large lesion on Tyrone's liver. Because of the trauma on the liver, he couldn't remove the duodenum because of the risk of death on the table. While he was sharing this, Tyrone's mother walked in the room. The surgeon tried to continue talking but I could tell that he didn't want to with her in the room. He decided to end the conversation with me and told me that he would call me later. At the time, I didn't know what these few details meant. All I could do is anticipate the call that would come later. I shared what I knew, went to the back and waited on Ty to regain consciousness after the surgery. I needed him to see me right there next to him when his eyes opened. This is where I would stay.

Ty stayed in the hospital for two weeks. The surgery took a toll on his body. They cut him open from his rib cage to below his belly button. He was stapled all the way down. He could barely breathe without pain. The first nine days were filled with a morphine pump and physical therapy. After Ty was able to get up and walk on his own, they began preparing us to take him home. We knew his arrival home was going to be a challenge because of the amount of pain he was in, but we had already committed to doing whatever was required for his total rehabilitation. Again, it was just the two of us in this. I put sheets on the couch where we slept for seven days together. I helped him to and from the bathroom. I bathed him until he was able to get in the shower alone. We started walking up and down two steps, then four, then eight, until he was completely up all sixteen. As he progressed, we went for walks to the mailbox and back two to three times daily. Soon, he was back up and walking.

Three weeks after surgery I texted the surgeon to get a full understanding of what happened in the operating room and to see what was next. The surgeon called me around 7:30 that evening. He apologized for not giving me the full picture on the day he did the operation but said that he was uncomfortable speaking in front of someone who made their way in the consultation room uninvited. He told me that while Ty was on the operating table, the intention was for him to go in, remove the duodenum where the tumor was located, and seal him back up. Unfortunately, while he was checking inside, he saw the lesion and knew that it was too large to leave. With that, he had to make the choice to either remove it or the duodenum. What made the choice to remove the lesion easier was the fact that the tumor had begun to take on a life of its own as it was too close to one of Ty's main veins that was supplying blood to his vital organs. He told me that cutting that close would've put Tyrone in a near death position and he didn't feel comfortable doing it. He told me that more chemotherapy would be required to get the tumor under control because it was being fed by the vein's blood flow. I had him on speaker so that Ty could also hear everything he was saying. After hanging up, I asked Tyrone what he wanted to do, chemo or natural. He made it clear that he hated the chemo, but this was the option that he wanted to go with. Knowing that this was his body and his decision, I encouraged the holistic route and left it alone for him to ponder on. We were back at the oncologist for his first post-surgery chemo treatment on March 4, 2019.

We were back to the same routine of on-site chemo treatment on Mondays, sleeping with a chemo pump in the middle of us like an infant for the next two nights, toilet hugging accompanied by back rubs, prayers, and bleach cleaning for the next three days, then back to the oncologist to get disconnected from the pump, and sleepless nights. By now, Tyrone had lost at least 100 pounds. I was doing everything I could to get him the proper nutrition, but he was throwing everything up multiple times a day. We tried smoothies, soft foods, all veggies, everything, but nothing would stay down. He was getting weaker by the day, until one day, he looked like he was knocking on Death's door. His skin had turned a pale gray color, his eyes were sunken in, and he could barely stand. I got him dressed, helped him to the car and took him to the hospital. We were sitting in the back waiting for the doctor to come in when Tyrone went limp. I panicked and started yelling for the doctor and nurse who rushed in immediately. Tyrone's blood pressure had dropped to 69/42. Standing at the top of the bed in an attempt to get out of the way of the staff that needed to work on Ty, I noticed that I was panicking. I stood straight, gathered myself, grabbed Tyrone's head and started praying immediately. I commanded that he wake up. I told satan that he was a lie and my husband wasn't going out like this. After 11 seconds Tyrone woke up and looked me in my face. Confused and wondering what had happened, I told him that he passed out. He told me that he heard everything that was going on around him, but he couldn't respond. After they saw that he was now fully conscious, everyone left as the nurse monitored his vitals. The doctor came in with the diagnosis of Ileus which included severe dehydration and malnutrition. He explained this diagnosis by telling us that the severity of the cancer had caused Tyrone's stomach to be paralyzed. He told us that the likelihood of his stomach regaining activity was slim to none. He decided to keep Tyrone in the hospital due to the instability in his blood pressure and the lack of nutrition.

Tyrone and I spent five days in the hospital, one of those days was May 30th, our son's graduation day. On that day, Lil Ty got dressed for graduation and went up to the hospital for his dad to see him prior to going to the actual graduation. Every single person on the hospital staff was crying as we made our way to Ty's room for him to see his son. When Ty saw him, he broke down. He told Lil Ty how proud he was of him and how he was so grateful that GOD was giving him the chance to see this day. So that Ty wouldn't miss it, we used Instagram Live for him to see his son walk across the stage. During graduation, I was on an emotional rollercoaster. It was a mixture of feelings bringing on a flurry of tears. On one hand, I was sad because my husband wasn't there with the rest of the family to witness his son graduate. On the other hand, I was grateful that my son didn't have to walk across the stage and point to the sky in his father's absence because he had died. That day was an emotional roller coaster.

Seems like we were at the hospital every other week after graduation. I had him back in the hospital on Friday, June 14th for the same symptoms. He was weak, vomiting, and pale again. The ileus hadn't gotten better, and according to the doctors, the disease was progressing. By now, there was no other treatment they could give Ty because his body was far too weak to tolerate it. Father's Day was spent in the hospital room with the four of us joking, laughing, and praying together. I brought Tyrone home 6 days after Father's Day. That following week Tyrone had a visit from a bunch of the brothers from our former church. I figured that Dana and I would leave the house for them to have it to themselves. After being gone for about 2 hours, I had to return home to grab my laptop; Dana and I were going to go to the coffee shop and do some homework together. The sight that I saw when I walked in the house was breathtaking. There were about 12 men sitting in a circle encouraging and loving on each other. This was what my husband needed in this moment. Although I had been there every step, praying and encouraging him through this battle, there was a different version of strength and encouragement that he needed in that moment that not even I could give him. This is where these men made the impact. I was grateful to them that day.

Our Last Ride Together

*J*une 30th was Ty's last trip to the hospital. When we woke up that morning, he was so weak that he couldn't get out of the bed. "Babe, I'm about to get you dressed so that we could go back to the hospital, O.K.?" I told him. He was so defiant, and I totally understood why. He was tired of going back and forth. He was tired of going in and staying. He was tired of me running so much. He was tired, and so was I but I wasn't about to let him sit here and slip away from me. He was in severe pain, was severely malnourished, and his eyes were showing signs of jaundice. In his attempt to compromise with me, he told me to just give him an hour to gather himself. I don't know what he was trying to gather but I agreed, knowing he just trying to stall. I told him that if I didn't see any improvement, to the hospital we were headed. After the hour passed, I took his blood pressure with a blood pressure cuff our friends let us borrow. His pressure came back as 79/52. "Let's go baby. You are not about to pass out on me like you did before." He was too weak to walk, so I had to have Lil Ty carry him from our bedroom, down the stairs, and to the car. When Lil Ty sat him in the car, he Tyrone grabbed his arm, stared in his face and started crying. With the little bit of strength he had, he pulled his son in for a hug. They sat there in that position until Lil Ty felt his dad release the grasp.

By now, the entire ER staff knew us, as did the nursing staff on both the ICU (2nd) and Med/ Surg (5th) floors. After tests, they moved us to the 5th floor and got us settled as we waited for the doctor to come in with results. When he did come in, the doctor told us that Tyrone's gall bladder had been backing up with bile. To fix this, they inserted a drain which consisted of a small tube being pushed through one of the bile ducts of the liver to drain the bile that he had been throwing up. Because we were standing strong on the fact that GOD was going to heal Tyrone, we asked the doctor was this something that could be removed once he was healed. His response was, "Yes, anything we put in can be taken out." They took him down shortly after that conversation and surgically implanted the drain. I sat in the room praying that GOD was the Master Surgeon in that room while they were performing the procedure. When he came back, he had a tube sticking out of his side with a bag attached. The bag had already started catching the green bile that he had previously been throwing up. They had also already inserted a PIC line into the main vein in his arm as a feeding mechanism since his stomach was still paralyzed. He was in pain from the surgery, so they were giving him medicine to manage it. Once he got the medicine, he was good, but they had to give it to him every two hours, as the wounds to his liver and his side were fresh. We spent that night talking about GOD's complete healing and our plans once cancer was in our rear view. This was the night that we started writing the outline for this book.

When I woke up the next day, Tyrone told me to get out of the hospital room and go do something. I hated leaving him alone, but he hated me being there 24/7. He told me to call Dana and see if she was down with going to the movies to see The Lion King because he knew I had been wanting to see it. Luckily, the theatre was right across the street from the hospital. I called Dana and she agreed to meet me at the theatre. While watching the movie, I was nervous. I hated leaving his side. I knew what he was going through and I couldn't stomach the vision of him being fully awake and alone in the hospital room, starring at the walls. I couldn't enjoy myself knowing he was lying in a hospital bed fighting for his life. As much as I wanted to see this movie, I couldn't get Ty off my mind. I hated that he was there, and I was in the theatre. I had my phone sitting in my lap, face up just in case he called. We had gotten toward the end of the movie when Scar and Simba were about to fight when my phone rang. I answered to Tyrone screaming, "BABE! PLEASE COME! I'M HURTING SO BAD!" I grabbed my jacket and took off down the stairs. Somewhere in that action, I told Dana that her dad had called and he was in pain. Running to the car, I thought "See! I knew I shouldn't have left!" as if my being there would've prevented the pain, or whatever this episode was. When I got to Ty's room, he was screaming. The nurses were in there with him, but they had no idea what to do. One had already placed a call to the doctor to see if they could give him something for it until they figure out what was going on. I sat on the edge of the bed, stroked his face and tried to calm him down, knowing that the more worked up he gets, the worse the symptoms would be. "Baby, try to breathe. Don't hold your breath. Try to calm down until the doctor comes." I said to him calmly. "DON'T TELL ME TO CALM DOWN! IT HURTS! DON'T TELL ME TO CALM DOWN! YOU'RE FRUSTRATING ME!" I knew that it was the pain that was causing him to behave like this. This wasn't his normal demeanor at all. I kept encouraging him to breathe because he had the bad habit of holding his breath when he was in pain. I didn't care if he was yelling at me. I was willing to be his punching bag during this time, as long as he was breathing through the pain. A nurse came in with a needle letting us know that the doctor had approved the pain meds. She gave it to him via his IV and he began to calm down. By now, Dana had followed me to the hospital and was in the room with us, sitting on the couch encouraging her dad. Praying, I sat on the side of the bed stroking his head when his eyes rolled back in his head. "Tyrone, don't you do this. This ain't it. This is not how you're leaving" I said to him calmly as I tapped the left side of his face with my right hand. All of a sudden, his head slumped in my hands. "Tyrone, no. Wake up now." I said calmly, trying to support his head. The nurses were scrambling with tears running down their faces. Dana stood up and said, "DAD! NO! DAD!" and ran out. I wanted to go after her, but I knew I needed to be right here next to him because this was not the end. "Tyrone, the devil is a liar. You will not go like this. This is not how GOD has this planned. Wake up now." I said calmly to him with less than an inch between our faces. Our noses were practically touching. His body had stiffened, and he felt clammy. "Wake up now." The nurses were now prepared to code him. The only thing they knew was that he wasn't responding, so they went into rescue mode. "Tyrone, wake up now." His eyes rolled and he closed his mouth which had been hanging open. He blinked and in a weak voice said, "I'm good". The nurses turned around in complete shock to see that he had regained consciousness. They rushed over to him to take his vitals. As they were doing what they were required to do, I sat there staring in his eyes and praying as they worked around me. "I love you" he said with a much stronger voice. "I love you more" I told him while still holding his head in my hands as we stared at each other. His vitals were good. He was back.

Now that he was stable, I needed to go find my baby girl. As I walked down the hall, I prayed for strength. There was no time to be weak. I was trying to be the strength for Tyrone, both of my children, our parents and siblings, as well as close friends. I was in a fog, not knowing where I was going or where I was. Once I snapped out of it, I was driven to the bathroom in the lobby. I put my ear to the door and heard whimpering. I knew it was my baby. I knocked and asked her to open the door, which she did. I assured her that her dad was stable and was talking. She was a complete mess, understandably. She was shaking and her face had "fear" written all over it. In that moment, she thought she had witnessed her father pass away. After I was able to get her to a good place, I had to go back to be at Tyrone's side.

The ultrasound tech came in to do an ultrasound on his torso. Ty had been juiced up on pain meds, so he didn't even mind the tech moving him around to get the film behind him, which was usually a bother to him. Because I had to step out during the ultrasound, I walked around the corner to get a cup of ice. Throughout the stays we had at that hospital, I had become addicted to the ice. Although I have never smoked a cigarette, it had become like a cigarette to me. I chewed it when I was stressed, when I was aggravated, and just because it was so good. When I came back from getting ice, the tech was gone. I sat on the edge of the bed and said, "This is going to be a story to tell baby". Looking at me, he shook his head from left to right "Real talk." We sat there and talked more about this book and started putting the pieces together. We were eager to get on the other side of this battle so that we could share the story of victory. I just wanted to talk to him about anything, anything that would keep his mind as far away from the situation as possible. He was fully engaged, and so was I.

The results from the ultrasound came back and the doctor was standing in front of us telling us that the pain was coming from three blood clots that had traveled to Tyrone's left lung. He went on to tell us that they usually treat the blood clots with a heparin IV drip which was effective at dissolving blood clots. However, he told us that there was a catch to this situation. He said that they could treat the blood clots with the medicine, but that there would be a chance that once they do, the tumor in Tyrone's stomach could start bleeding. He also told us that if the clots went untreated, they could travel causing a fatal stroke. After educating us, he looked to us for direction. I asked him to step out for a minute so that we could discuss this without the pressure. Once he stepped out and closed the door, I looked at Ty to ask what he wanted to do. He agreed to the IV drip. I beckoned for the doctor to return and Ty told the doctor to start the IV drip. The doctor told us that we could adjust if necessary. The nurse started the drip about fifteen minutes later. Just like clockwork, after the drip had been going for about 20 minutes, Tyrone started throwing up blood. They placed a NG tube up his nose and into his stomach to pump the blood that was pouring out of his stomach. His oncologist just so happened to be at the hospital that evening and came in the room to see Tyrone. He told them to stop the heparin immediately to see if the bleeding would stop. They stopped the drip but the blood kept coming so the doctor ordered for a blood transfusion.

For days, the blood poured from Ty's stomach through the tube, and into a canister. For days Tyrone was getting transfusion after transfusion. We joked about him breaking the blood bank. For days, I reminded GOD about the woman with the issue of blood in the Bible. For days, Ty and I prayed that this blood shed stopped. For days, Ty's hemoglobin fluctuated from anywhere between 6 and 10. One morning, I walked in his room after a sleepless night. He was laying there sleeping but there was no blood pumping through the NG tube. I sat on the couch, pulled my laptop out and started doing homework while munching on my ice as usual until he woke up. I saw him starting to stir, so I closed my laptop and turned my attention to him. He opened his eyes and smiled so big when he saw me. "Good morning baby" I greeted him. "Good morning sweetheart" he said back to me in a soft voice. "Babe, the NG tube is empty." I said to him. He lifted the tube, looked at it and shrugged his shoulders in confusion. I called the nurse in to ask about this hemoglobin. She told me that at last check, it was at a 9. I asked if they had done any blood transfusions overnight and she said no. This was a positive sign that the bleeding had stopped and that his body was producing blood the way to was supposed to do on its own. We began to worship GOD because after seeing the amount of blood that had been pouring from his stomach, we knew that this was a miracle.

Tyrone's progress had the doctors feeling good about his prospects of going home soon. They had gone in and placed a filter that would catch any travelling blood clots so the possibilities of a stroke were lowered. The nurse had begun talking to us about physical therapy to strengthen Ty's body prior to him going home. We were on the move and grateful for the progress. During the time that we were at the hospital waiting on a room to open up at the physical therapy facility, we finished the outline for this book. We were required to stay in the hospital until insurance approved to pay for the special nutrition Tyrone was getting through the PIC line. For days, we'd sit there and make plans for the years after we received the cancer-free report. He had me writing down ideas he came up with. I had him adding color to the ideas I came up with. We began writing this book. We were moving forward, knowing that GOD was going to manifest the healing.

One day, while sitting and talking, Tyrone started feeling nauseous. He asked me to give him the pale that he had been using to hold his toiletries. Before he could grab it completely, he started throwing up dark blood. I called for the nurse who rushed in to see the blood spewing out. The nurse called the doctor and told him it was urgent that he come. Once the doctor came in and saw the blood, his face shifted to hopelessness. He told us that he was calling in an emergency team to see if they could perform an endoscopy and try to stop the bleeding. After the doctor and nurse left the room, Ty and I looked at each other and didn't say a word. I don't know what was going through his head at the time. All I know is that I was fuming mad. I felt heat coming from the top of my head. Once the bleeding had stopped a few days prior, we knew we were moving in the right direction. This detour took us both by surprise. I was enraged on the inside, trying not to let it translate on the outside.

The team was ready to take Ty down to the operating room for the endoscopy, in hopes of stopping the bleeding. It was late on a Sunday evening. Two nurses came in to transport him downstairs. I sat in the room eating ice and praying but not even sure what I was praying for. The sun had already gone down. I stared at the headlights of the cars as they drove by. My mind was everywhere and nowhere at the same time. I was exhausted, more spiritually and mentally than physically. When the nurses returned an hour later, the team that performed the endoscopy came in following him. The surgeon came to me with the most depressing look on his face. "When we went down in his stomach, we couldn't even see anything because there was too much blood. Unfortunately, there is nothing else that can be done. You know ma'am, there's dignity in life, just like there is dignity in death. I hate that he's so young going through this. I'll be praying for you." Because my face can't hide anything, I'm sure that he read the "Man, if you don't get outta my face with that death bull" expression that was clearly all over it. I was not willing to hear anything about death because that was not a part of what we were believing. After the team walked out, the nurse came back in the room and told us that they were transferring us downtown to the main hospital. They were limited on what they could do at this campus, but the team downtown was able to go through his groin area to see if anything could be done. They switched Ty to a stretcher and loaded him into the ambulance to take him to the downtown campus. I beat them there and was waiting on him to arrive. Upon arrival, they put us in a room where we would wait until the morning for the procedure.

The next morning, they came in to get Ty for the procedure. I kissed him and walked with them to the elevator. We locked eyes as the elevator doors closed. I sat in the hallway praying and staring until they wheeled him back up. When the surgical team walked in, they told us that they went in through his groin and attempted to cauterize the veins that were feeding the tumor without cutting off any main blood flow, but they don't think they were as successful as they wanted to be. After leaving us, the attending doctor came in to talk to us about their Do Not Resuscitate policy. He was so persistent about Tyrone's current health situation and how pointless it would be to resuscitate him knowing that they aren't healing the cancer. As persistent as he was about the condition, Ty was just as persistent letting them know that if something happened to him, he expected them to do whatever they had to do to try and resuscitate him. The attending doctor squatted down at the bottom of Ty's bed and said, "You know you've got less than six months to live right?" "WAIT! EXCUSE ME? THIS IS HOW Y'ALL BREAK THAT KIND OF NEWS TO PEOPLE? GET OUT! NOW!" I felt fire. I didn't even give Ty an option to say anything. The doctor stood up and walked out. I was fuming. I could feel Ty staring at me as I paced the floor ready to follow the doctor and punch him in his face. Ugh! I could hear Ty praying in a still soft voice. I eventually calmed down and sat on the side of the bed. Ty grabbed my shaking hands and started to pray a little louder, eventually calming me down.

I had been the point of contact for all the family and friends when asking about his status, but he was still taking phone calls and visitors. Once we moved to the downtown campus, he decided to go on a sabbatical. He told me that he no longer wanted visitors, which he had been getting almost every day at the other hospital. He didn't even want the kids to come to the hospital. He said that he needed to hear GOD and he wanted time for just the two of us. Although I was confused as to what this meant for me, I was in agreement. I asked how I was supposed to deal with family and friends when they were trying to talk to him and see him. What I didn't want was for his family to think that I was trying to keep him away from them. Although I didn't know why they would, I knew the possibilities of them thinking this and wanted to eliminate the thoughts of this being my doing all together. He told me that he would communicate the parameters of his sabbatical to them and that we needed to fully trust GOD in the process. "I'm with you baby. Whatever it takes." I told him. That day, he sent texts to the men who had been faithfully coming to visit and pray with him. He then called his mother. He knew this would be the hardest to communicate this message, so he left her call for last. He sat in the bed staring off for about 10 minutes before picking the phone up to call her. "What's wrong baby?" I asked. "She's not going to understand" he responded. I stepped out to go get ice and give him privacy to speak with his mom. When I returned, he was sitting there crying with the phone in his hand. I took the phone and sat on the edge of the bed to see what was wrong. "I knew she wouldn't understand" he said to me. He was hurt. I encouraged him in his decision and explained to him that as a mom, I could see how she could not understand not being able to talk to or seeing her son while he's going through this. I did, however, tell him that I pray that my children always see me as a prayer warrior and not a worrier. This way, they'd never feel the need to disconnect from me to seek GOD. My children will always know that momma is going to pray first and pray hard.

During the next month, Ty and I played cards, prayed, worshipped, prayed, praised, prayed, laughed, prayed, cried, prayed, ate ice, danced, and prayed. He was getting blood transfusion after blood transfusion. They had him on two different blood pressure medicines at the same time to keep his pressure at a safe level. The goal was to keep it from dropping too low due to the loss of blood and fluids. They were giving him fluids left and right to keep his heart from overworking. He had started retaining fluids. Throughout all of this, he was still smiling and being Tyrone. We had a routine. I was confessing and speaking life over his body every single day. I'd anoint the windows and doors and told the spirit of death that it was unwelcomed in his room and that it could not and would not steal my husband's life. I'd do this every evening before I headed home to cook dinner and spend some time with the kids. I spent every day with him watching him sleep while I was doing homework, playing music and dancing at his bedside. The nurses had fallen in love with us, and we them. They had Ty spoiled, and so did I. One day I told him that he was rotten and that he wasn't to expect all of this when we returned home. We giggled when he told me that he was expecting me to do all of this plus more. "N-word please" I said, laughing with him.

On Sundays, we would watch Pastor John Gray's service on YouTube. One Sunday, the Pastor mentioned a healing service that was happening that Wednesday, August 14th. "I wish I could be there" Tyrone said in a subdued voice. "Want me to go stand in the gap for you?" I asked. Without hesitation, he responded a strong "YES". "Say less, I got you babe." I knew this was strong on his heart because Tyrone never wanted me to travel alone. Pastor John Gray's church was in Greenville. The fact that he wanted me to take a five-and-a-half-hour trip alone said to me that I had to be there. I called my mom, who was in Columbia, SC and asked her to go with me. She responded immediately saying she would and that she would get a room for us to prevent us having to get right back on the road to return home after the service. That Monday when I got to the hospital, I told Ty that my mom and I were headed to Greenville that Wednesday and would be returning that Thursday. He was so grateful. I only had one problem;

I didn't want him there alone Wednesday through Thursday morning. He gave me the OK to call his best friend and brother, Rico, to come to the hospital and stay with him while I was gone.

That Wednesday morning, I woke up and was on my way to Columbia to pick up my mom before heading to Greenville. When I got there, she was ready to head out. We made our way to Greenville and checked in at the hotel. We figured we'd get some rest prior to the service. I called Rico to check on Ty. He told me that they had been talking, but that Tyrone had dosed off to sleep and was resting peacefully. My prayer while I was gone for that one day was that nothing happened to my husband and I wasn't there with him.

When we got to the church, I walked in with the highest expectations. I knew that GOD was going to heal my husband, and if this is what was required, I'm all in. The service was SPIRIT-filled and during it, something happened. I found myself totally exposed to GOD. I heard stuff that scared me, not about Tyrone's health but about GOD's plan for my life. I saw things that shocked me about where we were headed. This visit was required for me, and I was sure that I got the healing that I came for while I was there.

I dropped my mom off the next day, got right back on the road to Jacksonville, and headed straight to the hospital. I couldn't wait to get back to Ty to tell him what I had experienced and about the healing he was receiving. I walked in the room to him sleeping. He heard me moving the chair to sit down and he woke up. I kissed him and asked him how he was feeling. He smiled and said he was feeling pretty good. "Babe, GOD is requiring a "yes" from us" I told Tyrone. "I'm not sure what the "yes" is for, but I know that HE's requiring it. GOD, yes. I'm saying yes to whatever it is that YOU'RE doing in this season." Tyrone looked at me and said, "Yes GOD. Yes." I started telling him about the service the night before and his eyes lit up like lightbulbs. As I'm telling the story and what GOD is going to do, I'm seeing the blood pour from his body into the canister through the tube that they still had inserted through his nose into his stomach. I was determined that I wasn't going to get discouraged nor distracted by what was in front of me at the moment. I went on to tell Ty about the atmosphere that was there.

While telling him about that night, the nurse walked in. I asked her how Ty's night went. She said that his blood pressure dropped so they had to put him on what they called "pressers". "What is that and how does it work?" I asked. She explained that the purpose of the presser medicine is to constrict the blood vessels in order to get the blood pumping throughout the entire body and to the vital organs. "Why does he need this medicine?" I asked. She explained that because he had been losing so much blood, the remaining blood needs to be able to make it around his 6'3" frame. She said even with the transfusions, at the rate the blood is pouring out, his blood pressure won't stay stable enough for him to survive. After she was done checking his vitals and answering my questions, she left the room. I turned back around, and Ty had dosed off. I sat there for hours watching T.V. and reading until he'd wake up briefly. Apparently, one of the side effects of the presser was drowsiness. I sat there until 6:30 that evening watching him dose on and off. Before leaving to get some rest for the night, I prayed, confessed, and anointed as I did every day.

The next week was scary. I'd ask him if I could call his mom to let her know what was going on and he'd tell me no, "I don't need the worry right now. I just need you to stand with me on this." When he first started the sabbatical, I told him that because he felt lead to do it, he was to take the lead and I'd follow. Therefore, when he told me no, I followed. One day, we were sitting having a conversation when he blacked out on me. "Babe. Babe, wake up." I pressed the nurse call button. The nurse came in, saw his state and rushed out to get the doctor and the Anesthesiologist. They ran in and tried to get him to respond, but he wouldn't. The group of 9 walked out and left the doctor, the anesthesiologist, Ty and me in the room. He was standing over me on the opposite side of the bed pressing me to allow him to intubate Tyrone. He told me that in order to save Ty's life right now, this was a must. He was trying his hardest to persuade me that this was required because Tyrone needed to have breath in his body in order to say goodbye to his kids. He kept pressing while I'm talking to Tyrone trying to wake him up. All of this was happening within a matter of about fifteen seconds. "PLEASE LEAVE NOW" I said in a firm voice. "GO NOW". The anesthesiologist looked at the doctor and they both walked out and closed the door behind them. I sat next to a limp Tyrone on the bed with tears streaming down my face.

"Baby, I need you to wake up. I told you this was not it. This is not how this is going to happen. You remember us talking about this? Wake up now. I need direction. They want to intubate you. I don't think that's what should be done, but if you don't wake up, I'll have no choice. Wake up. This is not it! Wake up now! Right now!"

Tyrone's eyes opened. He looked at me confused. "What's wrong sweetheart?" he asked.

"Baby, you blacked out on me and they're trying to get me to put the tube down your throat."

"I don't need that crap."

"I know but they want me to tell them you do and I'm not. But you've got to wake all the way up" I'm exclaiming to him as the tears are still flowing.

"Baby, I'm good. Call them in here."

I stood up, dried my face, and walked to the door without taking my eyes off Tyrone. The anesthesiologist walked in and was in total shock that Tyrone was wide awake. "Man! What's going on?" he said to Ty with a surprised look on his face. "Look man, I apologize. I just blacked out for a minute. I don't need a tube down my throat. I'm good." Tyrone said to the young doctor. "You don't have to apologize man. Now you're making me feel bad" he told Ty. He walked out amazed. The other 8 who were in the room were looking through the glass with the same amazement. "Baby, satan cannot take your life. You hear me? He can't. You're not leaving here until you're ready, and that better not be any time soon. You can't leave me. Do you hear me?"

At one point during this period, they had to not only max out the presser medication they were already giving him, but added another because he was bleeding so profusely. When they did, I started to see changes in his behavior. He'd sleep even more. He'd process things a bit slower. His body would respond slower. His arms and legs began to get weak. While watching and interacting with him, all I could think about was what I could do to help him recover from all the negative effects of the medicine. "God, I don't know what's going on, but I know what you promised me. Where's the manifestation?" I said out loud while walking to my car that evening. I cried from the time I exited the hospital doors until I got to our driveway. After I pulled into the garage, I got myself together as to not alarm the kids when I walked in the house.

I Wanna Go Home

On Thursday, August 22nd, I woke up with a plan. I remember the exact day so well because it was my mom's birthday. I couldn't wait to get to the hospital to tell him what I was thinking. When I got there, it was like he was waiting on me to get there. I told him that starting today, we would work on building his leg strength. It was time to get up and out of that hospital. I was so excited when he agreed because this meant that he would give me his full effort. I started by lifting his legs one-by-one and putting it on my shoulder so that he could pump his feet at the ankles. Doing this would get the fluids circulating around his body. We then went to the arms. I had him lifting his harms with minimal help from me. The nurse walked in and became his cheerleader when she saw us working. We were determined. I told him that when I come back tomorrow, I'll have the resistance bands and lite dumbbells. He agreed. After our 20-minute workout, he dosed off and stayed asleep until it was close to time for me to leave for the evening.

Friday morning, I arrived and walked past the nurses and gave them my sincere yet routine welcome. I walked in the room to find Tyrone sitting straight up in the bed. "Hey sweetheart" he greeted me. I rushed over to the bed to give him a kiss, "Hey baby! What in the world? What's up?" I looked and saw there was no more blood coming from the tube. I also saw that the presser medicine was no longer hanging. "Hold on." I walked out the room to look for Ty's nurse. She saw me hanging around the door and came to make sure that everything was good.

"Hey! I saw that Ty's meds were gone. What happened overnight?"

Well, his blood pressure started bouncing back so we started weening him until we were able to remove them completely."

"Praise GOD!"

"Did you notice he's not bleeding?"

"I sure did!"

"He's progressing wonderfully."

"Praise GOD! Babe! Your healing is here! It's done!"

Tyrone and I praised GOD for about thirty minutes. We thanked HIM for the manifestation of the healing that HE promised. We cried tears of gratefulness. We were so appreciative. The next two days were the most peaceful days we'd had in the hospital in the almost two months we were in the hospital.

Sunday morning, I walked in Ty's room and found him sitting up with a cup in his hands. When I kissed him, I smelled what I knew wasn't water. "Baby, what's that?" I asked. "Ginger Ale" he responded. With a confused look, I asked, "Baby, why are you drinking Ginger Ale on an empty stomach?" He looked at me with the guilty eyes as he took a few more sips. "But it's so good babe" he responded. The nurse giggled as we went back and forth about the fact that I felt that he shouldn't have been drinking it, but that he was so satisfied while drinking it. However, within an hour of him drinking the Ginger Ale, things took a drastic turn. I noticed his face changing from content to discomfort. "What's wrong baby?" I asked. "My chest is hurting. It's hurting bad sweetheart." I called the nurse in to him cringing in pain. She rushed out to get the doctor, who came immediately with a partner. "What's wrong Mr. Johnson?" the male doctor asked. "My chest. My chest." Tyron responded. They immediately started ordering an EKG and an ultrasound. "I don't think it's anything with his heart, I think it's related to him drinking the Ginger Ale he just had about an hour ago" I told the doctor. The female doctor recommended that they do the EKG and ultrasound just to confirm, which I was cool with. The pain started to move from his chest to his back. "It's acid reflux" I said. "He has gas." After the EKG and ultrasound proved there was nothing wrong with his lungs and heart, they agreed that it was probably acid reflux. Tyrone was in so much pain that he begged for pain meds. Although I hated to see him in pain, I warned him that if he took the pain meds, his blood pressure would tank, and they'd have to put him back on the presser medicine. At this point, he didn't even care. All he wanted was for the pain to leave. The nurse gave him the same warning, but he didn't even give it a second thought. He just wanted the pain to leave. She injected the medicine into his I.V. and within a matter of minutes, his blood pressure dropped severely, he was back on the presser with blood being pumped out of his stomach, and he was sleep. I spent the night with him that night, laid back in the recliner next to him praying and dozing.

When I opened my eyes Monday morning, Ty was awake. I asked how he was feeling. He told me that he wasn't in any pain at all.

"Praise GOD babe!"

"I wanna go home."

"I want you home baby, but you've gotta get off of this medicine first. They can't send you home on this medicine"

"They told me this is not a prison. I'm ready to leave."

"Then let's do what we need to do to get you off these meds, O.K.?"

I made note that the fluid and swelling in his legs had begun to decrease. We worked his legs and arms. We move around as much as we could without him getting lite headed. When I laid him back down, he told me again, "Baby, I wanna go home." I assured him again that we were getting out of there soon. He didn't say much that day. I could tell he was in his head about something. As I sat doing homework, I'd glance up to see him either sleeping or laying in silence. "Can I call momma?" I asked. "No, please." he responded. We sat for the remainder of the day, mostly in silence. I hadn't showered nor rested since I got there yesterday morning, so I headed home to shower and try to sleep. I didn't sleep well that night. Tyrone's "I wanna go home" talk gave me zero peace.

Tuesday morning was no different. When I walked in the room, Tyrone was asleep. When he heard me setting up my laptop to do homework, he opened his eyes. "Good morning baby" I greeted him with a kiss. "Good morning sweetheart" he smiled back. I cleaned him up, as usual and asked him how he was feeling. He told me that he had no pain and that he was ready to go home. I couldn't tell him anything more than what I had already told him previously, "Babe, we're going." He was a little more talkative this day. We laughed about the kids. We worked on his strength and leg movement. We prayed. We confessed. We told each other how much we loved each other. We giggled about our Shaw days. When it was time for me to leave, as I did daily, I anointed the windows and doors and told the death angel he was not welcomed, and he couldn't come and steal Ty's life. I kissed my husband and told him goodnight. I left him watching "Martin".

Wednesday morning, I walked in the room to a bright-eyed Mr. Johnson. "Hey babe!" Smiling, he responded, "Hey sweetheart. How was your night?" I told him that I rested well and couldn't wait to get to him this morning. I cleaned him up, helped him brush his teeth, and sat next to him in the chair that had become my designated spot when I wasn't sitting next to him in the bed. He wanted to talk about the kids, so we did. I caught him up on everything from Lil Ty and his girlfriend to Dana and her internship. He expressed how proud he was of his "babies" although they are adults at this point. He told me how he wouldn't have made it this far without me, and how much he loved and adored me. Although it felt good hearing this from him, I really didn't want to hear it, because I didn't like the circumstances in which he was saying it. My insides were crying, but I kept a strong face. We had talked well into the evening when he fell silent on me.

"Sweetheart, thank you for never dropping your end. I'm ready to go home."

I had already felt in my spirit that this was coming so I had a prepared remark for him: "Babe, we can talk to the doctor to get a plan for you to go home within the next few days. That way, they can ween you from these meds slowly and you'll be good. Cool?"

"Yeah, call the doctor in here so that we could talk to her."

"Now?"

"Yeah."

Instead of pushing the nurse call button, I went to the desk and asked the attending doctor to come in and speak to us. She followed right behind me.

"Hey Mr. Johnson! You're looking pretty good. What's up sir?

"I'm ready to go home. I no longer want this medicine. I want it stopped now."

"Wait babe, this is not what we talked about."

Turning and looking me in my face, "Can I please say something?"

"O.K. We'll talk when she leaves."

Mr. Johnson, if we stop these medicines immediately, it's not going to be good. Your blood pressure will immediately drop, and you won't make it through the hour. We've got another option. We can try to ween you over the next few days. This way, we can monitor your blood pressure and adjust accordingly. How does that sound?"

"No, I don't want that. I want them gone now.?

Behind his back. I'm looking at the doctor giving her the fast "NO" head shake. I knew this was not what we talked about and I needed to get into Ty's head space to see where he was. Seeing my face, the doctor stood up and said, "Mr. Johnson, let me go talk to my senior. I'll be back within the hour." She looked in my eyes as to acknowledge that she saw and understood my gesture behind Ty's back before she walked out the room.

"Babe! That was so not the plan we just talked about."

"I know and I'm sorry. I'm just ready."

We went back and forth about what needed to happen in order for him to get home. After about 30 minutes, we both just stopped talking. I did my anointing, kissed him, stared at him for a brief minute and left. My heart was aching. In my spirit, I began to realize that his "home" wasn't the home that I was referencing, but my flesh wasn't hearing nor having it.

Thursday morning, August 29th, I walked in Tyrone's room. He was still sleeping but I noticed the NG tube that was suctioning the blood from Tyrone's stomach was gone. When he heard the movement in the room, he opened his eyes. "Good morning Babe" I greeted him as I leaned over to give him a kiss. "Good morning Sweetheart" he greeted me back with his normal smile. "Babe, why is the NG tube out?" I asked with a confused look on my face. Ty looked at me, just as confused as I was, "I have no idea. Maybe it came out in my sleep. I don't know." Joking, I asked him was he trying to be rebellious. He laughed and said, "No baby, I'm not. But I am ready to go home though." I wasn't ready for this today, especially after the day we had just had the day before, so I didn't acknowledge that he said anything. I started cleaning Tyrone up and got his toothbrush ready for him to brush his teeth. When I walked over to him, he looked up at me, grabbed my hand and said, "Baby, I'm ready to go home." I gave him the toothbrush and walked back to the sink. I gave him the cup for him to rinse his mouth and wiped it after he was done. I took the cup a walked back to the sink. I was trying to avoid eye contact because the look in his eyes was different than the past days. This look was indescribable. It wasn't a look of pain, exhaustion, or anything negative. It was hopeful and positive. It was bright, life filled and happy. Yet, it was a look that I didn't want to see because I didn't know what was tied to it.

After he was completely clean, he told me to come sit down next to him. "Sweetheart, I'm ready to go home. I need you to be in agreement with me on this." The sense of urgency in his voice broke me. I started crying instantly. "Baby, are we talking about the same home?" I asked Ty. He looked at me and smiled. "I need you to be in agreement with me sweetheart." I stood up and started pacing the floor. My heart started pounding so loud that I could hear it. I was instantly sick to my stomach. "I'll be right back babe." I walked out the room and down the hall where I called his best friend and prayer warrior. "Bro, Ty just told me that he's ready to go home. He wants them to stop the medicine immediately." Hesitantly, he asked me what I thought about it. Hesitantly, I told him that I was in agreement. He told me "Then, that's what it is". I stopped to get a cup of ice before I went back in the room to Tyrone's eyes staring at me, waiting for a response. I paced the floor eating the ice like it was my cigarette. I paced and crunched vigorously. He never took his eyes off me. I could feel him staring at me, almost piercing my soul, but I wasn't ready to say anything yet. I paced in silence for a good 45 minutes, remembering a conversation that I had with one of his friends. He asked me if Ty was done fighting, would I allow him to leave. I told him that I would have to not only consider my own selfish feelings, but I'd have to consider Ty; and the fact that he was the one laying in the bed fighting so I'd have no choice but to let him go. After reflecting on that conversation in my mind, I looked up at Ty and said, "O.K." The look on Tyrone's face was a look of amazement. I had never in our 23 years of life together seen this level of excitement in his eyes. It was as if I could see his insides dancing through his eyes. "O.K.?" he asked me. "Yes" I responded. "Call the doctor now." I pressed the nurse call button. Seems like the nurse was sitting there waiting because she was in the room in less than 10 seconds. "I want the medicines to stop now. I'm ready." he told the nurse. She acknowledged what he said and went to get the doctor. When he came in, he started telling Ty all of the possibilities and suggested the same weening that the other doctor suggested Tuesday evening. He told the doctor that he understood, but was ready for the medicine to stop immediately. The doctor looked up at me to get my feedback. Trying to keep myself together, I gave a nod of agreement and the doctor walked out.

Tyrone had a smile on his face as he stared out the window. "Baby, what are you thinking about? What are you feeling?" I asked, making sure that he had a full grasp on what he wanted. He looked at me and started rolling his shoulders backwards, "I feel free. I feel like I've got wings growing from my back." I looked at him, knowing what was happening but again, not wanting to acknowledge it. The nurse and a CNA walked in the room to pray with us. We held hands as the CNA began to pray. At a point during the prayer, I broke down. Once we all said "Amen" she looked at Ty, still holding our hands, "Wow, you are so good with this. God is so pleased. It is so well with you." The three of them then turned their attention to me sobbing almost uncontrollably. She squeezed my hand, looked at Ty who had a look of concern on his face, and said "She will be too. Give her some time. She's going to be good." The nurse and the CNA left the room. Tyrone looked at me and said, "Are you O.K?" Still crying, but trying to gather myself, I nodded a "Yes". He looked me in my eyes and said. "If you're O.K., everyone else will be O.K." Again, I nodded, "Yes". He smiled. I wept.

Things began to move fast. The doctor came in and asked Tyrone if he'd wanted to be resuscitated if anything happened. He said no, which was a drastic change from his adamant demands that they do what they had to do to keep him alive the entire two months he had been in the hospital. The Palliative Care nurse came up to discuss what was about to happen. She told us that the goal was to get Tyrone home, since this is what he was requesting, not knowing that his "home" didn't mean the same as our understanding of "home". She looked at me and said, "Kendra, call your kids and get them here. I know what we're believing GOD for but they need to be here just in case." She left the room and made the calls for hospice to deliver all equipment to the house for Ty's future care. She also made the call for transportation to get Ty home. Dana was already on her way to the hospital to bring his clothes, but Lil Ty was at work at a huge warehouse. It took three phone calls and an hour for my son to call me. I told him what was going on. He left his job immediately and made his way to the hospital to join Ty, Dana, and me. While waiting, the nurse and her trainee came in to make sure that all of Tyrone's dressings were clean. While doing so, Tyrone was in full entertainment mode. It was the most lively I'd seen him while in the hospital. Within the hour that they were cleaning him up, they had learned of our love story, what the kids were in school for, how much we loved East Cleveland and Shaw High School. They had learned about polish boys and wings with sauce. Tyrone had given them the rundown on how proud he was of his "babies". He told them about how much he loved me and would give anything for me. He had them laughing about the stories when our kids were growing up. As they were cleaning Ty's drain site in his side, the nurse said, "If y'all lives have been just as good as the time that I've observed the two of you in these past 30 days, you guys have lived a great life together and I love it." By this time, the nurse trainee had giggled so hard until her face had turned beet red. As she was cleaning up the linen that they had changed underneath Ty, she looked at me and said, "This is the best first day I've ever had".

When Dana arrived, the palliative nurse was back in the room telling us that we needed someone to be at the house for the delivery of the supplies by hospice care. Dana called one of her sorority sisters to come, get the keys, and go home to wait on their arrival and delivery. When she came back in the room, Tyrone's smile lit up the room. The palliative nurse saw the look on his face and how he was staring at Dana and said, "You must really like her." "With the proudest and most loving look on his face, he looked at Dana and said, "I love her." Dana giggled and blushed as she would normally do when only her dad gushed with love and pride over her. Shortly afterwards, Lil Ty entered the room. With the four of us in there together, which hadn't happened since Father's Day because of the sabbatical, it felt complete. Dana said, "Dad, you sure you don't want them to ween you off the medicine?" followed by an agreement from Lil Ty. "Yes, I'm sure" he responded.

"What's taking them so long?" Ty asked with a hint of frustration about an hour after everyone had arrived. Baby, they're making sure that everything is good for you to make it home. As I was answering his frustration, hospice transport showed up and parked the stretcher right outside his room. He looked to his right to see them waiting for instructions. His nurse and the palliative nurse came in. The nurse typed something in the system and the medication screen went black. That's it Mr. Johnson. He looked at her and asked was the medicine done. She answered with the confirmation that they were done. He smiled. Hospice transport rushed in to get him on the stretcher. As they moved him, I could see that he went from extremely lively to mediocre. "Babe, you good?" I asked. He shook his head and gave us the thumbs up. The blood pressure cuff was still on his arm during the transition from the bed to the stretcher. It reflected a blood pressure of 73 over 42. Transport got Ty strapped in and walked him out the intensive care doors to the elevator and pushed the button to go down. I looked at Ty's face and could see in his eyes that he wasn't alert. "Babe, you O.K.? Babe, wake up. Baby, talk to me." He wasn't responding. The doctor who had followed us to the elevator to say bye, with a sense of urgency told the transporters to rush him back to the room. After getting him back in the same room, they transferred him from the stretcher back to the bed. Because of the Do Not Resuscitate order that had been given earlier that day, there was nothing they could do.

I was standing at Ty's right side, holding his head in my arms as my son stood next to me holding Ty's hand and begging GOD not to take his dad. Dana was on this left side with her head resting on his heart, literally listening to his heartbeat. Tyrone regained consciousness for a brief second and at his son's request, gave us a thumbs up. I kissed him, told him how much I love him, made sure that he knew that he is the best man I know, and thanked him for allowing GOD to use him to help me break down the walls I had built up due to my childhood. As I was saying these things, he was looking me in my eyes. Shortly after, he went limp again. We were encouraging him to breathe but at this point, his breaths became further apart. The palliative nurse came in as a form of comfort. "Can you tell me what his blood pressure is?" I asked in desperation. Before she could answer Dana responded, "Mom, he's taking a breath every 10 seconds. It's not going to matter." The nurse walked back out and closed the blinds to give the four of us some privacy. I heard my baby boy praying as my baby girl demanded that we showed no signs of doubt. Tyrone took a deep breath in and released a long peaceful sigh. He did the same thing about six times with ten seconds between each. It was the most tranquil sound ever. My husband took his last breath at 6:58 P.M.

My son broke down. I hugged him in pure pain. "Mom, I've gotta go. I can't be here right now." I understood but didn't want him to leave in the height of these emotions. But he was adamant, and I couldn't stop him. Dana was crying but had not lifted her head from Ty's chest. Not only did she not move her head, she took his arm, wrapped it around her waist, and laid there not wanting anyone to touch her. As I looked around the room, I felt numb. I didn't know what or how to think at this point. My best friend was gone. The palliative nurse was back. Dana stood up crying and said, "Mom, he didn't even tell me that he loved me before he left." The nurse reminded Dana when she walked in the room and looked at Ty's face, she mentioned liking Dana and he looked at her and said, "No, I love her." "He did tell me" she remembered as she laid her head back on his chest. I could do nothing but kiss his lifeless body.

I made all of the necessary calls. His brother, his best friend, my cousin, and my best friend came to the hospital. Saying "see you later" was hard. I can't even remember the feeling that I had walking out of the room knowing that I wouldn't return again. Dana's uncle had to pick her up out of Ty's arms to get her out of the room. This was the hardest thing I had ever had to do in my life. Not only had I never witnessed anything like this, but I had to witness it with my best friend and the father of my children. This was a gut punch of massive proportions. "Now what GOD? Now what?"

We left the hospital around 9:30 p.m. I drove home in silence, followed by my brother-n-law and Ty's best friend. I heard my son walking down the steps as I opened the door. I sat everything down and sat on the ottoman. My son, sitting at the dinner table, looked at me and said, "Mom, I just want you to know you were a good wife and mom, especially while all of this was going on. It was a lot, but you did good." The tears began to flow again. I was afraid for the two guys to leave because I knew it was going to get quiet and I was afraid of the quiet time. Nonetheless, they left, and I was left in a big house with my two children. I showered and got in the bed. I couldn't sleep so I just laid there with my back to the door. I felt a presence but was too scared to turn around. It was Dana. She walked up to my side of the bed weeping. I moved over, peeled the covers back, and invited her in. I held her in my arms, and we cried together until we fell asleep. The next day, I woke up like clockwork to get dressed and head to the hospital. It wasn't until I was on my way to the bathroom to shower that I realized there were no more trips to the hospital, I'd be lying alone, and my best friend was never coming back. Life had shifted.

God Honored My Husband

For a full 15 months, although some people had let him down, he never lost faith in God. Every single day post-diagnosis, I'd ask Ty what he was thinking and how was he feeling. He'd always assure me that he was good mentally and spiritually and that "God's got it". This, by far, is the hardest thing I've ever gone through in my entire life. I had my hand in or was able to control everything around me for the past twenty plus years. Things that happened while I was younger made me feel the need to have some sort of influence in everything around me to avert disaster. However, in this case I couldn't. The one thing that I should've been able to and wanted to be able to control, to prevent, was never in my hands nor in my control. This forced me to trust God and even in my husband's promotion, I still trust Him. God spoke to me one day. He asked me if I trusted Him. I, of course, answered "Yes". He then reminded me that I had no choice but to trust Him because there was nothing I could do about the situation. I then saw a picture of a single basket of eggs. In the same instance, He asked, "But why didn't you trust me when you had two baskets? You still chose to put all of your eggs in your own basket, instead of Mine?" That's when I saw two baskets, one smaller with plenty of eggs and one bigger with no eggs. I immediately repented. It's easy to say you're trusting God when you have the capabilities of working it out yourself, just in case He doesn't "come through". But how easy is it to trust Him when you have other options? Can you then make the choice to trust Him with everything?

Tyrone was diagnosed on May 27, 2018. He graduated on August 29, 2019. God loved him so much that He allowed Ty to make the choice of laying down his life and honored the agreement between the two of us. I know that if we weren't in agreement, Tyrone would not have made the decision nor the transition. God honored my husband on that day. As Ty took his last breaths, the sounds that he made was far too perfect for me to believe anything else than the fact that he saw God in all His glory. In that, I couldn't be upset about him leaving us. If I witnessed what he was witnessing in that moment, as much as I love Ty and my children, I wouldn't have come back either. I miss you Tyrone D. Johnson, Sr.

I trust you GOD.

Legacy

Being a father has been without a doubt one of my greatest sources of inspiration. Giving my son something I wish I had growing up is fulfilling. I know now it's easier for a father to have a child than for a child to have… a real father.

I thank God for this woman. Looking at my maturity, my success, and my life as a whole… I'm so happy with who I've become. I never understood what my wife meant when she said divorce is not an option because she refuses to allow another woman to benefit from her sacrifices… but now I do. I can humbly say that I'm a product of her tears, her faith and her patience to watch me shape into the man I am today.

Some think love can be measured by the amount of butterflies in my belly. Others think love can be measured in tons of flowers, or by using the words "for ever". But TRUE love can only be measured by actions. You have to make it last for ever ON PURPOSE… it's a choice. "takes2totango

I'm so blessed to be celebrating 16yrs of marriage with this beautiful woman. The ultimate blessing is I don't have to fake it for social media. This smile on my face is genuinely my daily expression with this woman. Thank you baby for your personal growth, your commitment, your love and your patience. I love you Kendra Johnson. Happy Anniversary!

I love this lil woman so much. She will always be daddy's baby girl no matter how old she gets. #proudfather #daddysgirl

Based on the lump sum of decisions I've made in my life... I should be either dead, in jail, homeless, divorced, broke, depressed, or disabled. Nothing but His grace. #feelinggrateful

It isn't what you have, who you have, who you are, where you are, or what you are doing that makes you happy or unhappy. It is what you choose to think about. Maturity develops mind over matter. And when you learn to stop minding, it won't matter.

If your life inspires others to fream more, learn more, do more or become more, you are a leader. #livelife #inspire

Stop worrying about what people think about you. Sometimes you're behind and sometimes you're ahead, it's life. The sad part is haters could be the moon... and still be jealous of the stars. Jealousy... is a mental cancer. #livelife #doyou

Success is NOT a good teacher. Failure should be your trusted advisor. Remember talent is "God-given", stay humble. Conceit is "self-given", be careful.

As I watched… I witnessed people being elevated because of my situation, people being encouraged in their situations because they don't see me throwing in the towel, people's true hears being exposed and some even being moved out of the way and things shifted in my favor. I may never sknow the full purpose of this season in my life, but I do know… nothing just happens.

I encourage anybody that's facing anything that makes you want to say "why me?" to keep your eyes on Him. You may never know the full purpose, but know it's bigger than you. There's a plan and a purpose behind it all. Take it day by day, stay encouraged, and keep pressing. #HisTiming #HisPurpose #MyTestimony

Printed in the United States
By Bookmasters

Tiny Python Projects

KEN YOUENS-CLARK

MANNING
SHELTER ISLAND

For online information and ordering of this and other Manning books, please visit
www.manning.com. The publisher offers discounts on this book when ordered in quantity.
For more information, please contact

> Special Sales Department
> Manning Publications Co.
> 20 Baldwin Road
> PO Box 761
> Shelter Island, NY 11964
> Email: orders@manning.com

Manning Publications Co.
20 Baldwin Road
PO Box 761
Shelter Island, NY 11964

Development editor:	Elesha Hyde
Technical development editor:	Al Scherer
Review editor:	Aleksandar Dragosavljević
Production editor:	Deirdre S. Hiam
Copy editor:	Andy Carroll
Proofreader:	Katie Tennant
Technical proofreader:	Mathijs Affourtit
Typesetter:	Dennis Dalinnik
Cover designer:	Marija Tudor

ISBN: 9781617297519
Printed in the United States of America

brief contents

Getting started: Introduction and installation guide   1

1 ■ How to write and test a Python program   15

2 ■ The crow's nest: Working with strings   35

3 ■ Going on a picnic: Working with lists   55

4 ■ Jump the Five: Working with dictionaries   76

5 ■ Howler: Working with files and STDOUT   92

6 ■ Words count: Reading files and STDIN, iterating lists,
       formatting strings   107

7 ■ Gashlycrumb: Looking items up in a dictionary 118

8 ■ Apples and Bananas: Find and replace   128

9 ■ Dial-a-Curse: Generating random insults from
       lists of words   150

10 ■ Telephone: Randomly mutating strings   165

11 ■ Bottles of Beer Song: Writing and
        testing functions   178

12 ■ Ransom: Randomly capitalizing text   195

13 ■ Twelve Days of Christmas: Algorithm design   207

iii

14 ■ Rhymer: Using regular expressions to create rhyming words 225

15 ■ The Kentucky Friar: More regular expressions 248

16 ■ The Scrambler: Randomly reordering the middles of words 268

17 ■ Mad Libs: Using regular expressions 281

18 ■ Gematria: Numeric encoding of text using ASCII values 295

19 ■ Workout of the Day: Parsing CSV files, creating text table output 311

20 ■ Password strength: Generating a secure and memorable password 331

21 ■ Tic-Tac-Toe: Exploring state 351

22 ■ Tic-Tac-Toe redux: An interactive version with type hints 367

contents

preface   xv
acknowledgments   xvii
about this book   xix
about the author   xxii
about the cover   xxiii

Getting started: Introduction and installation guide   1

Writing command-line programs   1

Using test-driven development   4

Setting up your environment   4

Code examples   5

Getting the code   8

Installing modules   10

Code formatters   10

Code linters   11

How to start writing new programs   11

Why not Notebooks?   12

The scope of topics we'll cover   12

Why not object-oriented programming?   13

A note about the lingo   13

1 How to write and test a Python program 15

1.1   Creating your first program   15

1.2   Comment lines   16

1.3   Testing your program   17

1.4   Adding the #! (shebang) line   18

1.5   Making a program executable   20

1.6   Understanding $PATH   20

Altering your $PATH   21

1.7   Adding a parameter and help   22

1.8   Making the argument optional   24

1.9   Running our tests   26

1.10 Adding the main() function   26

1.11 Adding the get_args() function   27

Checking style and errors   28

1.12 Testing hello.py   29

1.13 Starting a new program with new.py   30

1.14 Using template.py as an alternative to new.py   33

2 The crow's nest: Working with strings 35

2.1   Getting started   36

How to use the tests   36 ▪ *Creating programs with new.py   37*
Write, test, repeat   38 ▪ *Defining your arguments   39*
Concatenating strings   41 ▪ *Variable types   42* ▪ *Getting
just part of a string   43* ▪ *Finding help in the REPL   44*
String methods   44 ▪ *String comparisons   45* ▪ *Conditional
branching   47* ▪ *String formatting   48* ▪ *Time to write   49*

2.2   Solution   49

2.3   Discussion   50

Defining the arguments with get_args()   50 ▪ *The main()
thing   51* ▪ *Classifying the first character of a word   51*
Printing the results   52 ▪ *Running the test suite   52*

2.4   Going further   53

3 Going on a picnic: Working with lists 55

3.1   Starting the program   56

3.2   Writing picnic.py   58

3.3 Introducing lists 59

Adding one element to a list 60 ▪ Adding many elements to a list 61 ▪ Indexing lists 63 ▪ Slicing lists 64 ▪ Finding elements in a list 64 ▪ Removing elements from a list 65 Sorting and reversing a list 67 ▪ Lists are mutable 69 Joining a list 70

3.4 Conditional branching with if/elif/else 70

Time to write 71

3.5 Solution 71

3.6 Discussion 73

Defining the arguments 73 ▪ Assigning and sorting the items 73 Formatting the items 73 ▪ Printing the items 74

3.7 Going further 75

4 **Jump the Five: Working with dictionaries 76**

4.1 Dictionaries 77

Creating a dictionary 78 ▪ Accessing dictionary values 80 Other dictionary methods 81

4.2 Writing jump.py 82

4.3 Solution 84

4.4 Discussion 85

Defining the parameters 85 ▪ Using a dict for encoding 85 Various ways to process items in a series 86 ▪ (Not) using str.replace() 90

4.5 Going further 91

5 **Howler: Working with files and STDOUT 92**

5.1 Reading files 93

5.2 Writing files 97

5.3 Writing howler.py 99

5.4 Solution 101

5.5 Discussion 102

Defining the arguments 102 ▪ Reading input from a file or the command line 103 ▪ Choosing the output file handle 104 Printing the output 104 ▪ A low-memory version 104

5.6 Going further 106

6 **Words count: Reading files and STDIN, iterating lists, formatting strings 107**

6.1 Writing wc.py 109

Defining file inputs 110 ▪ Iterating lists 111 ▪ What you're counting 111 ▪ Formatting your results 112

6.2 Solution 114

6.3 Discussion 115

Defining the arguments 115 ▪ Reading a file using a for loop 115

6.4 Going further 117

7 **Gashlycrumb: Looking items up in a dictionary 118**

7.1 Writing gashlycrumb.py 119

7.2 Solution 122

7.3 Discussion 123

Handling the arguments 123 ▪ Reading the input file 124 Using a dictionary comprehension 125 ▪ Dictionary lookups 126

7.4 Going further 126

8 **Apples and Bananas: Find and replace 128**

8.1 Altering strings 130

Using the str.replace() method 131 ▪ Using str.translate() 131 Other ways to mutate strings 132

8.2 Solution 133

8.3 Discussion 134

Defining the parameters 134 ▪ Eight ways to replace the vowels 135

8.4 Refactoring with tests 149

8.5 Going further 149

9 **Dial-a-Curse: Generating random insults from lists of words 150**

9.1 Writing abuse.py 151

Validating arguments 153 ▪ Importing and seeding the random module 154 ▪ Defining the adjectives and nouns 155 ▪ Taking random samples and choices 156 ▪ Formatting the output 156

9.2   Solution   157

9.3   Discussion   159

Defining the arguments   159 ▪ *Using parser.error()   160*
Program exit values and STDERR   160 ▪ *Controlling randomness*
with random.seed()   161 ▪ *Iterating with range() and using*
throwaway variables   162 ▪ *Constructing the insults   162*

9.4   Going further   163

10 Telephone: Randomly mutating strings   165

10.1   Writing telephone.py   167

Calculating the number of mutations   168 ▪ *The mutation*
space   169 ▪ *Selecting the characters to mutate   169*
Mutating a string   172 ▪ *Time to write   173*

10.2   Solution   173

10.3   Discussion   175

Mutating a string   175 ▪ *Using a list instead of a str   176*

10.4   Going further   177

11 Bottles of Beer Song: Writing and testing functions   178

11.1   Writing bottles.py   179

Counting down   180 ▪ *Writing a function   181* ▪ *Writing*
a test for verse()   182 ▪ *Using the verse() function   186*

11.2   Solution   187

11.3   Discussion   189

Counting down   189 ▪ *Test-driven development   189*
The verse() function   190 ▪ *Iterating through the verses   191*
1,500 other solutions   194

11.4   Going further   194

12 Ransom: Randomly capitalizing text   195

12.1   Writing ransom.py   197

Mutating the text   197 ▪ *Flipping a coin   198* ▪ *Creating*
a new string   198

12.2   Solution   199

12.3   Discussion   200

Iterating through elements in a sequence   200 ▪ *Writing a function*
to choose the letter   202 ▪ *Another way to write list.append()   202*
Using a str instead of a list   203 ▪ *Using a list comprehension   203*
Using a map() function   204

12.4   Comparing methods   204

12.5   Going further   205

13   Twelve Days of Christmas: Algorithm design   207

13.1   Writing twelve_days.py   208

Counting   209 ▪ *Creating the ordinal value   211* ▪ *Making the verses   213* ▪ *Using the verse() function   215* ▪ *Printing   215 Time to write   215*

13.2   Solution   216

13.3   Discussion   218

Making one verse   218 ▪ *Generating the verses   221 Printing the verses   222*

13.4   Going further   223

14   Rhymer: Using regular expressions to create rhyming words   225

14.1   Writing rhymer.py   227

Breaking a word   228 ▪ *Using regular expressions   229 Using capture groups   232* ▪ *Truthiness   236* ▪ *Creating the output   238*

14.2   Solution   238

14.3   Discussion   240

Stemming a word   240 ▪ *Formatting and commenting the regular expression   242* ▪ *Using the stemmer() function outside your program   243* ▪ *Creating rhyming strings   244* ▪ *Writing stemmer() without regular expressions   245*

14.4   Going further   246

15   The Kentucky Friar: More regular expressions   248

15.1   Writing friar.py   250

Splitting text using regular expressions   251 ▪ *Shorthand classes   252* ▪ *Negated shorthand classes   254* ▪ *Using re.split() with a captured regex   255* ▪ *Writing the fry() function   256 Using the fry() function   261*

15.2   Solution   262

15.3   Discussion   263

Writing the fry() function manually   264 ▪ *Writing the fry() function with regular expressions   266*

15.4   Going further   266

16 The Scrambler: Randomly reordering the middles of words 268

16.1   Writing scrambler.py 269

  Breaking the text into lines and words 270 ▪ Capturing, non-capturing, and optional groups 272 ▪ Compiling a regex 272
  Scrambling a word 273 ▪ Scrambling all the words 275

16.2   Solution 276

16.3   Discussion 277

  Processing the text 277 ▪ Scrambling a word 279

16.4   Going further 280

17 Mad Libs: Using regular expressions 281

17.1   Writing mad.py 282

  Using regular expressions to find the pointy bits 284
  Halting and printing errors 287 ▪ Getting the values 288
  Substituting the text 289

17.2   Solution 289

17.3   Discussion 290

  Substituting with regular expressions 291 ▪ Finding the placeholders without regular expressions 291

17.4   Going further 293

18 Gematria: Numeric encoding of text using ASCII values 295

18.1   Writing gematria.py 296

  Cleaning a word 297 ▪ Ordinal character values and ranges 298 ▪ Summing and reducing 300 ▪ Using functools.reduce 302 ▪ Encoding the words 303
  Breaking the text 304

18.2   Solution 304

18.3   Discussion 305

  Writing word2num() 306 ▪ Sorting 308 ▪ Testing 309

18.4   Going further 309

19 Workout of the Day: Parsing CSV files, creating text table output 311

19.1   Writing wod.py 312

  Reading delimited text files 313 ▪ Manually reading a CSV file 315 ▪ Parsing with the csv module 318 ▪ Creating a

function to read a CSV file   320 ▪ *Selecting the exercises   321*
Formatting the output   322 ▪ *Handling bad data   322*
Time to write   323

19.2   Solution   323

19.3   Discussion   325

Reading a CSV file   325 ▪ *Potential runtime errors   326*
Using pandas.read_csv() to parse the file   327 ▪ *Formatting
the table   328*

19.4   Going further   330

**20   Password strength: Generating a secure and memorable
password   331**

20.1   Writing password.py   334

Creating a unique list of words   335 ▪ *Cleaning the text   337*
Using a set   339 ▪ *Filtering the words   340* ▪ *Titlecasing the
words   341* ▪ *Sampling and making a password   341*
l33t-ify   342 ▪ *Putting it all together   343*

20.2   Solution   343

20.3   Discussion   346

Cleaning the text   346 ▪ *A king's ransom   347* ▪ *How to
l33t()   347* ▪ *Processing the files   347* ▪ *Sampling and
creating the passwords   348*

20.4   Going further   349

21   Tic-Tac-Toe: Exploring state   351

21.1   Writing tictactoe.py   353

Validating user input   355 ▪ *Altering the board   355*
Printing the board   356 ▪ *Determining a winner   356*
Solution   357 ▪ *Validating the arguments and mutating
the board   360* ▪ *Formatting the board   363* ▪ *Finding the
winner   364*

21.2   Going further   366

**22   Tic-Tac-Toe redux: An interactive version
with type hints   367**

22.1   Writing itictactoe.py   368

Tuple talk   369 ▪ *Named tuples   371* ▪ *Adding type
hints   372* ▪ *Type verification with Mypy   373* ▪ *Updating*

immutable structures   375 ▪ *Adding type hints to function definitions   376*

22.2   Solution   377

A version using TypedDict   379 ▪ *Thinking about state   381*

22.3   Going further   381

Epilogue   383

appendix   Using argparse   385

index   405

preface

Why write Python?

Python is an excellent, general-purpose programming language. You can write a program to send secret messages to your friends or to play chess. There are Python modules to help you wrangle complex scientific data, explore machine learning algorithms, and generate publication-ready graphics. Many college-level computer science programs have moved away from languages like C and Java to Python as their introductory language because Python is a relatively easy language to learn. We can use Python to study fundamental and powerful ideas from computer science. As I show you ideas like regular expressions and higher-order functions, I hope to encourage you to study further.

Why did I write this book?

Over the years, I've had many opportunities to help people learn programming, and I always find it rewarding. The structure of this book comes from my own experience in the classroom, where I think formal specifications and tests can be useful aids in learning how to break a program into smaller problems that need to be solved to create the whole program.

The biggest barrier to entry I've found when I'm learning a new language is that small concepts of the language are usually presented outside of any useful context. Most programming language tutorials will start with printing "HELLO, WORLD!" (and this is book is no exception). Usually that's pretty simple. After that, I usually struggle to write a complete program that will accept some arguments and do something *useful*.

In this book, I'll show you many, many examples of programs that do useful things, in the hopes that you can modify these programs to make more programs for your own use.

More than anything, I think you need to practice. It's like the old joke: "What's the way to Carnegie Hall? Practice, practice, practice." These coding challenges are short enough that you could probably finish each in a few hours or days. This is more material than I could work through in a semester-long university-level class, so I imagine the whole book will take you several months. I hope you will solve the problems, then think about them, and then return later to see if you can solve them differently, maybe using a more advanced technique or making them run faster.

acknowledgments

This being my first book, it has been interesting to note the many people who have helped me create it. It all started with a call with Mike Stephens, the acquisitions editor for Manning, who entertained the idea of a book on learning how to produce serious, tested software by writing silly games and puzzles. That eventually led to a call with Marjan Bace, the publisher, who was enthusiastic about using test-driven development ideas to motivate readers to actively engage with writing the programs.

My first development editor, Susanna Kline, had to help me wrestle the first few chapters of the book into something people would actually want to read. My second development editor, Elesha Hyde, provided patient and thoughtful guidance through months of writing, editing, and reviews. I thank my technical editors, Scott Chaussee, Al Scherer, and Mathijs Affourtit, for carefully checking all my code and text for mistakes. I appreciated the efforts of Manning's MEAP team, especially Mehmed Pasic for producing the PDFs and giving me technical guidance on how to use AsciiDoc. I would also like to thank my project editor Deirdre Hiam, my copyeditor Andy Carroll, my proofreader Katie Tennant, and my review editor Aleksandar Dragosavljević. Also, the readers of the liveBook edition and the many technical reviewers who provided such great feedback: Amanda Debler, Conor Redmond, Drew Leon, Joaquin Beltran, José Apablaza, Kimberly Winston-Jackson, Maciej Jurkowski, Mafinar Khan, Manuel Ricardo Gonzalez Cova, Marcel van den Brink, Marcin Sęk, Mathijs Affourtit, Paul R Hendrik, Shayn Cornwell, Víctor M. Pérez.

I especially want to acknowledge the countless people who create the open source software upon which all of this is built. From the people who maintain the Python language and modules and documentation to the countless hackers who answer questions on the internet, I thank you for all that you do.

Of course, none of this would have ever been possible without the love and support of my family, especially my wife, Lori Kindler, who has been an unbelievable source of love and support for over 27 years. (I'm still really, really sorry about wrecking on my mountain bike and the year it took for me to recover!) Our three children bring me such challenges and joy, and I hope that I am making them proud. They constantly have to feign interest in topics they know and care nothing about, and they have shown such patience for the many hours I've spent writing this book.

about this book

Who should read this book

After you read this book and write all the programs, I would hope that you will be a zealot for creating programs that are documented, tested, and reproducible.

I think my ideal reader is someone who's been trying to learn to code well but isn't quite sure how to level up. Perhaps you are someone who's been playing with Python or some other language that has a similar syntax, like Java(Script) or Perl. Maybe you've cut your teeth on something really different, like Haskell or Scheme, and you're wondering how to translate your ideas to Python. Maybe you've been writing Python for a while and are looking for interesting challenges with enough structure to help you know when you're moving in the right direction.

This is a book that will teach you to write well-structured, documented, testable code in Python. The material introduces best practices from industry such as *test-driven development*—that's when the *tests* for a program exist even before the program itself is written! I will show you how to read documentation and Python Enhancement Proposals (PEPs) and how to write idiomatic code that other Python programmers would immediately recognize and understand.

This is probably not an ideal book for the absolute beginning programmer. I assume no prior knowledge of the Python language specifically, because I'm thinking of someone who is coming from another language. If you've never written a program in *any* language at all, you might do well to come back to this material when you are comfortable with ideas like variables, loops, and functions.

How this book is organized: A roadmap

The book is written with chapters building on previous chapters, so I really recommend you start at the beginning and work sequentially through the material.

- Every program uses command-line arguments, so we start off discussing how to use argparse to handle this. Every program is also tested, so you'll have to learn how to install and use pytest. The introduction and chapter 1 will get you up and running.
- Chapters 2–4 discuss the basic Python structures like strings, lists, and dictionaries.
- Chapters 5 and 6 move into how we can work with files as input and output and how files are related to "standard in" and "standard out" (STDIN/STDOUT).
- Chapters 7 and 8 start combining ideas so you can write more complicated programs.
- Chapters 9 and 10 introduce the random module and how to control and test random events.
- In chapters 11–13 you'll learn more about compartmentalizing code into functions and how to write and run tests for them.
- In chapters 14–18 we'll start digging into denser topics like higher-order functions as well as regular expressions to find patterns of text.
- In chapters 19–22 we'll start writing more complex, "real-world" programs that will put all your skills together while pushing your knowledge of the Python language and testing.

About the code

Every program and test shown in the book can be found at https://github.com/kyclark/tiny_python_projects.

Software/hardware requirements

All the program were written and tested with Python 3.8, but version 3.6 would be sufficient for almost every program. Several additional modules are required, such as pytest for running the tests. There are instructions for how to use the pip module to install these.

liveBook discussion forum

Purchase of *Tiny Python Projects* includes free access to a private web forum run by Manning Publications where you can make comments about the book, ask technical questions, and receive help from the author and from other users. To access the forum, go to https://livebook.manning.com/book/tiny-python-projects/welcome/v-6. You can also learn more about Manning's forums and the rules of conduct at https://livebook.manning.com/#!/discussion.

   Manning's commitment to our readers is to provide a venue where a meaningful dialogue between individual readers and between readers and the author can take place. It is not a commitment to any specific amount of participation on the part of the author, whose contribution to the forum remains voluntary (and unpaid). We suggest you try asking him some challenging questions lest his interest stray! The forum and the archives of previous discussions will be accessible from the publisher's website as long as the book is in print.

Other online resources

One element missing from many programming courses is a demonstration of how one can go from having no program to having one that works. In my classroom teaching, I spend a lot of time showing students how to start writing a program and then how to work through the process of adding and testing new features. I've recorded videos for each chapter and shared them at www.youtube.com/user/kyclark. There is a playlist for each chapter, and the videos follow the pattern of each chapter by introducing the problem and the language features you might use to write your program, followed by a discussion of the solution(s).

about the author

My name is Ken Youens-Clark. I work as a Senior Scientific Programmer at the University of Arizona. Most of my career has been spent working in bioinformatics, using computer science ideas to study biological data.

I began my undergraduate degree as a Jazz Studies major on the drum set at the University of North Texas in 1990. I changed my major a few times and eventually ended up with a BA in English literature in 1995. I didn't really have a plan for my career, but I did like computers.

Around 1995, I stared tinkering with databases and HTML at my first job out of college, building the company's mailing list and first website. I was definitely hooked! After that, I managed to learned Visual Basic on Windows 3.1 and, during the next few years, I programmed in several languages and companies before landing in a bioinformatics group at Cold Spring Harbor Laboratory in 2001, led by Lincoln Stein, a prominent author of books and modules in Perl and an early advocate for open software, data, and science. In 2014 I moved to Tucson, AZ, to work at the University of Arizona, where I completed my MS in Biosystems Engineering in 2019.

When I'm not coding, I like playing music, riding bikes, cooking, reading, and being with my wife and children.

about the cover

The figure on the cover of *Tiny Python Projects* is captioned "Femme Turc allant par les rues," or "Turkish woman going through the streets." The illustration is taken from a collection of dress costumes from various countries by Jacques Grasset de Saint-Sauveur (1757–1810), titled *Costumes de Différents Pays*, published in France in 1788. Each illustration is finely drawn and colored by hand. The rich variety of Grasset de Saint-Sauveur's collection reminds us vividly of how culturally apart the world's towns and regions were just 200 years ago. Isolated from each other, people spoke different dialects and languages. In the streets or in the countryside, it was easy to identify where they lived and what their trade or station in life was just by their dress.

The way we dress has changed since then, and the diversity by region, so rich at the time, has faded away. It is now hard to tell apart the inhabitants of different continents, let alone different towns, regions, or countries. Perhaps we have traded cultural diversity for a more varied personal life—certainly for a more varied and fast-paced technological life.

At a time when it is hard to tell one computer book from another, Manning celebrates the inventiveness and initiative of the computer business with book covers based on the rich diversity of regional life of two centuries ago, brought back to life by Grasset de Saint-Sauveur's pictures.

Getting started: Introduction and installation guide

This book will teach you how to write Python programs that run on the command line. If you have never used the command line before, don't worry! You can use programs like PyCharm (see figure 0.1) or Microsoft's VS Code to help you write and run these programs. If you are completely new to programming or to the Python language, I will try to cover everything I think you'll need to know, although you might find it useful to read another book first if you've never heard of things like variables and functions.

In this introduction, we'll discuss

- Why you should learn to write command-line programs
- Tools and environments for writing code
- How and why we test software

Writing command-line programs

Why do I want you to write command-line programs? For one, I think they strip a program down to its most bare essentials. We're not going to try to write complicated programs like an interactive 3D game that requires lots of other software to work. The programs in this book will all work with the barest of inputs and create only text output. We're going to focus on learning the core Python language and how to write *and test* programs.

Another reason for focusing on command-line programs is that I want to show you how to write programs that can run on any computer that has Python installed. I'm writing this book on my Mac laptop, but I can run all the programs on any of

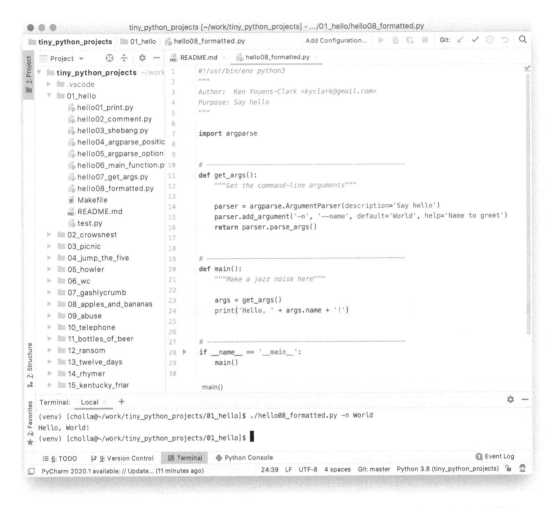

Figure 0.1   This is the PyCharm tool being used to edit and run the hello.py program from chapter 1. "Hello, World!"

the Linux machines I use in my work or on a friend's Windows machine. Any computer with the same version of Python can run any of these programs, and that is pretty cool.

The biggest reason I want to show you how to write command-line programs, though, is because I want to show you how to *test* programs to make sure they work. While I don't think anyone will die if I make a mistake in one of my programs, I still really, really want to be sure that my code is as perfect as possible.

What does it mean to test a program? Well, if my program is supposed to add two numbers together, I'll need to run it with many pairs of numbers and check that it prints the correct sum. I might also give it a number and a word, to make sure that it doesn't try to add "3" plus "seahorse" but instead complains that I didn't give it two numbers. Testing gives me some measure of confidence in my code, and I hope you will come to see how testing can help you understand programming more deeply.

The exercises in this book are meant to be silly enough to pique your interest, but they each contain lessons that can be applied to all sorts of real-world problems. Almost every program I've ever written needs to accept some input data, whether from the user or from a file, and produce some output—sometimes text on the screen or maybe a new file. These are the kinds of skills you'll learn by writing these programs.

In each chapter, I'll describe some program that I want you to write and the tests you'll use to check if your program is working correctly. Then I'll show you a solution and discuss how it works. As the problems get harder, I'll start suggesting ways you might write your own tests to explore and verify your code.

When you're done with this book, you should be able to

- Write and run command-line Python programs
- Handle arguments to your programs
- Write and run tests for your programs and functions
- Use Python data structures like strings, lists, and dictionaries
- Have your programs read and write text files
- Use regular expressions to find patterns in text
- Use and control randomness to make your programs behave unpredictably

"Codes are a puzzle. A game, just like any other game."

—Alan Turing

Alan Turing is perhaps most famous for cracking the Enigma code that the Nazis used to encrypt messages during World War II. The fact that the Allies could read enemy messages is credited with shortening the war by years and saving millions of lives. *The Imitation Game* is a fun movie that shows how Turing published puzzles in newspapers to find people who could help him break what was supposed to be an unbreakable code.

I think we can learn tons from writing fun programs that generate random insults or produce verses to "The Twelve Days of Christmas" or play Tic-Tac-Toe. Some of the programs in this book even dabble a bit in cryptography, like in chapter 4 where we encode all the numbers in a piece of text or in chapter 18 where we create signatures for words by summing the numeric representations of their letters. I hope you'll find the programs both amusing and challenging.

The programming techniques in each exercise are not specific to Python. Most every language has variables, loops, functions, strings, lists, and dictionaries, as well as ways to parameterize and test programs. After you write your solutions in Python, I encourage you to write solutions in another language you know and compare what parts of the different languages make it easier or harder to write your programs. If your programs support the same command-line options, you can even use the included tests to verify those programs.

Using test-driven development

Test-driven development is described by Kent Beck in his 2002 book by that title as a method for creating more reliable programs. The basic idea is that we write tests even before we write code. The tests define what it means to say that our program works "correctly." *First* we write and run our tests to verify that our code fails. Then we write the code to make each test pass. We always run *all of the tests* so that, as we fix new tests, we ensure we don't break tests that were passing before. When all the tests pass, we have at least some assurance that the code we've written conforms to some manner of specification.

Each program you are asked to write in this book comes with tests that will tell you when the code is working acceptably. The first test in every exercise checks whether the expected program exists. The second test checks that the program will print a help message if we ask for help. After that, your program will be run with various inputs and options.

Since I've written around 250 tests for the programs in this book, and you have not yet written one of the programs, you're going to encounter many failed tests. That's OK! In fact, it's a really good thing, because when you pass all the tests, you'll know that your programs are correct. You'll learn to read the failed tests carefully to figure out what needs fixing. Then you'll correct the program and run the tests again. You may get another failed test, in which case you'll repeat the process until finally all the tests pass. Then you'll be done.

It doesn't matter if you solve the problems the same way as in the solution I provide. All that matters is that you figure out a way to pass the tests.

Setting up your environment

If you want to write these programs on your computer, you will need Python version 3.6 or later. It's quite possible that it's already installed on your computer.

You'll also need some way to execute the `python3` command—something we often call a *command line*. If you use a Windows computer, you may want to install Windows Subsystem for Linux (WSL). On a Mac, the default Terminal app is sufficient. You can also use a tool like VS Code (in figure 0.2) or PyCharm, which have terminals built into them.

I wrote and tested the programs for this book with Python version 3.8, but they should work with version 3.6 or newer. Python 2 reached its end of life at the end of 2019 and should no longer be used. To see what version of Python you have installed, open a terminal window and type `python3 --version`. If it says something like "command "python3" not found," then you need to install Python. You can download the latest version from the Python site (www.python.org/downloads).

If you are using a computer that doesn't have Python, and you don't have any way to install Python, you can do everything in this book using the Repl.it website (http://repl.it).

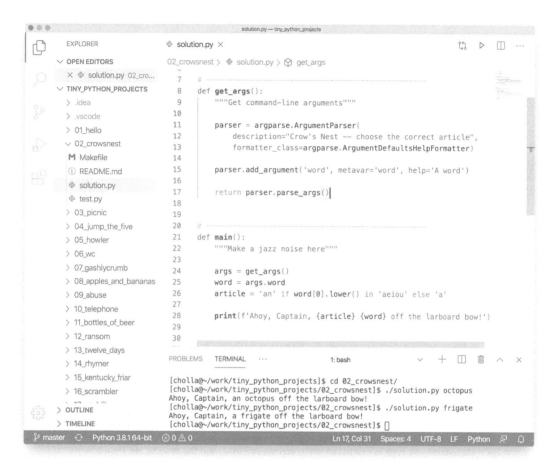

Figure 0.2 An IDE like VS Code combines a text editor for writing your code along with a terminal (lower-right window) for running your programs, and many other tools.

Code examples

Throughout the book, I will show commands and code using a `fixed-width font`. When the text is preceded with a dollar sign ($), that means it's something you can type on the command line. For instance, there is a program called `cat` (short for "concatenate") that will print the contents of a file to the screen. Here is how I can run it to print the contents of the spiders.txt file that lives in the inputs directory:

```
$ cat inputs/spiders.txt
Don't worry, spiders,
I keep house
casually.
```

If you want to run that command, *do not copy* the leading $, only the text that follows. Otherwise you'll probably get an error like "$: command not found."

Python has a really excellent tool called IDLE that allows you to interact directly with the language to try out ideas. You can start it with the command `idle3`. That should open a new window with a prompt that looks like >>> (see figure 0.3).

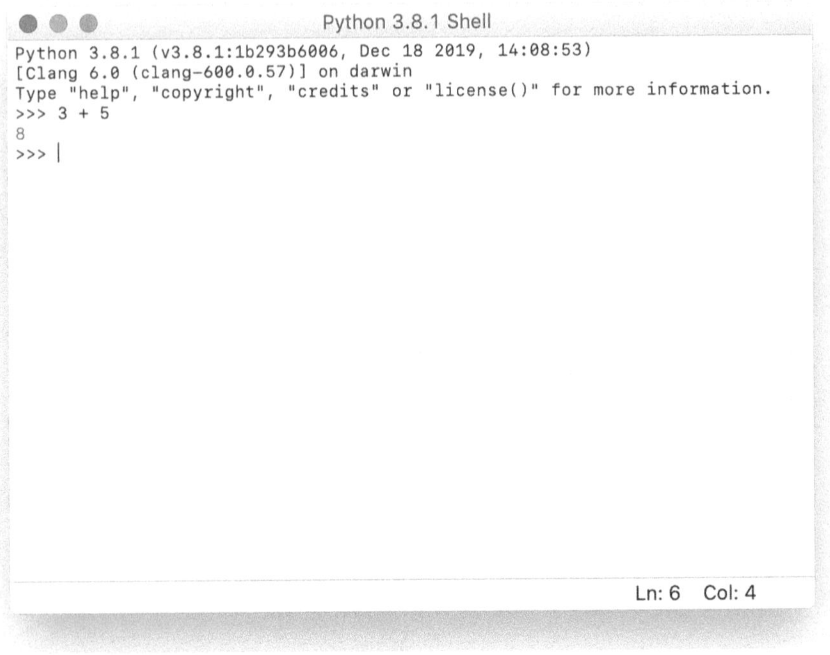

```
●  ●  ●                    Python 3.8.1 Shell
Python 3.8.1 (v3.8.1:1b293b6006, Dec 18 2019, 14:08:53)
[Clang 6.0 (clang-600.0.57)] on darwin
Type "help", "copyright", "credits" or "license()" for more information.
>>> 3 + 5
8
>>> |




                                                      Ln: 6   Col: 4
```

Figure 0.3   The IDLE application allows you to interact directly with the Python language. Each statement you type is evaluated when you press Enter, and the results are shown in the window.

You can type Python statements there, and they will be immediately evaluated and printed. For example, type 3 + 5 and press Enter, and you should see 8:

```
>>> 3 + 5
8
```

This interface is called a *REPL* because it's a Read-Evaluate-Print-Loop. (I pronounce this like "repple" in a way that sort of rhymes with "pebble.") You can get a similar tool by typing `python3` on the command line (see figure 0.4).

The IPython program is yet another "interactive Python" REPL that has many enhancements over IDLE and `python3`. Figure 0.5 shows what it looks like on my system.

I also recommend you look into using Jupyter Notebooks, as they allow you to interactively run code with the added bonus that you can save a Notebook as a file and share all your code with other people.

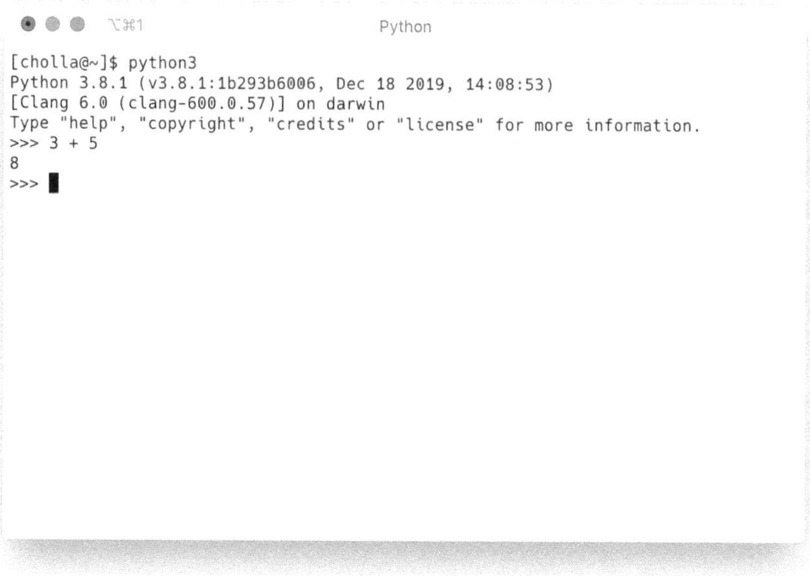

```
●  ●  ●     ⌥⌘1                    Python
[cholla@~]$ python3
Python 3.8.1 (v3.8.1:1b293b6006, Dec 18 2019, 14:08:53)
[Clang 6.0 (clang-600.0.57)] on darwin
Type "help", "copyright", "credits" or "license" for more information.
>>> 3 + 5
8
>>> ▮
```

Figure 0.4 Typing the command `python3` in the terminal will give you a REPL similar to the IDLE interface.

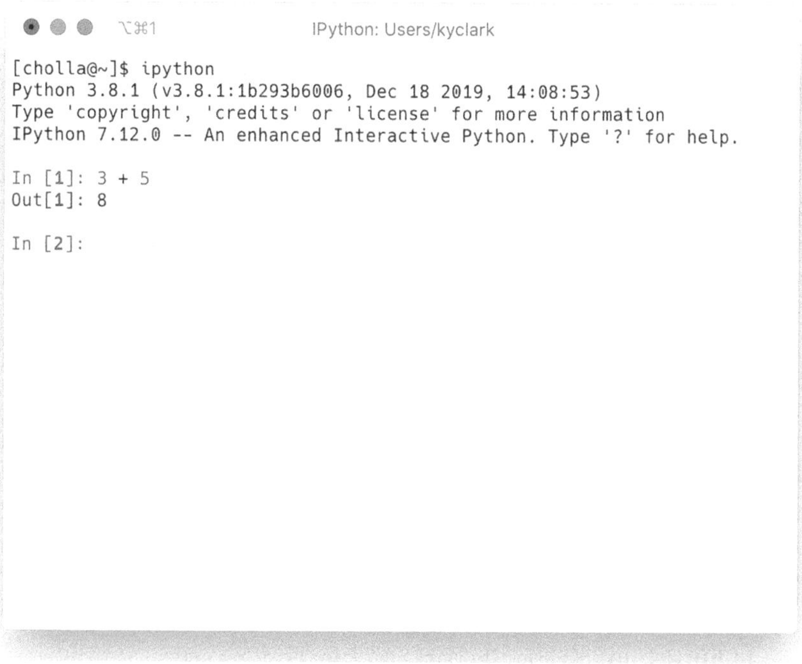

```
●  ●  ●     ⌥⌘1              IPython: Users/kyclark
[cholla@~]$ ipython
Python 3.8.1 (v3.8.1:1b293b6006, Dec 18 2019, 14:08:53)
Type 'copyright', 'credits' or 'license' for more information
IPython 7.12.0 -- An enhanced Interactive Python. Type '?' for help.

In [1]: 3 + 5
Out[1]: 8

In [2]:
```

Figure 0.5 The IPython application is another REPL interface you can use to try out your ideas with Python.

Whichever REPL interface you use, you can type Python statements like x = 10 and press Enter to assign the value 10 to the variable x:

```
>>> x = 10
```

As with the command-line prompt, $, do not copy the leading >>> or Python will complain:

```
>>> >>> x = 10
  File "<stdin>", line 1
    >>> x = 10
    ^
SyntaxError: invalid syntax
```

The IPython REPL has a magical %paste mode that removes the leading >>> prompts so that you can copy and paste all the code examples:

```
In [1]: >>> x = 10

In [2]: x
Out[2]: 10
```

Whichever way you choose to interact with Python, I suggest you *manually type all the code yourself* in this book, as this builds muscle memory and forces you to interact with the syntax of the language.

Getting the code

All the tests and solutions are available at https://github.com/kyclark/tiny_python_projects. You can use the program Git (which you may need to install) to copy that code to your computer with the following command:

```
$ git clone https://github.com/kyclark/tiny_python_projects
```

Now you should have a new directory called tiny_python_projects on your computer.

You may prefer to make a copy of the code into your own repository, so that you can track your changes and share your solutions with others. This is called "forking" because you're breaking off from my code and adding your own programs to the repository. If you plan to use Repl.it to write the exercises, I recommend you do fork my repo into your own account so that you can configure Repl.it to interact with your own GitHub repositories.

To fork, do the following:

1 Create an account on GitHub.com.
2 Go to https://github.com/kyclark/tiny_python_projects.
3 Click the Fork button (see figure 0.6) to make a copy of the repository into your account.

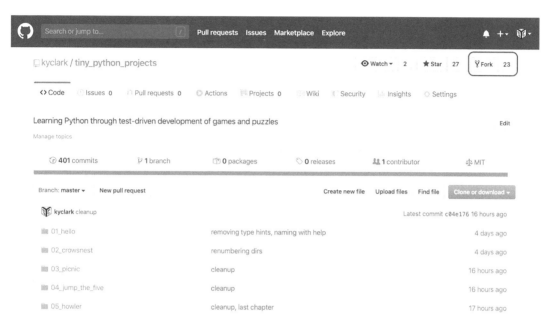

Figure 0.6   The Fork button on my GitHub repository will make a copy of the code into your account.

Now you have a copy of my all code in your own repository. You can use Git to copy that code to your computer. Be sure to replace "YOUR_GITHUB_ID" with your actual GitHub ID:

```
$ git clone https://github.com/YOUR_GITHUB_ID/tiny_python_projects
```

I may update the repo after you make your copy. If you would like to be able to get those updates, you will need to configure Git to set my repository as an "upstream" source. To do so, after you have cloned your repository to your computer, go into your tiny_python_projects directory:

```
$ cd tiny_python_projects
```

Then execute this command:

```
$ git remote add upstream https://github.com/kyclark/tiny_python_projects.git
```

Whenever you would like to update your repository from mine, you can execute this command:

```
$ git pull upstream master
```

Installing modules

I recommend using a few tools that may not be installed on your system. You can use the pip module to install them like so:

```
$ python3 -m pip install black flake8 ipython mypy pylint pytest yapf
```

I've also included a requirements.txt file in the top level of the repository. You can use it to install all the modules and tools with this command:

```
$ python3 -m pip install -r requirements.txt
```

If, for example, you wish to write the exercises on Repl.it, you will need to run this command to set up your environment, as the modules are not already installed.

Code formatters

Most IDEs and text editors will have tools to help you format your code so that it's easier to read and find problems. In addition, the Python community has created a standard for writing code so that other Python programmers can readily understand it. The PEP 8 (Python Enhancement Proposal) document at www.python.org/dev/peps/pep-0008/ describes best practices for formatting code, and most editors will automatically apply formatting for you. For instance, the Repl.it interface has an autoformat button (see figure 0.7), VS Code has a Format Document command, and PyCharm has a Reformat Code command.

Figure 0.7 The Repl.it tool has an autoformat button to reformat your code according to community standards. The interface also includes a command line for running and testing your program.

There are also command-line tools that integrate with your editor. I used YAPF (Yet Another Python Formatter, https://github.com/google/yapf) to format every program in the book, but another popular formatter is Black (https://github.com/psf/black). Whatever you use, I encourage you to use it *often*. For instance, I can tell YAPF to format the hello.py program that we will write in chapter 1 by running the following command. Note that the -i tells YAPF to format the code "in place," so that the original file will be overwritten with the newly formatted code.

```
$ yapf -i hello.py
```

Code linters

A *code linter* is a tool that will report problems in your code, such as declaring a variable but never using it. Two that I like are Pylint (www.pylint.org/) and Flake8 (http://flake8.pycqa.org/en/latest/), and both can find errors in your code that the Python interpreter itself will not complain about.

In the final chapter, I will show you how to incorporate *type hints* into your code that the Mypy tool (http://mypy-lang.org/) can use to find problems, such as using text when you should be using a number.

How to start writing new programs

I think it's much easier to start writing code with a standard template, so I wrote a program called new.py that will help you create new Python programs with boilerplate code that will be expected of every program. It's located in the bin directory, so if you are in the top directory of the repository, you can run it like this:

```
$ bin/new.py
usage: new.py [-h] [-s] [-n NAME] [-e EMAIL] [-p PURPOSE] [-f] program
new.py: error: the following arguments are required: program
```

Here you can see that new.py is asking you to provide the name of the "program" to create. For each chapter, the program you write needs to live in the directory that has the test.py file for that program.

For example, you can use new.py to start off chapter 2's crowsnest.py program in the 02_crowsnest directory like so:

```
$ bin/new.py 02_crowsnest/crowsnest.py
Done, see new script "02_crowsnest/crowsnest.py."
```

If you open that file now, you'll see that it has written a lot of code for you that I'll explain later. For now, just realize that the resulting crowsnest.py program is one that can be run like so:

```
$ 02_crowsnest/crowsnest.py
usage: crowsnest.py [-h] [-a str] [-i int] [-f FILE] [-o] str
crowsnest.py: error: the following arguments are required: str
```

Later you'll learn how to modify the program to do what the tests expect.

An alternative to running new.py is to copy the file template.py from the template directory to the directory and program name you need to write. You could create the crowsnest.py program file like so:

```
$ cp template/template.py 02_crowsnest/crowsnest.py
```

You do not have to use either new.py or copy the template.py file to start your programs. These are provided to save you time and provide your programs with an initial structure, but you are welcome to write your programs however you please.

Why not Notebooks?

Many people are familiar with Jupyter Notebooks, as they provide a way to integrate Python code and text and images into a document that other people can execute like a program. I really love Notebooks, especially for interactively exploring data, but I find them difficult to use in teaching for the following reasons:

- A Notebook is stored in JavaScript Object Notation (JSON), not as line-oriented text. This makes it really difficult to compare Notebooks to each other to find out how they differ.
- Code and text and images can live mixed together in separate cells. These cells can be interactively run in any order, which can lead to very subtle problems in the logic of a program. The programs we write in this book will always be run from top to bottom in entirety every time, which I think makes them easier to understand.
- There is no way for Notebooks to accept different values when they are run. That is, if you test a program with one input file and then want to change to a different file, you have to change *the program itself.* You will learn how to pass in a file as an *argument* to the program, so that you can change the value without changing the *code.*
- It's difficult to automatically run tests on a Notebook or on the functions they contain. We will use the `pytest` module to run our programs over and over with different input values and verify that the programs create the correct output.

The scope of topics we'll cover

The purpose of this book is to show you how amazingly useful all the built-in features of the Python language are. The exercises will push you to practice manipulating strings, lists, dictionaries, and files. We'll spend several chapters focusing on regular expressions, and every exercise except for the last requires you to accept and validate command-line arguments of varying types and numbers.

Every author is biased toward some subjects, and I'm no different. I've chosen these topics because they reflect ideas that are fundamental to the work I've done over the last 20 years. For instance, I have spent many more hours than I would care to admit parsing really messy data from countless Excel spreadsheets and XML files. The world of genomics that has consumed most of my career is based primarily on efficiently parsing text files, and much of my web development work is predicated on understanding how text is encoded and transferred to and from the web browser. For that reason, you'll find many exercises that entail processing text and files, and that will challenge you to think about how to transform inputs into outputs. If you work through every exercise, I believe you'll be a much improved programmer who understands the basic ideas that are common across many languages.

Why not object-oriented programming?

One topic that you'll notice is missing from this book is writing object-oriented code in Python. If you are not familiar with *object-oriented programming* (OOP), you can skip this section.

I think OOP is a somewhat advanced topic that is beyond the scope of this book. I prefer to focus on how to write small functions and their accompanying tests. I think this leads to more transparent code, because the functions should be short, should only use the values explicitly passed as arguments, and should have enough tests that you can completely understand how they will behave under both favorable and unfavorable circumstances.

The Python language is itself inherently object-oriented. Almost everything from strings to the lists and dictionaries that we'll use are actually *objects*, so you'll get plenty of practice using objects. But I don't think it's necessary to create objects to solve any of the problems I present. In fact, even though I spent many years writing object-oriented code, I haven't written in this style for the last few years. I tend to draw my inspiration from the world of purely functional programming, and I hope I can convince you by the end of this book that you can do anything you want by combining functions.

Although I personally avoid OOP, I would recommend you learn about it. There have been several seismic paradigm shifts in the world of programming from procedural to object-oriented and now functional. You can find dozens of books on OOP in general and on programming objects in Python specifically. This is a deep and fascinating topic, and I encourage you to try writing object-oriented solutions and compare them to my solutions.

A note about the lingo

Often in programming books you will see *foobar* used in examples. The word has no real meaning, but its origin probably comes from the military acronym "FUBAR" (Fouled Up Beyond All Recognition). If I use "foobar" in an example, it's because I don't want to talk about any specific thing in the universe, just the idea of a string of characters. If I need a list of items, usually the first item will be "foo" and the next will be "bar." After that, convention uses "baz" and "quux," again because they mean nothing at all. Don't get hung up on "foobar." It's just a placeholder for something that could be more interesting later.

Programmers also tend to call errors in code *bugs*. This comes from the days of computing before the invention of transistors. Early machines used vacuum tubes, and the heat from the machines would attract actual bugs like moths that could cause short circuits. The operators (the people running the machines) would have to hunt through the machinery to find and remove the bugs; hence, the term "to debug."

How to write and test a Python program

Before you start working on the exercises, I want to discuss how to write programs that are documented and tested. Specifically, we're going to

- Write a Python program to say "Hello, World!"
- Handle command-line arguments using `argparse`
- Run tests for the code with Pytest.
- Learn about $PATH
- Use tools like YAPF and Black to format the code
- Use tools like Flake8 and Pylint to find problems in the code
- Use the new.py program to create new programs

Hello, World!

1.1 Creating your first program

It's pretty common to write "Hello, World!" as your first program in any language, so let's start there. We're going to work toward making a version that will greet whichever name is passed as an argument. It will also print a helpful message when we ask for it, and we'll use tests to make sure it does everything correctly.

In the 01_hello directory, you'll see several versions of the hello program we'll write. There is also a program called test.py that we'll use to test the program.

Start off by creating a text file called hello.py in that directory. If you are working in VS Code or PyCharm, you can use File > Open to open the 01_hello directory as a project. Both tools have something like a File > New menu option that will allow you to create a new file in that directory. It's very important to create the hello.py file *inside* the 01_hello directory so that the test.py program can find it.

15

Once you've started a new file, add this line:

```
print('Hello, World!')
```

It's time to run your new program! Open a terminal window in VS Code or PyCharm or in some other terminal, and navigate to the directory where your hello.py program is located. You can run it with the command `python3 hello.py`—this causes Python version 3 to execute the commands in the file named hello.py. You should see this:

```
$ python3 hello.py
Hello, World!
```

Figure 1.1 shows how it looks in the Repl.it interface.

Figure 1.1   Writing and running our first program using Repl.it

If that was your first Python program, congratulations!

1.2   *Comment lines*

In Python, the # character and anything following it is ignored by Python. This is useful for adding comments to your code or temporarily disabling lines of code when testing and debugging. It's always a good idea to document your programs, indicating the purpose of the program or the author's name and email address, or both. We can use a comment for that:

```
# Purpose: Say hello
print('Hello, World!')
```

If you run this program again, you should see the same output as before because the "Purpose" line is ignored. Note that any text to the left of the # is executed, so you can add a comment to the end of a line if you like.

1.3 *Testing your program*

The most fundamental idea I want to teach you is how to test your programs. I've written a test.py program in the 01_hello directory that we can use to test our new hello.py program.

We will use pytest to execute all the commands and tell us how many tests we passed. We'll include the -v option, which tells pytest to create "verbose" output. If you run it like this, you should see the following output as the first several lines. After that will follow many more lines showing you more information about the tests that didn't pass.

> **NOTE**   If you get the error "pytest: command not found," you need to install the pytest module. Refer to the "Installing modules" section in the book's introduction.

The second test tries to run the program with python3 hello.py and then checks if the program printed "Hello, World!" If you miss even one character, like forgetting a comma, the test will point out the error, so read carefully!

```
$ pytest -v test.py
============================ test session starts ============================
...
collected 5 items                           The first test always checks that the expected
                                            file exists. Here the test looks for hello.py.
test.py::test_exists PASSED                                         [ 20%]
test.py::test_runnable PASSED                                       [ 40%]
test.py::test_executable FAILED                                     [ 60%]
test.py::test_usage FAILED                                          [ 80%]
test.py::test_input FAILED                                          [100%]

================================= FAILURES =================================
```

The fourth test asks the program for help and doesn't get anything. We're going to add the ability to print a "usage" statement that describes how to use our program.

The last test checks that the program can greet a name that we'll pass as an argument. Since our program doesn't yet accept arguments, we'll need to add that, too.

The third test checks that the program is "executable." This test fails, so next we'll talk about how to make that pass.

I've written the tests in an order that I hope will help you write the program in a logical fashion. If the program doesn't pass one of the tests, there's no reason to continue running the tests after it. I recommend you always run the tests with the flags -x, to stop on the first failing test, and -v, to print verbose output. You can combine these like -xv or -vx. Here's what our tests look like with those options:

```
$ pytest -xv test.py
============================ test session starts ============================
...
collected 5 items
```

```
test.py::test_exists PASSED                                              [ 20%]
test.py::test_runnable PASSED                                           [ 40%]
test.py::test_executable FAILED                                         [ 60%]
```

**This test fails. No more tests are run because
we ran pytest with the -x option.**

```
=================================== FAILURES ===================================
_____ test_executable _____

    def test_executable():
        """Says 'Hello, World!' by default"""

        out = getoutput({prg})
>       assert out.strip() == 'Hello, World!'
E       AssertionError: assert '/bin/sh: ./h...ission denied' == 'Hello, World!'
E         - /bin/sh: ./hello.py: Permission denied
E         + Hello, World!

test.py:30: AssertionError
!!!!!!!!!!!!!!!!!!!!!!!!!!!!! stopping after 1 failures !!!!!!!!!!!!!!!!!!!!!!!!!!!!!
========================= 1 failed, 2 passed in 0.09s =========================
```

**The angle bracket (>) at
the beginning of this line
shows the source of the
subsequent errors.**

**The hyphen character (-) is
showing that the actual
output from the command
is "Permission denied."**

**The plus character (+) shows
that the test expected to get
"Hello, World!"**

**The "E" at the beginning of this line shows that this is an
"Error" you should read. The AssertionError is saying that the
test.py program is trying to execute the command ./hello.py
to see if it will produce the text "Hello, World!"**

Let's talk about how to fix this error.

1.4   Adding the #! (shebang) line

One thing you have learned so far is that Python programs live in plain text files that
you ask `python3` to execute. Many other programming languages, such as Ruby and
Perl, work in the same way—we type Ruby or Perl commands into a text file and run
it with the right language. It's common to put a special comment line in programs
like these to indicate which language needs to be used to execute the commands in
the file.

This comment line starts off with #!, and the nickname for this is "shebang" (pronounced "shuh-bang"—I always think of the # as the "shuh" and the ! as the "bang!").
Just as with any other comment, Python will ignore the shebang, but the operating system (like macOS or Windows) will use it to decide which program to use to run the
rest of the file.

Here is the shebang you should add:

```
#!/usr/bin/env python3
```

The `env` program will tell you about your "environment." When I run `env` on my computer, I see many lines of output like `USER=kyclark` and `HOME=/Users/kyclark`. These
values are accessible as the variables `$USER` and `$HOME`:

```
$ echo $USER
kyclark
$ echo $HOME
/Users/kyclark
```

If you run env on your computer, you should see your login name and your home directory. They will, of course, have different values from mine, but we both (probably) have both of these concepts.

You can use the env command to find and run programs. If you run env python3, it will run a python3 program if it can find one. Here's what I see on my computer:

```
$ env python3
Python 3.8.1 (v3.8.1:1b293b6006, Dec 18 2019, 14:08:53)
[Clang 6.0 (clang-600.0.57)] on darwin
Type "help", "copyright", "credits" or "license" for more information.
>>>
```

The env program is looking for python3 in the environment. If Python has not been installed, it won't be able to find it, but it's also possible that Python has been installed more than once. You can use the which command to see which python3 it finds:

```
$ which python3
/Library/Frameworks/Python.framework/Versions/3.8/bin/python3
```

If I run this on Repl.it, I can see that python3 exists in a different place. Where does it exist on your computer?

```
$ which python3
/home/runner/.local/share/virtualenvs/python3/bin/python3
```

Just as my $USER name is different from yours, my python3 is probably different from yours. If the env command is able to find a python3, it will execute it. As shown previously, if you run python3 by itself, it will open a REPL.

If I were to put my python3 path as the shebang line, like so,

```
#!/Library/Frameworks/Python.framework/Versions/3.8/bin/python3
```

my program would not work on another computer that has python3 installed in a different location. I doubt it would work on your computer, either. This is why you should always use the env program to find the python3 that is specific to the machine on which it's running.

Now your program should look like this:

```
#!/usr/bin/env python3          The shebang line tells the operating system to use
# Purpose: Say hello            /usr/bin/env to find python3 to interpret this program.
print('Hello, World!')
                                A comment line documenting
                                the purpose of the program

                                A Python command to print
                                some text to the screen
```

1.5   *Making a program executable*

So far we've been explicitly telling python3 to run our program, but since we added the shebang, we can execute the program directly and let the OS figure out that it should use python3. The advantage of this is that we could copy our program to a directory where other programs live and execute it from anywhere on our computer.

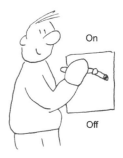

On

Off

The first step in doing this is to make our program "executable" using the command chmod (*change mode*). Think of it as turning your program "on." Run this command to make hello.py executable:

```
$ chmod +x hello.py
```
⟵ **The +x will add an "executable" attribute to the file.**

Now you can run the program like so:

```
$ ./hello.py
Hello, World!
```
⟵ **The ./ is the current directory, and it's necessary to run a program when you are in the same directory as the program.**

1.6   *Understanding $PATH*

One of the biggest reasons to set the shebang line and make your program executable is so that you can install your Python programs just like other commands and programs. We used the which command earlier to find the location of python3 on the Repl.it instance:

```
$ which python3
/home/runner/.local/share/virtualenvs/python3/bin/python3
```

How was the env program able to find it? Windows, macOS, and Linux all have a $PATH variable, which is a list of directories the OS will look in to find a program. For instance, here is the $PATH for my Repl.it instance:

```
> echo $PATH
/home/runner/.local/share/virtualenvs/python3/bin:/usr/local/bin:\
/usr/local/sbin:/usr/local/bin:/usr/sbin:/usr/bin:/sbin:/bin
```

The directories are separated by colons (:). Notice that the directory where python3 lives is the first one in $PATH. It's a pretty long string, so I broke it with the \ character to make it easier to read. If you copy your hello.py program to any of the directories listed in your $PATH, you can execute a program like hello.py without the leading ./ and without having to be in the same directory as the program.

Think about $PATH like this: If you lose your keys in your house, would you start looking in the upper-left kitchen cabinet and work your way through each cabinet, and then all the drawers where you keep your silverware and kitchen gadgets, and then move on to your bathrooms and bedroom closets? Or would you start by looking in places where you normally put your keys, like the key hooks beside the front door, and then move on to search the pockets of your favorite jacket and your purse or backpack, and then maybe look under the couch cushions, and so forth?

The $PATH variable is a way of telling your computer to only look in places where executable programs can be found. The only alternative is for the OS to search *every directory*, and that could take several minutes or possibly even hours! You can control both the names of the directories in the $PATH variable and their relative order so that the OS will find the programs you need.

It's very common for programs to be installed into /usr/local/bin, so we could try to copy our program there using the cp command. Unfortunately, I do not have permission to do this on Repl.it:

```
> cp 01_hello/hello.py /usr/local/bin
cp: cannot create regular file '/usr/local/bin/hello.py': Permission denied
```

But I can do this on my own laptop:

```
$ cp hello.py /usr/local/bin/
```

I can verify that the program is found:

```
$ which hello.py
/usr/local/bin/hello.py
```

And now I can execute it from any directory on my computer:

```
$ hello.py
Hello, World!
```

1.6.1   *Altering your $PATH*

Often you may find yourself working on a computer that won't allow you to install programs into your $PATH, such as on Repl.it. An alternative is to alter your $PATH to include a directory where you can put your programs. For instance, I often create a bin directory in my home directory, which can often be written with the tilde (~).

On most computers, ~/bin would mean "the bin directory in my home directory." It's also common to see $HOME/bin where $HOME is the name of your home directory. Here is how I create this directory on the Repl.it machine, copy a program to it, and then add it to my $PATH:

```
$ mkdir ~/bin
$ cp 01_hello/hello.py ~/bin
$ PATH=~/bin:$PATH
$ which hello.py
/home/runner/bin/hello.py
```

Use the mkdir ("make directory") command to create ~/bin.

Use the cp command to copy the 01_hello/hello.py program to the ~/bin directory.

Put the ~/bin directory first in $PATH.

Use the which command to look for the hello.py program. If the previous steps worked, the OS should now be able to find the program in one of the directories listed in $PATH.

Now I can be in any directory,

```
$ pwd
/home/runner/tinypythonprojects
```

and I can run it:

```
$ hello.py
Hello, World!
```

Although the shebang and the executable stuff may seem like a lot of work, the payoff is that you can create a Python program that can be installed onto your computer or anyone else's and run just like any other program.

1.7 *Adding a parameter and help*

Throughout the book, I'll use string diagrams to visualize the inputs and outputs of the programs we'll write. If we created one for our program now (as in figure 1.2), there would be no inputs, and the output would always be "Hello, World!"

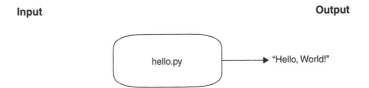

Input   **Output**

Figure 1.2   A string diagram representing our hello.py program that takes no inputs and always produces the same output

It's not terribly interesting for our program to always say "Hello, World!" It would be nice if it could say "Hello" to something else, like the entire universe. We could do this by changing the code as follows:

```
print('Hello, Universe')
```

But that would mean we'd have to change the code every time we wanted to make it greet a different name. It would be better to change the *behavior* of the program without always having to change *the program itself.*

We can do that by finding the parts of the program that we want to change—like the name to greet— and providing that value as as an *argument* to our program. That is, we'd like our program to work like this:

```
$ ./hello.py Terra
Hello, Terra!
```

How would the person using our program know to do this? *It's our program's responsibility to provide a help message!* Most command-line programs will respond to arguments like -h and --help with helpful messages about how to use the programs. We need our program to print something like this:

```
$ ./hello.py -h
usage: hello.py [-h] name

Say hello

positional arguments:
  name            Name to greet

optional arguments:
  -h, --help  show this help message and exit
```

Note that name is called a positional argument.

To do this, we can use the argparse module. Modules are files of code we can bring into our programs. We can also create modules to share our code with other people. There are hundreds to thousands of modules you can use in Python, which is one of the reasons why it's so exciting to use the language.

The argparse module will "parse" the "arguments" to the program. To use it, change your program as follows. I recommend you type everything yourself and don't copy and paste.

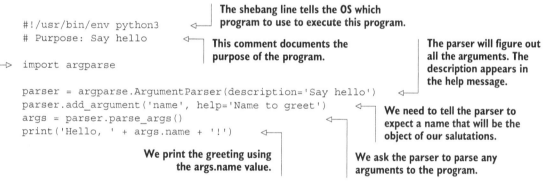

We must import the argparse module to use it.

The shebang line tells the OS which program to use to execute this program.

This comment documents the purpose of the program.

The parser will figure out all the arguments. The description appears in the help message.

```
#!/usr/bin/env python3
# Purpose: Say hello

import argparse

parser = argparse.ArgumentParser(description='Say hello')
parser.add_argument('name', help='Name to greet')
args = parser.parse_args()
print('Hello, ' + args.name + '!')
```

We need to tell the parser to expect a name that will be the object of our salutations.

We print the greeting using the args.name value.

We ask the parser to parse any arguments to the program.

Figure 1.3 shows a string diagram of our program now.

Now when you try to run the program like before, it triggers an error and a "usage" statement (notice that "usage" is the first word of the output):

We run the program with no arguments, but the program now expects a single argument (a "name").

```
$ ./hello.py
usage: hello.py [-h] name
hello.py: error: the following arguments are required: name
```

Since the program doesn't get the expected argument, it stops and prints a "usage" message to let the user know how to properly invoke the program.

The error message tells the user that they have not supplied a required parameter called "name."

Input   Output

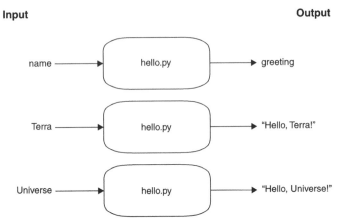

Figure 1.3 Now our string diagram shows that our program can take an argument and produce a message based on that value.

We've changed the program so that it requires a name or it won't run. That's pretty cool! Let's give it a name to greet:

```
$ ./hello.py Universe
Hello, Universe!
```

Try running your program with both the `-h` and `--help` arguments, and verify that you see the help messages.

The program works really well now and has nice documentation, all because we added those few lines using `argparse`. That's a big improvement.

1.8   *Making the argument optional*

Suppose we'd like to run the program like before, with no arguments, and have it print "Hello, World!" We can make the `name` optional by changing the name of the argument to `--name`:

```
#!/usr/bin/env python3
# Purpose: Say hello

import argparse

parser = argparse.ArgumentParser(description='Say hello')
parser.add_argument('-n', '--name', metavar='name',
                    default='World', help='Name to greet')
args = parser.parse_args()
print('Hello, ' + args.name + '!')
```

The only change to this program is adding -n and --name for the "short" and "long" option names. We also indicate a default value. "metavar" will show up in the usage to describe the argument.

Now we can run it like before:

```
$ ./hello.py
Hello, World!
```

Or we can use the --name option:

```
$ ./hello.py --name Terra
Hello, Terra!
```

And our help message has changed:

```
$ ./hello.py -h
usage: hello.py [-h] [-n NAME]

Say hello

optional arguments:
  -h, --help            show this help message and exit
  -n name, --name name  Name to greet
```

The argument is now optional and no longer a positional argument. It's common to provide both short and long names to make it easy to type the options. The metavar value of "name" appears here to describe what the value should be.

Figure 1.4 shows a string diagram that describes our program.

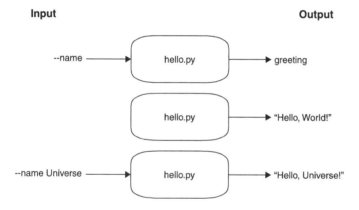

Input   **Output**

--name ⟶ hello.py ⟶ greeting

hello.py ⟶ "Hello, World!"

--name Universe ⟶ hello.py ⟶ "Hello, Universe!"

Figure 1.4   The name parameter is now optional. The program will greet a given name or will use a default value when it's missing.

Our program is really flexible now, greeting a default value when run with no arguments or allowing us to say "hi" to something else. Remember that parameters that start with dashes are *optional*, so they can be left out, and they may have default values. Parameters that *don't* start with dashes are *positional* and are usually required, so they do not have default values.

Table 1.1   Two kinds of command-line parameters

Type	Example	Required	Default
Positional	name	Yes	No
Optional	-n (short), --name (long)	No	Yes

1.9   *Running our tests*

Let's run our tests again to see how we are doing:

```
$ make test
pytest -xv test.py
============================== test session starts ==============================
...
collected 5 items

test.py::test_exists PASSED                                               [ 20%]
test.py::test_runnable PASSED                                            [ 40%]
test.py::test_executable PASSED                                         [ 60%]
test.py::test_usage PASSED                                              [ 80%]
test.py::test_input PASSED                                             [100%]

============================== 5 passed in 0.38s ==============================
```

Wow, we're passing all our tests! I actually get excited whenever I see my programs pass all their tests, even when I'm the one who wrote the tests. Before we were failing on the usage and input tests. Adding the `argparse` code fixed both of those because it allows us to accept arguments when our program runs, and it will also create documentation about how to run our program.

1.10   *Adding the main() function*

Our program works really well now, but it's not quite up to community standards and expectations. For instance, it's very common for computer programs—not just ones written in Python—to start at a place called `main()`. Most Python programs define a function called `main()`, and there is an idiom to call the `main()` function at the end of the code, like this:

```
#!/usr/bin/env python3
# Purpose: Say hello

import argparse

def main():
    parser = argparse.ArgumentParser(description='Say hello')
    parser.add_argument('-n', '--name', metavar='name',
                        default='World', help='Name to greet')
    args = parser.parse_args()
    print('Hello, ' + args.name + '!')

if __name__ == '__main__':
    main()
```

def defines a function, named main() in this case. The empty parentheses show that this function accepts no arguments.

Every program or module in Python has a name that can be accessed through the variable __name__. When the program is executing, __name__ is set to "__main__".[1]

If this is true, call the main() function.

---

[1] See Python's documentation of `main` for more information: https://docs.python.org/3/library/__main__.html.

As our programs get longer, we'll start creating more functions. Python programmers approach this in different ways, but in this book I will always create and execute a `main()` function to be consistent. To start off, we'll always put the main part of our program inside the `main()` function.

1.11 Adding the get_args() function

As a matter of personal taste, I like to put all the `argparse` code into a separate place that I always call `get_args()`. Getting and validating arguments is one concept in my mind, so it belongs by itself. For some programs, this function can get quite long.

I always put `get_args()` as the first function so that I can see it immediately when I read the source code. I usually put `main()` right after it. You are, of course, welcome to structure your programs however you like.

Here is what the program looks like now:

```
#!/usr/bin/env python3
# Purpose: Say hello

import argparse

def get_args():
    parser = argparse.ArgumentParser(description='Say hello')
    parser.add_argument('-n', '--name', metavar='name',
                        default='World', help='Name to greet')
    return parser.parse_args()

def main():
    args = get_args()
    print('Hello, ' + args.name + '!')

if __name__ == '__main__':
    main()
```

The get_args() function is dedicated to getting the arguments. All the argparse code now lives here.

We need to call return to send the results of parsing the arguments back to the main() function.

The main() function is much shorter now.

Call the get_args() function to get parsed arguments. If there is a problem with the arguments or if the user asks for --help, the program never gets to this point because argparse will cause it to exit. If our program does make it this far, the input values must have been OK.

Nothing has changed about the way the program works. We're just organizing the code to group ideas together—the code that deals with `argparse` now lives in the `get_args()` function, and everything else lives in `main()`. Just to be sure, go run the test suite!

1.11.1 *Checking style and errors*

Our program works really well now. We can use tools like Flake8 and Pylint to check if our program has problems. These tools are called *linters,* and their job is to suggest ways to improve a program. If you haven't installed them yet, you can use the `pip` module to do so now:

```
$ python3 -m pip install flake8 pylint
```

The Flake8 program wants me to put two blank lines between each of the function `def` definitions:

```
$ flake8 hello.py
hello.py:6:1: E302 expected 2 blank lines, found 1
hello.py:12:1: E302 expected 2 blank lines, found 1
hello.py:16:1: E305 expected 2 blank lines after class or function definition,
    found 1
```

And Pylint says that the functions are missing documentation ("docstrings"):

```
$ pylint hello.py
************* Module hello
hello.py:1:0: C0114: Missing module docstring (missing-module-docstring)
hello.py:6:0: C0116: Missing function or method docstring (missing-function-
    docstring)
hello.py:12:0: C0116: Missing function or method docstring (missing-function-
    docstring)

------------------------------------------------------------------
Your code has been rated at 7.00/10 (previous run: -10.00/10, +17.00)
```

A *docstring* is a string that occurs just after the `def` of the function. It's common to have several lines of documentation for a function, so programmers often will use Python's triple quotes (single or double) to create a multiline string. Following is what the program looks like when I add docstrings. I have also used YAPF to format the program and fix the spacing problems, but you are welcome to use Black or any other tool you like.

```
#!/usr/bin/env python3
"""
Author:  Ken Youens-Clark <kyclark@gmail.com>
Purpose: Say hello
"""

import argparse
```

Triple-quoted, multiline docstring for the entire program. It's common practice to write a long docstring just after the shebang to document the overall purpose of the function. I like to include at least my name, email address, and the purpose of the script so that any future person using the program will know who wrote it, how to get in touch with me if they have problems, and what the program is supposed to do.

```
# -------------------------------------------
def get_args():
    """Get the command-line arguments"""

    parser = argparse.ArgumentParser(description='Say hello')
    parser.add_argument('-n', '--
     name', default='World', help='Name to greet')
    return parser.parse_args()
```

A big horizontal "line" comment to help me find the functions. You can omit these if you don't like them.

The docstring for the get_args() function. I like to use triple quotes even for a single-line comment, as they help me to see the docstring better.

```
    # -------------------------------------------------
def main():
    """Make a jazz noise here"""

    args = get_args()
    print('Hello, ' + args.name + '!')
```

The main() function is simply where the program begins, so there's not much to say in the docstring. I think it's (at least a little) funny to always put "Make a jazz noise here," but you can put whatever you like.

```
    # -------------------------------------------------
if __name__ == '__main__':
    main()
```

To learn how to use YAPF or Black on the command line, run them with the -h or --help flag and read the documentation. If you are using an IDE like VS Code or PyCharm, or if you are using the Repl.it interface, there are commands to reformat your code.

1.12   Testing hello.py

We've made many changes to our program—are we sure it still works correctly? Let's run our test again.

This is something you will do literally hundreds of times, so I've created a short-cut you might like to use. In every directory, you'll find a file called Makefile that looks like this:

```
$ cat Makefile
.PHONY: test

test:
    pytest -xv test.py
```

If you have the program make installed on your computer, you can run make test when you are in the 01_hello directory. The make program will look for a Makefile in your current working directory and then look for a recipe called "test." There it will find that the command to run for the "test" target is pytest -xv test.py, so it will run that command for you.

```
$ make test
pytest -xv test.py
```

```
=========================== test session starts ===========================
...
collected 5 items

test.py::test_exists PASSED                                          [ 20%]
test.py::test_runnable PASSED                                       [ 40%]
test.py::test_executable PASSED                                     [ 60%]
test.py::test_usage PASSED                                          [ 80%]
test.py::test_input PASSED                                          [100%]


=========================== 5 passed in 0.75s ===========================
```

If you do not have `make` installed, you might like to install it and learn about how Makefiles can be used to execute complicated sets of commands. If you do not want to install or use `make`, you can always run `pytest -xv test.py` yourself. They both accomplish the same task.

The important point is that we were able to use our tests to verify that our program still does exactly what it is supposed to do. As you write programs, you may want to try different solutions. Tests give you the freedom to rewrite a program (also called "refactoring your code") and know that it still works.

1.13   *Starting a new program with new.py*

The `argparse` module is a standard module that is always installed with Python. It's widely used because it can save us so much time in parsing and validating the arguments to our programs. You'll be using `argparse` in every program for this book, and you'll learn how you can use it to convert text to numbers, to validate and open files, and much more. There are so many options that I created a Python program called new.py that will help you start writing new Python programs that use `argparse`.

I have put this new.py program into the bin directory of the GitHub repo. I suggest you use it to start every new program you write. For instance, you could create a new version of hello.py using new.py. Go to the top level of your repository and run this:

```
$ bin/new.py 01_hello/hello.py
"01_hello/hello.py" exists.  Overwrite? [yN] n
Will not overwrite. Bye!
```

The new.py program will not overwrite an existing file unless you tell it to, so you can use it without worrying that you might erase your work. Try using it to create a program with a different name:

```
$ bin/new.py 01_hello/hello2.py
Done, see new script "01_hello/hello2.py."
```

Now try executing that program:

```
$ 01_hello/hello2.py
usage: hello2.py [-h] [-a str] [-i int] [-f FILE] [-o] str
hello2.py: error: the following arguments are required: str
```

Let's look at the source code of the new program:

```
#!/usr/bin/env python3
"""
Author : Ken Youens-Clark <kyclark@gmail.com>
Date   : 2020-02-28
Purpose: Rock the Casbah
"""
```

The shebang line should use the env program to find the python3 program.

This docstring is for the program as a whole.

```
import argparse
import os
import sys
```

These lines import various modules that the program needs.

```
# --------------------------------------------------
def get_args():
    """Get command-line arguments"""

    parser = argparse.ArgumentParser(
        description='Rock the Casbah',
        formatter_class=argparse.ArgumentDefaultsHelpFormatter)

    parser.add_argument('positional',
                        metavar='str',
                        help='A positional argument')

    parser.add_argument('-a',
                        '--arg',
                        help='A named string argument',
                        metavar='str',
                        type=str,
                        default='')

    parser.add_argument('-i',
                        '--int',
                        help='A named integer argument',
                        metavar='int',
                        type=int,
                        default=0)

    parser.add_argument('-f',
                        '--file',
                        help='A readable file',
                        metavar='FILE',
                        type=argparse.FileType('r'),
                        default=None)

    parser.add_argument('-o',
                        '--on',
```

The get_args() function is responsible for parsing and validating arguments.

Define a "positional" argument like our first version of hello.py that had a name argument.

Define an "optional" argument like when we changed to use the --name option.

Define an optional argument that must be an integer value.

Define an optional argument that must be a file.

Define a "flag" option that is either "on" when present or "off" when absent. You'll learn more about these later.

```
                              help='A boolean flag',
                              action='store_true')
```

```
    return parser.parse_args()
```

← **Return the parsed arguments to main(). If there are any problems, like if the --int value is some text rather than a number like 42, argparse will print an error message and the "usage" for the user.**

```
# ------------------------------------------------
def main():
    """Make a jazz noise here"""
```

← **Define the main() function where the program starts.**

```
    args = get_args()
    str_arg = args.arg
    int_arg = args.int
    file_arg = args.file
    flag_arg = args.on
    pos_arg = args.positional
```

← **The first thing our main() functions will always do is call get_args() to get the arguments.**

Each argument's value is accessible through the long name of the argument. It is not required to have both a short and long name, but it is common and tends to make your program more readable.

```
    print(f'str_arg = "{str_arg}"')
    print(f'int_arg = "{int_arg}"')
    print('file_arg = "{}"'.format(file_arg.name if file_arg else ''))
    print(f'flag_arg = "{flag_arg}"')
    print(f'positional = "{pos_arg}"')
```

```
# ------------------------------------------------
if __name__ == '__main__':
    main()
```

← **If the condition is true, this calls the main() function.**

← **When the program is being executed, the __name__ value will be equal to the text "__main__."**

This program will accept the following arguments:

- A single positional argument of the type str. *Positional* means it is not preceded by a flag to name it but has meaning because of its position relative to the command name.
- An automatic -h or --help flag that will cause argparse to print the usage.
- A string option called either -a or --arg.
- A named option argument called -i or --int.
- A file option called -f or --file.
- A Boolean (off/on) flag called -o or --on.

Looking at the preceding list, you can see that new.py has done the following for you:

- Created a new Python program called hello2.py
- Used a template to generate a working program complete with docstrings, a main() function to start the program, a get_args() function to parse and document various kinds of arguments, and code to start the program running in the main() function
- Made the new program executable so that it can be run like ./hello2.py

The result is a program that you can immediately execute and that will produce documentation on how to run it. After you use new.py to create your new program, you should open it with your editor and modify the argument names and types to suit the needs of your program. For instance, in chapter 2 you'll be able to delete everything but the positional argument, which you should rename from `'positional'` to something like `'word'` (because the argument is going to be a word).

Note that you can control the "name" and "email" values that are used by new.py by creating a file called .new.py (note the leading dot!) in your home directory. Here is mine:

```
$ cat ~/.new.py
name=Ken Youens-Clark
email=kyclark@gmail.com
```

1.14 *Using template.py as an alternative to new.py*

If you don't want to use new.py, I have included a sample of the preceding program as template/template.py, which you can copy. For instance, in chapter 2 you will need to create the program 02_crowsnest/crowsnest.py.

You can do this with new.py from the top level of the repository:

```
$ bin/new.py 02_crowsnest/crowsnest.py
```

Or you can the use cp (copy) command to copy the template to your new program:

```
$ cp template/template.py 02_crowsnest/crowsnest.py
```

The main point is that you won't have to start every program from scratch. I think it's much easier to start with a complete, working program and modify it.

> **NOTE** You can copy new.py to your ~/bin directory. Then you can use it from any directory to create a new program.

Be sure to skim the appendix—it has many examples of programs that use `argparse`. You can copy many of those examples to help you with the exercises.

Summary

- A Python program is plain text that lives in a file. You need the `python3` program to interpret and execute the program file.
- You can make a program executable and copy it to a location in your `$PATH` so that you can run it like any other program on your computer. Be sure to set the shebang to use `env` to find the correct `python3`.
- The `argparse` module will help you document and parse all the parameters to your program. You can validate the types and numbers of arguments, which can be positional, optional, or flags. The usage will be automatically generated.

- We will use the pytest program to run the test.py programs for each exercise. The make test shortcut will execute pytest -xv test.py, or you can run this command directly.
- You should run your tests often to ensure that everything works.
- Code formatters like YAPF and Black will automatically format your code to community standards, making it easier to read and debug.
- Code linters like Pylint and Flake8 can help you correct both programmatic and stylistic problems.
- You can use the new.py program to generate new Python programs that use argparse.

The crow's nest: Working with strings

A narwhal!

An octopus!

Ahoy!

Avast, you corny-faced gollumpus! Ye are barrelman for this watch. D'ye ken what I mean, ye addle-pated blunderbuss?! Ah, landlubber ye be! OK, then, you are the lookout in the crow's nest—the little bucket attached to the top of a mast of a sailing ship. Your job is to keep a lookout for interesting or dangerous things, like a ship to plunder or an iceberg to avoid. When you see something like a narwhal, you are supposed to cry out, "Ahoy, Captain, *a narwhal* off the larboard bow!" If you see an octopus, you'll shout "Ahoy, Captain, *an octopus* off the larboard bow!" (We'll assume everything is "off the larboard bow" for this exercise. It's a great place for things to be.)

From this point on, each chapter will present a coding challenge that you should complete on your own. I will discuss the key ideas you'll need to solve the problems as well as how to use the provided tests to determine when your program is correct. You should have a copy of the Git repository locally (see the setup instructions in the book's introduction), and you should write each program in that chapter's directory. For example, this chapter's program should be written in the 02_crowsnest directory, where the tests for the program live.

In this chapter, we're going to start working with strings. By the end, you will be able to

- Create a program that accepts a positional argument and produces usage documentation
- Create a new output string depending on the inputs to the program
- Run a test suite

Your program should be called crowsnest.py. It will accept a single positional argument and will print the given argument inside the "Ahoy" bit, along with the word "a" or "an" depending on whether the argument starts with a consonant or a vowel.

That is, if given "narwhal," it should do this:

```
$ ./crowsnest.py narwhal
Ahoy, Captain, a narwhal off the larboard bow!
```

And if given "octopus,"

```
$ ./crowsnest.py octopus
Ahoy, Captain, an octopus off the larboard bow!
```

This means you're going to need to write a program that accepts some input on the command line, decides on the proper article ("a" or "an") for the input, and prints out a string that puts those two values into the "Ahoy" phrase.

2.1 Getting started

You're probably ready to start writing the program! Well, hold on just a minute longer, ye duke of limbs. We need to discuss how you can use the tests to know when your program is working and how you might get started programming.

2.1.1 How to use the tests

"The greatest teacher, failure is."

—Yoda

In the code repository, I've included tests that will guide you in the writing of your program. Before you even write the first line of code, I'd like you to run the tests so you can look at the first failed test:

```
$ cd 02_crowsnest
$ make test
```

Instead of make test you could also run pytest -xv test.py. Among the output, you'll see this line:

```
$ pytest -xv test.py
============================== test session starts ==============================
...
```

```
collected 6 items
```

→ `test.py::test_exists FAILED`   [16%]

**This test failed. There are more tests after this, but
testing stops here because of the -x flag to pytest.**

You'll also see lots of other output trying to convince you that the expected file, crows-nest.py, does not exist. Learning to read the test output is a skill in itself—it takes quite a bit of practice, so try not to feel overwhelmed. In my terminal (iTerm on a Mac), the output from `pytest` shows colors and bold print to highlight key failures. The text in bold, red letters is usually where I start, but your terminal may behave differently.

Let's take a gander at the output. It does look at bit daunting at first, but you'll get used to reading the messages and finding your errors.

**The "E" at the beginning of this line is the "Error" you should read. It's very
difficult to understand what the test is trying to tell you, but essentially the
./crowsnest.py file does not exist.**

```
===================================== FAILURES =====================================
_____ test_exists _____

        def test_exists():    ←——┐   This is the actual code inside      The ">" at the beginning of this line
            """exists"""          │   test.py that is running. It's a     indicates this is the line where the
                                  │   function called test_exists().      error starts. The test is checking if
                                                                          there is a file called crowsnest.py.
>           assert os.path.isfile(prg)              ←————————             If you haven't created it, this will
E           AssertionError: assert False                                 fail as expected.
E             +  where False = <function isfile at 0x1086f1310>('./crowsnest.py')
E             +    where <function isfile at 0x1086f1310> = <module 'posixpath'
from '/Library/Frameworks/Python.framework/Versions/3.8/lib/python3.8/posixpath.
    py'>.isfile
E             +      where <module 'posixpath' from
'/Library/Frameworks/Python.framework/Versions/3.8/lib/python3.8/posixpath.py'>
    = os.path

test.py:22: AssertionError
```
→ `!!!!!!!!!!!!!!!!!!!!!!!!!!! stopping after 1 failures !!!!!!!!!!!!!!!!!!!!!!!!!!!!!`
```
============================== 1 failed in 0.05s ==============================
```

**This warns that no more tests will run after the one failure. This is
because we ran it with the flag to stop testing at the first failure.**

The first test for every program in the book checks that the expected file exists, so let's create it!

2.1.2 Creating programs with new.py

In order to pass the first test, you need to create a file called crowsnest.py inside the 02_crowsnest directory where test.py is located. While it's perfectly fine to start writing from scratch, I suggest you use the new.py program to print some useful boilerplate code that you'll need in every exercise.

From the top level of the repository, you can run the following command to create the new program.

```
$ bin/new.py 02_crowsnest/crowsnest.py
Done, see new script "02_crowsnest/crowsnest.py."
```

If you don't want to use new.py, you can copy the template/template.py program:

```
$ cp template/template.py 02_crowsnest/crowsnest.py
```

You should now have the outline of a working program that accepts command-line arguments. If you run your new crowsnest.py with no arguments, it will print a short usage statement like the following (notice how "usage" is the first word of the output):

```
$ ./crowsnest.py
usage: crowsnest.py [-h] [-a str] [-i int] [-f FILE] [-o] str
crowsnest.py: error: the following arguments are required: str
```

Run it with `./crowsnest.py --help`. It will print a longer help message too.

NOTE   Those are not the correct parameters for our program, just the default examples supplied by new.py. You will need to modify them to suit this program.

2.1.3   *Write, test, repeat*

You just created the program, so you ought to be able to pass the first test. The cycle I hope you'll develop is to write a very small amount of code—literally one or two lines at most—and then run the program or the tests to see how you're doing.

Let's run the tests again:

The program will respond to -h and --help. The fact that the help is actually incorrect is not important at this point. The tests are only checking that you seem to have the outline of a program that will run and process the help flags.

```
$ make test
pytest -xv test.py
============================ test session starts ==============================
...
collected 6 items

test.py::test_exists PASSED                                              [ 16%]
test.py::test_usage PASSED                                              [ 33%]
test.py::test_consonant FAILED                                         [ 50%]
```

The expected file exists, so this test passes.

The test_consonant() test is failing. That's OK! We haven't even started writing the actual program, but at least we have a place to start.

As you can see, creating a new program with new.py will make you pass the first *two* tests:

1 Does the program exist? Yes, you just created it.
2 Does the program print a help message when you ask for help? Yes, you ran it above with no arguments and the `--help` flag, and you saw that it will produce help messages.

Now you have a working program that accepts some arguments (but not the right ones). Next you need to make your program accept the "narwhal" or "octopus" value that needs to be announced. We'll use command-line arguments to do that.

2.1.4 Defining your arguments

Figure 2.1 is sure to shiver your timbers, showing the inputs (or *parameters*) and output of the program. We'll use these diagrams throughout the book to imagine how code and data work together. In this program, the input is a word, and a phrase incorporating that word with the correct article is the output.

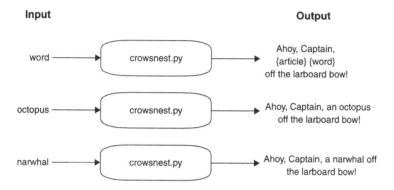

Figure 2.1 **The input to the program is a word, and the output is that word plus its proper article (and some other stuff).**

We need to modify the part of the program that gets the arguments—the aptly named get_args() function. This function uses the argparse module to parse the command-line arguments, and our program needs to accept a single, positional argument. If you're unsure what a "positional" argument is, be sure to read the appendix, especially section A.4.1.

The get_args() function created by the template names the first argument positional. Remember that positional arguments are defined by their positions and don't have names that start with dashes. You can delete all the arguments except for the positional word. Modify the get_args() part of your program until it will print this usage:

```
$ ./crowsnest.py
usage: crowsnest.py [-h] word
crowsnest.py: error: the following arguments are required: word
```

Likewise, it should print longer usage documentation for the -h or --help flag:

```
$ ./crowsnest.py -h
usage: crowsnest.py [-h] word
```

```
Crow's Nest -- choose the correct article
```

```
positional arguments:
    word         A word
```
⊲— **You need to define a word parameter. Notice that it is listed as a positional argument.**

```
optional arguments:
  -h, --help  show this help message and exit
```
⊲— **The -h and --help flags are created automatically by argparse. You are not allowed to use these as options. They are used to create the documentation for your program.**

Do not proceed until your usage matches the preceding!

When your program prints the correct usage, you can get the word argument inside the main function. Modify your program so that it will print the word:

```
def main():
    args = get_args()
    word = args.word
    print(word)
```

Then test that it works:

```
$ ./crowsnest.py narwhal
narwhal
```

And now run your tests again. You should still be passing two and failing the third. Let's read the test failure:

It's not terribly important right now to understand this line, but the getoutput() function is running the program with a word. We're going to talk about the f-string in this chapter. The output from running the program will go into the out variable, which will be used to see if the program created the correct output for a given word. None of the code in this function is anything you should worry about being able to write yet.

```
================================== FAILURES ==================================
_____ test_consonant _____

    def test_consonant():
        """brigantine -> a brigantine"""

        for word in consonant_words:
            out = getoutput(f'{prg} {word}')
>           assert out.strip() == template.format('a', word)
E           AssertionError: assert 'brigantine' == 'Ahoy, Captai...larboard bow!'
E             - brigantine
E             + Ahoy, Captain, a brigantine off the larboard bow!
```

⊲— **The line starting with ">" shows the code that produced an error. The output of the program is compared to an expected string. Since it didn't match, the assert produces an exception.**

This line starts with "E" to indicate the error.

The line starting with the plus sign (+) is what the test expected: "Ahoy, Captain, a brigantine off the larboard bow!"

The line starting with a hyphen (-) is what the test got when it ran with the argument "brigantine"—it got back the word "brigantine."

So we need to get the word into the "Ahoy" phrase. How can we do that?

2.1.5 *Concatenating strings*

Putting strings together is called *concatenating* or *joining* strings. To demonstrate, I'll enter some code directly into the Python interpreter. I want you to type along. No, really! Type everything you see, and try it for yourself.

Open a terminal and type `python3` or `ipython` to start a REPL. A REPL is a Read-Evaluate-Print-Loop—Python will *read* each line of input, *evaluate* it, and *print* the results in a *loop*. Here's what it looks like on my system:

```
$ python3
Python 3.8.1 (v3.8.1:1b293b6006, Dec 18 2019, 14:08:53)
[Clang 6.0 (clang-600.0.57)] on darwin
Type "help", "copyright", "credits" or "license" for more information.
>>>
```

The ">>>" is a prompt where you can type code. Remember *not* to type that part! To exit the REPL, either type `quit()` or press Ctrl-D (the Control key plus the letter *D*).

> **NOTE** You may prefer to use Python's IDLE (integrated development and learning environment) program, IPython, or Jupyter Notebooks to interact with the language. I'll stick to the python3 REPL throughout the book.

Let's start off by assigning the variable `word` to the value "narwhal." In the REPL, type `word = 'narwhal'` and press Enter:

```
>>> word = 'narwhal'
```

Note that you can put as many (or no) spaces around the = as you like, but convention and readability (and tools like Pylint and Flake8 that help you find errors in your code) ask you to use exactly one space on either side.

If you type `word` and press Enter, Python will print the current value of `word`:

```
>>> word
'narwhal'
```

Now type `werd` and press Enter:

```
>>> werd
Traceback (most recent call last):
  File "<stdin>", line 1, in <module>
NameError: name 'werd' is not defined
```

> **WARNING** There is no `werd` variable because we haven't set `werd` to be anything. Using an undefined variable causes an *exception* that will crash your program. Python will happily create `werd` for you when you assign it a value.

We need to insert the `word` between two other strings. The + operator can be used to join strings together:

```
>>> 'Ahoy, Captain, a ' + word + ' off the larboard bow!'
'Ahoy, Captain, a narwhal off the larboard bow!'
```

If you change your program to `print()` that string instead of just printing the `word`, you should be able to pass four tests:

```
test.py::test_exists PASSED                                      [ 16%]
test.py::test_usage PASSED                                       [ 33%]
test.py::test_consonant PASSED                                   [ 50%]
test.py::test_consonant_upper PASSED                             [ 66%]
test.py::test_vowel FAILED                                       [ 83%]
```

If you look closely at the failure, you'll see this:

```
E              - Ahoy, Captain, a aviso off the larboard bow!
E              + Ahoy, Captain, an aviso off the larboard bow!
E              ?                   +
```

We hardcoded the "a" before the `word`, but we really need to figure out whether to use "a" or "an" depending on whether the `word` starts with a vowel. How can we do that?

2.1.6 *Variable types*

Before we go much further, I need to take a small step back and point out that our `word` variable is a *string*. Every variable in Python has a *type* that describes the kind of data it holds. Because we put the value for `word` in quotes (`'narwhal'`), `word` holds a *string*, which Python represents with a class called `str`. (A *class* is a collection of code and functions that we can use.)

The `type()` function will tell you what kind of data Python thinks something is:

```
>>> type(word)
<class 'str'>
```

Whenever you put a value in single quotes (`''`) or double quotes (`""`), Python will interpret it as a `str`:

```
>>> type("submarine")
<class 'str'>
```

> **WARNING** If you forget the quotes, Python will look for some variable or function by that name. If there is no variable or function by that name, it will cause an exception:

```
>>> word = narwhal
Traceback (most recent call last):
  File "<stdin>", line 1, in <module>
NameError: name 'narwhal' is not defined
```

Exceptions are bad, and we will try to write code that avoids them, or at least knows how to handle them gracefully.

2.1.7   *Getting just part of a string*

Back to our problem. We need to put either "a" or "an" in front of the word we're given, based on whether the first character of word is a vowel or a consonant.

In Python, we can use square brackets and an *index* to get an individual character from a string. The index is the numeric position of an element in a sequence, and we must remember that indexing starts at 0.

```
>>> word = 'narwhal'
>>> word[0]
'n'
```

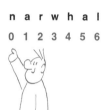

You can index into a literal string value too:

```
>>> 'narwhal'[0]
'n'
```

Because the index values start with 0, that means the last index is *one less than the length* of the string, which is often confusing. The length of "narwhal" is 7, but the last character is found at index 6:

```
>>> word[6]
'l'
```

You can also use negative index numbers to count backwards from the end, so the last index is also -1:

```
>>> word[-1]
'l'
```

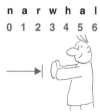

You can use *slice notation* [start:stop] to get a range of characters. Both start and stop are optional. The default value for start is 0 (the beginning of the string), and the stop value is *not inclusive*:

```
>>> word[:3]
'nar'
```

The default value for `stop` is the end of the string:

```
>>> word[3:]
'whal'
```

In the next chapter, you'll see that this is the same as the syntax for slicing lists. A string is (sort of) a list of characters, so this isn't too strange.

2.1.8 *Finding help in the REPL*

The `str` class has a ton of functions we can use to handle strings, but what are they? A large part of programming is knowing how to ask questions and where to look for answers. A common refrain you may hear is "RTFM"—Read the Fine Manual. The Python community has created reams of documentation, which are all available at https://docs.python.org/3/. You will need to refer to the documentation constantly to remind yourself (and discover) how to use certain functions. The docs for the string class are here: https://docs.python.org/ 3/library/string.html.

I prefer to read the docs directly inside the REPL, in this case by typing `help(str)`:

```
>>> help(str)
```

Inside the `help`, you move up and down in the text using the up and down cursor arrows on your keyboard. You can also press the space-bar or the letter *F* (or sometimes Ctrl-F) to jump forward to the next page, and the letter *B* (or sometimes Ctrl-B) to jump backward. You can search through the documentation by pressing / and then the text you want to find. If you press *N* (for "next") after a search, you will jump to the next place that string is found. To leave the help, press *Q* (for "quit").

2.1.9 *String methods*

Now that we know `word` is a string (`str`), we have all these incredibly useful methods we can call on the variable. (A *method* is a function that belongs to a variable like `word`.)

For instance, if I wanted to shout about the fact that we have a narwhal, I could print it in UPPERCASE LETTERS. If I search through the help, I will see that there is a function called `str.upper()`. Here is how you can *call* or *execute* that function:

```
>>> word.upper()
'NARWHAL'
```

You must include the parentheses, `()`, or else you're talking about the *function itself*:

```
>>> word.upper
<built-in method upper of str object at 0x10559e500>
```

That will actually come in handy later, when we use functions like `map()` and `filter()`, but for now we want Python to execute the `str.upper()` function on the variable `word`, so we add the parentheses. Note that the function returns an uppercase version of the word but *does not* change the value of `word`:

```
>>> word
'narwhal'
```

There is another `str` function with "upper" in the name called `str.isupper()`. The name helps you know that this will return a true/false type answer. Let's try it:

```
>>> word.isupper()
False
```

We can chain methods together like so:

```
>>> word.upper().isupper()
True
```

That makes sense. If I convert `word` to uppercase, then `word.isupper()` returns `True`.

I find it odd that the `str` class does not include a method to get the length of a string. For that, we must use a separate function called `len()`, short for "length":

```
>>> len('narwhal')
7
>>> len(word)
7
```

Are you typing all this into Python yourself? I recommend you do! Find other methods in the `str` help, and try them out.

2.1.10 *String comparisons*

You now know how to get the first letter of `word` by using `word[0]`. Let's assign it to the variable `char`:

```
>>> word = 'octopus'
>>> char = word[0]
>>> char
'o'
```

If you check the `type()` of your new `char` variable, it is a `str`. Even a single character is still considered by Python to be a string:

```
>>> type(char)
<class 'str'>
```

Now we need to figure out if `char` is a vowel or a consonant. We'll say that the letters "a," "e," "i," "o," and "u" make up our set of "vowels." You can use `==` to compare strings:

```
>>> char == 'a'
False
>>> char == 'o'
True
```

> **NOTE**   Be careful to always use one equal sign (=) when *assigning a value* to a variable, like word = 'narwhal' and two equal signs (==, which, in my head, I pronounce "equal-equal") when you *compare two values* like word == 'narwhal'. The first is a statement that changes the value of word, and the second is an *expression* that returns True or False (see figure 2.2).

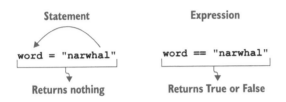

Figure 2.2   **An expression returns a value. A statement does not.**

We need to compare our char to *all* the vowels. You can use and and or in such comparisons, and they will be combined according to standard Boolean algebra:

```
>>> char == 'a' or char == 'e' or char == 'i' or char == 'o' or char == 'u'
True
```

What if the word is "Octopus" or "OCTOPUS"?

```
>>> word = 'OCTOPUS'
>>> char = word[0]
>>> char == 'a' or char == 'e' or char == 'i' or char == 'o' or char == 'u'
False
```

Do we have to make 10 comparisons in order to check the uppercase versions, too? What if we were to lowercase word[0]? Remember that word[0] returns a str, so we can chain other str methods onto that:

```
>>> word = 'OCTOPUS'
>>> char = word[0].lower()
>>> char == 'a' or char == 'e' or char == 'i' or char == 'o' or char == 'u'
True
```

An easier way to determine if char is a vowel would be to use Python's x in y construct, which will tell us if the value x is in the collection y. We can ask whether the letter 'a' is in the longer string 'aeiou':

```
>>> 'a' in 'aeiou'
True
```

But the letter `'b'` is not:

```
>>> 'b' in 'aeiou'
False
```

Let's use that to test the first character of the lowercased word (which is `'o'`):

```
>>> word = 'OCTOPUS'
>>> word[0].lower() in 'aeiou'
True
```

2.1.11 Conditional branching

Once you have figured out if the first letter is a vowel, you will need to select an article. We'll use a very simple rule: if the word starts with a vowel, choose "an"; otherwise, choose "a." This misses exceptions like when the initial "h" in a word is silent. For instance, we say "a hat" but "an honor." Nor will we consider the case where an initial vowel has a consonant sound, as in "union," where the "u" sounds like a "y."

We can create a new variable called `article` that we will set to the empty string, and we'll use an `if/else` statement to figure out what to put in it:

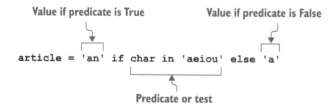

Here is a much shorter way to write that with an `if` *expression* (expressions return values; statements do not). The `if` expression is written a little backwards. First comes the value if the test (or "predicate") is `True`, then the predicate, and then the value if the predicate is `False` (figure 2.3).

Value if predicate is True   **Value if predicate is False**

```
article = 'an' if char in 'aeiou' else 'a'
```

Predicate or test

Figure 2.3 The `if` expression will return the first value if the predicate is `True` and the second value otherwise.

This approach is also safer because the `if` expression is *required* to have the `else`. There's no chance that we could forget to handle both cases:

```
>>> char = 'o'
>>> article = 'an' if char in 'aeiou' else 'a'
```

Let's verify that we have the correct `article`:

```
>>> article
'an'
```

2.1.12 *String formatting*

Now we have two variables, `article` and `word`, that need to be incorporated into our "Ahoy!" phrase. You saw earlier that we can use the plus sign (+) to concatenate strings. Another method for creating new strings from other strings is to use the `str.format()` method.

To do so, you create a string template with curly brackets {}, which indicate placeholders for values. The values that will be substituted are arguments to the `str.format()` method, and they are substituted in the same order that the {} appear (figure 2.4).

```
'Ahoy, Captain, {} {} off the larboard bow!' .format(article, word)
```

Figure 2.4   The `str.format()` method is used to expand the values of variables inside strings.

Here it is in code:

```
>>> 'Ahoy, Captain, {} {} off the larboard bow!'.format(article, word)
'Ahoy, Captain, an octopus off the larboard bow!'
```

Another method for combining strings uses the special "f-string" where you can put the variables directly into the curly brackets {}. It's a matter of taste which approach you choose; I tend to prefer this style because I don't have to think about which variable goes with which set of brackets:

```
>>> f'Ahoy, Captain, {article} {word} off the larboard bow!'
'Ahoy, Captain, an octopus off the larboard bow!'
```

NOTE In some programming languages, you have to declare the variable's name and what *type* of data it will hold. If a variable is declared to be a number, it can never hold a different type of value, like a string. This is called *static typing* because the type of the variable can never change.

Python is a *dynamically typed* language, which means you do not have to declare a variable or what kind of data the variable will hold. You can change the value and type of data at any time. This could be either great or terrible news. As Hamlet says, "There is nothing either good or bad, but thinking makes it so."

2.1.13 *Time to write*

Here are a few hints for writing your solution:

- Start your program with new.py and fill in get_args() with a single positional argument called word.
- You can get the first character of the word by indexing it like a list, word[0].
- Unless you want to check both upper- and lowercase letters, you can use either the str.lower() or str.upper() method to force the input to one case for checking whether the first character is a vowel or consonant.
- There are fewer vowels (five, if you recall) than consonants, so it's probably easier to check whether the first character is one of those.
- You can use the x in y syntax to see if the element x is in the collection y, with the collection here being a list.
- Use str.format() or f-strings to insert the correct article for the given word into the longer phrase.
- Run make test (or pytest -xv test.py) after *every* change to your program to ensure that your program compiles and is on the right track.

Now go write the program before you turn the page and study my solution. Look alive, you ill-tempered shabaroon!

2.2 Solution

Following is one way you could write a program that satisfies the test suite:

```python
#!/usr/bin/env python3
"""Crow's Nest"""

import argparse

# -------------------------------------------------
def get_args():
    """Get command-line arguments"""

    parser = argparse.ArgumentParser(
        description="Crow's Nest -- choose the correct article",
        formatter_class=argparse.ArgumentDefaultsHelpFormatter)

    parser.add_argument('word', metavar='word', help='A word')

    return parser.parse_args()


# -------------------------------------------------
def main():
    """Make a jazz noise here"""

    args = get_args()
    word = args.word
```

Define the function get_args() to handle the command-line arguments. I like to put this first so I can see it right away when I'm reading the code.

The parser will parse the arguments.

The description shows in the usage to describe what the program does.

Show the default values for each parameter in the usage.

Define a positional argument called word.

The result of parsing the arguments will be returned to main().

args contains the return value from the get_args() function.

Define the main() function where the program will start.

Put the args.word value from the arguments into the word variable.

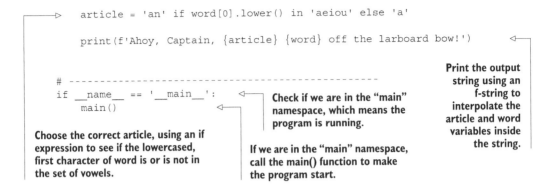

```
article = 'an' if word[0].lower() in 'aeiou' else 'a'

print(f'Ahoy, Captain, {article} {word} off the larboard bow!')


# ----------------------------------------------------
if __name__ == '__main__':
    main()
```

Choose the correct article, using an if expression to see if the lowercased, first character of word is or is not in the set of vowels.

Check if we are in the "main" namespace, which means the program is running.

If we are in the "main" namespace, call the main() function to make the program start.

Print the output string using an f-string to interpolate the article and word variables inside the string.

2.3   Discussion

I'd like to stress that the preceding listing is *a* solution, not *the* solution. There are many ways to express the same idea in Python. As long as your code passes the test suite, it is correct.

That said, I created my program with new.py, which automatically gives me two functions:

- get_args(), where I define the arguments to the program
- main(), where the program starts

Let's talk about these two functions.

2.3.1   Defining the arguments with get_args()

I prefer to put the get_args() function first so that I can see right away what the program expects as input. You don't have to define this as a separate function—you could put all this code inside main(), if you prefer. Eventually our programs are going to get longer, though, and I think it's nice to keep this as a separate idea. Every program I present will have a get_args() function that will define and validate the input.

Our program specifications (the "specs") say that the program should accept one positional argument. I changed the 'positional' argument name to 'word' because I'm expecting a single word:

```
parser.add_argument('word', metavar='word', help='Word')
```

I recommend you never leave the positional argument named 'positional' because it is an entirely nondescriptive term. Naming your variables according to *what they are* will make your code more readable.

The program doesn't need any of the other options created by new.py, so you can delete the rest of the parser.add_argument() calls.

The get_args() function will return the result of parsing the command-line arguments that I put into the variable args:

```
return parser.parse_args()
```

If `argparse` is not able to parse the arguments—for example, if there are none—it will never `return` from `get_args()` but will instead print the "usage" for the user and exit with an error code to let the operating system know that the program exited without success. (On the command line, an exit value of 0 means there were 0 errors. Anything other than 0 is considered an error.)

2.3.2 *The main() thing*

Many programming languages will automatically start from the `main()` function, so I always define a `main()` function and start my programs there. This is not a requirement, but it's an extremely common idiom in Python. Every program I present will start with a `main()` function that will first call `get_args()` to get the program's inputs:

```
def main():
    args = get_args()
```

I can now access the `word` by calling `args.word`. Note the lack of parentheses. It's not `args.word()` because it is not a function call. Think of `args.word` as being like a slot where the value of the word lives:

```
word = args.word
```

I like to work through my ideas using the REPL, so I'm going to pretend that `word` has been set to "octopus":

```
>>> word = 'octopus'
```

2.3.3 *Classifying the first character of a word*

To figure out whether the article I choose should be a or an, I need to look at the first character of the `word`. In the introduction, we used this:

```
>>> word[0]
'o'
```

I can check if the first character is `in` the string of vowels, both lower- and uppercase:

```
>>> word[0] in 'aeiouAEIOU'
True
```

I can make this shorter, however, if I use the `word.lower()` function. Then I'd only have to check the lowercase vowels:

```
>>> word[0].lower() in  'aeiou'
True
```

Remember that the x in y form is a way to ask if element x is in the collection y. You can use it for letters in a longer string (like the list of vowels):

```
>>> 'a' in 'aeiou'
True
```

You can use membership in the list of vowels as a condition to choose "an"; otherwise, we choose "a." As mentioned in the introduction, the if expression is the shortest and safest way to make a *binary* choice (where there are only two possibilities):

```
>>> article = 'an' if word[0].lower() in  'aeiou' else 'a'
>>> article
'an'
```

The safety of the if expression comes from the fact that Python will not even run this program if you forget the else. Try it and see what error you get.

Let's change the value of word to "galleon" and check that it still works:

```
>>> word = 'galleon'
>>> article = 'an' if word[0].lower() in  'aeiou' else 'a'
>>> article
'a'
```

2.3.4 *Printing the results*

Finally we need to print out the phrase with our article and word. As noted in the introduction, you can use the str.format() function to incorporate the variables into a string:

```
>>> article = 'a'
>>> word = 'ketch'
>>> print('Ahoy, Captain, {} {} off the larboard bow!'.format(article, word))
Ahoy, Captain, a ketch off the larboard bow!
```

Python's f-strings will *interpolate* any code inside the {} placeholders, so variables get turned into their contents:

```
>>> print(f'Ahoy, Captain, {article} {word} off the larboard bow!')
Ahoy, Captain, a ketch off the larboard bow!
```

However you choose to print out the article and word is fine, as long as it passes the tests. While it's a matter of personal taste which you choose, I find f-strings a bit easier to read, as my eyes don't have to jump back and forth from the {} placeholders to the variables that will go inside them.

2.3.5 *Running the test suite*

> *"A computer is like a mischievous genie. It will give you exactly what you ask for, but not always what you want."*
>
> —Joe Sondow

Computers are a bit like bad genies. They will do exactly what you tell them, but not necessarily what you *want*. In an episode of *The X-Files*, the character Mulder wishes for peace on Earth, and a genie removes all humans but him.

Tests are what we can use to verify that our programs are doing what we *actually* want them to do. Tests can never prove that our program is truly free from errors, only that the bugs we imagined or found while writing the program no longer exist. Still, we write and run tests because they are really quite effective and much better than not doing so.

This is the idea behind *test-driven development*:

- Write tests *before* we write the software.
- Run the tests to verify that our as-yet-unwritten software fails to deliver on some task.
- Write the software to fulfill the request.
- Run the tests to check that it now *does* work.
- Keep running all the tests to ensure that when we add some new code we do not break existing code.

We won't be discussing how to *write* tests just yet. That will come later. For now, I've written all the tests for you. I hope that by the end of this book, you will see the value of testing and will always start off by writing *tests first and code second*!

2.4   *Going further*

- Have your program match the case of the incoming word (for example, "an octopus" and "An Octopus"). Copy an existing `test_` function in test.py to verify that your program works correctly while still passing all the other tests. Try writing the test first, and then make your program pass the test. That's *test-driven development*!

- Accept a new parameter that changes "larboard" (the left side of the boat) to "starboard" (the right side[1]). You could either make an option called `--side` that defaults to "larboard," or you could make a `--starboard` flag that, if present, changes the side to "starboard."

- The provided tests only give you words that start with an actual alphabetic character. Expand your code to handle words that start with numbers or punctuation. Should your program reject these? Add more tests to ensure that your program does what you intend.

---

[1]   "Starboard" has nothing to do with stars but with the "steering board" or rudder, which typically was on the right side of the boat for right-handed sailors.

Summary

- All Python's documentation is available at https://docs.python.org/3/ and via the `help` command in the REPL.
- Variables in Python are dynamically typed according to whatever value you assign them, and they come into existence when you assign a value to them.
- Strings have methods like `str.upper()` and `str.isupper()` that you can call to alter them or get information.
- You can get parts of a string by using square brackets and indexes like `[0]` for the first letter or `[-1]` for the last.
- You can concatenate strings with the + operator.
- The `str.format()` method allows you to create a template with `{}` placeholders that get filled in with arguments.
- F-strings like `f'{article} {word}'` allow variables and code to go directly inside the brackets.
- The `x in y` expression will report whether the value `x` is present in the collection `y`.
- Statements like `if/else` do not return a value, whereas expressions like `x if y else z` do return a value.
- Test-driven development is a way to ensure programs meet some minimum criteria of correctness. Every feature of a program should have tests, and writing and running test suites should be an integral part of writing programs.

Going on a picnic: Working with lists

Writing code makes me hungry! Let's write a program to list some tasty foods we'd like to eat.

So far we've worked with single variables, like a name to say "hello" to or a nautical-themed object to point out. In this program, we want to keep track of one or more foods that we will store in a `list`, a variable that can hold any number of items. We use lists all the time in real life. Maybe it's your top-five favorite songs, your birthday wish list, or a bucket list of the best types of buckets.

In this chapter, we're going on a picnic, and we want to print a list of items to bring along. You will learn to

- Write a program that accepts multiple positional arguments
- Use `if`, `elif`, and `else` to handle conditional branching with three or more options
- Find and alter items in a list
- Sort and reverse lists
- Format a list into a new string

The items for the list will be passed as positional arguments. When there is only one item, you'll print that:

```
$ ./picnic.py salad
You are bringing salad.
```

What? Who just brings salad on a picnic? When there are two items, you'll print "and" between them:

```
$ ./picnic.py salad chips
You are bringing salad and chips.
```

Hmm, chips. That's an improvement. When there are three or more items, you'll separate the items with commas:

```
$ ./picnic.py salad chips cupcakes
You are bringing salad, chips, and cupcakes.
```

There's one other twist. The program will also need to accept a --sorted argument that will require you to sort the items before you print them. We'll deal with that in a bit.

So, your Python program must do the following:

- Store one or more positional arguments in a list
- Count the number of arguments
- Possibly sort the items
- Use the list to print a new a string that formats the arguments according to how many items there are

How should we begin?

3.1   *Starting the program*

I will always recommend you start programming by running new.py or by copying template/template.py to the program name. This time the program should be called picnic.py, and you need to create it in the 03_picnic directory.

You can do this using the new.py program from the top level of your repository:

```
$ bin/new.py 03_picnic/picnic.py
Done, see new script "03_picnic/picnic.py."
```

Now go into the 03_picnic directory and run make test or pytest -xv test.py. You should pass the first two tests (program exists, program creates usage) and fail the third:

```
test.py::test_exists PASSED                                          [ 14%]
test.py::test_usage PASSED                                           [ 28%]
test.py::test_one FAILED                                             [ 42%]
```

The rest of the output complains that the test expected "You are bringing chips" but got something else:

```
================================= FAILURES =====================================
_____ test_one _____

    def test_one():
        """one item"""

        out = getoutput(f'{prg} chips')          ◄──── The program is
>       assert out.strip() == 'You are bringing chips.'      being run with the
E       assert 'str_arg = ""'...nal = "chips"' == 'You are bringing chips.'   argument "chips."
E         + You are bringing chips.       ◄──────
E         - str_arg = ""           ◄─────   The line starting with a
E         - int_arg = "0"                    + sign shows what was
E         - file_arg = ""                    expected.
E         - flag_arg = "False"
E         - positional = "chips"            The lines starting with
                                            the - sign show what was
test.py:31: AssertionError                  returned by the program.
===================== 1 failed, 2 passed in 0.56 seconds =======================
```

**This line is causing the error. The output is tested to see if it
is equal (==) to the string "You are bringing chips."**

Let's run the program with the argument "chips" and see what it gets:

```
$ ./picnic.py chips
str_arg = ""
int_arg = "0"
file_arg = ""
flag_arg = "False"
positional = "chips"
```

Right, that's not correct at all! Remember, the template doesn't yet have the *correct* arguments, just some examples, so the first thing we need to do is fix the get_args() function. Your program should print a usage statement like the following if given *no arguments*:

```
$ ./picnic.py
usage: picnic.py [-h] [-s] str [str ...]
picnic.py: error: the following arguments are required: str
```

And here is the usage for the -h or --help flags:

```
$ ./picnic.py -h
usage: picnic.py [-h] [-s] str [str ...]

Picnic game

positional arguments:
  str              Item(s) to bring
```

```
optional arguments:
  -h, --help    show this help message and exit
  -s, --sorted  Sort the items (default: False)
```

We need one or more positional arguments and an optional flag called --sorted. Modify your get_args() until it produces the preceding output.

Note that there should be one or more of the item parameter, so you should define it with nargs='+'. Refer to section A.4.5 in the appendix for details.

3.2   *Writing picnic.py*

Figure 3.1 shows a tasty diagram of the inputs and outputs for the picnic.py program we'll write.

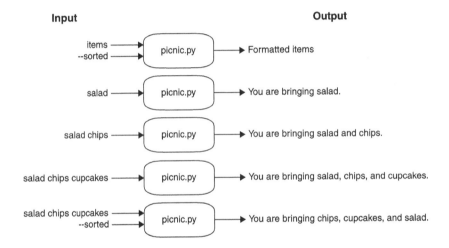

Figure 3.1   A string diagram of the picnic program showing the various inputs and outputs the program will handle

The program should accept one or more positional arguments for the items to bring on a picnic as well as an -s or --sorted *flag* to indicate whether or not to sort the items. The output will be "You are bringing" followed by the list of items formatted according to the following rules:

- If there's one item, state the item:

```
$ ./picnic.py chips
You are bringing chips.
```

- If there are two items, put "and" in between the items. Note that "potato chips" is just *one string* that happens to contain *two words*. If you leave out the quotes, there would be three arguments to the program. It doesn't matter here whether you use single or double quotes:

```
$ ./picnic.py "potato chips" salad
You are bringing potato chips and salad.
```

- If there are three or more items, place a comma and space between the items and the word "and" before the final element. Don't forget the comma before the "and" (sometimes called the "Oxford comma") because your author was an English lit major and, while I may have finally stopped using two spaces after the end of a sentence, you can pry the Oxford comma from my cold, dead hands:

```
$ ./picnic.py "potato chips" salad soda cupcakes
You are bringing potato chips, salad, soda, and cupcakes.
```

Be sure to sort the items if the -s or --sorted flag is specified:

```
$ ./picnic.py --sorted salad soda cupcakes
You are bringing cupcakes, salad, and soda.
```

To figure out how many items we have, how to sort and slice them, and how to format the output string, we need to talk about the list type in Python.

3.3   *Introducing lists*

It's time to learn how to define positional arguments so that they are available as a list. That is, if we run the program like this,

```
$ ./picnic.py salad chips cupcakes
```

the arguments salad chips cupcakes will be available as a list of strings inside the program. If you print() a list in Python, you'll see something like this:

```
['salad', 'chips', 'cupcakes']
```

The square brackets tell us this is a list, and the quotes around the elements tell us they are strings. Note that the items are shown in the same order as they were provided on the command line. Lists always keep their order!

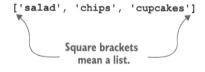

Let's go into the REPL and create a variable called items to hold some scrumptious victuals to bring on our picnic. I really want you to type these commands yourself, whether in the python3 REPL or IPython or a Jupyter Notebook. It's very important to interact in real time with the language.

To create a new, empty list, you can use the list() function:

```
>>> items = list()
```

Or you can use empty square brackets:

```
>>> items = []
```

Check what Python says for the type(). Yep, it's a list:

```
>>> type(items)
<class 'list'>
```

One of the first things we need to know is how many items we have for our picnic. Just as with a str, we can use len() (length) to get the number of elements in items:

```
>>> len(items)
0
```

The length of an empty list is 0.

3.3.1 *Adding one element to a list*

An empty list is not very useful. Let's see how we can add new items. We used help(str) in the last chapter to read documentation about the string methods—the functions that belong to every str in Python. Here I want you to use help(list) to learn about the list methods:

```
>>> help(list)
```

Remember that pressing the spacebar or *F* key (or Ctrl-F) will take you forward, and pressing *B* (or Ctrl-B) will take you back. Pressing the / key will let you search for a string.

You'll see lots of "double-under" methods, like __len__. Skip over those, and the first method is list.append(), which we can use to add items to the end of a list.

If we evaluate items, the empty brackets will tell us that it's empty:

```
>>> items
[]
```

Let's add "sammiches" to the end:

```
>>> items.append('sammiches')
```

Nothing happened, so how do we know if it worked? Let's check the length. It should be 1:

```
>>> len(items)
1
```

Hooray! That worked. In the spirit of testing, we'll use the assert statement to verify that the length is 1:

```
>>> assert len(items) == 1
```

The fact that nothing happens is good. When an assertion fails, it triggers an exception that results in a lot of messages.

If you type `items` and press Enter in the REPL, Python will show you the contents:

```
>>> items
['sammiches']
```

Cool, we added one element.

3.3.2 Adding many elements to a list

Let's try to add "chips" and "ice cream" to `items`:

```
>>> items.append('chips', 'ice cream')
Traceback (most recent call last):
  File "<stdin>", line 1, in <module>
TypeError: append() takes exactly one argument (2 given)
```

Here is one of those pesky exceptions, and these will cause your programs to *crash*, something we want to avoid at all costs. As you can see, `append()` takes exactly one argument, and we gave it two. If you look at `items`, you'll see that nothing was added:

```
>>> items
['sammiches']
```

OK, so maybe we were supposed to give it a `list` of items to add? Let's try that:

```
>>> items.append(['chips', 'ice cream'])
```

Well, that didn't cause an exception, so maybe it worked? We would expect there to be three `items`, so let's use an assertion to check that:

```
>>> assert len(items) == 3
Traceback (most recent call last):
  File "<stdin>", line 1, in <module>
AssertionError
```

We get another exception, because `len(items)` is not 3. What is the length?

```
>>> len(items)
2
```

Only 2? Let's look at `items`:

```
>>> items
['sammiches', ['chips', 'ice cream']]
```

Check that out! Lists can hold any type of data, like strings and numbers and even other lists (see figure 3.2). We asked `items.append()` to add `['chips', 'ice cream']`, which is a `list`, and that's just what it did. Of course, it's not what we wanted.

First item   Second item

Figure 3.2   A list can hold any mix of values, such as a string and another list of strings.

Let's reset `items` so we can fix this:

```
>>> items = ['sammiches']
```

If you read further into the help, you will find the `list.extend()` method:

```
|   extend(self, iterable, /)
|   Extend list by appending elements from the iterable.
```

Let's try that:

```
>>> items.extend('chips', 'ice cream')
Traceback (most recent call last):
  File "<stdin>", line 1, in <module>
TypeError: extend() takes exactly one argument (2 given)
```

Well that's frustrating! Now Python is telling us that `extend()` takes exactly one argument, which, if you refer to the `help`, should be an `iterable`. A `list` is something you can iterate (travel over from beginning to end), so that will work:

```
>>> items.extend(['chips', 'ice cream'])
```

Nothing happened. No exception, so maybe that worked? Let's check the length. It *should* be 3:

```
>>> assert len(items) == 3
```

Yes! Let's look at the items we've added:

```
>>> items
['sammiches', 'chips', 'ice cream']
```

Great! This is sounding like a pretty delicious outing.

If you know everything that will go into the `list`, you can create it like so:

```
>>> items = ['sammiches', 'chips', 'ice cream']
```

The `list.append()` and `list.extend()` methods add new elements to the *end* of a given list. The `list.insert()` method allows you to place new items at any position by specifying the index. I can use the index 0 to put a new element at the beginning of `items`:

```
>>> items.insert(0, 'soda')
>>> items
['soda', 'sammiches', 'chips', 'ice cream']
```

I recommend you read through all the `list` functions so you get an idea of just how powerful this data structure is. In addition to `help(list)`, you can also find lots of great documentation here: https://docs.python.org/3/tutorial/datastructures.html.

3.3.3 *Indexing lists*

We now have a `list` of items. We know how to use `len()` to find how many items there are in the `items` list, and now we need to know how to get parts of the `list` to format.

Indexing a `list` in Python looks exactly the same as indexing a `str` (figure 3.3). (This actually makes me a bit uncomfortable, so I tend to imagine a `str` as a `list` of characters, and then I feel somewhat better.)

```
    0           1            2          3
['soda',   'sammiches',   'chips', 'ice cream']
   -4          -3           -2          -1
```

Figure 3.3   Indexing lists and strings is the same. For both, you start counting at 0, and you can also use negative numbers to index from the end.

All indexing in Python is zero-offset, so the first element of `items` is at index `items[0]`:

```
>>> items[0]
'soda'
```

If the index is negative, Python starts counting backwards from the end of the `list`. The index -1 is the last element of the `list`:

```
>>> items[-1]
'ice cream'
```

You should be very careful when using indexes to reference elements in a `list`. This is unsafe code:

```
>>> items[10]
Traceback (most recent call last):
  File "<stdin>", line 1, in <module>
IndexError: list index out of range
```

WARNING   Referencing an index that is not present will cause an exception.

You'll soon learn how to safely *iterate*, or travel through, a list so that you don't have to use indexes to get at elements.

3.3.4   *Slicing lists*

You can extract "slices" (sub-lists) of a list by using list[start:stop]. To get the first two elements, you use [0:2]. Remember that the 2 is actually the index of the *third* element, but it's not inclusive, as shown in figure 3.4.

```
>>> items[0:2]
['soda', 'sammiches']
```

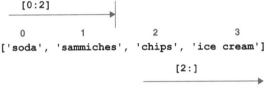

Figure 3.4   The stop value for a list slice is not included. If the stop value is omitted, the slice goes to the end of the list.

If you leave out start, it will default to a value of 0, so the following line does the same thing:

```
>>> items[:2]
['soda', 'sammiches']
```

If you leave out stop, it will go to the end of the list:

```
>>> items[2:]
['chips', 'ice cream']
```

Oddly, it is completely *safe* for slices to use list indexes that don't exist. For example, we can ask for all the elements from index 10 to the end, even though there is nothing at index 10. Instead of an exception, we get an empty list:

```
>>> items[10:]
[]
```

For this chapter's exercise, you're going to need to insert the word "and" into the list if there are three or more elements. Could you use a list index to do that?

3.3.5   *Finding elements in a list*

Did we remember to pack the chips?

Often you'll want to know if some item is in a list. The index method will return the location of an element in a list:

```
>>> items.index('chips')
2
```

Note that list.index() is unsafe code, because it will cause an exception if the argument is not present in the list. See what happens if we check for a fog machine:

```
>>> items.index('fog machine')
Traceback (most recent call last):
  File "<stdin>", line 1, in <module>
ValueError: 'fog machine' is not in list
```

You should never use `list.index()` unless you have first verified that an element is present. The `x in y` approach that we used in chapter 2 to see if a letter was in a string of vowels can also be used for lists. We get back a `True` value if x is in the collection of y:

```
>>> 'chips' in items
True
```

I hope they're salt and vinegar chips.

The same code returns `False` if the element is not present:

```
>>> 'fog machine' in items
False
```

We're going to need to talk to the planning committee. What's a picnic without a fog machine?

3.3.6 *Removing elements from a list*

The `list.pop()` method will remove *and return* the element at the index, as shown in figure 3.5. By default it will remove the *last* item (`-1`).

```
>>> items.pop()
'ice cream'
```

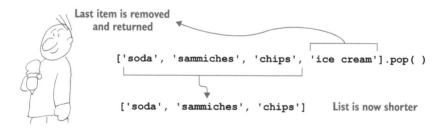

Last item is removed and returned

```
['soda', 'sammiches', 'chips', 'ice cream'].pop( )
```

```
['soda', 'sammiches', 'chips']     List is now shorter
```

Figure 3.5 The `list.pop()` method will remove an element from the list.

If we look at `items`, we will see it's now shorter by one:

```
>>> items
['soda', 'sammiches', 'chips']
```

We can use an index value to remove an element at a particular location. For instance, we can use 0 to remove the first element (see figure 3.6):

```
>>> items.pop(0)
'soda'
```

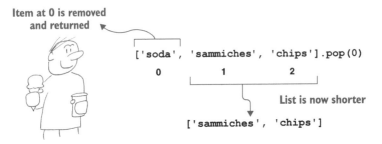

Figure 3.6   You can specify an index value to `list.pop()` **to remove a particular element.**

Now `items` is shorter still:

```
>>> items
['sammiches', 'chips']
```

You can also use the `list.remove()` method to remove the first occurrence of a given item (see figure 3.7):

```
>>> items.remove('chips')
>>> items
['sammiches']
```

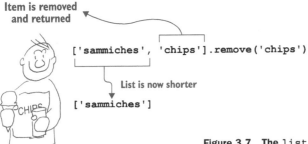

Figure 3.7   The `list.remove()` **method will remove an element matching a given value.**

WARNING   The `list.remove()` method will cause an exception if the element is not present.

If we try to use `items.remove()` to remove the chips again, we'll get an exception:

```
>>> items.remove('chips')
Traceback (most recent call last):
  File "<stdin>", line 1, in <module>
ValueError: list.remove(x): x not in list
```

So don't use this code unless you've verified that a given element is in the `list`:

```
item = 'chips'
if item in items:
    items.remove(item)
```

3.3.7 *Sorting and reversing a list*

If the `--sorted` flag is used to call our program, we're going to need to sort the items. You might notice in the help documentation that two methods, `list.reverse()` and `list.sort()`, stress that they work *in place*. That means that the `list` itself will be either reversed or sorted, and nothing will be returned. So, given this `list`,

```
>>> items = ['soda', 'sammiches', 'chips', 'ice cream']
```

the `items.sort()` method will return nothing:

None ◄────── items.sort()

```
>>> items.sort()
```

Items are sorted,
and nothing is returned.

If you inspect `items`, you will see that the items have been sorted alphabetically:

```
>>> items
['chips', 'ice cream', 'sammiches', 'soda']
```

As with `list.sort()`, nothing is returned from the `list.reverse()` call:

```
>>> items.reverse()
```

But the `items` are now in the opposite order:

```
>>> items
['soda', 'sammiches', 'ice cream', 'chips']
```

The `list.sort()` and `list.reverse()` *methods* are easily confused with the `sorted()` and `reversed()` *functions*. The `sorted()` *function* accepts a list as an argument and *returns* a new `list`:

```
>>> items = ['soda', 'sammiches', 'chips', 'ice cream']
>>> sorted(items)
['chips', 'ice cream', 'sammiches', 'soda']
```

It's crucial to note that the sorted() function *does not alter* the given list:

```
>>> items
['soda', 'sammiches', 'chips', 'ice cream']
```

Note that Python will sort a list of numbers *numerically*, so we've got that going for us, which is nice:

```
>>> sorted([4, 2, 10, 3, 1])
[1, 2, 3, 4, 10]
```

> **WARNING** Sorting a list that mixes strings and numbers will cause an exception!

```
>>> sorted([1, 'two', 3, 'four'])
Traceback (most recent call last):
  File "<stdin>", line 1, in <module>
TypeError: '<' not supported between instances of 'str' and 'int'
```

The list.sort() *method* is a function that belongs to the list. It can take arguments that affect the way the sorting happens. Let's look at help(list.sort):

```
sort(self, /, *, key=None, reverse=False)
    Stable sort *IN PLACE*.
```

That means we can also sort() items in reverse, like so:

```
>>> items.sort(reverse=True)
```

Now they look like this:

```
>>> items
['soda', 'sammiches', 'ice cream', 'chips']
```

The reversed() function works a bit differently:

```
>>> reversed(items)
<list_reverseiterator object at 0x10e012ef0>
```

I bet you were expecting to see a new list with the items in reverse. This is an example of a *lazy* function in Python. The process of reversing a list might take a while, so Python is showing that it has generated an *iterator object* that will provide the reversed list when we actually need the elements.

We can see the values of our reversed() list in the REPL by using the list() function to evaluate the iterator:

```
>>> list(reversed(items))
['ice cream', 'chips', 'sammiches', 'soda']
```

As with the `sorted()` function, the original `items` remains unchanged:

```
>>> items
['soda', 'sammiches', 'chips', 'ice cream']
```

If you use the `list.sort()` method instead of the `sorted()` function, you might end up deleting your data. Imagine you wanted to set `items` equal to the sorted list of items, like so:

```
>>> items = items.sort()
```

What is in `items` now? If you print `items` in the REPL, you won't see anything useful, so inspect the `type()`:

```
>>> type(items)
<class 'NoneType'>
```

It's no longer a `list`. We set it equal to the result of calling the `items.sort()` method, which changes `items` *in place* and returns `None`.

If the `--sorted` flag is given to your program, you will need to sort your items in order to pass the test. Will you use `list.sort()` or the `sorted()` function?

3.3.8 *Lists are mutable*

As you've seen, we can change a `list` quite easily. The `list.sort()` and `list.reverse()` methods change the whole list, but you can also change any single element by referencing it by index. Maybe we should make our picnic slightly healthier by swapping out the chips for apples:

```
>>> items
['soda', 'sammiches', 'chips', 'ice cream']        See if the string 'chips' is
>>> if 'chips' in items:                           in the list of items.
...     idx = items.index('chips')
...     items[idx] = 'apples'                       Assign the index of 'chips'
...                                                  to the variable idx.

                                                     Use the index idx to change
                                                     the element to 'apples'.
```

Let's look at `items` to verify the result:

```
>>> items
['soda', 'sammiches', 'apples', 'ice cream']
```

We can also write a couple of tests:

```
                    Make sure "chips" are no
                         longer on the menu.
>>> assert 'chips' not in items
>>> assert 'apples' in items

                    Check that we now have
                         some "apples."
```

You will need to get the word "and" into your list just before the last element when there are three or more items. Could you use this idea?

3.3.9   *Joining a list*

In this chapter's exercise, you'll need to print a string based on the number of elements in the given list. The string will intersperse other strings like a comma and a space (', ') between the elements of the list.

The following syntax will join a list with a string made of a comma and a space:

```
>>> ', '.join(items)
'soda, sammiches, chips, ice cream'
```

The preceding code uses the `str.join()` method and passes the `list` as an argument. It always feels backwards to me, but that's the way it goes.

The result of `str.join()` is a new string:

```
>>> type(', '.join(items))
<class 'str'>
```

The original `list` remains unchanged:

```
>>> items
['soda', 'sammiches', 'chips', 'apples']
```

We can do quite a bit more with Python's `list`, but that should be enough for you to solve this chapter's problem.

3.4   *Conditional branching with if/elif/else*

You need to use conditional branching, based on the number of items, to correctly format the output. In chapter 2's exercise, there were two conditions—either a vowel or not—so we used `if`/`else` statements. Here we have three options to consider, so you will have to use `elif` (else-if) as well.

For instance, suppose we want to classify someone by their age using three options:

- If their age is greater than 0, it is valid.
- If their age is less than 18, they are a minor.
- Otherwise, they are 18 years or older, which means they can vote.

Here is how we could write that code:

```
>>> age = 15
>>> if age < 0:
...     print('You are impossible.')
... elif age < 18:
...     print('You are a minor.')
... else:
...     print('You can vote.')
...
You are a minor.
```

See if you can use that example to figure out how to write the three options for picnic.py. First write the branch that handles one item. Then write the branch that handles two items. Then write the last branch for three or more items. Run the tests *after every change to your program.*

3.4.1 *Time to write*

Now go write the program yourself before you look at my solution. Here are a few hints:

- Go into your 03_picnic directory and run `new.py picnic.py` to create your program. Then run `make test` (or `pytest -xv test.py`). You should pass the first two tests.
- Next work on getting your `--help` usage looking like the example shown earlier in the chapter. It's very important to define your arguments correctly. For the `items` argument, look at `nargs` in `argparse`, as discussed in section A.4.5 of the appendix.
- If you use new.py to start your program, be sure to keep the Boolean flag and modify it for your `sorted` flag.
- Solve the tests in order! First handle one item, then handle two items, and then handle three. Then handle the sorted items.

You'll get the best benefit from this book if you try writing the programs and passing the tests before reading the solutions!

3.5 *Solution*

Here is one way to satisfy the tests. If you wrote something different that passed, that's great!

```
#!/usr/bin/env python3
"""Picnic game"""

import argparse

# -----------------------------------------------
def get_args():
    """Get command-line arguments"""
```

The get_args() function is placed first so we can easily see what the program accepts when we read it. Note that the function order here is not important to Python, only to us readers.

```python
parser = argparse.ArgumentParser(
    description='Picnic game',
    formatter_class=argparse.ArgumentDefaultsHelpFormatter)

parser.add_argument('item',
                    metavar='str',
                    nargs='+',
                    help='Item(s) to bring')

parser.add_argument('-s',
                    '--sorted',
                    action='store_true',
                    help='Sort the items')

return parser.parse_args()
```

The item argument uses nargs='+' so that it will accept one or more positional arguments, which will be strings.

The dashes in the short (-s) and long (--sorted) names make this an option. There is no value associated with this argument. It's either present (in which case it will be True) or absent (False).

Process the command-line arguments and return them to the caller.

The main() function is where the program will start.

```python
# ------------------------------------------------
def main():
    """Make a jazz noise here"""

    args = get_args()
    items = args.item
    num = len(items)

    if args.sorted:
        items.sort()

    bringing = ''
    if num == 1:
        bringing = items[0]
    elif num == 2:
        bringing = ' and '.join(items)
    else:
        items[-1] = 'and ' + items[-1]
        bringing = ', '.join(items)

    print('You are bringing {}.'.format(bringing))

# ------------------------------------------------
if __name__ == '__main__':
    main()
```

Call the get_args() function and put the returned value into the variable args. If there is a problem parsing the arguments, the program will fail before the values are returned.

Copy the item list from args into the new variable items.

Use the length function len() to get the number of items in the list. There can never be zero items because we defined the argument using nargs='+', which always requires at least one value.

The args.sorted value will be either True or False.

If we are supposed to sort the items, call the items.sort() method to sort them in place.

Use an empty string to initialize a variable to hold the items we are bringing.

If the number of items is 1, we will assign the one item to bringing.

If the number of items is 2, put the string ' and ' in between the items.

Join the items on a string of comma and space.

Otherwise, alter the last element in items to append the string 'and ' before whatever is already there.

Print the output string, using the str.format() method to interpolate the bringing variable.

When Python runs the program, it will read all the lines to this point but will not run anything. Here we look to see if we are in the "main" namespace. If we are, we call the main() function to make the program begin.

3.6 Discussion

How did it go? Did it take you long to write your version? How different was it from mine? Let's talk about my solution. It's fine if yours is different from mine, just as long as you pass the tests!

3.6.1 Defining the arguments

This program can accept a variable number of arguments that are all the same thing (strings). In my get_args() method I define an item like so:

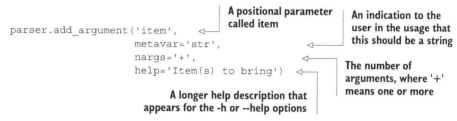

This program also accepts -s and --sorted arguments. They are "flags," which typically means that they are True if they are present and False if absent. Remember that the leading dashes makes them optional.

```
parser.add_argument('-s',                  The short flag name          The long flag name
                    '--sorted',                                         If the flag is present, store
                    action='store_true',                               a True value. The default
                    help='Sort the items')                             value will be False.

                                           The longer help description
```

3.6.2 Assigning and sorting the items

In main() I call get_args() to get the arguments, and I assign them to the args variable. Then I create the items variable to hold the args.item value(s):

```
def main():
    args = get_args()
    items = args.item
```

If args.sorted is True, I need to sort items. I chose the in-place sort method here:

```
if args.sorted:
    items.sort()
```

Now I have the items, sorted if needed, and I need to format them for output.

3.6.3 Formatting the items

I suggested you solve the tests in order. There are four conditions we need to solve:

- Zero items
- One item

- Two items
- Three or more items

The first test is actually handled by argparse—if the user fails to provide any arguments, they get a usage message:

```
$ ./picnic.py
usage: picnic.py [-h] [-s] str [str ...]
picnic.py: error: the following arguments are required: str
```

Since argparse handles the case of no arguments, we have to handle the other three conditions. Here's one way to do that:

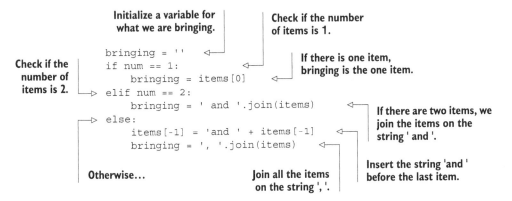

Can you come up with any other ways to do this?

3.6.4   *Printing the items*

Finally, to print() the output, I used a format string where the {} indicate a placeholder for a value, like so:

```
>>> print('You are bringing {}.'.format(bringing))
You are bringing salad, soda, and cupcakes.
```

If you prefer, you could use an f''-string:

```
>>> print(f'You are bringing {bringing}.')
You are bringing salad, soda, and cupcakes.
```

They both get the job done.

3.7 Going further

- Add an option so the user can choose not to print with the Oxford comma (even though that is a morally indefensible option).
- Add an option to separate items with a character passed in by the user (like a semicolon if the list of items needs to contain commas).

Be sure to add tests to the test.py program to ensure your new features are correct!

Summary

- Python lists are ordered sequences of other Python data types, such as strings and numbers.
- There are methods like `list.append()` and `list.extend()` to add elements to a `list`. Use `list.pop()` and `list.remove()` to remove elements.
- You can use `x in y` to ask if element `x` is in the list `y`. You can also use `list.index()` to find the index of an element, but this will cause an exception if the element is not present.
- Lists can be sorted and reversed, and elements within lists can be modified. Lists are useful when the order of the elements is important.
- Strings and lists share many features, such as using `len()` to find their lengths, using zero-based indexing where `0` is the first element and `-1` is the last, and using slices to extract smaller pieces from the whole.
- The `str.join()` method can be used to make a new `str` from a `list`.
- `if/elif/else` can be used to branch code depending on conditions.

Jump the Five:
Working with dictionaries

"When I get up, nothing gets me down."

—D. L. Roth

In an episode of the television show *The Wire*, drug dealers assume the police are intercepting their text messages. Whenever a phone number needs to be texted in the course of a criminal conspiracy, the dealers will obfuscate the number. They use an algorithm we'll call "Jump the Five" because each number is changed to its mate on the opposite of a US telephone pad if you jump over the 5. In this exercise, we'll discuss how to encrypt messages using this algorithm, and then we'll see how to use it to decrypt the encrypted messages, you feel me?

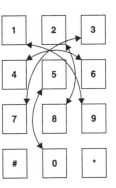

If we start with the 1 button and jump across the 5, we get to 9. The 6 jumps the 5 to become 4, and so forth. The numbers 5 and 0 will swap with each other.

In this exercise, we're going to write a Python program called jump.py that will take in some text as a positional argument. Each number in the text will be encoded using this algorithm. All non-number text will pass through unchanged. Here are a couple of examples:

```
$ ./jump.py 867-5309
243-0751
$ ./jump.py 'Call 1-800-329-8044 today!'
Call 9-255-781-2566 today!
```

You will need some way to inspect each character in the input text to identify the numbers—you will learn how to use a for loop for this. Then you'll see how a for loop can be rewritten as a "list comprehension." You'll need some way to associate a number like 1 with the number 9, and so on for all the numbers—you'll learn about a data structure in Python called a *dictionary* that will allow you to do exactly that.

In this chapter, you will learn to

- Create a dictionary
- Use a for loop and a list comprehension to process text, character by character
- Check if items exist in a dictionary
- Retrieve values from a dictionary
- Print a new string with the numbers substituted with their encoded values

Before we start writing, you need to learn about Python's dictionaries.

4.1   *Dictionaries*

A Python dictionary allows us to relate some *thing* (a "key") to some other *thing* (a "value"). An actual dictionary does this. If we look up a word like "quirky" in a dictionary (www.merriam-webster.com/dictionary/quirky), we can find a definition, as in figure 4.1. We can think of the word itself as the "key" and the definition as the "value."

> quirky ⊳ unusual, esp. in an interesting or appealing way

Figure 4.1   You can find the definition of a word by looking it up in a dictionary.

Dictionaries actually provide quite a bit more information about words, such as pronunciation, part of speech, derived words, history, synonyms, alternate spellings, etymology, first known use, and so on. (I really love dictionaries.) Each of those attributes has a value, so we could also think of the dictionary entry for a word as itself being another "dictionary" (see figure 4.2).

> definition   ⊳ unusual, esp. in an interesting or appealing way
> pronunciation ⊳ ˈkwər-kē
> part of speech ⊳ adjective

Figure 4.2   The entry for "quirky" can contain much more than a single definition.

Let's see how we can use Python's dictionaries to go beyond word definitions.

4.1.1   Creating a dictionary

In the film *Monty Python and the Holy Grail*, King Arthur and his knights must cross The Bridge of Death. Anyone who wishes to cross must correctly answer three questions from the Keeper. Those who fail are cast into the Gorge of Eternal Peril.

Let us ride to CAMELOT.... No, sorry, let us create and use a dictionary to keep track of the questions and answers as key/value pairs. Once again, I want you to fire up your `python3` or IPython REPL or Jupyter Notebook and type these out for yourself.

Lancelot goes first. We can use the `dict()` function to create an empty dictionary for his answers.

```
>>> answers = dict()
```

Or we can use empty curly brackets (both methods are equivalent):

```
>>> answers = {}
```

The Keeper's first question is, "What is your name?" Lancelot answers, "My name is Sir Lancelot of Camelot." We can add the key "name" to the `answers` dictionary by using square brackets (`[]`—not curlies!) and the literal string `'name'`:

```
>>> answers['name'] = 'Sir Lancelot'
```

If you type `answers` and press Enter in the REPL, Python will show you a structure in curlies (see figure 4.3) to indicate that this is a `dict`:

```
>>> answers
{'name': 'Sir Lancelot'}
```

You can verify this with the `type()` function:

```
>>> type(answers)
<class 'dict'>
```

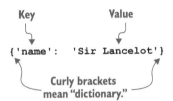

Figure 4.3   A dictionary is printed inside curly braces. The keys are separated from the values by a colon.

Next the Keeper asks, "What is your quest?" to which Lancelot answers "To seek the Holy Grail." Let's add "quest" to `answers`:

```
>>> answers['quest'] = 'To seek the Holy Grail'
```

There's no return value to let us know something happened, so type answers to inspect the variable again to ensure the new key/value was added:

```
>>> answers
{'name': 'Sir Lancelot', 'quest': 'To seek the
    Holy Grail'}
```

Finally the Keeper asks, "What is your favorite color?" and Lancelot answers, "Blue."

```
>>> answers['favorite_color'] = 'blue'
>>> answers
{'name': 'Sir Lancelot', 'quest': 'To seek the Holy Grail', 'favorite_color':
    'blue'}
```

> **NOTE**   I'm using "favorite_color" (with an underscore) as the key, but I could use "favorite color" (with a space) or "FavoriteColor" or "Favorite color," but each one of those would be a separate and distinct string, or key. I prefer to use the PEP 8 naming conventions for dictionary keys and variable and functions names. PEP 8, the "Style Guide for Python Code" (www.python.org/dev/peps/pep-0008/), suggests using lowercase names with words separated by underscores.

If you knew all the answers beforehand, you could create answers using the dict() function with the following syntax, where you do *not* have to quote the keys, and the keys are separated from the values with equal signs:

```
>>> answers = dict(name='Sir Lancelot', quest='To seek the Holy Grail',
    favorite_color='blue')
```

Or you could use the following syntax using curlies {}, where the keys must be quoted and they are followed by a colon (:):

```
>>> answers = {'name': 'Sir Lancelot', 'quest': 'To seek the Holy Grail',
    'favorite_color': 'blue'}
```

It might be helpful to think of the answers dictionary as a box holding key/value pairs that describe Lancelot's answers (see figure 4.4), just the way the "quirky" dictionary holds all the information about that word.

answers

name	⇨ Sir Lancelot
quest	⇨ To seek the Holy Grail
favorite color	⇨ blue

Figure 4.4   Just like the "quirky" dictionary entry, a Python dictionary can contain many key/value pairs.

4.1.2 Accessing dictionary values

To retrieve the values, you use the key name inside square brackets ([]). For instance, you can get the name like so:

```
>>> answers['name']
'Sir Lancelot'
```

Let's request his "age":

```
>>> answers['age']
Traceback (most recent call last):
  File "<stdin>", line 1, in <module>
KeyError: 'age'
```

As you can see, you will cause an exception if you ask for a dictionary key that doesn't exist!

Just as with strings and lists, you can use x in y to first see if a key exists in the dict:

```
>>> 'quest' in answers
True
>>> 'age' in answers
False
```

The dict.get() method is a *safe* way to ask for a value:

```
>>> answers.get('quest')
'To seek the Holy Grail'
```

When the requested key does not exist in the dict, it will return the special value None:

```
>>> answers.get('age')
```

That doesn't print anything because the REPL won't print a None, but we can check the type(). Note that the type of None is the NoneType:

```
>>> type(answers.get('age'))
<class 'NoneType'>
```

There is an optional second argument you can pass to dict.get(), which is the value to return *if the key does not exist*:

```
>>> answers.get('age', 'NA')
'NA'
```

That's going to be important for the solution because we will only need to represent the characters 0–9.

4.1.3 *Other dictionary methods*

If you want to know how "big" a dictionary is, the `len()` (length) function on a `dict` will tell you how many key/value pairs are present:

```
>>> len(answers)
3
```

The `dict.keys()` method will give you just the keys:

```
>>> answers.keys()
dict_keys(['name', 'quest', 'favorite_color'])
```

And `dict.values()` will give you just the values:

```
>>> answers.values()
dict_values(['Sir Lancelot', 'To seek the Holy Grail', 'blue'])
```

Often we want both together, so you might see code like this:

```
>>> for key in answers.keys():
...     print(key, answers[key])
...
name Sir Lancelot
quest To seek the Holy Grail
favorite_color blue
```

An easier way to write this would be to use the `dict.items()` method, which will return the contents of the dictionary as a new `list` containing each key/value pair:

```
>>> answers.items()
dict_items([('name', 'Sir Lancelot'), ('quest', 'To seek the Holy Grail'),
('favorite_color', 'blue')])
```

The preceding `for` loop could also be written using the `dict.items()` method:

```
>>> for key, value in answers.items():
...     print(f'{key:15} {value}')
...
name           Sir Lancelot
quest          To seek the Holy Grail
favorite_color blue
```

Unpack each key/value pair into the variables key and value (see figure 4.5). Note that you don't have to call them key and value. You could use k and v or question and answer.

Print the key in a left-justified field 15 characters wide. The value is printed normally.

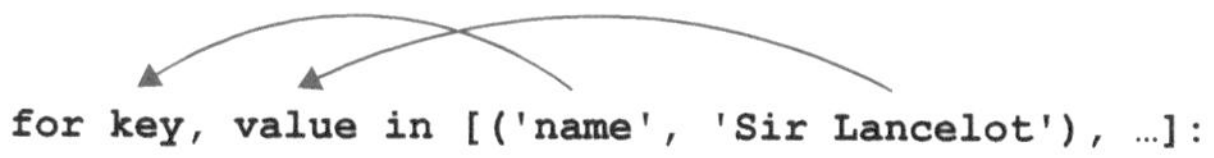

```
for key, value in [('name', 'Sir Lancelot'), …]:
```

Figure 4.5 We can unpack the key/value pairs returned by `dict.items()` into variables.

In the REPL you can execute `help(dict)` to see all the methods available to you, like `dict.pop()`, which removes a key/value, or `dict.update()`, which merges one dictionary with another.

TIP Each key in the `dict` is unique.

That means if you set a value for a given key twice,

```
>>> answers = {}
>>> answers['favorite_color'] = 'blue'
>>> answers
{'favorite_color': 'blue'}
```

you will not have two entries but one entry with the *second* value:

```
>>> answers['favorite_color'] = 'red'
>>> answers
{'favorite_color': 'red'}
```

Keys don't have to be strings—you can also use numbers like the `int` and `float` types. Whatever value you use must be immutable. For instance, lists could not be used because they are mutable, as you saw in the previous chapter. You'll learn which types are immutable as we go further.

4.2   *Writing jump.py*

Now let's get started with writing our program. You'll need to create a program called jump.py in the 04_jump_the_five directory so you can use the test.py that is there. Figure 4.6 shows a diagram of the inputs and outputs. Note that your program will only affect the numbers in the text. Anything that is *not* a number will remain unchanged.

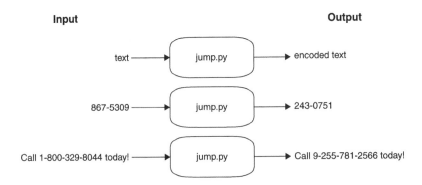

Figure 4.6   A string diagram for the jump.py program. Any number in the input text will be changed to a corresponding number in the output text.

When your program is run with no arguments, -h, or --help, it should print a usage message:

```
$ ./jump.py -h
usage: jump.py [-h] str

Jump the Five

positional arguments:
  str          Input text

optional arguments:
  -h, --help  show this help message and exit
```

Note that we will be processing *text* representations of the "numbers," so the string '1' will be converted to the string '9'. We won't be changing the actual integer value 1 to the integer value 9. Keep that in mind as you figure out a way to represent the substitutions in table 4.1.

Table 4.1 The encoding table for the numeric characters in the text

```
1 => 9
2 => 8
3 => 7
4 => 6
5 => 0
6 => 4
7 => 3
8 => 2
9 => 1
0 => 5
```

How would you represent this using a dict? Try creating a dict called jumper in the REPL with the preceding key/value pairs, and then see if the following assert statements will execute with exceptions. Remember that assert will return nothing if the statement is True.

```
>>> assert jumper['1'] == '9'
>>> assert jumper['5'] == '0'
```

Next, you will need a way to visit each character. I suggest you use a for loop, like so:

```
>>> for char in 'ABC123':
...     print(char)
...
A
B
C
1
2
3
```

Rather than printing the char, print the value of char in the jumper table, or print the char itself. Look at the dict.get() method! Also, if you read help(print), you'll see there is an end option to replace the newline that gets stuck onto the end with something else.

Here are some other hints:

- The numbers can occur anywhere in the text, so I recommend you process the input character by character with a for loop.
- Given any one character, how can you look it up in your table?
- If the character is in your table, how can you get the value (the translation)?
- How can you print() the translation or the value without printing a newline? Look at help(print) in the REPL to read about the options for print().
- If you read help(str) on Python's str class, you'll see that there is a str.replace() method. Could you use that?

Now spend the time to write the program on your own before you look at the solutions. Use the tests to guide you.

4.3   Solution

Here is one solution that satisfies the tests. I will show some variations after we discuss this first version.

```python
#!/usr/bin/env python3
"""Jump the Five"""

import argparse


# --------------------------------------------------
def get_args():
    """Get command-line arguments"""

    parser = argparse.ArgumentParser(
        description='Jump the Five',
        formatter_class=argparse.ArgumentDefaultsHelpFormatter)

    parser.add_argument('text', metavar='str', help='Input text')

    return parser.parse_args()


# --------------------------------------------------
def main():
    """Make a jazz noise here"""

    args = get_args()
    jumper = {'1': '9', '2': '8', '3': '7', '4': '6', '5': '0',
              '6': '4', '7': '3', '8': '2', '9': '1', '0': '5'}
```

Define the get_args() function first, so it's easy to find when I read the program.

Define one positional argument called "text."

Define a main() function where the program starts.

Get the command-line arguments from get_args ().

Create a dictionary for the lookup table.

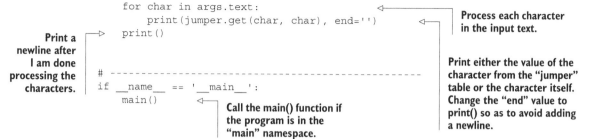

Print a newline after I am done processing the characters.

```
        for char in args.text:
            print(jumper.get(char, char), end='')
        print()

    # -------------------------------------------------
    if __name__ == '__main__':
        main()
```

Process each character in the input text.

Print either the value of the character from the "jumper" table or the character itself. Change the "end" value to print() so as to avoid adding a newline.

Call the main() function if the program is in the "main" namespace.

4.4 Discussion

Let's break this program down into the big ideas, like how we define the parameters, define and use a dictionary, process the input text, and print the output.

4.4.1 Defining the parameters

As usual, the get_args() function is defined first. The program needs to define one positional argument. Since I'm expecting some "text," I call the argument 'text' and then assign that to a variable called text:

```
parser.add_argument('text', metavar='str', help='Input text')
```

While that seems rather obvious, I think it's very important to name things for *what they are*. That is, please don't leave the name of the argument as 'positional'—that does not describe what it *is*.

It may seem like overkill to use argparse for such a simple program, but it handles the validation of the correct *number* and *type* of the arguments as well as generating help documentation, so it's well worth the effort.

4.4.2 Using a dict for encoding

I suggested you could represent the substitution table as a dict, where each number key has its substitute as the value in the dict. For instance, I know that if I jump from 1 over the 5, I should land on 9:

```
>>> jumper = {'1': '9', '2': '8', '3': '7', '4': '6', '5': '0',
...           '6': '4', '7': '3', '8': '2', '9': '1', '0': '5'}
>>> jumper['1']
'9'
```

Since there are only 10 numbers to encode, this is probably the easiest way to write this. Note that the numbers are written with quotes around them, so they are actually of the type str and not int (integers). I do this because I will be reading characters from a str. If I stored them as actual numbers, I would have to coerce the str types using the int() function:

```
>>> type('4')
<class 'str'>
```

```
>>> type(4)
<class 'int'>
>>> type(int('4'))
<class 'int'>
```

4.4.3   *Various ways to process items in a series*

As you've seen before, strings and lists in Python are similar in how you can index them. Both strings and lists are essentially sequences of elements—strings are sequences of characters, and lists can be sequences of anything at all.

There are several different ways to process any sequence of items, which here will be characters in a string.

METHOD 1: USING A FOR LOOP TO PRINT() EACH CHARACTER

As I suggested in the introduction, we can process each character of the text using a for loop. To start, I might first see if each character of the text is in the jumper table using the x in y construct:

```
>>> text = 'ABC123'
>>> for char in text:
...     print(char, char in jumper)
...
A False
B False
C False
1 True
2 True
3 True
```

> **NOTE**   When print() is given more than one argument, it will put a space between each bit of text. You can change that with the sep argument. Read help(print) to learn more.

Now let's try to translate the numbers. I could use an if expression, where I print the value from the jumper table if char is present, and, otherwise, print the char:

```
>>> for char in text:
...     print(char, jumper[char] if char in jumper else char)
...
A A
B B
C C
1 9
2 8
3 7
```

It's a bit laborious to check for every character, but it's necessary because, for instance, the letter "A" is not in jumper. If I try to retrieve that value, I'll get an exception:

```
>>> jumper['A']
Traceback (most recent call last):
```

```
   File "<stdin>", line 1, in <module>
KeyError: 'A'
```

The dict.get() method allows me to safely ask for a value if it is present. Asking for "A" will not produce an exception, but it will also not show anything in the REPL because it returns the None value:

```
>>> jumper.get('A')
```

It's a bit easier to see if we try to print() the values:

```
>>> for char in text:
...     print(char, jumper.get(char))
...
A None
B None
C None
1 9
2 8
3 7
```

I can provide a second, optional argument to dict.get(), which is the default value to return when the key does not exist. In this program, I want to print the character itself when it does not exist in jumper. For instance, if I had "A," I'd want to print "A":

```
>>> jumper.get('A', 'A')
'A'
```

But if I have "5," I want to print "0":

```
>>> jumper.get('5', '5')
'0'
```

I can use that to process all the characters:

```
>>> for char in text:
...     print(jumper.get(char, char))
...
A
B
C
9
8
7
```

I don't want that newline printing after every character, so I can use end='' to tell Python to put the empty string at the end instead of a newline.

   When I run this in the REPL, the output is going to look funny because I have to press Enter after the for loop to run it. Then I'll be left with ABC987 with no newline, and then the >>> prompt:

```
>>> for char in text:
...     print(jumper.get(char, char), end='')
...
ABC987>>>
```

In your code, you'll have to add another `print()`.

It's useful that you can change what is added at the end, and that you can `print()` with no arguments to print a newline. There are several other really cool things `print()` can do, so I encourage you to read `help(print)` and try them out.

METHOD 2: USING A FOR LOOP TO BUILD A NEW STRING

There are several other ways you could solve this. While it was fun to explore all the things we can do with `print()`, that code is a bit ugly. I think it's cleaner to create a new_text variable and call `print()` once with that:

```
def main():
    args = get_args()
    jumper = {'1': '9', '2': '8', '3': '7', '4': '6', '5': '0',
              '6': '4', '7': '3', '8': '2', '9': '1', '0': '5'}
    new_text = ''                          ◁─────────────┐   Create an empty
    for char in args.text:                 ◁────────────┐│   new_text variable.
        new_text += jumper.get(char, char) ◁───────────┐││
    print(new_text)   ◁──┐                              ││└── Use the same
                         │   Append either the encoded  │    for loop.
        Print the new_text.│   number or the original   │
                            │   char to the new_text.   │
```

In this version, I start by setting new_text equal to the empty string:

```
>>> new_text = ''
```

I use the same `for` loop to process each character in the `text`. Each time through the loop, I use `+=` to append the right side of the equation to the left side. The `+=` adds the value on the right to the variable on the left:

```
>>> new_text += 'a'
>>> assert new_text == 'a'
>>> new_text += 'b'
>>> assert new_text == 'ab'
```

On the right, I'm using the `jumper.get()` method. Each character will be appended to the new_text, as shown in figure 4.7.

```
>>> new_text = ''
>>> for char in text:
...     new_text += jumper.get(char, char)
...
```

```
new_text += jumper.get(char, char)
```

The result of jumper.get() is appended to new_text.

Figure 4.7 The += operator will append the string on the right to the variable on the left.

Now I can call `print()` once with the new value:

```
>>> print(new_text)
ABC987
```

METHOD 3: USING A FOR LOOP TO BUILD A NEW LIST

This method is the same as the preceding one, but rather than new_text being a str, it's a list:

```
def main():
    args = get_args()
    jumper = {'1': '9', '2': '8', '3': '7', '4': '6', '5': '0',
              '6': '4', '7': '3', '8': '2', '9': '1', '0': '5'}
    new_text = []
    for char in args.text:
        new_text.append(jumper.get(char, char))
    print(''.join(new_text))
```

Initialize new_text as an empty list.

Iterate through each character of the text.

Append the results of the jumper.get () call to the new_text variable.

Join the new_text on the empty string to create a new string to print.

As we go through the book, I'll keep reminding you how Python treats strings and lists similarly. Here I'm using new_text exactly the same as I did before, starting with an empty structure and then making it longer for each character. I could actually use the exact same += syntax instead of the list.append() method:

```
for char in args.text:
    new_text += jumper.get(char, char)
```

After the for loop is done, I have all the new characters that need to be put back together using str.join() into a new string that I can print().

METHOD 4: TURNING A FOR LOOP INTO A LIST COMPREHENSION

A shorter solution uses a *list comprehension*, which is basically a one-line for loop inside square brackets ([]) that results in a new list (see figure 4.8).

```
def main():
    args = get_args()
    jumper = {'1': '9', '2': '8', '3': '7', '4': '6', '5': '0',
              '6': '4', '7': '3', '8': '2', '9': '1', '0': '5'}
    print(''.join([jumper.get(char, char) for char in args.text]))
```

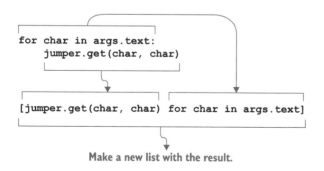

```
for char in args.text:
    jumper.get(char, char)
```

```
[jumper.get(char, char) for char in args.text]
```

Make a new list with the result.

Figure 4.8 A list comprehension will generate a new list with the results of iterating with a for statement.

A list comprehension is read backwards from a for loop, but it's all there. It's one line of code instead four!

```
>>> text = '867-5309'
>>> [jumper.get(char, char) for char in text]
['2', '4', '3', '-', '0', '7', '5', '1']
```

You can use str.join() on the empty string to turn that list into a new string you can print():

```
>>> print(''.join([jumper.get(char, char) for char in text]))
243-0751
```

The purpose of a list comprehension is to create a new list, which is what we were trying to do with the for loop code before. A list comprehension makes much more sense and uses far fewer lines of code.

METHOD 5: USING THE STR.TRANSLATE() FUNCTION

This last approach uses a really powerful method from the str class to change all the characters in one step:

```
def main():
    args = get_args()
    jumper = {'1': '9', '2': '8', '3': '7', '4': '6', '5': '0',
              '6': '4', '7': '3', '8': '2', '9': '1', '0': '5'}
    print(args.text.translate(str.maketrans(jumper)))
```

The argument to str.translate() is a translation table that describes how each character should be translated. That's exactly what jumper does.

```
>>> text = 'Jenny = 867-5309'
>>> text.translate(str.maketrans(jumper))
'Jenny = 243-0751'
```

I'll explain this in much greater detail in chapter 8.

4.4.4   *(Not) using str.replace()*

I asked earlier whether you could use str.replace() to change all the numbers. It turns out you cannot, because you'll end up changing some of the values twice so that they end up at their original values.

Watch how we start off with this string:

```
>>> text = '1234567890'
```

When you change "1" to "9," now you have two 9's:

```
>>> text = text.replace('1', '9')
>>> text
'9234567890'
```

This means that when you try to change all the 9's to 1's, you end up with two 1's. The 1 in the first position is changed to 9 and then back to 1 again:

```
>>> text = text.replace('9', '1')
>>> text
'1234567810'
```

So if you go through each number in "1234567890" and try to change them using `str.replace()`, you'll end up with the value "1234543215":

```
>>> text = '1234567890'
>>> for n in jumper.keys():
...     text = text.replace(n, jumper[n])
...
>>> text
'1234543215'
```

But the correctly encoded string is "9876043215." The `str.translate()` function exists to change all the values in one move, all while leaving the unchanging characters alone.

4.5   *Going further*

- Try creating a similar program that encodes the numbers with strings (for example, "5" becomes "five," "7" becomes "seven"). Be sure to write the necessary tests in `test.py` to check your work!
- What happens if you feed the output of the program back into itself? For example, if you run `./jump.py 12345`, you should get `98760`. If you run `./jump.py 98760`, do you recover the original numbers? This is called *round-tripping*, and it's a common operation with algorithms that encode and decode text.

Summary

- You can create a new dictionary using the `dict()` function or with empty curly brackets (`{}`).
- Dictionary values are retrieved using their keys inside square brackets or by using the `dict.get()` method.
- For a `dict` called x, you can use `'key' in x` to determine if a key exists.
- You can use a `for` loop to iterate through the characters of a `str` just like you can iterate through the elements of a `list`. You can think of strings as lists of characters.
- The `print()` function takes optional keyword arguments like `end=''`, which you can use to print a value to the screen without a newline.

Howler: Working with files and STDOUT

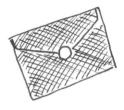

In the Harry Potter stories, a "Howler" is a nasty-gram that arrives by owl at Hogwarts. It will tear itself open, shout a blistering message at the recipient, and then combust. In this exercise, we're going to write a program that will transform text into a rather mild-mannered version of a Howler by MAKING ALL THE LETTERS UPPERCASE. The text that we'll process will be given as a single positional argument.

For instance, if our program is given the input, "How dare you steal that car!" it should scream back "HOW DARE YOU STEAL THAT CAR!" Remember spaces on the command line delimit arguments, so multiple words need to be enclosed in quotes to be considered one argument:

```
$ ./howler.py 'How dare you steal that car!'
HOW DARE YOU STEAL THAT CAR!
```

The argument to the program may also name a file, in which case we need to read the file for the input:

```
$ ./howler.py ../inputs/fox.txt
THE QUICK BROWN FOX JUMPS OVER THE LAZY DOG.
```

Our program will also accept an `-o` or `--outfile` option that names an output file into which the output text should be written. In that case, *nothing* will be printed on the command line:

```
$ ./howler.py -o out.txt 'How dare
    you steal that car!'
```

There should now be a file called out.txt that has the output:

```
$ cat out.txt
HOW DARE YOU STEAL THAT CAR!
```

In this exercise, you will learn to

- Accept text input from the command line or from a file
- Change strings to uppercase
- Print output either to the command line or to a file that needs to be created
- Make plain text behave like a file handle

5.1 Reading files

This is our first exercise that will involve reading files. The argument to the program will be some text that might name an input file, in which case you will open and read the file. If the text is not the name of a file, you'll use the text itself.

The built-in `os` (operating system) module has a method for detecting whether a string is the name of a file. To use it, you must import the `os` module. For instance, there's probably not a file called "blargh" on your system:

```
>>> import os
>>> os.path.isfile('blargh')
False
```

The `os` module contains loads of useful submodules and functions. Consult the documentation at https://docs.python.org/3/library/os.html or use `help(os)` in the REPL.

For instance, `os.path.basename()` and `os.path.dirname()` can return a file's name or directory from a path, respectively (see figure 5.1):

```
>>> file = '/var/lib/db.txt'
>>> os.path.dirname(file)
'/var/lib'
>>> os.path.basename(file)
'db.txt'
```

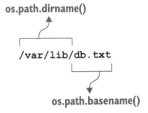

os.path.dirname()

/var/lib/db.txt

os.path.basename()

Figure 5.1 **The os module has handy functions like os.path.dirname() and os.path.basename() for getting parts of file paths.**

In the top level of the GitHub source repository, there is a directory called "inputs" that contains several files we'll use for many of the exercises. Here I'll use a file called inputs/fox.txt. Note that you will need to be in the main directory of the repo for this to work.

```
>>> file = 'inputs/fox.txt'
>>> os.path.isfile(file)
True
```

Once you've determined that the argument is the name of a file, you must open() it to read() it. The return from open() is a *file handle*. I usually call this variable fh to remind me that it's a file handle. If I have more than one open file handle, like both input and output handles, I may call them in_fh and out_fh.

```
>>> fh = open(file)
```

> **NOTE** Per PEP 8 (www.python.org/dev/peps/pep-0008/#function-and-variable-names), function and variable "names should be lowercase, with words separated by underscores as necessary to improve readability."

If you try to open() a file that does not exist, you'll get an exception. This is unsafe code:

```
>>> file = 'blargh'
>>> open(file)
Traceback (most recent call last):
  File "<stdin>", line 1, in <module>
FileNotFoundError: [Errno 2] No such file or directory: 'blargh'
```

Always check that the file exists!

```
>>> file = 'inputs/fox.txt'
>>> if os.path.isfile(file):
...     fh = open(file)
```

We will use the fh.read() method to get the contents of the file. It might be helpful to think of a file as a can of tomatoes. The file's name, like "inputs/fox.txt," is the label on the can, which is not the same as the *contents*. To get at the text inside (or the "tomatoes"), we need to *open* the can.

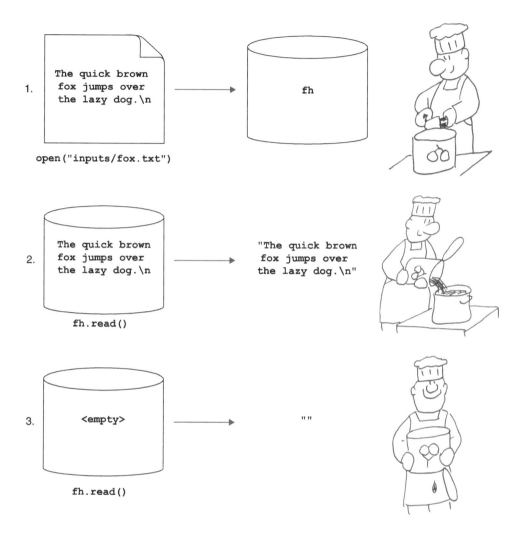

Figure 5.2 A file is a bit like a can of tomatoes. We have to open it first so that we can read it, after which the file handle is exhausted.

Take a look at figure 5.2:

1 The file handle (`fh`) is a mechanism we can use to get at the contents of the file. To get at the tomatoes, we need to `open()` the can.

2 The `fh.read()` method returns what is inside the `file`. With the can opened, we can get at the contents.

3 Once the file handle has been read, there's nothing left.

NOTE You can use `fh.seek(0)` to reset the file handle to the beginning if you really want to read it again.

Let's see what `type()` the `fh` is:

```
>>> type(fh)
<class '_io.TextIOWrapper'>
```

In computer lingo, "io" means "input/output." The `fh` object is something that handles I/O operations. You can use `help(fh)` (using the name of the variable itself) to read the docs on the `class TextIOWrapper`.

The two methods you'll use quite often are `read()` and `write()`. Right now, we care about `read()`. Let's see what that gives us:

```
>>> fh.read()
'The quick brown fox jumps over the lazy dog.\n'
```

Do me a favor and execute that line one more time. What do you see?

```
>>> fh.read()
''
```

A file handle is different from something like a `str`. Once you read a file handle, it's empty. It's like pouring the tomatoes out of the can. Now that the can is empty, you can't empty it again.

We can actually compress `open()` and `fh.read()` into one line of code by *chaining* those methods together. The `open()` method returns a file handle that can be used for the call to `fh.read()` (see figure 5.3). Run this:

```
>>> open(file).read()
'The quick brown fox jumps over the lazy dog.\n'
```

Figure 5.3   The `open()` function returns a file handle, so we can chain it to a call to `read()`.

And now run it again:

```
>>> open(file).read()
'The quick brown fox jumps over the lazy dog.\n'
```

Each time you `open()` the file, you get a fresh file handle to `read()`.

If we want to preserve the contents, we'll need to copy them into a variable.

```
>>> text = open(file).read()
>>> text
'The quick brown fox jumps over the lazy dog.\n'
```

The type() of the result is a str:

```
>>> type(text)
<class 'str'>
```

If you want, you can chain any str method onto the end of that. For instance, maybe you want to remove the trailing newline. The str.rstrip() method will remove any whitespace (which includes newlines) from the *right* end of a string (see figure 5.4).

```
>>> text = open(file).read().rstrip()
>>> text
'The quick brown fox jumps over the lazy dog.'
```

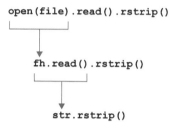

Figure 5.4 The open() method returns a file handle, to which we chain read(), which returns a string, to which we chain the str.rstrip() call.

Once you have your input text—whether it is from the command line or from a file—you need to UPPERCASE it. The str.upper() method is probably what you want.

5.2 Writing files

The output of the program should either appear on the command line or be written to a file. Command-line output is also called *standard out* or STDOUT. (It's the *standard* or normal place for *output* to occur.) Now let's look at how to write the output to a file.

We still need to open() a file handle, but we have to use an optional second argument, the string 'w', to instruct Python to open it for *writing*. Other modes include 'r' for *reading* (the default) and 'a' for *appending*, as listed in table 5.1.

Table 5.1 File-writing modes

Mode	Meaning
w	Write
r	Read
a	Append

You can additionally describe the kind of content, whether 't' for *text* (the default) or 'b' for *binary*, as listed in table 5.2.

Table 5.2   File-content modes

Mode	Meaning
t	Text
b	Bytes

You can combine the values in these two tables, like 'rb' to *read* a *binary* file or 'at' to *append* to a *text* file. Here we will use 'wt' to *write* a *text* file.

I'll call my variable out_fh to remind me that this is the output file handle:

```
>>> out_fh = open('out.txt', 'wt')
```

If the file does not exist, it will be created. If the file does exist, it will be *overwritten*, which means that all the previous data will be lost! If you don't want an existing file to be lost, you can use the os.path.isfile() function you saw earlier to first check if the file exists, and perhaps use open() in the "append" mode instead. For this exercise, we'll use the 'wt' mode to write text.

You can use the write() method of the file handle to put text into the file. Whereas the print() function will append a newline (\n) unless you instruct it not to, the write() method will *not* add a newline, so you have to explicitly add one.

If you use the out_fh.write() method in the REPL, you will see that it returns the number of bytes written. Here each character, including the newline (\n), is a byte:

```
>>> out_fh.write('this is some text\n')
18
```

You can check that this is correct:

```
>>> len('this is some text\n')
18
```

Most code tends to ignore this return value; that is, we don't usually bother to capture the results in a variable or check that we got a nonzero return. If write() fails, there's usually some much bigger problem with your system.

You can also use the print() function with the optional file argument. Notice that I don't include a newline with print() because it will add one. This method returns None:

```
>>> print('this is some more text', file=out_fh)
```

When you are done writing to a file handle, you should out_fh.close() it so that Python can clean up the file and release the memory associated with it. This method also returns None:

```
>>> out_fh.close()
```

Let's check if the lines of text we printed to our out.txt file made it by opening the file and reading it. Note that the newline appears here as \n. We need to print() the string for it to create an actual newline:

```
>>> open('out.txt').read()
'this is some text\nthis is some more text\n'
```

When we print() on an open file handle, the text will be appended to any previously written data. Look at this code, though:

```
>>> print("I am what I am an' I'm not ashamed.", file=open('hagrid.txt', 'wt'))
```

If you run that line twice, will the file called hagrid.txt have the line once or twice? Let's find out:

```
>>> open('hagrid.txt').read()
"I am what I am an' I'm not ashamed\n"
```

Just once! Why is that? Remember, each call to open() gives us a new file handle, so calling open() twice results in new file handles. Each time you run that code, the file is opened anew in *write* mode and the existing data is *overwritten*. To avoid confusion, I recommend you write code more along these lines:

```
fh = open('hagrid.txt', 'wt')
fh.write("I am what I am an' I'm not ashamed.\n")
fh.close()
```

5.3   *Writing howler.py*

You'll need to create a program called howler.py in the 05_howler directory. You can use the new.py program for this, copy template.py, or start however you prefer. Figure 5.5 is a string diagram showing an overview of the program and some example inputs and outputs.

When run with no arguments, it should print a short usage message:

```
$ ./howler.py
usage: howler.py [-h] [-o str] text
howler.py: error: the following arguments are required: text
```

When run with -h or --help, the program should print a longer usage statement:

```
$ ./howler.py -h
usage: howler.py [-h] [-o str] text

Howler (upper-cases input)

positional arguments:
  text                  Input string or file

optional arguments:
  -h, --help            show this help message and exit
  -o str, --outfile str
                        Output filename (default: )
```

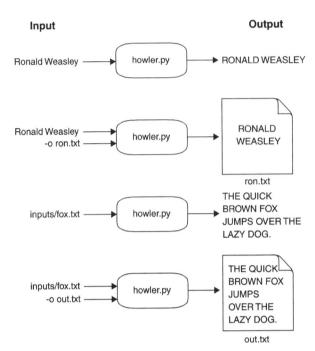

Figure 5.5   A string diagram showing that our howler.py program will accept strings or files as inputs and possibly an output filename.

If the argument is a regular string, it should uppercase that:

```
$ ./howler.py 'How dare you steal that car!'
HOW DARE YOU STEAL THAT CAR!
```

If the argument is the name of a file, it should uppercase the *contents of the file*:

```
$ ./howler.py ../inputs/fox.txt
THE QUICK BROWN FOX JUMPS OVER THE LAZY DOG.
```

If given an `--outfile` filename, the uppercased text should be written to the indicated file and nothing should be printed to STDOUT:

```
$ ./howler.py -o out.txt ../inputs/fox.txt
$ cat out.txt
THE QUICK BROWN FOX JUMPS OVER THE LAZY DOG.
```

Here are a few hints:

- Start with new.py and alter the `get_args()` section until your usage statements match the ones above.
- Run the test suite and try to pass just the first test that handles text on the command line and prints the uppercased output to STDOUT.
- The next test is to see if you can write the output to a given file. Figure out how to do that.

- The next test is for reading input from a file. Don't try to pass all the tests at once!
- There is a special file handle that always exists called "standard out" (often STDOUT). If you `print()` without a `file` argument, it defaults to `sys.stdout`. You will need to `import sys` in order to use it.

Be sure you really try to write the program and pass all the tests before moving on to read the solution. If you get stuck, maybe whip up a batch of Polyjuice Potion and freak out your friends.

5.4   Solution

Here is a solution that will pass the tests. It's rather short because Python allows us to express some really powerful ideas very concisely.

```python
#!/usr/bin/env python3
"""Howler"""

import argparse
import os
import sys


# --------------------------------------------------
def get_args():
    """get command-line arguments"""

    parser = argparse.ArgumentParser(
        description='Howler (upper-case input)',
        formatter_class=argparse.ArgumentDefaultsHelpFormatter)

    parser.add_argument('text',
                        metavar='text',
                        type=str,
                        help='Input string or file')

    parser.add_argument('-o',
                        '--outfile',
                        help='Output filename',
                        metavar='str',
                        type=str,
                        default='')

    args = parser.parse_args()

    if os.path.isfile(args.text):
        args.text = open(args.text).read().rstrip()

    return args
```

The text argument is a string that may be the name of a file.

The --outfile option is also a string that names a file.

Parse the command-line arguments into the variable args so that we can manually check the text argument.

Check if args.text is the name of an existing file.

If so, overwrite the value of args.text with the results of reading the file.

Return the arguments to the caller.

```
# -------------------------------------------------
def main():
    """Make a jazz noise here"""

    args = get_args()
    out_fh = open(args.outfile, 'wt') if args.outfile else sys.stdout
    out_fh.write(args.text.upper() + '\n')
    out_fh.close()

# -------------------------------------------------
if __name__ == '__main__':
    main()
```

Use the opened file handle to write the output converted to uppercase.

Call get_args () to get the arguments to the program.

Close the file handle.

Use an if expression to choose either sys.stdout or a newly opened file handle to write the output.

5.5   *Discussion*

How did it go for you this time? I hope you didn't sneak into Professor Snape's office again. You really don't want more Saturday detentions.

5.5.1   *Defining the arguments*

The get_args() function, as always, comes first. Here I define two arguments. The first is a positional text argument. Since it may or may not name a file, all I can know is that it will be a string.

```
parser.add_argument('text',
                    metavar='text',
                    type=str,
                    help='Input string or file')
```

> **NOTE**   If you define multiple positional parameters, their order *relative to each other* is important. The first positional parameter you define will handle the first positional argument provided. It's not important, however, to define positional parameters before or after options and flags. You can declare those in any order you like.

The other argument is an option, so I give it a short name of -o and a long name of --outfile. Even though the default type for all arguments is str, I like to state this explicitly. The default value is the empty string. I could just as easily use the special None type, which is also the default value, but I prefer to use a defined argument like the empty string.

```
parser.add_argument('-o',
                    '--outfile',
                    help='Output filename',
                    metavar='str',
                    type=str,
                    default='')
```

5.5.2 *Reading input from a file or the command line*

This is a deceptively simple program that demonstrates a couple of very important elements of file input and output. The text input might be a plain string, or it might be the name of a file. This pattern will come up repeatedly in this book:

```
if os.path.isfile(args.text):
    args.text = open(args.text).read().rstrip()
```

The `os.path.isfile()` function will tell me if there is a file with the specified name in `text`. If that returns `True`, I can safely `open(file)` to get a file handle, which has a method called `read` and which will return *all* the contents of the file.

> **WARNING** You should be aware that `fh.read()` will return the *entire file* as a single string. Your computer must have more memory available than the size of the file. For all the programs in this book, you will be safe as the files are small. In my day job, I regularly deal with gigabyte-sized files, so calling `fh.read()` would likely crash my program if not my whole system, because I would exceed my available memory.

The result of `open(file).read()` is a `str`, which has a method called `str.rstrip()` that will return a copy of the string *stripped* of any whitespace on the *right* side (see figure 5.6). I call this so that the input text will look the same whether it comes from a file or directly from the command line. When you provide the input text directly on the command line, you have to press Enter to terminate the command. That Enter is a newline, and the operating system automatically removes it before passing it to the program.

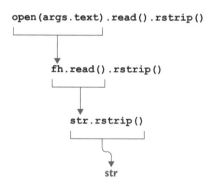

Figure 5.6 The `open()` function returns a file handle (`fh`). The `fh.read()` function returns a `str`. The `str.rstrip()` function returns a new `str` with the whitespace removed from the right side. All these functions can be chained together.

The longer way to write the preceding statement would be

```
if os.path.isfile(text):
    fh = open(text)
    text = fh.read()
    text = text.rstrip()
    fh.close()
```

In my version, I chose to handle this inside the `get_args()` function. This is the first time I've shown you that you can intercept and alter arguments before passing them on to `main()`. We'll use this idea quite a bit in later exercises.

I like to do all the work to validate the user's arguments inside `get_args()`. I could just as easily do this in `main()` after the call to `get_args()`, so this is entirely a style issue.

5.5.3 *Choosing the output file handle*

The following line decides where to put the output of the program:

```
out_fh = open(args.outfile, 'wt') if args.outfile else sys.stdout
```

The `if` expression will open args.outfile for writing text (`wt`) if the user provided that argument; otherwise, it will use `sys.stdout`, which is a file handle to STDOUT. Note that I don't have to call `open()` on `sys.stdout` because it is always available and open for business (figure 5.7).

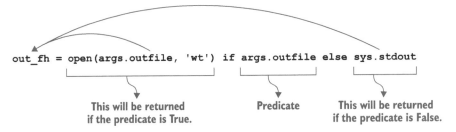

Figure 5.7   An `if` expression succinctly handles a binary choice. Here we want the output file handle to be the result of opening the outfile argument if present; otherwise, it should be `sys.stdout`.

5.5.4 *Printing the output*

To get the uppercase text, I can use the `text.upper()` method. Then I need to find a way to print it to the output file handle. I chose to do this:

```
out_fh.write(text.upper())
```

Alternatively, you could do this:

```
print(text.upper(), file=out_fh)
```

Finally, I need to close the file handle with `out_fh.close()`.

5.5.5 *A low-memory version*

There is a potentially serious problem waiting to bite us in this program. In `get_args()`, we're reading the entire file into memory with this line:

```
if os.path.isfile(args.text):
    args.text = open(args.text).read().rstrip()
```

We could, instead, only `open()` the file:

```
if os.path.isfile(args.text):
    args.text = open(args.text)
```

Later we could read it line by line:

```
for line in args.text:
    out_fh.write(line.upper())
```

The problem, though, is how to handle the times when the `text` argument is actually text and not the name of a file. The `io` (input-output) module in Python has a way to represent text as a *stream*:

```
>>> import io          ⟵⎯⎯|    Import the io module.                        ⎯⎯⎯|   Use the io.StringIO() function to turn
>>> text = io.StringIO('foo\nbar\nbaz\n')              ⟵⎯⎯|                      the given str value into something we
>>> for line in text:                      ⟵⎯⎯⎯|                                can treat like an open file handle.
...     print(line, end='')            ⟵⎯⎯|          Use a for loop to iterate
...                                                   through the "lines" of text
foo                     Print the line using the      separated by newlines.
bar                     end=" option to avoid
baz                     having two newlines.
```

This is the first time you're seeing that you can treat a regular string value as if it were a generator of values similar to a file handle. This is a particularly useful technique for testing any code that needs to read an input file. You can use the return from `io.StreamIO()` as a "mock" file handle so that your code doesn't have to read an *actual* file, just a given value that can produce "lines" of text.

To make this work, we can change how we handle `args.text`, like so:

```
#!/usr/bin/env python3
"""Low-memory Howler"""

import argparse
import os
import io
import sys


# --------------------------------------------------
def get_args():
    """get command-line arguments"""

    parser = argparse.ArgumentParser(
        description='Howler (upper-cases input)',
        formatter_class=argparse.ArgumentDefaultsHelpFormatter)

    parser.add_argument('text',
                        metavar='text',
                        type=str,
                        help='Input string or file')

    parser.add_argument('-o',
                        '--outfile',
                        help='Output filename',
```

```
                              metavar='str',
                              type=str,
                              default='')
      args = parser.parse_args()

      if os.path.isfile(args.text):
          args.text = open(args.text)
      else:
          args.text = io.StringIO(args.text + '\n')

      return args
```

Check if args.text is a file.

If it is, replace args.text with the file handle created by opening the file.

Otherwise, replace args.text with an io.StringIO() value that will act like an open file handle. Note that we need to add a newline to the text so that it will look like the lines of input coming from an actual file.

```
# --------------------------------------------------
def main():
    """Make a jazz noise here"""

    args = get_args()
    out_fh = open(args.outfile, 'wt') if args.outfile else sys.stdout
    for line in args.text:
        out_fh.write(line.upper())
    out_fh.close()

# --------------------------------------------------
if __name__ == '__main__':
    main()
```

Read the input (whether io.StringIO() or a file handle) line by line.

Process the line as before.

5.6   *Going further*

- Add a flag that will lowercase the input instead. Maybe call it --ee for the poet e e cummings, who liked to write poetry devoid of uppercase letters.
- Alter the program to handle multiple input files. Change --outfile to --outdir, and write each input file to the same filename in the output directory.

Summary

- To read or write files, you must first open() them.
- The default mode for open() is for reading a file.
- To write a text file, you must use 'wt' as the second argument to open().
- Text is the default type of data that you write() to a file handle. You must use the 'b' flag to indicate that you want to write binary data.
- The os.path module contains many useful functions, such as os.path.isfile(), that will tell you if a file exists with a given name.
- STDOUT (standard output) is always available via the special sys.stdout file handle, which is always open.
- The print() function takes an optional file argument specifying where to put the output. That argument must be an open file handle, such as sys.stdout (the default) or the result of open().

Words count: Reading files and STDIN, iterating lists, formatting strings

"I love to count!"

—Count von Count

Counting things is a surprisingly important programming skill. Maybe you're trying to find out how many pizzas were sold each quarter or how many times you see certain words in a set of documents. Usually the data we deal with in computing comes to us in files, so in this chapter, we're going to push a little further into reading files and manipulating strings.

We're going to write a Python version of the venerable `wc` ("word count") program. Ours will be called wc.py, and it will count the lines, words, and bytes found in each input supplied as one or more positional arguments. The counts will appear in columns eight characters wide, and they will be followed by the name of the file. For instance, here is what wc.py should print for one file:

```
$ ./wc.py ../inputs/scarlet.txt
    7035    68061   396320 ../inputs/scarlet.txt
```

When counting multiple files, there will be an additional "total" line summing each column:

```
$ ./wc.py ../inputs/const.txt ../inputs/sonnet-29.txt
     865     7620    44841 ../inputs/const.txt
      17      118      661 ../inputs/sonnet-29.txt
     882     7738    45502 total
```

There may also be *no* arguments, in which case we'll read from *standard in*, which is often written as STDIN. We started talking about STDOUT in chapter 5 when we used sys.stdout as a file handle. STDIN is the complement to STDOUT—it's the "standard" place to read input on the command line. When our program is given *no* positional arguments, it will read from sys.stdin.

STDIN and STDOUT are common file handles that many command-line programs recognize. We can chain the STDOUT from one program to the STDIN of another to create ad hoc programs. For instance, the cat program will print the contents of a file to STDOUT. We can use the pipe operator (|) to funnel that output as input into our program via STDIN:

```
$ cat ../inputs/fox.txt | ./wc.py
      1       9      45 <stdin>
```

Another option is to use the < operator to redirect input from a file:

```
$ ./wc.py < ../inputs/fox.txt
      1       9      45 <stdin>
```

One of the handiest command-line tools is grep, which can find patterns of text in files. If, for instance, we wanted to find all the lines of text that contain the word "scarlet" in all the files in the inputs directory, we could use this command:

```
$ grep scarlet ../inputs/*.txt
```

On the command line, the asterisk (*) is a wildcard that will match anything, so *.txt will match any file ending with ".txt." If you run the preceding command, you'll see quite a bit of output.

To count the lines found by grep, we can pipe that output into our wc.py program like so:

```
$ grep scarlet ../inputs/*.txt | ./wc.py
    108    1192    9201 <stdin>
```

We can verify that this matches what wc finds:

```
$ grep scarlet ../inputs/*.txt | wc
    108    1192    9201
```

In this chapter, you will

- Learn how to process zero or more positional arguments
- Validate input files
- Read from files or from standard input
- Use multiple levels of for loops
- Break files into lines, words, and bytes
- Use counter variables
- Format string output

6.1   *Writing wc.py*

Let's get started! Create a program called wc.py in the 06_wc directory, and modify the arguments until it will print the following usage if run with the -h or --help flags:

```
$ ./wc.py -h
usage: wc.py [-h] [FILE [FILE ...]]

Emulate wc (word count)

positional arguments:
  FILE          Input file(s) (default: [<_io.TextIOWrapper name='<stdin>'
                mode='r' encoding='UTF-8'>])

optional arguments:
  -h, --help  show this help message and exit
```

Given a nonexistent file, your program should print an error message and exit with a nonzero exit value:

```
$ ./wc.py blargh
usage: wc.py [-h] [FILE [FILE ...]]
wc.py: error: argument FILE: can't open 'blargh': \
[Errno 2] No such file or directory: 'blargh'
```

Figure 6.1 is a string diagram that will help you think about how the program should work.

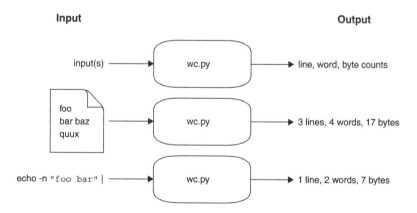

Figure 6.1   A string diagram showing that wc.py will read one or more file inputs or possibly STDIN and will produce a summary of the words, lines, and bytes contained in each input.

6.1.1 *Defining file inputs*

Let's talk about how we can define the program's parameters using argparse. This program takes *zero or more* positional arguments and nothing else. Remember that you never have to define the -h or --help arguments, as argparse handles those automatically.

In chapter 3 we used nargs='+' to indicate one or more items for our picnic. Here we want to use nargs='*' to indicate *zero* or more. When there are no arguments, the default value will be None. For this program, we'll read STDIN when there are no arguments.

All of the possible values for nargs are listed in table 6.1.

Table 6.1 Possible values for nargs

Symbol	Meaning
?	Zero or one
*	Zero or more
+	One or more

Any arguments that are provided to our program *must be readable files*. In chapter 5 you learned how to test whether the input argument was a file by using os.path.isfile(). The input was allowed to be either plain text or a filename, so you had to check this yourself.

In this program, the input arguments are required to be readable text files, so we can define our arguments using type=argparse.FileType('rt'). This means that argparse takes on all the work of validating the inputs from the user and producing useful error messages. If the user provides valid input, argparse will provide a list of *open file handles*. All in all, this will save us quite a bit of time. (Be sure to review section A.4.6 on file arguments in the appendix.)

In chapter 5 we used sys.stdout to write to STDOUT. To read from STDIN here, we'll use Python's sys.stdin file handle. Like sys.stdout, the sys.stdin file handle does not need an open()—it's always present and available for reading.

Because we are using nargs='*' to define our argument, the result will always be a list. To set sys.stdin as the default value, we should place it in a list like so:

```
parser.add_argument('file',                          Zero or more of
                    metavar='FILE',                  this argument
                    nargs='*',
                    type=argparse.FileType('rt'),    If arguments are provided,
                    default=[sys.stdin],             they must be readable text
                    help='Input file(s)')            files. The files will be opened
                                                     by argparse and will be
    The default will be a list containing sys.stdin, which is like an    provided as file handles.
    open file handle to STDIN. We do not need to open it.
```

6.1.2 *Iterating lists*

Your program will end up with a `list` of file handles that will need to be processed. In chapter 4 we used a `for` loop to iterate through the characters in the input text. Here we can use a `for` loop over the `args.file` inputs, which will be open file handles:

```
for fh in args.file:
    # read each file
```

You can give whatever name you like to the variable you use in your `for` loop, but I think it's very important to give it a semantically meaningful name. Here the variable name `fh` reminds me that this is an open file handle. You saw in chapter 5 how to manually `open()` and `read()` a file. Here `fh` is already open, so we can use it directly to read the contents.

There are many ways to read a file. The `fh.read()` method will give you the *entire contents* of the file in one go. If the file is large—if it exceeds the available memory on your machine—your program will crash. I would recommend, instead, that you use another `for` loop on the `fh`. Python will understand this to mean that you wish to read each `line` of the file handle, one at a time.

```
for fh in args.file: # ONE LOOP!
    for line in fh:  # TWO LOOPS!
        # process the line
```

That's two levels of `for` loops, one for each file handle and then another for each line in each file handle. ONE LOOP! TWO LOOPS! I LOVE TO COUNT!

6.1.3 *What you're counting*

The output for each file will be the number of lines, words, and bytes (like characters and whitespace), each of which is printed in a field eight characters wide, followed by a space and then the name of the file, which will be available to you via `fh.name`.

Let's take a look at the output from the standard `wc` program on my system. Notice that when it's run with just one argument, it produces counts only for that file:

```
$ wc fox.txt
       1       9      45 fox.txt
```

The fox.txt file is short enough that you could manually verify that it does in fact contain 1 line, 9 words, and 45 bytes, which includes all the characters, spaces, and the trailing newline (see figure 6.2).

When run with multiple files, the standard `wc` program also shows a "total" line:

```
$ wc fox.txt sonnet-29.txt
       1       9      45 fox.txt
      17     118     669 sonnet-29.txt
      18     127     714 total
```

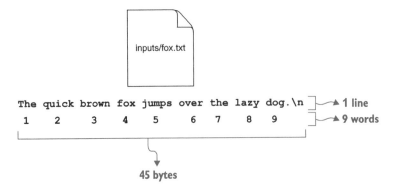

Figure 6.2   **The fox.txt file contains 1 line of text, 9 words, and a total of 45 bytes.**

We are going to emulate the behavior of this program. For each file, you will need to create variables to hold the numbers of lines, words, and bytes. For instance, if you use the `for line in fh` loop that I suggest, you will need to have a variable like `num_lines` to increment on each iteration.

That is, somewhere in your code you will need to set a variable to `0` and then, inside the `for` loop, make it go up by 1. The idiom in Python is to use the `+=` operator to add some value on the right side to the variable on the left side (as shown in figure 6.3):

This number

`num_lines += 1`

Added to the variable

```
num_lines = 0
for line in fh:
    num_lines += 1
```

Figure 6.3   **The `+=` operator will add the value on the right to the variable on the left.**

You will also need to count the number of words and bytes, so you'll need similar `num_words` and `num_bytes` variables.

To get the words, we'll use the `str.split()` method to break each `line` on spaces. You can then use the length of the resulting `list` as the number of words. For the number of bytes, you can use the `len()` (length) function on the `line` and add that to a `num_bytes` variable.

> **NOTE**   Splitting the text on spaces doesn't actually produce "words" because it won't separate the punctuation, like commas and periods, from the letters, but it's close enough for this program. In chapter 15, we'll look at how to use a regular expression to separate strings that look like words from others that do not.

6.1.4   *Formatting your results*

This is the first exercise where the output needs to be formatted in a particular way. Don't try to handle this part manually—that way lies madness. Instead, you need to learn the magic of the `str.format()` method. The `help` doesn't have much in the way of documentation, so I recommend you read PEP 3101 on advanced string formatting (www.python.org/dev/peps/pep-3101/).

The str.format() method uses a template that contains curly brackets ({}) to create placeholders for the values passed as arguments. For example, we can print the raw value of math.pi like so:

```
>>> import math
>>> 'Pi is {}'.format(math.pi)
'Pi is 3.141592653589793'
```

You can add formatting instructions after a colon (:) to specify how you want the value displayed. If you are familiar with printf() from C-type languages, this is the same idea. For instance, I can print math.pi with two numbers after the decimal by specifying 0.02f:

```
>>> 'Pi is {:0.02f}'.format(math.pi)
'Pi is 3.14'
```

In the preceding example, the colon (:) introduces the formatting options, and the 0.02f describes two decimal points of precision.

You can also use the f-string method, where the variable comes *before* the colon:

```
>>> f'Pi is {math.pi:0.02f}'
'Pi is 3.14'
```

In this chapter's exercise, you need to use the formatting option {:8} to align each of the lines, words, and characters into columns. The 8 describes the width of the field. The text is usually left-justified, like so:

```
>>> '{:8}'.format('hello')
'hello   '
```

But the text will be right-justified when you are formatting numeric values:

```
>>> '{:8}'.format(123)
'     123'
```

You will need to place a single space between the last column and the name of the file, which you can find in fh.name.

Here are a few hints:

- Start with new.py and delete all the nonpositional arguments.
- Use nargs='*' to indicate zero or more positional arguments for your file argument.
- Try to pass one test at a time. Create the program, get the help right, and then worry about the first test, then the next, and so on.
- Compare the results of your version to the wc installed on your system. Note that not every system has the same version of wc, so results may vary.

It's time to write this yourself before you read the solution. Fear is the mind killer. You can do this.

6.2   Solution

Here is one way to satisfy the tests. Remember, it's fine if you wrote it differently, as long as it's correct and you understand your code!

```python
#!/usr/bin/env python3
"""Emulate wc (word count)"""

import argparse
import sys


# --------------------------------------------------
def get_args():
    """Get command-line arguments"""

    parser = argparse.ArgumentParser(
        description='Emulate wc (word count)',
        formatter_class=argparse.ArgumentDefaultsHelpFormatter)

    parser.add_argument('file',
                        metavar='FILE',
                        nargs='*',
                        default=[sys.stdin],
                        type=argparse.FileType('rt'),
                        help='Input file(s)')

    return parser.parse_args()


# --------------------------------------------------
def main():
    """Make a jazz noise here"""

    args = get_args()

    total_lines, total_bytes, total_words = 0, 0, 0
    for fh in args.file:
        num_lines, num_words, num_bytes = 0, 0, 0
        for line in fh:
            num_lines += 1
            num_bytes += len(line)
            num_words += len(line.split())

        total_lines += num_lines
        total_bytes += num_bytes
        total_words += num_words
```

If you set the default to a list with sys.stdin, you have handled the STDIN option.

If the user supplies any arguments, argparse will check if they are valid file inputs. If there is a problem, argparse will halt execution of the program and show the user an error message.

These are the variables for the "total" line, if I need them.

Iterate through the list of arg.file inputs. I use the variable fh to remind me that these are open file handles, even STDIN.

Iterate through each line of the file handle.

For each line, increment the number of lines by 1.

Initialize variables to count the lines, words, and bytes in just this file.

To get the number of words, we can call line.split() to break the line on whitespace. The length of that list is added to the count of words.

The number of bytes is incremented by the length of the line.

Add all the counts for lines, words, and bytes for this file to the variables for counting the totals.

```
        print(f'{num_lines:8}{num_words:8}{num_bytes:8} {fh.name}')

    if len(args.file) > 1:
        print(f'{total_lines:8}{total_words:8}{total_bytes:8} total')


# --------------------------------------------------
if __name__ == '__main__':
    main()
```

Print the "total" line.

Check if we had more than 1 input.

Print the counts for this file using the {:8} option to print in a field 8 characters wide followed by a single space and then the name of the file.

6.3   Discussion

This program is rather short and seems rather simple, but it's not exactly easy. Let's break down the main ideas in the program.

6.3.1   Defining the arguments

One point of this exercise is to get familiar with argparse and the trouble it can save you. The key is in defining the file parameter. We use type=argparse.File-Type('rt') to indicate that any arguments provided must be readable text files. We use nargs='*' to indicate zero or more arguments, and we set the default to be a list containing sys.stdin. This means we know that argparse will always give us a list of one or more open file handles.

That's really quite a bit of logic packed into a small space, and most of the work validating the inputs, generating error messages, and handling the defaults is all done for us!

6.3.2   Reading a file using a for loop

The values that argparse returns for args.file will be a list of *open file handles*. We can create such a list in the REPL to mimic what we'd get from args.file:

```
>>> files = [open('../inputs/fox.txt')]
```

Before we use a for loop to iterate through them, we need to set up three variables to track the *total* number of lines, words, and characters. We could define them on three separate lines:

```
>>> total_lines = 0
>>> total_words = 0
>>> total_bytes = 0
```

Or we can declare them on a single line like the following:

```
>>> total_lines, total_words, total_bytes = 0, 0, 0
```

Technically we're creating a `tuple` on the right side by placing commas between the three zeros and then "unpacking" them into three variables on the left side. I'll have more to say about tuples much later.

Inside the `for` loop for each file handle, we initialize three more variables to hold the count of lines, characters, and words *for this particular file*. We can then use another `for` loop to iterate over each line in the file handle (`fh`). For `lines`, we can add `1` on each pass through the `for` loop. For `bytes`, we can add the length of the line (`len(line)`) to track the number of "characters" (which may be printable characters or whitespace, so it's easiest to call them "bytes"). Lastly, for `words`, we can use `line.split()` to break the line on whitespace to create a `list` of "words." It's not a perfect way to count actual words, but it's close enough. We can use the `len()` function on the `list` to add to the `words` variable.

The `for` loop ends when the end of the file is reached. Next we can `print()` out the counts and the filename, using `{:8}` placeholders in the print template to indicate a text field 8 characters wide:

```
>>> for fh in files:
...     lines, words, bytes = 0, 0, 0
...     for line in fh:
...         lines += 1
...         bytes += len(line)
...         words += len(line.split())
...     print(f'{lines:8}{words:8}{bytes:8} {fh.name}')
...     total_lines += lines
...     total_bytes += bytes
...     total_words += words
...
       1       9      45 ../inputs/fox.txt
```

Notice that the preceding call to `print()` lines up with the *second* `for` loop, so that it will run after we're done iterating over the lines in `fh`. I chose to use the f-string method to print each of `lines`, `words`, and `bytes` in a space eight characters wide, followed by one space and then the `fh.name` of the file.

After printing, we can add the counts to the "total" variables to keep a running total.

Lastly, if the number of file arguments is greater than 1, we need to print the totals:

```
if len(args.file) > 1:
    print(f'{total_lines:8}{total_words:8}{total_bytes:8} total')
```

6.4   *Going further*

- By default, wc will print all the columns like our program does, but it will also accept flags to print -c for number of characters, -l for number of lines, and -w for number of words. When any of these flags are present, only columns for the specified flags are shown, so wc.py -wc would show just the columns for words and characters. Add short and long flags for these options to your program so that it behaves exactly like wc.

- Write your own implementation of other system tools like cat (to print the contents of a file to STDOUT), head (to print just the first *n* lines of a file), tail (to print the last *n* lines of a file), and tac (to print the lines of a file in reverse order).

Summary

- The nargs (number of arguments) option to argparse allows you to validate the number of arguments from the user. The asterisk ('*') means zero or more, whereas '+' means one or more.

- If you define an argument using type=argparse.FileType('rt'), argparse will validate that the user has provided a readable text file and will make the value available in your code as an open file handle.

- You can read and write from the standard in/out file handles by using sys.stdin and sys.stdout.

- You can nest for loops to handle multiple levels of processing.

- The str.split() method will split a string on spaces.

- The len() function can be used on both strings and lists. For lists, it will tell you the number of elements the list contains.

- Both str.format() and Python's f-strings recognize printf-style formatting options to allow you to control how a value is displayed.

Gashlycrumb: Looking items up in a dictionary

In this chapter, we're going to look up lines of text from an input file that start with the letters provided by the user. The text will come from an input file that will default to Edward Gorey's "The Gashlycrumb Tinies," an abecedarian book that describes various and ghastly ways in which children expire. For instance, figure 7.1 shows that "N is for Neville who died of ennui."

Figure 7.1 N is for Neville who died of ennui.

Our gashlycrumb.py program will take one or more letters as positional arguments and will look up the lines of text that start with that letter from an *optional* input file. We will look up the letters in a *case-insensitive* fashion.

The input file will have the value for each letter on a separate line:

```
$ head -2 gashlycrumb.txt
A is for Amy who fell down the stairs.
B is for Basil assaulted by bears.
```

118

When our unfortunate user runs this program, here is what they will see:

```
$ ./gashlycrumb.py e f
E is for Ernest who choked on a peach.
F is for Fanny sucked dry by a leech.
```

In this exercise, you will

- Accept one or more positional arguments that we'll call `letter`.
- Accept an optional `--file` argument, which must be a readable text file. The default value will be `'gashlycrumb.txt'` (provided).
- Read the file, find the first letter of each line, and build a data structure that associates the letter to the line of text. (We'll only be using files where each line starts with a single, unique letter. This program would fail with any other format of text.)
- For each `letter` provided by the user, either print the line of text for the `letter` if present, or print a message if it isn't.
- Learn how to "pretty-print" a data structure.

You can draw from several previous programs:

- From chapter 2 you know how to get the first letter of a bit of text.
- From chapter 4 you know how to build a dictionary and look up a value.
- From chapter 6 you know how to accept a file input argument and read it line by line.

Now you'll put all those skills together to recite morbid poetry!

7.1 Writing gashlycrumb.py

Before you begin writing, I encourage you to run the tests with `make test` or `pytest -xv test.py` in the 07_gashlycrumb directory. The first test should fail:

```
test.py::test_exists FAILED
```

This is just a reminder that the first thing you need to do is create the file called gashlycrumb.py. You can do this however you like, such as by running `new.py gashlycrumb.py` in the 07_gashlycrumb directory, by copying the template/template.py file, or by just starting a new file from scratch. Run your tests again, and you should pass the first test and possibly the second if your program produces a usage statement.

Next, let's get the arguments straight. Modify your program's parameters in the `get_args()` function so that it will produce the following usage statement when the program is run with no arguments or with the `-h` or `--help` flags:

```
$ ./gashlycrumb.py -h
usage: gashlycrumb.py [-h] [-f FILE] letter [letter ...]
```

```
Gashlycrumb

positional arguments:
  letter                    Letter(s)

optional arguments:
  -h, --help                show this help message and exit
  -f FILE, --file FILE      Input file (default: gashlycrumb.txt)
```

letter is a required positional argument that accepts one or more values.

The -h and --help arguments are created automatically by argparse.

The -f or --file argument is an option with a default value of gashlycrumb.txt.

Figure 7.2 shows a string diagram of how the program will work.

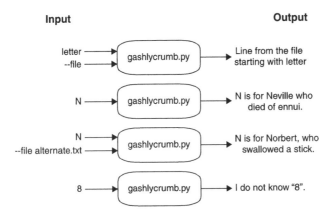

Figure 7.2 Our program will accept some letter(s) and possibly a file. It will then look up the line(s) of the file starting with the given letter(s).

In the main() function, start off by echoing each of the letter arguments:

```
def main():
    args = get_args()
    for letter in args.letter:
        print(letter)
```

Try running it to make sure it works:

```
$ ./gashlycrumb.py a b
a
b
```

Next, read the file line by line using a for loop:

```
def main():
    args = get_args()
```

```
    for letter in args.letter:
        print(letter)

    for line in args.file:
        print(line, end='')
```

Note that I'm using `end=''` with `print()` so that it won't print the newline that's already attached to each `line` of the file:

Try running it to ensure you can read the input file:

```
$ ./gashlycrumb.py a b | head -4
a
b
A is for Amy who fell down the stairs.
B is for Basil assaulted by bears.
```

Use the alternate.txt file too:

```
$ ./gashlycrumb.py a b --file alternate.txt | head -4
a
b
A is for Alfred, poisoned to death.
B is for Bertrand, consumed by meth.
```

If your program is provided a `--file` argument that does not exist, it should exit with an error and message. Note that if you declare the parameter in `get_args()` using `type=argparse.FileType('rt')` as we did in the previous chapter, this error should be produced automatically by `argparse`:

```
$ ./gashlycrumb.py -f blargh b
usage: gashlycrumb.py [-h] [-f FILE] letter [letter ...]
gashlycrumb.py: error: argument -f/--file: can't open 'blargh': \
[Errno 2] No such file or directory: 'blargh'
```

Now think about how you can use the first letter of each `line` to create an entry in a dict. Use `print()` to look at your dictionary. Figure out how to check if the given `letter` is *in* (wink, wink, nudge, nudge) your dictionary.

If your program is given a value that does not exist in the list of first characters on the lines from the input file (when searched without regard to case), you should print a message:

```
$ ./gashlycrumb.py 3
I do not know "3".
$ ./gashlycrumb.py CH
I do not know "CH".
```

If the given `letter` is in the dictionary, print the value for it (see figure 7.3):

```
$ ./gashlycrumb.py a
A is for Amy who fell down the stairs.
```

```
$ ./gashlycrumb.py z
Z is for Zillah who drank too much gin.
```

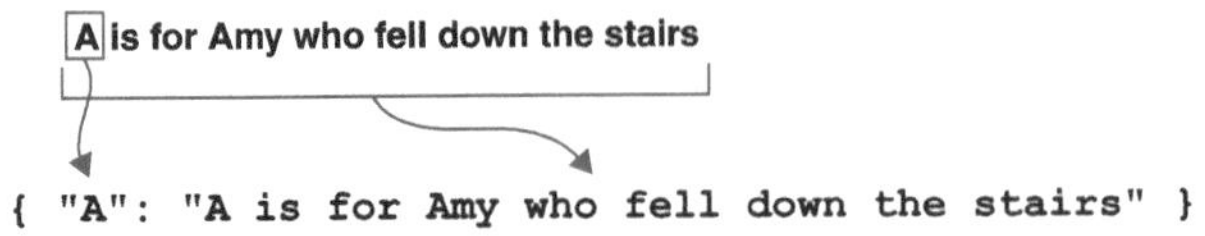

```
{ "A": "A is for Amy who fell down the stairs" }
```

Figure 7.3 We need to create a dictionary where the first letter of each line is the key and the line is the value.

Run the test suite to ensure your program meets all the requirements. Read the errors closely and fix your program.

Here are some hints:

- Start with new.py and remove everything but the positional `letter` and optional `--file` parameters.
- Use `type=argparse.FileType('rt')` to validate the `--file` argument.
- Use `nargs='+'` to define the positional argument `letter` so it will require one or more values.
- A dictionary is a natural data structure for associating a value like the letter "A" to a phrase like "A is for Amy who fell down the stairs." Create a new, empty `dict`.
- Once you have an open file handle, you can read the file line by line with a `for` loop.
- Each line of text is a string. How can you get the first character of a string?
- Create an entry in your dictionary using the first character as the key and the line itself as the value.
- Iterate through each `letter` argument. How can you check that a given value is in the dictionary?

No skipping ahead to the solution until you have written your own version! If you peek, you will die a horrible death: stampeded by kittens.

7.2   Solution

I really hope you looked at Gorey's artwork for his book. Now let's talk about how to build a dictionary from a file input:

```
#!/usr/bin/env python3
"""Lookup tables"""

import argparse
```

```
# --------------------------------------------------
def get_args():
    """get command-line arguments"""

    parser = argparse.ArgumentParser(
        description='Gashlycrumb',
        formatter_class=argparse.ArgumentDefaultsHelpFormatter)

    parser.add_argument('letter',
                        help='Letter(s)',
                        metavar='letter',
                        nargs='+',
                        type=str)

    parser.add_argument('-f',
                        '--file',
                        help='Input file',
                        metavar='FILE',
                        type=argparse.FileType('rt'),
                        default='gashlycrumb.txt')

    return parser.parse_args()
```

A positional argument called letter uses nargs='+' to indicate that one or more values are required.

The optional --file argument must be a readable file because of type=argparse.FileType('rt'). The default value is gashlycrumb.txt, which I know exists.

```
# --------------------------------------------------
def main():
    """Make a jazz noise here"""

    args = get_args()

    lookup = {}
    for line in args.file:
        lookup[line[0].upper()] = line.rstrip()

    for letter in args.letter:
        if letter.upper() in lookup:
            print(lookup[letter.upper()])
        else:
            print(f'I do not know "{letter}".')
# --------------------------------------------------
if __name__ == '__main__':
    main()
```

Create an empty dictionary to hold the lookup table.

Iterate through each line of the args.file, which will be an open file handle.

Uppercase the first character of the line to use as the key into the lookup table and set the value to be the line stripped of whitespace on the right side.

Use a for loop to iterate over each letter in args.letter.

If so, print the line of text from the lookup for the letter.

Check if the letter is in the lookup dictionary, using letter.upper() to disregard case.

Otherwise, print a message saying the letter is unknown.

7.3   Discussion

Did the frightful paws of the kittens hurt much? Let's talk about how I solved this problem. Remember, mine is just one of many possible solutions.

7.3.1   Handling the arguments

I prefer to have all the logic for parsing and validating the command-line arguments in the get_args() function. In particular, argparse can do a fine job of verifying tedious things, such as an argument being an existing, readable text file, which is why

I use `type=argparse.FileType('rt')` for that argument. If the user doesn't supply a valid argument, `argparse` will throw an error, printing a helpful message along with the short usage statement, and will exit with an error code.

By the time I get to the line `args = get_args()`, I know that I have one or more "letter" arguments and a valid, open file handle in the `args.file` slot. In the REPL, I can use `open` to get a file handle, which I usually like to call `fh`. For copyright purposes, I'll use my alternate text:

```
>>> fh = open('alternate.txt')
```

7.3.2   *Reading the input file*

We want to use a dictionary where the keys are the first letters of each line and the values are the lines themselves. That means we need to start by creating a new, empty dictionary, either by using the `dict()` function or by setting a variable equal to an empty set of curly brackets (`{}`). Let's call the variable `lookup`:

```
>>> lookup = {}
```

We can use a `for` loop to read each `line` of text. From the Crow's Nest program in chapter 2, you know we can use `line[0].upper()` to get the first letter of `line` and uppercase it. We can use that as the key into `lookup`.

Each `line` of text ends with a newline that I'd like to remove. The `str.rstrip()` method will strip whitespace from the right side of the `line` ("rstrip" = *right strip*). The result of that will be the value for my `lookup`:

```
for line in fh:
    lookup[line[0].upper()] = line.rstrip()
```

Let's look at the resulting `lookup` dictionary. We can `print()` it from the program or type `lookup` in the REPL, but it's going to be hard to read. I encourage you to try it.

Luckily there is a lovely module called `pprint` to "pretty-print" data structures. Here is how you can import the `pprint()` function from the `pprint` module with the alias `pp`:

```
>>> from pprint import pprint as pp
```

Figure 7.4 illustrates how this works.

from pprint import pprint as pp

Module   Function   Alias

Figure 7.4   We can specify exactly which functions to import from a module and even give the function an alias.

Now let's take a peek at the `lookup` table:

```
>>> pp(lookup)
{'A': 'A is for Alfred, poisoned to death.',
 'B': 'B is for Bertrand, consumed by meth.',
 'C': 'C is for Cornell, who ate some glass.',
 'D': 'D is for Donald, who died from gas.',
 'E': 'E is for Edward, hanged by the neck.',
 'F': 'F is for Freddy, crushed in a wreck.',
 'G': 'G is for Geoffrey, who slit his wrist.',
 'H': "H is for Henry, who's neck got a twist.",
 'I': 'I is for Ingrid, who tripped down a stair.',
 'J': 'J is for Jered, who fell off a chair,',
 'K': 'K is for Kevin, bit by a snake.',
 'L': 'L is for Lauryl, impaled on a stake.',
 'M': 'M is for Moira, hit by a brick.',
 'N': 'N is for Norbert, who swallowed a stick.',
 'O': 'O is for Orville, who fell in a canyon,',
 'P': 'P is for Paul, strangled by his banyan,',
 'Q': 'Q is for Quintanna, flayed in the night,',
 'R': 'R is for Robert, who died of spite,',
 'S': 'S is for Susan, stung by a jelly,',
 'T': 'T is for Terrange, kicked in the belly,',
 'U': "U is for Uma, who's life was vanquished,",
 'V': 'V is for Victor, consumed by anguish,',
 'W': "W is for Walter, who's socks were too long,",
 'X': 'X is for Xavier, stuck through with a prong,',
 'Y': 'Y is for Yoeman, too fat by a piece,',
 'Z': 'Z is for Zora, smothered by a fleece.'}
```

Hey, that looks like a handy data structure. Hooray for us! Please don't discount the value of using lots of `print()` calls when you are trying to write and understand a program, and of using the `pprint()` function whenever you need to see a complex data structure.

7.3.3   *Using a dictionary comprehension*

In chapter 4 you saw that you can use a list comprehension to build a list by putting a `for` loop inside `[]`. If we change the brackets to curlies (`{}`), we create a dictionary comprehension:

```
>>> fh = open('gashlycrumb.txt')
>>> lookup = { line[0].upper(): line.rstrip() for line in fh }
```

See in figure 7.5 how we can rearrange three lines of our `for` loop into a single line of code.

   If you print the `lookup` table again, you should see the same output as before. It may seem like showing off to write one line of code instead of three, but it really does make a good deal of sense to write compact, idiomatic code. More code always means more chances for bugs, so I usually try to write code that is as simple as possible (but no simpler).

```
lookup = {}
for line in fh:
    lookup[line[0].upper()] = line.rstrip()


lookup = { line[0].upper(): line.rstrip() for line in fh }
```

Figure 7.5 The for loop we used to build a dictionary can be written using a dictionary comprehension.

7.3.4 *Dictionary lookups*

Now that I have a `lookup` table, I can ask whether some value is `in` the keys. I know the letters are in uppercase, and since the user could give me a lowercase letter, I use `letter.upper()` to only compare that case:

```
>>> letter = 'a'
>>> letter.upper() in lookup
True
>>> lookup[letter.upper()]
'A is for Amy who fell down the stairs.'
```

If the letter is found, I can print the line of text for that letter; otherwise, I can print a message saying that I don't know that letter:

```
>>> letter = '4'
>>> if letter.upper() in lookup:
...     print(lookup[letter.upper()])
... else:
...     print('I do not know "{}".'.format(letter))
...
I do not know "4".
```

An even shorter way to write that would be to use the `dict.get()` method:

```
def main():                 lookup.get() will return the value for letter.upper() or the
    args = get_args()           warning about a value not being found in our lookup.
    lookup = {line[0].upper(): line.rstrip() for line in args.file}

    for letter in args.letter:
        print(lookup.get(letter.upper(), f'I do not know "{letter}".'))
```

7.4 *Going further*

- Write a phonebook that reads a file and creates a dictionary from the names of your friends and their email or phone numbers.
- Create a program that uses a dictionary to count the number of times you see each word in a document.

- Write an interactive version of the program that takes input directly from the user. Use while True to set up an infinite loop and keep using the input() function to get the user's next letter:

```
$ ./gashlycrumb_interactive.py
    Please provide a letter [! to quit]: t
    T is for Titus who flew into bits.
    Please provide a letter [! to quit]: 7
    I do not know "7".
    Please provide a letter [! to quit]: !
    Bye
```

- Interactive programs are fun to write, but how would you go about testing them? In chapter 17 I'll show you one way to do this.

Summary

- A dictionary comprehension is a way to build a dictionary in a one-line for loop.
- Defining file input arguments using argparse.FileType saves you time and code.
- Python's pprint module is used to pretty-print complex data structures.

Apples and Bananas: Find and replace

Have you ever misspelled a word? I haven't, but I've heard that many other people often do. We can use computers to find and replace all instances of a misspelled word with the correction. Or maybe you'd like to replace all mentions of your ex's name in your poetry with your new love's name? Find and replace is your friend.

To get us started, let's consider the children's song "Apples and Bananas," wherein we intone our favorite fruits to consume:

```
I like to eat, eat, eat apples and bananas
```

Subsequent verses substitute the main vowel sound in the fruits for various other vowel sounds, such as the long "a" sound (as in "hay"):

```
I like to ate, ate, ate ay-ples and ba-nay-nays
```

Or the ever-popular long "e" (as in "knee"):

```
I like to eat, eat, eat ee-ples and bee-nee-nees
```

And so forth. In this exercise, we'll write a Python program called apples.py that takes some text, given as a single positional argument, and replaces all the vowels in the text with the given -v or --vowel options (with the default being a).

The program should be written in the 08_apples_and_bananas directory and should handle text on the command line:

```
$ ./apples.py foo
faa
```

And accept the -v or --vowel option:

```
$ ./apples.py foo -v i
fii
```

Your program should *preserve the case* of the input vowels:

```
$ ./apples.py -v i "APPLES AND BANANAS"
IPPLIS IND BININIS
```

As with the Howler program in chapter 5, the text argument may name a file, in which case your program should read the contents of the file:

```
$ ./apples.py ../inputs/fox.txt
Tha qaack brawn fax jamps avar tha lazy dag.
$ ./apples.py --vowel e ../inputs/fox.txt
The qeeck brewn fex jemps ever the lezy deg.
```

Figure 8.1 shows a diagram of the program's inputs and output.

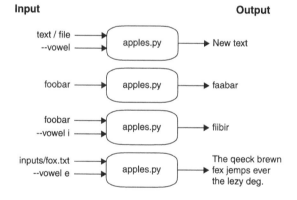

Figure 8.1 Our program will accept some text and possibly a vowel. All the vowels in the given text will be changed to the same vowel, resulting in hilarity.

Here is the usage statement that should print when there are no arguments:

```
$ ./apples.py
usage: apples.py [-h] [-v vowel] text
apples.py: error: the following arguments are required: text
```

And the program should always print usage for the -h and --help flags:

```
$ ./apples.py -h
usage: apples.py [-h] [-v vowel] text
```

```
Apples and bananas

positional arguments:
  text                    Input text or file

optional arguments:
  -h, --help              show this help message and exit
  -v vowel, --vowel vowel
                          The vowel to substitute (default: a)
```

The program should complain if the --vowel argument is
not a single, lowercase vowel:

```
$ ./apples.py -v x foo
usage: apples.py [-h] [-v str] str
apples.py: error: argument -v/--vowel: \
invalid choice: 'x' (choose from 'a', 'e', 'i', 'o', 'u')
```

Your program is going to need to do the following:

- Take a positional argument that might be some plain text or may name a file
- If the argument is a file, use the contents as the input text
- Take an optional -v or --vowel argument that should default to the letter "a"
- Verify that the --vowel option is in the set of vowels "a," "e," "i," "o," and "u"
- Replace all instances of vowels in the input text with the specified (or default)
  --vowel argument
- Print the new text to STDOUT

8.1   *Altering strings*

So far in our discussions of Python strings, numbers, lists, and dictionaries, we've seen
how easily we can change or *mutate* variables. There is a problem, however, in that
strings are immutable. Suppose we have a text variable that holds our input text:

```
>>> text = 'The quick brown fox jumps over the lazy dog.'
```

If we wanted to turn the first "e" (at index 2) into an "i," we cannot do this:

```
>>> text[2] = 'i'
Traceback (most recent call last):
  File "<stdin>", line 1, in <module>
TypeError: 'str' object does not support item assignment
```

To change text, we need to set it equal to an entirely new value. In chapter 4 you saw
that you can use a for loop to iterate over the characters in a string. For instance, I
could laboriously uppercase text like so:

```
new = ''
for char in text:
    new += char.upper()
```

Initialize a variable equal to the empty string.

Iterate through each character in the text.

Append the uppercase version of the character to the variable.

We can inspect the value of new to verify that it is all uppercase:

```
>>> new
'THE QUICK BROWN FOX JUMPS OVER THE LAZY DOG.'
```

Using this idea, you could iterate through the characters of text and build up a new string. Whenever the character is a vowel, you could change it for the given vowel; otherwise, you could use the character itself. We had to identify vowels in chapter 2, so you can refer back to how you did that.

8.1.1 Using the str.replace() method

In chapter 4 we talked about using the str.replace() method to replace all the numbers in a string with a different number. Maybe that would be a good way to solve this problem? Let's look at the documentation for that using help(str.replace) in the REPL:

```
>>> help(str.replace)
replace(self, old, new, count=-1, /)
    Return a copy with all occurrences of substring old replaced by new.

      count
        Maximum number of occurrences to replace.
        -1 (the default value) means replace all occurrences.

    If the optional argument count is given, only the first count occurrences
    are replaced.
```

Let's give that a try. We could replace "T" with "X":

```
>>> text.replace('T', 'X')
'Xhe quick brown fox jumps over the lazy dog.'
```

This seems promising! Can you see a way to replace all the vowels using this idea? Remember that this method never mutates the given string but instead returns a new string that you will need to assign to a variable.

8.1.2 Using str.translate()

We also looked at the str.translate() method in chapter 4. There we created a dictionary that described how to turn one character, like "1," into another string like "9." Any character not mentioned in the dictionary was left alone.

The documentation for this method is a bit more cryptic:

```
>>> help(str.translate)
translate(self, table, /)
    Replace each character in the string using the given translation table.

    table
      Translation table, which must be a mapping of Unicode ordinals to
      Unicode ordinals, strings, or None.

    The table must implement lookup/indexing via __getitem__, for instance a
    dictionary or list.  If this operation raises LookupError, the character is
    left untouched.  Characters mapped to None are deleted.
```

In my solution, I created the following dictionary:

```
jumper = {'1': '9', '2': '8', '3': '7', '4': '6', '5': '0',
          '6': '4', '7': '3', '8': '2', '9': '1', '0': '5'}
```

That is the argument to the `str.maketrans()` function, which creates a translation table that is then used with `str.translate()` to change all the characters present as keys in the dictionary to their corresponding values:

```
>>> '876-5309'.translate(str.maketrans(jumper))
'234-0751'
```

What keys and values should you have in a dictionary if you want to change all the vowels, both lower- and uppercase, to some other value?

8.1.3   *Other ways to mutate strings*

If you know about regular expressions, that's a strong solution. If you haven't heard of them, don't worry—I'll introduce them in the discussion.

The point is for you to *play* with this and come up with a solution. I found eight ways to change all the vowels to a new character, so there are many ways you could approach this. How many *different* methods can you find on your own before you look at my solution?

Here are a few hints:

- Consider using the `choices` option in the `argparse` documentation to constrain the `--vowel` options. Be sure to read section A.4.3 in the appendix for an example.
- Be sure to change both lower- and uppercase versions of the vowels, preserving the case of the input characters.

Now is the time to dig in and see what you can do before you look at my solution.

8.2   *Solution*

Here is the first solution I wanted to share. After this, we'll explore several more.

```python
#!/usr/bin/env python3
"""Apples and Bananas"""

import argparse
import os


# --------------------------------------------------
def get_args():
    """get command-line arguments"""

    parser = argparse.ArgumentParser(
        description='Apples and bananas',
        formatter_class=argparse.ArgumentDefaultsHelpFormatter)

    parser.add_argument('text', metavar='text', help='Input text or file')

    parser.add_argument('-v',
                        '--vowel',
                        help='The vowel(s) allowed',
                        metavar='vowel',
                        type=str,
                        default='a',
                        choices=list('aeiou'))

    args = parser.parse_args()

    if os.path.isfile(args.text):
        args.text = open(args.text).read().rstrip()

    return args


# --------------------------------------------------
def main():
    """Make a jazz noise here"""

    args = get_args()
    text = args.text
    vowel = args.vowel
    new_text = []

    for char in text:
        if char in 'aeiou':
            new_text.append(vowel)
        elif char in 'AEIOU':
            new_text.append(vowel.upper())
        else:
            new_text.append(char)
```

The input might be text or a filename, so I defined it as a string.

Use "choices" to restrict the user to one of the listed vowels.

Check if the text argument is a file.

If it is, read the file using str.rstrip() to remove any trailing whitespace.

Create a new list to hold the characters for the transformed text.

Iterate through each character of the text.

Check if the current character is in the list of lowercase vowels.

If it is, use the vowel value instead of the character.

Check if the current character is in the list of uppercase vowels.

If it is, use the value of vowel.upper() instead of the character.

Otherwise, use the character itself.

```
    print(''.join(new_text))        ◁──┐ Print a new string made by joining the
                                        │ new text list on the empty string.

# --------------------------------------------------
if __name__ == '__main__':
    main()
```

8.3   Discussion

I came up with eight ways to write my solution. All of them start with the same
get_args() function, so let's look at that first.

8.3.1   Defining the parameters

This is one of those problems that has many valid and interesting solutions. The first
problem to solve is, of course, getting and validating the user's input. As always, I will
use argparse.

I usually define all my required parameters first. The text parameter is a positional string that *might* be a filename:

```
parser.add_argument('text', metavar='str', help='Input text or file')
```

The --vowel option is also a string, and I decided to use the choices option to have
argparse validate that the user's input is in the list('aeiou'):

```
parser.add_argument('-v',
                    '--vowel',
                    help='The vowel to substitute'',
                    metavar='str',
                    type=str,
                    default='a',
                    choices=list('aeiou'))
```

That is, choices wants a list of options. I could pass in ['a', 'e', 'i', 'o', 'u'],
but that's a lot of typing on my part. It's much easier to type list('aeiou') and have
Python turn the str "aeiou" into a list of the characters. Both approaches produce
the same results, because list(str) creates a list of the individual characters in a
given string. And remember, the use of single or double quotes doesn't matter. Any
value enclosed in either type of quotes is a str, even if it's just one character:

```
>>> ['a', 'e', 'i', 'o', 'u']
['a', 'e', 'i', 'o', 'u']
>>> list('aeiou')
['a', 'e', 'i', 'o', 'u']
```

We can even write a test for this. The absence of any error means that it's OK:

```
>>> assert ['a', 'e', 'i', 'o', 'u'] == list('aeiou')
```

The next task is detecting whether text is the name of a file that should be read for
the text, or if it is the text itself. This is the same code I used in chapter 5, and again I

chose to handle the `text` argument inside the `get_args()` function so that, by the time I get `text` inside `main()`, it's all been handled. Figure 8.2 illustrates how we can chain the `open()` function to the `read()` method of a file handle to the `rstrip()` method of a string.

```
if os.path.isfile(args.text):
    args.text = open(args.text).read().rstrip()
```

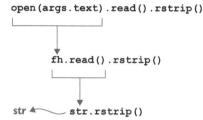

Figure 8.2   **We can chain methods together to create pipelines of operations. The open() returns a file handle that we can read. The `read()` operation returns a string that we strip of whitespace.**

At this point, the user's arguments to the program have been fully vetted. We've got `text` either from the command line or from a file, and we've verified that the `--vowel` value is one of the allowed characters. To me, this code is a single "unit" where I've handled the arguments. Processing can now go forward by returning the arguments:

```
return args
```

8.3.2   *Eight ways to replace the vowels*

How many ways did you find to replace the vowels? You only needed one, of course, to pass the tests, but I hope you probed the edges of the language to see how many different techniques there are. I know that the Zen of Python says

> *There should be one—and preferably only one—obvious way to do it.*

www.python.org/dev/peps/pep-0020/

But I really come from the Perl mentality, where "There Is More Than One Way To Do It" (TIMTOWTDI or "Tim Toady").

METHOD 1: ITERATING THROUGH EVERY CHARACTER
The first method is similar to what we did in chapter 4, where we used a `for` loop on a string to access each character. Here is some code you can copy and paste into the `ipython` REPL:

Set the new_text variable to an empty list.   Set text to the string "Apples and Bananas!"

```
>>> text = 'Apples and Bananas!'
>>> vowel = 'o'
>>> new_text = []
>>> for char in text:
```

Set the vowel variable to the string "o". That is, we'll replace all the vowels with this one.

Use a for to iterate text, putting each character into the char variable.

```
...        if char in 'aeiou':
...            new_text.append(vowel)
...        elif char in 'AEIOU':
...            new_text.append(vowel.upper())
...        else:
...            new_text.append(char)
...
>>> text = ''.join(new_text)
>>> text
'Opplos ond Bononos!'
```

> If the character is in the set of lowercase vowels, add the vowel "o" to the new text.

> If the character is in the set of uppercase vowels, substitute the vowel.upper() version "O" into the new text.

> Otherwise, add the current character to the new text.

> Turn the new_text list into a new str by joining it on the empty string (").

Note that it would be just fine to start off making new_text an empty string and then concatenating the new characters. With that approach, you wouldn't have to str.join() them at the end. Whatever you prefer:

```
new_text += vowel
```

Next I'm going to show you several alternate solutions. They're all functionally equivalent because they all pass the tests—the point here is to explore the Python language and understand it. For the alternate solutions, I'll just show the main() function.

METHOD 2: USING THE STR.REPLACE() METHOD

Here is a way to solve the problem using the str.replace() method:

```
def main():
    args = get_args()
    text = args.text
    vowel = args.vowel

    for v in 'aeiou':
        text = text.replace(v, vowel).replace(v.upper(), vowel.upper())

    print(text)
```

> Iterate through the list of vowels. We don't have to say list('aeiou') here—Python will automatically treat the string 'aeiou' like a list because we are using it in a list context with the for loop.

> Use the str.replace() method twice to replace both the lower- and uppercase versions of the vowel in the text.

Earlier in the chapter, I mentioned the str.replace() method, which will return a new string with all instances of one string replaced by another:

```
>>> s = 'foo'
>>> s.replace('o', 'a')
'faa'
>>> s.replace('oo', 'x')
'fx'
```

Note that the original string remains unchanged:

```
>>> s
'foo'
```

You don't have to chain the two str.replace() methods. It could be written as two separate statements, as illustrated in figure 8.3.

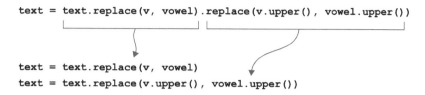

```
text = text.replace(v, vowel).replace(v.upper(), vowel.upper())


text = text.replace(v, vowel)
text = text.replace(v.upper(), vowel.upper())
```

Figure 8.3 The chained calls to `str.replace()` **can be written as two separate statements if you prefer.**

METHOD 3: USING THE STR.TRANSLATE() METHOD

Can we use the `str.translate()` method to solve this? I showed in chapter 4 how you could use a dictionary called `jumper` to change a character like "1" to the character "9." In this problem, we need to change all the lower- and uppercase vowels (10 total) to some given `vowel`. For instance, to change all the vowels into the letter "o," we could create a translation table t like so:

```
t = {'a': 'o',
     'e': 'o',
     'i': 'o',
     'o': 'o',
     'u': 'o',
     'A': 'O',
     'E': 'O',
     'I': 'O',
     'O': 'O',
     'U': 'O'}
```

We could use t with the `str.translate()` method:

```
>>> 'Apples and Bananas'.translate(str.maketrans(t))
'Opplos ond Bononos'
```

If you read the documentation for `str.maketrans()`, you will find that another way to specify the translation table is to supply two strings of equal lengths:

```
maketrans(x, y=None, z=None, /)
    Return a translation table usable for str.translate().

    If there is only one argument, it must be a dictionary mapping Unicode
    ordinals (integers) or characters to Unicode ordinals, strings or None.
    Character keys will be then converted to ordinals.
    If there are two arguments, they must be strings of equal length, and
    in the resulting dictionary, each character in x will be mapped to the
    character at the same position in y. If there is a third argument, it
    must be a string, whose characters will be mapped to None in the result.
```

The first string should contain the letters you want to replace, which are the lower- and uppercase vowels `'aeiouAEIOU'`. The second string is composed of the letters to use for substitution. We want to use `'ooooo'` for `'aeiou'` and `'OOOOO'` for `'AEIOU'`.

We can repeat vowel five times using the * operator that you'll normally associate with numeric multiplication. This is (sort of) "multiplying" a string, so, OK, I guess:

```
>>> vowel * 5
'ooooo'
```

Next we handle the uppercase version:

```
>>> vowel * 5 + vowel.upper() * 5
'oooooOOOOO'
```

And now we can make the translation table in one line of code like this:

```
>>> trans = str.maketrans('aeiouAEIOU', vowel * 5 + vowel.upper() * 5)
```

Let's inspect the trans table. We'll use the pprint.pprint() (pretty-print) function so we can read it easily:

```
>>> from pprint import pprint as pp
>>> pp(trans)
{65: 79,
 69: 79,
 73: 79,
 79: 79,
 85: 79,
 97: 111,
 101: 111,
 105: 111,
 111: 111,
 117: 111}
```

The enclosing curlies {} tell us that trans is a dict. Each character is represented by its *ordinal* value, which is the character's position in the ASCII table (www.asciitable.com).

You can go back and forth between characters and their ordinal values by using the chr() and ord() functions. We will explore and use these functions later in chapter 18. Here are the ord() values for the vowels:

```
>>> for char in 'aeiou':
...     print(char, ord(char))
...
a 97
e 101
i 105
o 111
u 117
```

You can create the same output by starting with the ord() values to get the chr() values:

```
>>> for num in [97, 101, 105, 111, 117]:
...     print(chr(num), num)
...
a 97
e 101
```

```
i 105
o 111
u 117
>>>
```

If you'd like to inspect all the ordinal values for all the printable characters, you can run this:

```
>>> import string
>>> for char in string.printable:
...     print(char, ord(char))
```

I haven't included the output because there are 100 printable characters:

```
>>> print(len(string.printable))
100
```

So the `trans` table is a mapping from one character to another, just like in the "Jump the Five" exercise in chapter 4. The lowercase vowels ("aeiou") all map to the ordinal value 111, which is "o." The uppercase vowels ("AEIOU") map to 79, which is "O." You can use the `dict.items()` method to iterate over the key/value pairs of `trans` to verify that this is the case:

```
>>> for x, y in trans.items():
...     print(f'{chr(x)} => {chr(y)}')
...
a => o
e => o
i => o
o => o
u => o
A => O
E => O
I => O
O => O
U => O
```

The original `text` will be unchanged by the `str.translate()` method, so we can over-write `text` with the new version. Here's how I wrote that idea in my solution:

Create a translation table from each of the vowels, both lower- and uppercase, to their respective characters. The lowercase vowels will be matched to the lowercase vowel argument, and the uppercase vowels will be matched to the uppercase vowel argument.

```
def main():
    args = get_args()
    vowel = args.vowel
    trans = str.maketrans('aeiouAEIOU', vowel * 5 + vowel.upper() * 5)
    text = args.text.translate(trans)
    print(text)
```

Call the str.translate() method on the text variable, passing the translation table as an argument.

That was a lot of explanation about `ord()` and `chr()` and dictionaries and such, but look how simple and elegant that solution is. This is much shorter than method 1. Fewer lines of code (LOC) means fewer opportunities for bugs!

METHOD 4: USING A LIST COMPREHENSION

Following up on method 1, we can use a *list comprehension* to significantly shorten the `for` loop. In chapter 7 we looked at a dictionary comprehension as a one-line method to create a new dictionary using a `for` loop. Here we can do the same, creating a new `list`:

```
def main():
    args = get_args()          Use a list comprehension to process
    vowel = args.vowel         all the characters in args.text to
    text = [                   create a new list called text.
        vowel if c in 'aeiou' else vowel.upper() if c in 'AEIOU' else c
        for c in args.text
    ]                          Print the translated      Use a compound if expression
    print(''.join(text))       string by joining the text   to handle three cases:
                               list on the empty string.   lowercase vowel, uppercase
                                                           vowel, and the default.
```

Let's talk just a bit more about list comprehensions. As an example, we can generate a list of the squared values of the numbers 1 through 4 by using the `range()` function to get the numbers from a starting number to an ending number (not inclusive). In the REPL, we must use the `list()` function to force the production of the values, but usually your code won't need to do this:

```
>>> list(range(1, 5))
[1, 2, 3, 4]
```

> **NOTE** `range()` is another example of a *lazy* function in Python, which means it won't actually produce values until your program needs them—a lazy function is a promise to do something. If your program branches in such a way that you never need to produce the values, the work is never done, meaning your code is more efficient.

We can write a `for` loop to `print()` the squares:

```
>>> for num in range(1, 5):
...     print(num ** 2)
...
1
4
9
16
```

Instead of printing the values, imagine that we wanted to create a new `list` that contains those values. One way to do this would be to create an empty `list` and then use `list.append()` to add each value in a `for` loop:

```
>>> squares = []
>>> for num in range(1, 5):
...     squares.append(num ** 2)
```

Now we can verify that we have our squares:

```
>>> assert len(squares) == 4
>>> assert squares == [1, 4, 9, 16]
```

We can achieve the same result in fewer lines of code using a list comprehension to generate our new list, as shown in figure 8.4.

```
>>> [num ** 2 for num in range(1, 5)]
[1, 4, 9, 16]
```

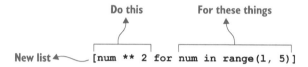

Figure 8.4 A list comprehension creates a new list using a `for` loop to iterate over the source values.

We can assign this list to the variable `squares` and verify that we still have what we expected. Ask yourself which version of the code you'd rather maintain: the longer one with the `for` loop, or the shorter one with the list comprehension?

```
>>> squares = [num ** 2 for num in range(1, 5)]
>>> assert len(squares) == 4
>>> assert squares == [1, 4, 9, 16]
```

For this version of the program, we'll condense the `if`/`elif`/`else` logic from method 1 into a compound `if` expression. First let's see how we could shorten the `for` loop version:

```
>>> text = 'Apples and Bananas!'
>>> new = []
>>> for c in text:
...     new.append(vowel if c in 'aeiou' else vowel.upper() if c in 'AEIOU'
        else c)
...
>>> ''.join(new)
'Opplos ond Bononos!'
```

Figure 8.5 shows how the parts of the expression match up to the original `if`/`elif`/`else`:

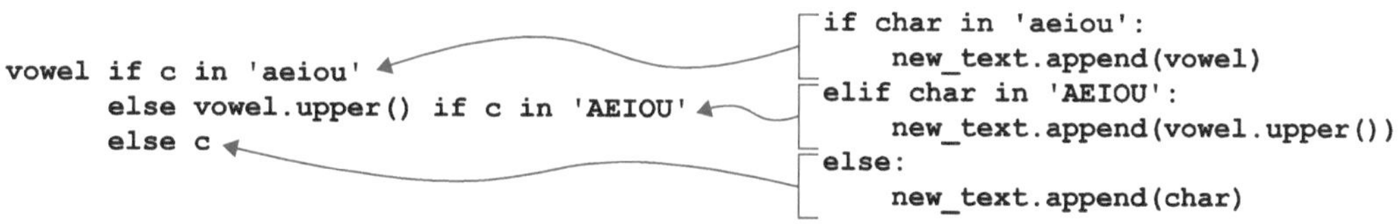

```
vowel if c in 'aeiou'                       if char in 'aeiou':
      else vowel.upper() if c in 'AEIOU'        new_text.append(vowel)
      else c                                elif char in 'AEIOU':
                                                new_text.append(vowel.upper())
                                            else:
                                                new_text.append(char)
```

Figure 8.5 The three conditional branches can be written using two `if` expressions.

Now let's turn that into a list comprehension:

```
>>> text = 'Apples and Bananas!'
>>> new_text = [
...     vowel if c in 'aeiou' else vowel.upper() if c in 'AEIOU' else c
...     for c in text ]
...
>>> ''.join(new_text)
'Opplos ond Bononos!'
```

Select the character using the compound if expression.

Perform this action for each character in the text.

The code is denser than the previous `for` loop, but it has advantages in that

- The list comprehension is shorter and generates our list rather than using the side effects of `list.append()`.
- The compound `if` expression will not compile if we forget one of the conditional branches.

METHOD 5: USING A LIST COMPREHENSION WITH A FUNCTION

The compound `if` expression inside the list comprehension is complicated enough that it probably should be a function. We can *define* a new function with the `def` statement and call it `new_char()`. It accepts a character we'll call `c`. After that, we can use the same compound `if` expression as before:

```
def main():
    args = get_args()
    vowel = args.vowel

    def new_char(c):
        return vowel if c in 'aeiou' else vowel.upper() if c in 'AEIOU' else c

    text = ''.join([new_char(c) for c in args.text])

    print(text)
```

Define a function to choose a new character. Note that it uses the vowel variable because the function has been declared in the same scope. This is called a closure, because new_char() closes over the variable.

Use the compound if expression to select the correct character.

Use a list comprehension to process all the characters in text.

You can play with the `new_char()` function by putting this into your REPL:

```
vowel = 'o'
def new_char(c):
    return vowel if c in 'aeiou' else vowel.upper() if c in 'AEIOU' else c
```

It should always return the letter "o" if the argument is a lowercase vowel:

```
>>> new_char('a')
'o'
```

It should return "O" if the argument is an uppercase vowel:

```
>>> new_char('A')
'O'
```

Otherwise, it should return the given character:

```
>>> new_char('b')
'b'
```

We can use the `new_char()` function to process all the characters in `text`, using a list comprehension:

```
>>> text = 'Apples and Bananas!'
>>> text = ''.join([new_char(c) for c in text])
>>> text
'Opplos ond Bononos!'
```

Note that the `new_char()` function is declared *inside* the `main()` function. Yes, you can do that! The function is then only "visible" inside the `main()` function. I've done this because we want to reference the `vowel` variable inside the function without passing it as an argument.

As an example, let's define a `foo()` function that has a `bar()` function inside it. We can call `foo()`, and it will call `bar()`. But from outside of `foo()`, the `bar()` function does not exist (it "is not visible" or "is not in scope").

```
>>> def foo():
...     def bar():
...         print('This is bar')
...     bar()
...
>>> foo()
This is bar
>>> bar()
Traceback (most recent call last):
  File "<stdin>", line 1, in <module>
NameError: name 'bar' is not defined
```

I declared the `new_char()` function inside `main()` because I wanted to reference the vowel variable inside the function, as shown in figure 8.6. Because `new_char()` "closes" around the `vowel`, it is a special type of function called a *closure*.

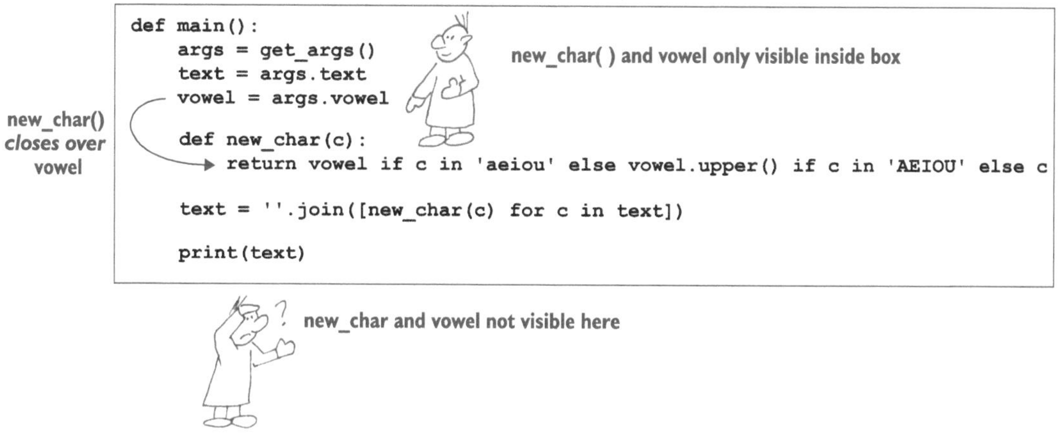

Figure 8.6 The `new_char()` function can only be seen within the `main()` function. It creates a closure because it references the `vowel` variable. Code outside of `main()` cannot see or call `new_char()`.

If we don't write this as a closure, we will have to pass the vowel as an argument:

```
def main():
    args = get_args()
    print(''.join([new_char(c, args.vowel) for c in args.text]))

def new_char(char, vowel):
    return vowel if char in 'aeiou' else \
        vowel.upper() if char in 'AEIOU' else char
```

We need to pass args.vowel as an argument to the new_char() function.

The vowel is only visible inside the main() function. Since new_char() is no longer declared in the same scope, we need to accept vowel as an argument.

While the closure method is interesting, this version is arguably easier to understand. It would also be easier to write a unit test for it, which is something we'll start doing soon.

METHOD 6: USING THE MAP() FUNCTION

For this method, I'll introduce the map() function, as it's quite similar to a list comprehension. The map() function accepts two arguments:

- A function
- An iterable like a list, a lazy function, or a generator

I like to think of map() like a paint booth—you load up the booth with, say, blue paint. Unpainted cars go in, blue paint is applied, and blue cars come out.

We can create a function to "paint" cars by adding the string "blue" to the beginning:

```
>>> list(map(lambda car: 'blue ' + car, ['BMW', 'Alfa Romeo', 'Chrysler']))
['blue BMW', 'blue Alfa Romeo', 'blue Chrysler']
```

The first argument you see here starts with the keyword lambda, which is used to create an *anonymous* function. With the regular def keyword, the function name follows. With lambda, there is no name, only the list of parameters and the function body.

For example, an add1() function that adds 1 to a value is a regular named function:

```
def add1(n):
    return n + 1
```

It works as expected:

```
>>> assert add1(10) == 11
>>> assert add1(add1(10)) == 12
```

Compare the preceding definition to one created using lambda, which we assign to the variable add1:

```
>>> add1 = lambda n: n + 1
```

This definition of add1 is functionally equivalent to the first version. We call it just like the add1() function:

```
>>> assert add1(10) == 11
>>> assert add1(add1(10)) == 12
```

The body for a lambda is a brief (usually one-line) expression. There is no return statement because the final evaluation of the expression is returned automatically. In figure 8.7, you can see that the lambda will return the result of n + 1.

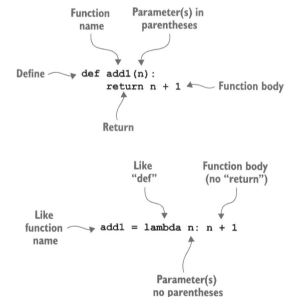

Figure 8.7 Both def and lambda are used to create functions.

In both versions of the add1 definition, using def and lambda, the argument to the function is n. In the usual named function, def add(n), the argument is defined in the parentheses just after the function name. In the lambda n version, there is no function name and no parentheses around the function's parameter, n.

There is no difference in how you can use the two types of functions. They are both functions:

```
>>> type(lambda x: x)
<class 'function'>
```

If you are comfortable with using add1() in a list comprehension, like this,

```
>>> [add1(n) for n in [1, 2, 3]]
[2, 3, 4]
```

it's a short step to using the map() function.

The map() function is a lazy function, like the range() function we looked at earlier. It won't create the values until you actually need them, as compared to a list comprehension, which will produce the resulting list immediately. I don't personally tend to worry about the performance of the code as much as I do the readability. When I write code for myself, I prefer to use map(), but you should write code that makes the most sense for you and your teammates.

To force the results from map() in the REPL, we need to use the list() function:

```
>>> list(map(add1, [1, 2, 3]))
[2, 3, 4]
```

We can write the list comprehension with the add1() code in line:

```
>>> [n + 1 for n in [1, 2, 3]]
[2, 3, 4]
```

That looks very similar to the lambda code (as illustrated in figure 8.8):

```
>>> list(map(lambda n: n + 1, [1, 2, 3]))
[2, 3, 4]
```

```
map(lambda n: n + 1, [1, 2, 3])

[2, 3, 4]
```

Figure 8.8 The map() function will create a new list from processing each element of an iterable through a given function.

Here is how we could use map():

```
def main():
    args = get_args()
    vowel = args.vowel
    text = map(
        lambda c: vowel if c in 'aeiou' else vowel.upper()
        if c in 'AEIOU' else c, args.text)

    print(''.join(text))
```

The map() function wants a function for the first argument and an iterable for the second.

Use lambda to create an anonymous function that accepts a character, c.

args.text is the second argument to map(). Technically, args.text is a string, but, because map() expects this argument to be a list, the string will be coerced to a list.

map() returns a new list to the text variable. We join it on the empty string to print it.

Higher-order functions

The map() function is called a *higher-order function* (HOF) because it takes *another function* as an argument, which is wicked cool. Later we'll use another HOF called filter().

Method 7: Using map() with a named function

We are not required to use map() with a lambda expression. Any function at all will work, so let's go back to using our new_char() function:

```
def main():
    args = get_args()
    vowel = args.vowel

    def new_char(c):
        return vowel if c in 'aeiou' else vowel.upper() if c in 'AEIOU' else c

    print(''.join(map(new_char, args.text)))
```

Define a function that will return the proper character. Note that I'm using the closure version so as to reference the "vowel" argument.

Use map() to apply new_char() to all the characters in args.text. The result is a list of characters, and we can use str.join() to turn them into a new string for print().

Notice that map() uses new_char *without parentheses* as the first argument. If you added the parentheses, you'd be *calling* the function and would see this error:

```
>>> text = ''.join(map(new_char(), text))
Traceback (most recent call last):
  File "<stdin>", line 1, in <module>
TypeError: new_char() missing 1 required positional argument: 'c'
```

As shown in figure 8.9, map() takes each character from text and passes it as the argument to the new_char() function, which decides whether to return a vowel or the original character. The result of mapping these characters is a new list of characters that we str.join() on the empty string to create a new version of text.

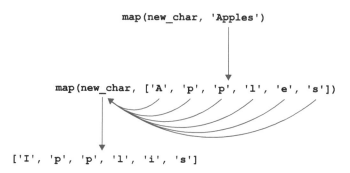

Figure 8.9 map() will apply a given function to each element of an iterable. A string will be processed as a list of characters.

METHOD 8: USING REGULAR EXPRESSIONS

A *regular expression* is a way to describe patterns of text. Regular expressions (also called "regexes") are a separate domain-specific language (DSL). They really have nothing whatsoever to do with Python. They have their own syntax and rules, and they are used in many places, from command-line tools to databases. Regexes are incredibly powerful and well worth the effort to learn.

To use regular expressions, you must `import re` in your code to import the regular expression module:

```
>>> import re
```

In this example, we're trying to find characters that are vowels, which we can define as the letters "a," "e," "i," "o," and "u." To describe this idea using a regular expression, we put those characters inside square brackets:

```
>>> pattern = '[aeiou]'
```

We can use the "substitute" function, `re.sub()`, to find all the vowels and replace them with the given `vowel`. The square brackets around the vowels `'[aeiou]'` create a *character class*, meaning anything matching one of the characters listed inside the brackets.

The second argument is the string that will replace the found strings—here it is the `vowel` provided by the user. The third argument is the string we want to change, which is the `text` from the user:

```
>>> vowel = 'o'
>>> re.sub(pattern, vowel, 'Apples and bananas!')
'Applos ond bononos!'
```

That misses the capital "A," so we'll have to handle both lower- and uppercase. Here is how we could write that:

```
def main():
    args = get_args()
    text = args.text
    vowel = args.vowel
    text = re.sub('[aeiou]', vowel, text)          ◁─── Substitute any of the lowercase
                                                         vowels with the given vowel
                                                         (which is lowercase because of
                                                         the restrictions in get_args()).
    text = re.sub('[AEIOU]', vowel.upper(), text)  ◁─┐ Substitute any of the
    print(text)                                       │ uppercase vowels with
                                                      │ the uppercase vowel.
```

If you prefer, we could squash the two calls to `re.sub()` into one, just as we did with the `str.replace()` method shown earlier:

```
>>> text = 'Apples and Bananas!'
>>> text = re.sub('[AEIOU]', vowel.upper(), re.sub('[aeiou]', vowel, text))
>>> text
'Opplos ond Bononos!'
```

One of the biggest differences between this solution and all the others is that we use regular expressions to describe what we are looking for. We didn't have to write the code to identify the vowels. This is more along the lines of *declarative* programming. We declare what we want, and the computer does the grunt work!

8.4 Refactoring with tests

There are many ways to solve this problem. The most important step is to get your program to work properly. Tests let you know when you've reached that point. From there, you can explore other ways to solve the problem and keep using the tests to ensure you still have a correct program.

Tests provide you with great freedom to be creative. Always be thinking about tests you can write for your own programs, so that when you change them later, they will always keep working.

I showed many ways to solve this seemingly trivial problem. Some of the techniques using higher-order functions and regular expression are quite advanced techniques. It might seem like driving a finishing nail with a sledgehammer, but I want to start introducing you to programming ideas that I'll visit again and again in later chapters.

If you only really understood the first few solutions, that's fine! Just stick with me. The more times you see these ideas applied in different contexts, the more they will begin to make sense.

8.5 Going further

Write a version of the program that collapses multiple adjacent vowels into a single substituted value. For example, "quick" should become "qack" and not "qaack."

Summary

- You can use `argparse` to limit an argument's values to a `list` of `choices` that you define.
- Strings cannot be directly modified, but the `str.replace()` and `str.translate()` methods can create a *new, modified string* from an existing string.
- A `for` loop on a string will iterate the characters of the string.
- A list comprehension is a shorthand way to write a `for` loop inside `[]` to create a new `list`.
- Functions can be defined inside other functions. Their visibility is then limited to the enclosing function.
- Functions can reference variables declared within the same scope, creating a closure.
- The `map()` function is similar to a list comprehension. It will create a new, modified list by applying some function to every member of a given list. The original list will not be changed.
- Regular expressions provide a syntax for describing patterns of text with the `re` module. The `re.sub()` method will substitute found patterns with new text. The original text will be unchanged.

Dial-a-Curse: Generating random insults from lists of words

"He or she is a slimy-sided, frog-mouthed, silt-eating slug with the brains of a turtle."

—Dial-A-Curse

Random events are at the heart of interesting games and puzzles. Humans quickly grow bored of things that are always the same. I think one reason people may choose to have pets and children is to inject some randomness into their lives. Let's learn how to make our programs more interesting by having them behave differently each time they are run.

This exercise will show you how to randomly select one or more elements from lists of options. To explore randomness, we'll create a program called abuse.py that will insult the user by randomly selecting adjectives and nouns to create slanderous epithets.

In order to test randomness, though, we need to control it. It turns out that "random" events on computers are rarely truly random but only *pseudo-random*, which means we can control them by using a "seed."[1] Each time you use the same seed, you will get the same "random" choices!

Shakespeare had some of the best insults, so we'll draw from the vocabulary of his works. Here is the list of adjectives you should use:

bankrupt base caterwauling corrupt cullionly detestable dishonest false filthsome filthy foolish foul gross heedless indistinguishable infected insatiate irksome lascivious

---

[1] "The generation of random numbers is too important to be left to chance."—Robert R. Coveyou

lecherous loathsome lubbery old peevish rascaly rotten ruinous scurilous scurvy slanderous sodden-witted thin-faced toad-spotted unmannered vile wall-eyed

And these are the nouns:

Judas Satan ape ass barbermonger beggar block boy braggart butt carbuncle coward coxcomb cur dandy degenerate fiend fishmonger fool gull harpy jack jolthead knave liar lunatic maw milksop minion ratcatcher recreant rogue scold slave swine traitor varlet villain worm

For instance, it might produce the following:

```
$ ./abuse.py
You slanderous, rotten block!
You lubbery, scurilous ratcatcher!
You rotten, foul liar!
```

In this exercise, you will learn to

- Use `parser.error()` from `argparse` to throw errors
- Control randomness with random seeds
- Take random choices and samples from Python lists
- Iterate an algorithm a specified number of times with a `for` loop
- Format output strings

9.1 Writing abuse.py

You should go into the 09_abuse directory to create your new program. Let's start by looking at the usage statement it should produce:

```
$ ./abuse.py -h
usage: abuse.py [-h] [-a adjectives] [-n insults] [-s seed]

Heap abuse

optional arguments:
  -h, --help            show this help message and exit
  -a adjectives, --adjectives adjectives
                        Number of adjectives (default: 2)
  -n insults, --number insults
                        Number of insults (default: 3)
  -s seed, --seed seed  Random seed (default: None)
```

All parameters are options that have default values, so our program will be able to run with no arguments at all.

For instance, the -n or --number option will have a default of 3 and will control the number of insults:

```
$ ./abuse.py --number 2
You filthsome, cullionly fiend!
You false, thin-faced minion!
```

The -a or --adjectives option should default to 2 and will determine how many adjectives are used in each insult:

```
$ ./abuse.py --adjectives 3
You caterwauling, heedless, gross coxcomb!
You sodden-witted, rascaly, lascivious varlet!
You dishonest, lecherous, foolish varlet!
```

Lastly, the -s or --seed option will control the random choices in the program by setting an initial value. The default should be the special None value, which is like an undefined value.

Because the program will use a random seed, the following output should be exactly reproducible by any user on any machine at any time:

```
$ ./abuse.py --seed 1
You filthsome, cullionly fiend!
You false, thin-faced minion!
You sodden-witted, rascaly cur!
```

When run with no arguments, the program should generate insults using the defaults:

```
$ ./abuse.py
You foul, false varlet!
You filthy, insatiate fool!
You lascivious, corrupt recreant!
```

I recommend you start by copying the template/template.py file to abuse/abuse.py or by using new.py to create the abuse.py program in the 09_abuse directory of your repository.

Figure 9.1 is a string diagram that illustrates the parameters for the program.

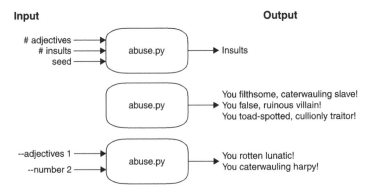

Figure 9.1   The abuse.py program will accept options for the number of insults to create, the number of adjectives per insult, and a random seed value.

9.1.1 Validating arguments

The options for the number of insults and adjectives and the random seed should all be int values. If you define each using type=int (remember, there are no quotes around the int), argparse will handle the validation and conversion of the arguments to int values for you. That is, just by defining type=int, the following error will be generated for you if a string is entered:

```
$ ./abuse.py -n foo
usage: abuse.py [-h] [-a adjectives] [-n insults] [-s seed]
abuse.py: error: argument -n/--number: invalid int value: 'foo'
```

Not only must the value be a number, but it must be an *integer* which means it must be a whole number, so argparse will complain if you give it something that looks like a float. Note that you can use type=float when you actually want a floating-point value:

```
$ ./abuse.py -a 2.1
usage: abuse.py [-h] [-a adjectives] [-n insults] [-s seed]
abuse.py: error: argument -a/--adjectives: invalid int value: '2.1'
```

Additionally, if either --number or --adjectives is less than 1, your program should exit with an error code and message:

```
$ ./abuse.py -a -4
usage: abuse.py [-h] [-a adjectives] [-n insults] [-s seed]
abuse.py: error: --adjectives "-4" must be > 0
$ ./abuse.py -n -4
usage: abuse.py [-h] [-a adjectives] [-n insults] [-s seed]
abuse.py: error: --number "-4" must be > 0
```

As you start to write your own programs and tests, I recommend you steal from the tests I've written.[2] Let's take a look at one of the tests in test.py to see how the program is tested:

Run the program using getstatusoutput() from the subprocess[3] module using a bad -a value. This function returns the exit value (which I put into rv for "return value") and standard out (out).

The name of the function must start with "test_" in order for Pytest to find and run it.

Use the random.choice() function to randomly select a value from the range() of numbers from -10 to 0. We will use this same function in our program, so note here how it is called.

```
def test_bad_adjective_num():
    """bad_adjectives"""

    n = random.choice(range(-10, 0))
    rv, out = getstatusoutput(f'{prg} -a {n}')
    assert rv != 0
    assert re.search(f'--adjectives "{n}" must be > 0', out)
```

Assert that the return value (rv) is not 0, where "0" would indicate success (or "zero errors").

Assert that the output somewhere contains the statement that the --adjectives argument must be greater than 0.

---

[2] "Good composers borrow. Great ones steal." — Igor Stravinsky

[3] The subprocess module allows you to run a command from inside your program. The subprocess .getoutput() function will capture the output from the command, while the subprocess.getstatusoutput() will capture both the exit value and the output from the command.

There's no simple way to tell `argparse` that the numbers for adjectives and insults must be greater than zero, so we'll have to check those values ourselves. We'll use the verification ideas from section A.4.7 in the appendix. There I introduce the `parser.error()` function, which you can call inside the `get_args()` function to do the following:

1 Print the short usage statement
2 Print an error message to the user
3 Stop execution of the program
4 Exit with a nonzero exit value to indicate an error

That is, `get_args()` normally finishes with this:

```
return args.parse_args()
```

Instead, we'll put the `args` into a variable and check the `args.adjectives` value to see if it's less than 1. If it is, we'll call `parser.error()` with an error message to report to the user:

```
args = parser.parse_args()

if args.adjectives < 1:
    parser.error(f'--adjectives "{args.adjectives}" must be > 0')
```

We'll also do this for `args.number`. If they are both fine, you can `return` the arguments to the calling function:

```
return args
```

9.1.2 *Importing and seeding the random module*

Once you have defined and validated all the program's arguments, you are ready to heap scorn upon the user. First, we need to add `import random` to our program so we can use functions from that module to select adjectives and nouns. It's best practice to list all the `import` statements, one module at a time, at the top of a program.

In `main()`, the first thing we need to do is call `get_args()` to get our arguments. The next step is to pass the `args.seed` value to the `random.seed()` function:

```
def main()
    args = get_args()
    random.seed(args.seed)   ◄──
```

We call the random.seed() function to set the initial value of the random module's state. There is no return value from random.seed()—the only change is internal to the random module.

You can read about the `random.seed()` function in the REPL:

```
>>> import random
>>> help(random.seed)
```

There you'll learn that the function will "initialize internal state [of the `random` module] from hashable object." That is, we set an initial value from some *hashable* Python type. Both the `int` and `str` types are hashable, but the tests are written with the expectation that you will define the seed argument as an `int`. (Remember that the character `'1'` is different from the *integer value* `1`!)

The default value for `args.seed` should be `None`. If the user has not indicated any seed, then setting `random.seed(None)` is the same as not setting it at all.

If you look at the test.py program, you will notice that all the tests that expect a particular output will pass an `-s` or `--seed` argument. Here is the first test for output:

Run the program using getoutput() from the subprocess module using a seed value of 1 and requesting 1 insult. This function returns only the output from the program.

```
def test_01():
    out = getoutput(f'{prg} -s 1 -n 1')
    assert out.strip() == 'You filthsome, cullionly fiend!'
```

Verify that the entire output is the one expected insult.

This means test.py will run your program and capture the output into the `out` variable:

```
$ ./abuse.py -s 1 -n 1
You filthsome, cullionly fiend!
```

It will then verify that the program did in fact produce the expected number of insults with the expected selection of words.

9.1.3   *Defining the adjectives and nouns*

Earlier in the chapter, I gave you a long list of adjectives and nouns that you should use in your program. You could create a `list` by individually quoting each word:

```
>>> adjectives = ['bankrupt', 'base', 'caterwauling']
```

Or you could save yourself a good bit of typing by using the `str.split()` method to create a new `list` from a `str` by splitting on spaces:

```
>>> adjectives = 'bankrupt base caterwauling'.split()
>>> adjectives
['bankrupt', 'base', 'caterwauling']
```

If you try to make one giant string of all the adjectives, it will be very long and so will wrap around in your code editor and look ugly. I recommend you use triple quotes (either single or double quotes), which will allow you to include newlines:

```
>>> """
... bankrupt base
... caterwauling
... """.split()
['bankrupt', 'base', 'caterwauling']
```

Once you have variables for `adjectives` and `nouns`, you should check that you have the right number of each:

```
>>> assert len(adjectives) == 36
>>> assert len(nouns) == 39
```

NOTE   In order to pass the tests, your adjectives and nouns must be in alphabetical order as they were provided.

9.1.4   *Taking random samples and choices*

In addition to the random.seed() function, we will also use the random.choice() and random.sample() functions. In the test_bad_adjective_num function in section 9.1.1, you saw one example of using random .choice(). We can use it similarly to select a noun from the list of nouns.

```
harpy
jack
jolthead
knave
liar
```

Notice that this function returns a single item, so, given a list of str values, it will return a single str:

```
>>> random.choice(nouns)
'braggart'
>>> random.choice(nouns)
'milksop'
```

For the adjectives, you should use random.sample(). If you read the help(random .sample) output, you will see that this function takes some list of items and a k parameter for how many items to return:

```
sample(population, k) method of random.Random instance
    Chooses k unique random elements from a population sequence or set.
```

Note that this function returns a new list:

```
>>> random.sample(adjectives, 2)
['detestable', 'peevish']
>>> random.sample(adjectives, 3)
['slanderous', 'detestable', 'base']
```

There is also a random.choices() function that works similarly but which might select the same items twice because it samples "with replacement." We will not use that.

9.1.5   *Formatting the output*

The output of the program is a --number of insults, which you could generate using a for loop and the range() function. It doesn't matter here that range() starts at zero. What's important is that it generates three values:

```
>>> for n in range(3):
...    print(n)
...
0
1
2
```

You can loop the --number of times needed, select your sample of adjectives and your noun, and then format the output. Each insult should start with the string "You", then have the adjectives joined on a comma and a space, then the noun, and finish with an exclamation point (figure 9.2). You could use either an f-string or the str.format() function to print() the output to STDOUT.

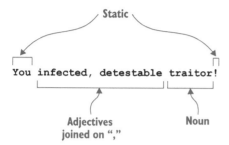

Figure 9.2   Each insult will combine the chosen adjectives joined on commas with the selected noun and some static bits of text.

Here are a few hints:

- Perform the check for positive values for --adjectives and --number *inside* the get_args() function, and use parser.error() to throw the error while printing a message and the usage.
- If you set the default of args.seed to None and use type=int, you can directly pass the value to random.seed(). When the value is None, it will be like not setting the value at all.
- Use a for loop with the range() function to create a loop that will execute the --number of times to generate each insult.
- Look at the random.sample() and random.choice() functions for help in selecting some adjectives and a noun.
- You can use three single quotes (''') or double quotes (""") to create a multi-line string and then use str.split() to get a list of strings. This is easier than individually quoting a long list of shorter strings (such as the list of adjectives and nouns).
- To construct an insult to print, you can use the + operator to concatenate strings, use the str.join() method, or use format strings.

Now give this your best shot before reading ahead to the solution, you snotty-faced heap of parrot droppings!

9.2   *Solution*

This is the first solution where I use parser.error() to augment the validation of the arguments. I also incorporate triple-quoted strings and introduce the random module, which is quite fun unless you're a vacuous, coffee-nosed, malodorous git.

```
#!/usr/bin/env python3
"""Heap abuse"""

import argparse
import random
```

Bring in the random module so we can call functions.

```
# --------------------------------------------------
def get_args():
    """Get command-line arguments"""

    parser = argparse.ArgumentParser(
        description='Heap abuse',
        formatter_class=argparse.ArgumentDefaultsHelpFormatter)

    parser.add_argument('-a',
                        '--adjectives',
                        help='Number of adjectives',
                        metavar='adjectives',
                        type=int,
                        default=2)
```

Define the parameter for the number of adjectives, setting type=int and the default value.

```
    parser.add_argument('-n',
                        '--number',
                        help='Number of adjectives',
                        metavar='adjectives',
                        type=int,
                        default=3)
```

Similarly define the parameter for the number of insults as an integer with a default.

The random seed default should be None.

```
    parser.add_argument('-s',
                        '--seed',
                        help='Random seed',
                        metavar='seed',
                        type=int,
                        default=None)
```

Get the result of parsing the command-line arguments. The argparse module will handle errors such as non-integer values.

```
    args = parser.parse_args()

    if args.adjectives < 1:
        parser.error('--adjectives "{}" must be > 0'.format(args.adjectives))
```

Check that args.adjectives is greater than 0. If there is a problem, call parser.error() with the error message.

Similarly check args.number.

```
    if args.number < 1:
        parser.error('--number "{}" must be > 0'.format(args.number))

    return args
```

At this point, all the user's arguments have been validated, so return the arguments to the caller.

```
# --------------------------------------------------
def main():
    """Make a jazz noise here"""

    args = get_args()
    random.seed(args.seed)

    adjectives = """
bankrupt base caterwauling corrupt cullionly detestable dishonest false
filthsome filthy foolish foul gross heedless indistinguishable infected
```

This is where the program actually begins as it is the first action inside main(). I always start off by getting the arguments.

Set random.seed() using whatever value was passed by the user. Any integer value is valid, and I know that argparse has handled the validation and conversion of the argument to an integer.

Create a list of adjectives by splitting the very long string contained in the triple quotes.

```
insatiate irksome lascivious lecherous loathsome lubbery old peevish
rascaly rotten ruinous scurilous scurvy slanderous sodden-witted
thin-faced toad-spotted unmannered vile wall-eyed
""".strip().split()
```

Do the same for the list of nouns.

```
nouns = """
Judas Satan ape ass barbermonger beggar block boy braggart butt
carbuncle coward coxcomb cur dandy degenerate fiend fishmonger fool
gull harpy jack jolthead knave liar lunatic maw milksop minion
ratcatcher recreant rogue scold slave swine traitor varlet villain worm
""".strip().split()
```

```
    for _ in range(args.number):
        adjs = ', '.join(random.sample(adjectives, k=args.adjectives))
        print(f'You {adjs} {random.choice(nouns)}!')


# --------------------------------------------------
if __name__ == '__main__':
    main()
```

Use an f-string to format the output to print().

Use a for loop over the range() of the args.number. Since I don't actually need the value from range(), I can use the _ to disregard it.

Use the random.sample() function to select the correct number of adjectives and join them on the comma-space string.

9.3   *Discussion*

I trust you did not peek at the solution before you passed all the tests or else you are a rascaly, filthsome swine.

9.3.1   *Defining the arguments*

More than half of my solution is defining the program's arguments to argparse. The effort is well worth the result. Because I set type=int, argparse will ensure that each argument is a valid integer value. Notice that there are no quotes around the int—it's not the string 'int' but a reference to the class in Python:

```
parser.add_argument('-a',
                    '--adjectives',
                    help='Number of adjectives',
                    metavar='adjectives',
                    type=int,
                    default=2)
```

The short flag

The long flag

The help message

A description of the parameter

The actual Python type for converting the input; note that this is the bare word int for the integer class

The default value for the number of adjectives per insult

I set reasonable defaults for all the program's options so that no input is required from the user. The --seed option should default to None so that the default behavior is to generate pseudo-random insults. This value is only important for testing purposes.

9.3.2   *Using parser.error()*

I really love the `argparse` module for all the work it saves me. In particular, I often use `parser.error()` when I find there is a problem with an argument. This function will do four things:

1 Print the short usage of the program to the user
2 Print a specific message about the problem
3 Halt execution of the program
4 Return an error code to the operating system

I'm using `parser.error()` here because, while I can ask `argparse` to verify that a given value is an `int`, I can't as easily say that it must be a *positive* value. I can, however, inspect the value myself and halt the program if there is a problem. I do all this inside `get_args()` so that, by the time I get the `args` in my `main()` function, I know they have been validated.

I highly recommend you tuck this tip into your back pocket. It can prove quite handy, saving you loads of time validating user input and generating useful error messages. (And it's quite likely that the future user of your program will be *you*, so you will really appreciate your efforts.)

9.3.3   *Program exit values and STDERR*

I would like to highlight the exit value of the program. Under normal circumstances, programs should exit with a value of 0. In computer science, we often think of 0 as a `False` value, but here it's quite positive. In this instance we should think of it as "zero errors."

If you use `sys.exit()` in your code to exit a program prematurely, the default exit value is 0. If you want to indicate to the operating system or some calling program that your program exited with an error, you should return *any value other than* 0. You can also call the function with a string, which will be printed as an error message, and Python will exit with the value 1. If you run this in the REPL, you will be returned to the command line:

```
>>> import sys
>>> sys.exit('You gross, thin-faced worm!')
You gross, thin-faced worm!
```

Additionally, it's common for all error messages to be printed not to STDOUT (standard out) but to STDERR (standard error). Many command shells (like Bash) can segregate these two output channels using 1 for STDOUT and 2 for STDERR. When using the Bash shell, note how I can use 2> to redirect STDERR to the file called err so that nothing appears on STDOUT:

```
$ ./abuse.py -a -1 2>err
```

I can verify that the expected error messages are in the err file:

```
$ cat err
usage: abuse.py [-h] [-a adjectives] [-n insults] [-s seed]
abuse.py: error: --adjectives "-1" must be > 0
```

If you were to handle all of this yourself, you would need to write something like this:

> Print the short usage. You can also use parser.print_help() to print the more verbose output for -h.

```
if args.adjectives < 1:
    parser.print_usage()
    print(f'--adjectives "{args.adjectives}" must be > 0', file=sys.stderr)
    sys.exit(1)
```

> Exit the program with a value that is not 0 to indicate an error.

> Print the error message to the sys.stderr file handle. This is similar to the sys.stdout file handle we used in chapter 5.

Writing pipelines

As you write more and more programs, you may eventually start chaining them together. We often call these *pipelines*, as the output of one program is "piped" to become the input for the next program. If there is an error in any part of the pipeline, you'll generally want the entire operation to stop so that the problems can be fixed. A nonzero return value from any program is a warning flag to halt operations.

9.3.4 *Controlling randomness with random.seed()*

The pseudo-random events in the random module follow from a given starting point. That is, each time you start from a given state, the events will happen in the same way. We can use the random.seed() function to set that starting point.

The seed value must be *hashable*. According to the Python documentation (https:// docs.python.org/3.1/glossary.html), "all of Python's immutable built-in objects are hashable, while no mutable containers (such as lists or dictionaries) are." In this program, we have to use an integer value because the tests were written using integer seeds. When you write you own programs, you may choose to use a string or other hashable type.

The default for our seed is the special None value, which is a bit like an undefined state. Calling random.seed(None) is essentially the same as not setting the seed at all, so it makes it safe to write this:

```
random.seed(args.seed)
```

9.3.5   *Iterating with range() and using throwaway variables*

To generate some --number of insults, we can use the range() function. Because we don't need the numbers returned by range(), we use the underscore (_) as the variable name to indicate this is throwaway value:

```
>>> num_insults = 2
>>> for _ in range(num_insults):
...     print('An insult!')
...
An insult!
An insult!
```

The underscore is a valid variable name in Python. You can assign to it and use it:

```
>>> _ = 'You indistinguishable, filthsome carbuncle!'
>>> _
'You indistinguishable, filthsome carbuncle!'
```

The use of the underscore as a variable name is a convention to indicate that we don't intend to use the value. That is, if we had said for num in range(...), some tools like Pylint will see that the num variable is not used and will report this as a possible error (and well it could be). The _ indicates that you're throwing this value away, which is good information for your future self, some other user, or external tools to know.

Note that you can use multiple _ variables in the same statement. For instance, I can unpack a 3-tuple so as to get the middle value:

```
>>> x = 'Jesus', 'Mary', 'Joseph'
>>> _, name, _ = x
>>> name
'Mary'
```

9.3.6   *Constructing the insults*

To create my list of adjectives, I used the str.split() method on a long, multiline string enclosed in triple quotes. I think this is probably the easiest way to get all these strings into my program. The triple quotes allow us to enter line breaks, which single quotes would not allow:

```
>>> adjectives = """
... bankrupt base caterwauling corrupt cullionly detestable dishonest
... false filthsome filthy foolish foul gross heedless indistinguishable
... infected insatiate irksome lascivious lecherous loathsome lubbery old
... peevish rascaly rotten ruinous scurilous scurvy slanderous
... sodden-witted thin-faced toad-spotted unmannered vile wall-eyed
... """.strip().split()
>>> nouns = """
... Judas Satan ape ass barbermonger beggar block boy braggart butt
... carbuncle coward coxcomb cur dandy degenerate fiend fishmonger fool
... gull harpy jack jolthead knave liar lunatic maw milksop minion
... ratcatcher recreant rogue scold slave swine traitor varlet villain worm
... """.strip().split()
```

```
>>> len(adjectives)
36
>>> len(nouns)
39
```

Because we need one or more adjectives, the random.sample() function is a good choice. It will return a list of items randomly selected from a given list:

```
>>> import random
>>> random.sample(adjectives, k=3)
['filthsome', 'cullionly', 'insatiate']
```

The random.choice() function is appropriate for selecting just one item from a list, such as the noun for our invective:

```
>>> random.choice(nouns)
'boy'
```

Next we need to concatenate the epithets using ', ' (a comma and a space) similar to what we did in chapter 3 for our picnic items. The str.join() function is perfect for this:

```
>>> adjs = random.sample(adjectives, k=3)
>>> adjs
['thin-faced', 'scurvy', 'sodden-witted']
>>> ', '.join(adjs)
'thin-faced, scurvy, sodden-witted'
```

To create the insult, we can combine the adjectives and nouns inside our template using an f-string:

```
>>> adjs = ', '.join(random.sample(adjectives, k=3))
>>> print(f'You {adjs} {random.choice(nouns)}!')
You heedless, thin-faced, gross recreant!
```

And now I have a handy way to make enemies and influence people.

9.4 Going further

- Read your adjectives and nouns from files that are passed as arguments.
- Add tests to verify that the files are processed correctly and new insults are still stinging.

Summary

- Use the parser.error() function to print a short usage statement, report the problem, and exit the program with an error value.
- Triple-quoted strings may contain line breaks, unlike regular single- or double-quoted strings.

- The `str.split()` method is a useful way to create a `list` of string values from a long string.
- The `random.seed()` function can be used to make reproducible pseudo-random selections each time a program is run.
- The `random.choice()` and `random.sample()` functions are useful for randomly selecting one or several items from a list of choices, respectively.

Telephone: Randomly mutating strings

"What we have here is a failure to communicate."

—Captain

Now that we've played with randomness, let's apply the idea to randomly mutating a string. This is interesting, because strings are actually *immutable* in Python. We'll have to figure out a way around that.

To explore these ideas, we'll write a version of the game of Telephone where a secret message is whispered through a line or circle of people. Each time the message is transmitted, it's usually changed in some unpredictable way. The last person to receive the message will say it out loud to compare it to the original message. Often the results are nonsensical and possibly comical.

We will write a program called telephone.py that will mimic this game. It will print "You said: " and the original text, followed by "I heard: " with a modified version of the message. As in chapter 5, the input text may come from the command line:

```
$ ./telephone.py 'The quick brown fox jumps over the lazy dog.'
You said: "The quick brown fox jumps over the lazy dog."
I heard : "TheMquick brown fox jumps ovMr t:e lamy dog."
```

Or it may come from a file:

```
$ ./telephone.py ../inputs/fox.txt
You said: "The quick brown fox jumps over the lazy dog."
I heard : "The quick]b'own fox jumps ovek the la[y dog."
```

The program should accept an -m or --mutations option, which should be a floating-point number between 0 and 1 with a default value of 0.1 (10%). This will be the percentage of the number of letters that should be altered. For instance, .5 means that 50% of the letters should be changed:

```
$ ./telephone.py ../inputs/fox.txt -m .5
You said: "The quick brown fox jumps over the lazy dog."
I heard : "F#eYquJsY ZrHnna"o. Muz/$ Nver t/Relazy dA!."
```

Because we are using the random module, we'll accept an int value for the -s or --seed option, so that we can reproduce our pseudo-random selections:

```
$ ./telephone.py ../inputs/fox.txt -s 1
You said: "The quick brown fox jumps over the lazy dog."
I heard : "The 'uicq brown *ox jumps over the l-zy dog."
```

Figure 10.1 shows a string diagram of the program.

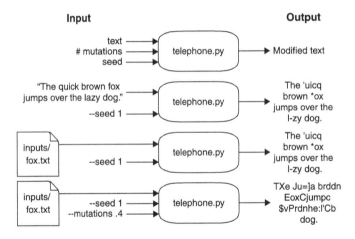

Figure 10.1 The telephone program will accept text and possibly some percentage of mutations, along with a random seed. The output will be a randomly mutated version of the input text.

In this exercise, you will learn to

- Round numbers
- Use the string module
- Modify strings and lists to introduce random mutations

10.1 Writing telephone.py

I recommend you use the new.py program to create a new program called tele-
phone.py in the 10_telephone directory. You could do this from the top level of the
repository like so:

```
$ ./bin/new.py 10_telephone/telephone.py
```

You could also copy template/template.py to 10_telephone/telephone.py. Modify the
get_args() function until your -h output matches the following. I would recommend
you use type=float for the mutations parameter:

```
$ ./telephone.py -h
usage: telephone.py [-h] [-s seed] [-m mutations] text

Telephone

positional arguments:
  text                  Input text or file

optional arguments:
  -h, --help            show this help message and exit
  -s seed, --seed seed  Random seed (default: None)
  -m mutations, --mutations mutations
                        Percent mutations (default: 0.1)
```

Now run the test suite. You should pass at least the first two tests (the telephone.py
program exists and prints a usage statement when run with -h or --help).

The next two tests check that your --seed and --mutations options both reject non-
numeric values. This should happen automatically if you define these parameters using
the int and float types, respectively. That is, your program should behave like this:

```
$ ./telephone.py -s blargh foo
usage: telephone.py [-h] [-s seed] [-m mutations] text
telephone.py: error: argument -s/--seed: invalid int value: 'blargh'
$ ./telephone.py -m blargh foo
usage: telephone.py [-h] [-s seed] [-m mutations] text
telephone.py: error: argument -m/--mutations: invalid float value: 'blargh'
```

The next test checks if the program rejects values for --mutations outside the range
0–1 (where both bounds are inclusive). This is not a check that you can easily describe
to argparse, so I suggest you look at how we handled the validation of the arguments
in abuse.py in chapter 9. In the get_args() function of that program, we manually
checked the value of the arguments and used the parser.error() function to throw
an error. Note that a --mutations value of 0 is acceptable, in which case we will print
out the input text without modifications. Your program should do this:

```
$ ./telephone.py -m -1 foobar
usage: telephone.py [-h] [-s seed] [-m mutations] text
telephone.py: error: --mutations "-1.0" must be between 0 and 1
```

This is another program that accepts input text either from the command line or from a file, and I suggest you look at the solution in chapter 5. Inside the get_args() function, you can use os.path.isfile() to detect whether the text argument is a file. If it is a file, read the contents of the file for the text value.

Once you have taken care of all the program parameters, start your main() function with setting the random.seed() and echoing back the given text:

```
def main():
    args = get_args()
    random.seed(args.seed)
    print(f'You said: "{args.text}"')
    print(f'I heard : "{args.text}"')
```

Your program should handle command-line text:

```
$ ./telephone.py 'The quick brown fox jumps over the lazy dog.'
You said: "The quick brown fox jumps over the lazy dog."
I heard : "The quick brown fox jumps over the lazy dog."
```

And it should handle an input file:

```
$ ./telephone.py ../inputs/fox.txt
You said: "The quick brown fox jumps over the lazy dog."
I heard : "The quick brown fox jumps over the lazy dog."
```

At this point, your code should pass up to test_for_echo(). The next tests start asking you to mutate the input, so let's discuss how to do that.

10.1.1 *Calculating the number of mutations*

The number of letters that need to be changed can be calculated by multiplying the length of the input text by the args.mutations value. If we want to change 20% of the characters in "The quick brown fox..." string, we'll find that it is not a whole number:

```
>>> text = 'The quick brown fox jumps over the lazy dog.'
>>> mutations = .20
>>> len(text) * mutations
8.8
```

We can use the round() function to give us the nearest integer value. Read help(round) to learn how to round floating-point numbers to a specific number of digits:

```
>>> round(len(text) * mutations)
9
```

Note that you could also convert a float to an int by using the int function, but this truncates the fractional part of the number rather than rounding it:

```
>>> int(len(text) * mutations)
8
```

You will need this value for later, so let's save it in a variable:

```
>>> num_mutations = round(len(text) * mutations)
>>> assert num_mutations == 9
```

10.1.2 The mutation space

When we change a character, what will we change it to? For this, we'll use the `string` module. I encourage you to take a look at the documentation by importing the module and reading `help(string)`:

```
>>> import string
>>> help(string)
```

We can, for instance, get all the lowercase ASCII letters as follows. Note that this is not a method call as there are no parentheses `()` at the end:

```
>>> string.ascii_lowercase
'abcdefghijklmnopqrstuvwxyz'
```

This returns a `str`:

```
>>> type(string.ascii_lowercase)
<class 'str'>
```

For our program, we can use `string.ascii_letters` and `string.punctuation` to get strings of all the letters and punctuation. To concatenate the two strings together, we can use the + operator. We'll draw from this string to randomly select a character to replace another:

```
>>> alpha = string.ascii_letters + string.punctuation
>>> alpha
'abcdefghijklmnopqrstuvwxyzABCDEFGHIJKLMNOPQRSTUVWXYZ!"#$%&\'()*+,-
    ./:;<=>?@[\\]^_`{|}~'
```

Note that even if we both use the same random seed, you and I will get different results if our letters are in a different order. To ensure our results match, we'll both need to sort the `alpha` characters so they are in a consistent order.

10.1.3 Selecting the characters to mutate

There are at least two approaches we could take to choosing which characters to change: a *deterministic approach* where the results are always guaranteed to be the same and a *non-deterministic approach* where we employ chance to get close to a target. Let's examine the latter one first.

NON-DETERMINISTIC SELECTION

One way to choose the characters to change would be to mimic method 1 in chapter 8. We could iterate through each of the characters in our text and select a random number to decide whether to keep the original character or change it to some randomly selected value. If our random number is less than or equal to our mutations setting, we should change the character:

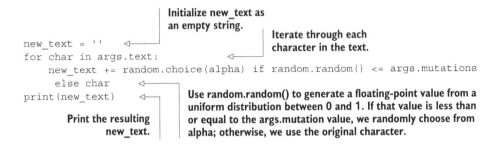

We used the `random.choice()` function in abuse.py in chapter 9 to randomly select *one* value from a list of choices. We can use it here to select a character from `alpha` if the `random.random()` value falls within the range of the `args.mutation` value (which we know is also a `float`).

The problem with this approach is that, by the end of the `for` loop, we are not guaranteed to have made exactly the correct number of changes. That is, we calculated that we should change 9 characters out of 44 when the mutation rate is 20%. We would expect to end up changing about 20% of the characters with this code, because a random value from a uniform distribution of values between 0 and 1 should be less than or equal to 0.2 about 20% of the time. Sometimes we might end up only changing 8 characters or other times we might change 10. Because of this uncertainty, this is approach would be considered *non-deterministic*.

Still, this is a really useful technique that you should note. Imagine you have an input file with millions or potentially billions of lines of text, and you want to randomly sample approximately 10% of the lines. The preceding approach would be reasonably fast and accurate. A larger sample size will help you get closer to the desired number of mutations.

RANDOMLY SAMPLING CHARACTERS

A deterministic approach to the million-line file would require first reading the entire input to count the number of lines, choosing which lines to take, and then going back through the file a second time to take those lines. This approach would take *much* longer than the method described above. Depending on how large the input file is, how the program is written, and how much memory your computer has, the program could possibly even crash your computer!

Our input is rather small, however, so we will use this algorithm because it has the advantages of being exact and testable. Rather than focusing on lines of text, though, we'll consider indexes of characters. You've seen the `str.replace()` method (in chapter 8), which allows us to change all instances of one string to another:

```
>>> 'foo'.replace('o', 'a')
'faa'
```

We can't use `str.replace()` because it will change every occurrence of some character, and we only want to change individual characters. Instead we can use the `random.sample()` function to select some indexes of the characters in the text. The first argument to `random.sample()` needs to be something like a `list`. We can give it a `range()` of numbers up to the length of our `text`.

Suppose our `text` is 44 characters long:

```
>>> text
'The quick brown fox jumps over the lazy dog.'
>>> len(text)
44
```

We can use the `range()` function to make a `list` of numbers up to 44:

```
>>> range(len(text))
range(0, 44)
```

Note that `range()` is a lazy function. It won't actually produce the 44 values until we force it, which we can do in the REPL using the `list()` function:

```
>>> list(range(len(text)))
```

We calculated earlier that the `num_mutations` value for altering 20% of `text` is 9. Here is one selection of indexes that could be changed:

```
>>> indexes = random.sample(range(len(text)), num_mutations)
>>> indexes
[13, 6, 31, 1, 24, 27, 0, 28, 17]
```

I suggest you use a `for` loop to iterate through each of these index values:

```
>>> for i in indexes:
...     print(f'{i:2} {text[i]}')
...
13 w
 6 i
31 t
 1 h
24 s
```

```
27 v
 0 T
28 e
17 o
```

You should replace the character at each index position with a randomly selected character from `alpha`:

```
>>> for i in indexes:
...     print(f'{i:2} {text[i]} changes to {random.choice(alpha)}')
...
13 w changes to b
 6 i changes to W
31 t changes to B
 1 h changes to #
24 s changes to d
27 v changes to :
 0 T changes to C
28 e changes to %
17 o changes to ,
```

I will introduce one other twist—we don't want the replacement value to ever be the same as the character it is replacing. Can you figure out how to get a subset of `alpha` that *does not* include the character at the position?

10.1.4 *Mutating a string*

Python `str` variables are *immutable*, meaning we cannot directly modify them. For instance, suppose we want to change the character `'w'` at position 13 to a `'b'`. It would be handy to directly modify `text[13]`, but that will create an exception:

```
>>> text[13] = 'b'
Traceback (most recent call last):
  File "<stdin>", line 1, in <module>
TypeError: 'str' object does not support item assignment
```

The only way to modify the `str` value `text` is to overwrite it with a new `str`. We need to create a new `str` with the following, as shown in figure 10.2:

- The part of `text` before a given index
- The randomly selected value from `alpha`
- The part of `text` after a given index

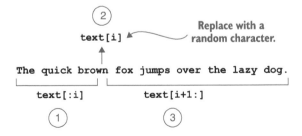

Figure 10.2 Create a new string by selecting the portion of the string up to the index, a new character, and the portion of the string after the index.

For 1 and 3, you can use string *slices*. For example, if the index i is 13, the slice before it is

```
>>> text[:13]
'The quick bro'
```

The part after it is

```
>>> text[14:]
'n fox jumps over the lazy dog.'
```

Using the three parts listed earlier, your for loop should be

```
for i in index:
    text = 1 + 2 + 3
```

Can you figure that out?

10.1.5 *Time to write*

OK, the lesson is over. You have to go write this now. Use the tests. Solve them one at a time. You can do this.

10.2 *Solution*

How different was your solution from mine? Let's look at one way to write a program that satisfies the tests:

```
#!/usr/bin/env python3
"""Telephone"""

import argparse
import os
import random
import string
```

Import the string module we'll need to select a random character.

```
# --------------------------------------------------
def get_args():
    """Get command-line arguments"""

    parser = argparse.ArgumentParser(
        description='Telephone',
        formatter_class=argparse.ArgumentDefaultsHelpFormatter)

    parser.add_argument('text', metavar='text', help='Input text or file')

    parser.add_argument('-s',
                        '--seed',
                        help='Random seed',
                        metavar='seed',
                        type=int,
                        default=None)
```

Define a positional argument for the text. This could be either a string of text or a file that needs to be read.

The --seed parameter is an integer value with a default of None.

If args.mutations is not in the acceptable range of 0–1, use
parser.error() to halt the program and print the given message. Note
the use of feedback to echo the bad args.mutation value to the user.

The --mutations parameter
is a floating-point value
with a default of 0.1.

```
parser.add_argument('-m',
                    '--mutations',
                    help='Percent mutations',
                    metavar='mutations',
                    type=float,
                    default=0.1)
```

Process the arguments from the
command line. If argparse detects
problems, such as non-numeric values
for the seed or mutations, the program
dies here and the user sees an error
message. If this call succeeds, argparse
has validated the arguments and
converted the values.

```
    args = parser.parse_args()

    if not 0 <= args.mutations <= 1:
        parser.error(f'--mutations "{args.mutations}" must be between 0 and 1')

    if os.path.isfile(args.text):
        args.text = open(args.text).read().rstrip()

    return args
```

If args.text names an existing
file, read that file for the
contents and overwrite the
original value of args.text.

Return the processed
arguments to the caller.

```
# --------------------------------------------------
def main():
    """Make a jazz noise here"""

    args = get_args()
    text = args.text
    random.seed(args.seed)
    alpha = ''.join(sorted(string.ascii_letters + string.punctuation))
    len_text = len(text)
    num_mutations = round(args.mutations * len_text)
    new_text = text

    for i in random.sample(range(len_text), num_mutations):
        new_char = random.choice(alpha.replace(new_text[i], ''))
        new_text = new_text[:i] + new_char + new_text[i + 1:]

    print(f'You said: "{text}"\nI heard : "{new_text}"')


# --------------------------------------------------
if __name__ == '__main__':
    main()
```

Set the random.seed() to the value
provided by the user. Remember
that the default value for args.seed
is None, which is the same as not
setting the seed.

Make a copy
of text.

Print the text.

Overwrite the text by concatenating the slice
before the current index with the new_char and
then the slice after the current index.

Figure the num_mutations by multiplying
the mutation rate by the length of the text.

Use random.choice () to select a new_char from
a string created by replacing the current
character (text[i]) in the alpha variable with
nothing. This ensures that the new character
cannot be the same as the one we are replacing.

Since we use len(text) more than
once, we put it into a variable.

Use random.sample () to get num_mutations
indexes to change. This function returns a list
that we can iterate using the for loop.

Set alpha to be the characters we'll use for replacements.
The sorted() function will return a new list of the
characters in the right order, and then we can use the
str.join() function to turn that back into a str value.

10.3 *Discussion*

There's nothing in get_args() that you haven't seen before. The --seed argument is an int that we will pass to the random.seed() function so as to control the randomness for testing. The default seed value is None so that we can call random.seed(args.seed) where None is the same as not setting it. The --mutations parameter is a float with a reasonable default, and we use parser.error() to create an error message if the value is not in the proper range. As in other programs, we test whether the text argument is a file and read the contents if it is.

10.3.1 *Mutating a string*

You saw earlier that we can't just change the text string:

```
>>> text = 'The quick brown fox jumps over the lazy dog.'
>>> text[13] = 'b'
Traceback (most recent call last):
  File "<stdin>", line 1, in <module>
TypeError: 'str' object does not support item assignment
```

We have to create a *new* string using the text before and after i, which we can get with string slices using text[start:stop]. If you leave out start, Python starts at 0 (the beginning of the string), and if you leave out stop, it goes to the end, so text[:] is a copy of the entire string.

If i is 13, the bit before i is

```
>>> i = 13
>>> text[:i]
'The quick bro'
```

The bit after i + 1 is

```
>>> text[i+1:]
'n fox jumps over the lazy dog.'
```

Now for what to put in the middle. I noted that we should use random.choice() to select a character from alpha, which is the combination of all the ASCII letters and punctuation *without* the current character. I use the str.replace() method to get rid of the current letter:

```
>>> alpha = ''.join(sorted(string.ascii_letters + string.punctuation))
>>> alpha.replace(text[i], '')
'!"#$%&\'()*+,-
     ./:;<=>?@ABCDEFGHIJKLMNOPQRSTUVWXYZ[\\]^_`abcdefghijklmnopqrstuvxyz{|}~'
```

Then I use that to get a new letter that won't include what it's replacing:

```
>>> new_char = random.choice(alpha.replace(text[i], ''))
>>> new_char
'Q'
```

There are many ways to join strings together into new strings. The + operator is perhaps the simplest:

```
>>> text = text[:i] + new_char + text[i+1:]
>>> text
'The quick broQn fox jumps over the lazy dog.'
```

I do this for each index in the `random.sample()` of indexes, each time overwriting `text`. After the `for` loop is done, I have mutated all the positions of the input string, and I can `print()` it.

10.3.2 *Using a list instead of a str*

Strings are immutable, but lists are not. You've seen that a move like `text[13] = 'b'` creates an exception, but we can change `text` into a list and directly modify it with the same syntax:

```
>>> text = list(text)
>>> text[13] = 'b'
```

We can then turn that `list` back into a `str` by joining it on the empty string:

```
>>> ''.join(text)
'The quick brobn fox jumps over the lazy dog.'
```

Here is a version of `main()` that uses this approach:

```
def main():
    args = get_args()
    text = args.text
    random.seed(args.seed)
    alpha = ''.join(sorted(string.ascii_letters + string.punctuation))
    len_text = len(text)
    num_mutations = round(args.mutations * len_text)
    new_text = list(text)                    ◄─────┤ Initialize new_text as a list
                                                    of the original text value.

    for i in random.sample(range(len_text), num_mutations):
  ┌─▷    new_text[i] = random.choice(alpha.replace(new_text[i], ''))
  │
  │     print('You said: "{}"\nI heard : "{}"'.format(text, ''.join(new_text)))   ◄──┐
  │
Now we can directly modify                          Join new_list on the empty     │
a value in new_text.                                string to make a new str.  ────┘
```

There's no particular advantage of one approach over the other, but I would personally choose the second method because I don't like messing around with slicing strings. To me, modifying a `list` in place makes much more sense than repeatedly chopping up and piecing together a `str`.

Mutations in DNA

For what it's worth, this program mimics (kind of, sort of) how DNA changes over time. The machinery to copy DNA makes mistakes, and mutations randomly occur. Often the change has no deleterious effect on the organism.

Our example only changes characters to other characters—what biologists call "point mutations," "single nucleotide variations" (SNV), or "single nucleotide polymorphisms" (SNP). We could instead write a version that would also randomly delete or insert new characters, which are called "in-dels" (insertion-deletions). Mutations (that don't result in the demise of the organism) occur at a fairly standard rate, so counting the number of mutations between a conserved region of any two organisms can allow an estimate of how long ago they diverged from a common ancestor.

10.4 Going further

- Apply the mutations to randomly selected words instead of the whole string.
- Perform insertions and deletions in addition to mutations; maybe create arguments for the percentage of each, and choose to add or delete characters at the indicated frequency.
- Add an option for -o or --output that names a file to write the output to. The default should be to print to STDOUT.
- Add a flag to limit the replacements to character values only (no punctuation).
- Add tests to test.py for every new feature, and ensure your program works properly.

Summary

- A string cannot be directly modified, but the variable containing the string can be repeatedly overwritten with new values.
- Lists can be directly modified, so it can sometimes help to use list on a string to turn it into a list, modify that list, and then use str.join() to change it back to a str.
- The string module has handy definitions of various strings.

Bottles of Beer Song: Writing and testing functions

Few songs are as annoying as "99 Bottles of Beer on the Wall." Hopefully you've never had to ride for hours in a van with middle school boys who like to sing this. I have. It's a fairly simple song that we can write an algorithm to generate. This will give us an opportunity to play with counting up and down, formatting strings, and—new to this exercise—writing functions and tests for those functions!

Our program will be called bottles.py and will take one option, -n or --num, which must be a *positive* int (the default will be 10). The program should print all the verses from --num down to 1. There should be two newlines between each verse to visually separate them, but there must be only one newline after the last verse (for one bottle), which should print "No more bottles of beer on the wall" rather than "0 bottles":

```
$ ./bottles.py -n 3
3 bottles of beer on the wall,
3 bottles of beer,
Take one down, pass it around,
2 bottles of beer on the wall!

2 bottles of beer on the wall,
2 bottles of beer,
Take one down, pass it around,
1 bottle of beer on the wall!
```

```
1 bottle of beer on the wall,
1 bottle of beer,
Take one down, pass it around,
No more bottles of beer on the wall!
```

In this exercise, you will

- Learn how to produce a list of numbers decreasing in value
- Write a function to create a verse of the song, using a test to verify when the verse is correct
- Explore how for loops can be written as list comprehensions, which in turn can be written with the map() function

11.1   *Writing bottles.py*

We'll be working in the 11_bottles_of_beer directory. Start off by copying template.py or using new.py to create your bottles.py program there. Then modify the get_args() function until your usage matches the following usage statement. You need to define only the --num option with type=int and default=10:

```
$ ./bottles.py -h
usage: bottles.py [-h] [-n number]

Bottles of beer song

optional arguments:
  -h, --help            show this help message and exit
  -n number, --num number
                        How many bottles (default: 10)
```

If the --num argument is not an int value, your program should print an error message and exit with an error value. This should happen automatically if you define your parameter to argparse properly:

```
$ ./bottles.py -n foo
usage: bottles.py [-h] [-n number]
bottles.py: error: argument -n/--num: invalid int value: 'foo'
$ ./bottles.py -n 2.4
usage: bottles.py [-h] [-n number]
bottles.py: error: argument -n/--num: invalid int value: '2.4'
```

Since we can't sing zero or fewer verses, we'll need to check if --num is less than 1. To handle this, I suggest you use parser.error() inside the get_args() function, as in previous exercises:

```
$ ./bottles.py -n 0
usage: bottles.py [-h] [-n number]
bottles.py: error: --num "0" must be greater than 0
```

Figure 11.1 shows a string diagram of the inputs and outputs.

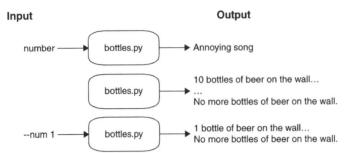

Figure 11.1   The bottles program may take a number for the verse to start, or it will sing the song starting at 10.

11.1.1 Counting down

The song starts at the given --num value, like 10, and needs to count down to 9, 8, 7, and so forth. How can we do that in Python? We've seen how to use range(start, stop) to get a list of integers that go *up* in value. If you give it just one number, that will be considered the stop, and it will assume 0 as the start:

```
>>> list(range(5))
[0, 1, 2, 3, 4]
```

Because this is a lazy function, we must use the list() function in the REPL to force it to produce the numbers. Remember that the stop value is never included in the output, so the preceding output stopped at 4, not 5.

If you give range() two numbers, they are considered to be start and stop:

```
>>> list(range(1, 5))
[1, 2, 3, 4]
```

To reverse this sequence, you might be tempted to swap the start and stop values. Unfortunately, if start is greater than stop, you get an empty list:

```
>>> list(range(5, 1))
[]
```

You saw in chapter 3 that we can use the reversed() function to reverse a list. This is another lazy function, so again I'll use the list() function to force the values in the REPL:

```
>>> list(reversed(range(1, 5)))
[4, 3, 2, 1]
```

The `range()` function can also take an optional third argument for a `step` value. For instance, you could use this to count by fives:

```
>>> list(range(0, 50, 5))
[0, 5, 10, 15, 20, 25, 30, 35, 40, 45]
```

Another way to count down is to swap the `start` and `stop` and use `-1` for the step:

```
>>> list(range(5, 0, -1))
[5, 4, 3, 2, 1]
```

So you have couple of ways to count in reverse.

11.1.2 Writing a function

Up to this point, I've suggested that all your code go into the `main()` function. This is the first exercise where I suggest you write a function. I would like you to consider how to write the code to sing *just one verse*. The function could take the number of the verse and return the text for that verse.

You can start off with something like the example in figure 11.2. The `def` keyword "defines" a function, and the name of the function follows. Function names should contain only letters, numbers, and underscores and cannot start with a number. After the name comes parentheses, which describe any parameters that the function accepts. Here our function will be called `verse()`, and it has the parameter `bottle` (or `number` or whatever you want to call it). After the parameters comes a colon to indicate the end of the `def` line. The function body comes next, with all lines being indented at least four spaces.

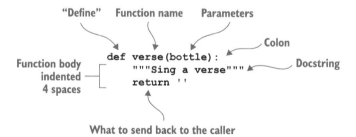

Figure 11.2   The elements of a function definition in Python

The docstring in figure 11.2 is a string just after the function definition. It will show up in the help for your function.

You can enter this function into the REPL:

```
>>> def verse(bottle):
...     """Sing a verse"""
...     return ''
...
>>> help(verse)
```

When you do, you will see this:

```
Help on function verse in module __main__:

verse(bottle)
    Sing a verse
```

The `return` statement tells Python what to send back from the function. It's not very interesting right now because it will just send back the empty string:

```
>>> verse(10)
''
```

It's also common practice to use the `pass` statement for the body of a dummy function. The `pass` will do nothing, and the function will return `None` instead of the empty string, as we have done here. When you start writing your own functions and tests, you might like to use `pass` when you stub out a new function, until you decide what the function will do.

11.1.3 *Writing a test for verse()*

In the spirit of *test-driven development,* let's write a test for `verse()` before we go any further. The following listing shows a test you can use. Add this code into your bottles.py program just after your `main()` function :

```
def verse(bottle):
    """Sing a verse"""

    return ''


def test_verse():
    """Test verse"""

    last_verse = verse(1)
    assert last_verse == '\n'.join([
        '1 bottle of beer on the wall,', '1 bottle of beer,',
        'Take one down, pass it around,',
        'No more bottles of beer on the wall!'
    ])

    two_bottles = verse(2)
    assert two_bottles == '\n'.join([
        '2 bottles of beer on the wall,', '2 bottles of beer,',
```

```
        'Take one down, pass it around,', '1 bottle of beer on the wall!'
    ])
```

There are many, many ways you could write this program. I have in mind that my `verse()` function will produce a single verse of the song, returning a new `str` value that is the lines of the verse joined on newlines.

You don't have to write your program this way, but I'd like you to consider what it means to write a function and a *unit test*. If you read about software testing, you'll find that there are different definitions of what a "unit" of code is. In this book, I consider a *function* to be a *unit*, so my unit tests are tests of individual functions.

Even though the song has potentially hundreds of verses, these two tests should cover everything you need to check. It may help to look at the musical notation in figure 11.3 for the song, as this does a nice job of graphically showing the structure of the song and, hence, our program.

99 Bottles of Beer

Anonymous

Figure 11.3 **The musical notation for the song shows there are two cases to handle: one for all the verses up to the last, and then the last one.**

I've taken a few liberties with the notation by mixing in some programming ideas. If you don't know how to read music, let me briefly explain the important parts. The `N` is the current *number*, like "99" so that `(N - 1)` would be "98." The endings are noted `1 - (N - 1)`, which is a bit confusing because we're using the hyphen to indicate both a range and subtraction in the same "equation." Still, the first ending is used for the first time through the penultimate repeat. The colon before the bar lines in the first ending means to repeat the song from the beginning. Then the `N` ending is taken on the last repeat, and the double bar indicates the end of the song/program.

What we can see from the music is that there are only two cases we need to handle: the last verse, and all the other verses. So first we check the last verse. We're looking for "1 bottle" (singular) and not "1 bottles" (plural). We also need to check that the last line says "No more bottles" instead of "0 bottles." The second test, for "2 bottles of beer," is making sure that the numbers are "2 bottles" and then "1 bottle." If we managed to pass these two tests, our program ought to be able to handle all the verses.

I wrote `test_verse()` to test just the `verse()` function. The name of the function matters because I am using the `pytest` module to find all the functions in my code that start with `test_` and run them. If your bottles.py program has the preceding functions for `verse()` and `test_verse()`, you can run `pytest bottles.py`.

Try it, and you should see something like this:

```
$ pytest bottles.py
============================ test session starts ============================
...
collected 1 item

bottles.py F                                                         [100%]

================================== FAILURES ==================================
_____ test_verse _____

    def test_verse():
        """Test verse"""

        last_verse = verse(1)
>       assert last_verse == '\n'.join([
            '1 bottle of beer on the wall,', '1 bottle of beer,',
            'Take one down, pass it around,',
            'No more bottles of beer on the wall!'
        ])
E       AssertionError: assert '' == '1 bottle of beer on the wal...ottles of
        beer on the wall!'
E           + 1 bottle of beer on the wall,
E           + 1 bottle of beer,
E           + Take one down, pass it around,
E           + No more bottles of beer on the wall!

bottles.py:49: AssertionError
========================== 1 failed in 0.10 seconds ==========================
```

Call the verse() function with the argument 1 to get the last verse of the song.

The > at the beginning of this line indicates this is the source of the error. The test checks if the value of last_verse is equal to an expected str value. Since it's not, this line throws an exception, causing the assertion to fail.

The "E" lines show the difference between what was received and what was expected. The value of last_verse is the empty string ("), which does not match the expected string "1 bottle of beer..." and so on.

To pass the first test, you could copy the code for the expected value of `last_verse` directly from the test. Change your `verse()` function to match this:

```
def verse(bottle):
    """Sing a verse"""

    return '\n'.join([
        '1 bottle of beer on the wall,', '1 bottle of beer,',
        'Take one down, pass it around,',
        'No more bottles of beer on the wall!'
    ])
```

Now run your test again. The first test should pass, and the second one should fail. Here are the relevant error lines:

```
================================== FAILURES ==================================
_____ test_verse _____

    def test_verse() -> None:
        """Test verse"""

        last_verse = verse(1)                          │ This test now passes.
        assert last_verse == '\n'.join([     ◄────┘
            '1 bottle of beer on the wall,', '1 bottle of beer,',
            'Take one down, pass it around,',
            'No more bottles of beer on the wall!'
        ])
                                                   │ Call verse() with the value of 2 to
        two_bottles = verse(2)         ◄────┘ get the "Two bottles..." verse.
>       assert two_bottles == '\n'.join([
            '2 bottles of beer on the wall,', '2 bottles of beer,',
            'Take one down, pass it around,', '1 bottle of beer on the wall!'
        ])
E       AssertionError: assert '1 bottle of ... on the wall!' == '2 bottles of
   ... on the wall!'
E         - 1 bottle of beer on the wall,          │ These E lines are showing you
E         ? ^                                      │ the problem. The verse()
E         + 2 bottles of beer on the wall,         │ function returned '1 bottle'
E         ? ^        +                             │ but the test expected '2
E         - 1 bottle of beer,                      │ bottles', etc.
E         ? ^
E         + 2 bottles of beer,...
E
E         ...Full output truncated (7 lines hidden), use '-vv' to show
```

Assert that this verse is equal to the expected string.

Go back and look at your verse() definition. Look at figure 11.4 and think about which parts need to change—the first, second, and fourth lines. The third line is always the same. You're given a value for bottle that needs to be used in the first two lines, along with either "bottle" or "bottles," depending on the value of bottle. (Hint: It's only singular for the value 1; otherwise, it's plural.) The fourth line needs the value of bottle - 1 and, again, the proper singular or plural depending on that value. Can you figure out how to write this?

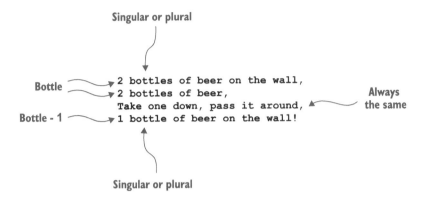

Figure 11.4   Each verse has four lines, where the first two and last are very similar. The third line is always the same. Find the parts that vary.

Focus on passing those two tests before you move to the next stage of printing the whole song. That is, do not attempt anything until you see this:

```
$ pytest bottles.py
============================ test session starts ==============================
...
collected 1 item

bottles.py .                                                          [100%]

========================= 1 passed in 0.05 seconds ===========================
```

11.1.4 *Using the verse() function*

At this point, you know

- That the `--num` value is a valid integer value greater than 0
- How to count from that `--num` value backwards down to 0
- That the `verse()` function will print any one verse properly

Now you need to put them together. I suggest you start by using a `for` loop with the `range()` function to count down. Use each value from that to produce a `verse()`. There should be two newlines after every verse except for the last.

You will use `pytest -xv test.py` (or `make test`) to test the program at this point. In the parlance of testing, test.py is an *integration test* because it checks that the program *as a whole* is working. From this point on, we'll focus on how to write *unit* tests to check individual functions in addition to integration tests to ensure that all the functions work together.

Once you can pass the test suite using a `for` loop, try to rewrite it using either a list comprehension or a `map()`. Rather than starting again from scratch, I suggest you comment out your working code by adding # to the beginnings of the lines, and then try other ways to write the algorithm. Use the tests to verify that your code still passes. If it is at all motivating, my solution is one line long. Can you write a single line of code that combines the range() and verse() functions to produce the expected output?

Here are a few hints:

- Define the --num argument as an int with a default value of 10.
- Use parser.error() to get argparse to print an error message for a negative --num value.
- Write the verse() function. Use the test_verse() function and Pytest to make that work properly.
- Combine the verse() function with range() to create all the verses.

Do try your best to write the program before reading the solution. Also feel free to solve the problem in a completely different way, even writing your own unit tests.

11.2 Solution

I've decided to show you a slightly fancy-pants version that uses map(). Later I'll show you how to write it using a for loop and a list comprehension.

```python
#!/usr/bin/env python3
"""Bottles of beer song"""

import argparse


# --------------------------------------------------
def get_args():
    """Get command-line arguments"""

    parser = argparse.ArgumentParser(
        description='Bottles of beer song',
        formatter_class=argparse.ArgumentDefaultsHelpFormatter)

    parser.add_argument('-n',
                        '--num',
                        metavar='number',
                        type=int,
                        default=10,
                        help='How many bottles')
```

Define the --num argument as an int with a default value of **10**.

Parse the command-line argument into the variable args.

```python
    args = parser.parse_args()

    if args.num < 1:
        parser.error(f'--num "{args.num}" must be greater than 0')

    return args
```

If args.num is less than 1, use parser.error() to display an error message and exit the program with an error value.

The map() function expects a function as the first argument and some iterable as the second argument. Here I feed the descending numbers from the range() function to my verse() function. The result from map() is a new list of verses that can be joined on two newlines.

```python
# --------------------------------------------------
def main():
    """Make a jazz noise here"""

    args = get_args()
    print('\n\n'.join(map(verse, range(args.num, 0, -1))))
```

Define a function that can create a single verse().

```python
# --------------------------------------------------
def verse(bottle):
    """Sing a verse"""

    next_bottle = bottle - 1
    s1 = '' if bottle == 1 else 's'
    s2 = '' if next_bottle == 1 else 's'
    num_next = 'No more' if next_bottle == 0 else next_bottle
    return '\n'.join([
        f'{bottle} bottle{s1} of beer on the wall,',
        f'{bottle} bottle{s1} of beer,',
        f'Take one down, pass it around,',
        f'{num_next} bottle{s2} of beer on the wall!',
    ])
```

Define a next_bottle that is one less than the current bottle.

Define an s1 (the first "s") that is either the character 's' or the empty string, depending on the value of current bottle.

Do the same for s2 (the second "s"), depending on the value of next_bottle.

Define a value for next_num depending on whether the next value is 0 or not.

Create a return string by joining the four lines of text on the newline. Substitute in the variables to create the correct verse.

```python
# --------------------------------------------------
def test_verse():
    """Test verse"""

    last_verse = verse(1)
    assert last_verse == '\n'.join([
        '1 bottle of beer on the wall,', '1 bottle of beer,',
        'Take one down, pass it around,',
        'No more bottles of beer on the wall!'
    ])

    two_bottles = verse(2)
    assert two_bottles == '\n'.join([
        '2 bottles of beer on the wall,', '2 bottles of beer,',
        'Take one down, pass it around,', '1 bottle of beer on the wall!'
    ])
```

Define a unit test called test_verse() for the verse() function. The test_ prefix means that the pytest module will find this function and execute it.

Test the last verse() with the value 1.

Test a verse() with the value 2.

```python
# --------------------------------------------------
if __name__ == '__main__':
    main()
```

11.3   *Discussion*

There isn't anything new in the `get_args()` function in this program. By this point, you have had several opportunities to define an optional integer parameter with a default argument and to use `parser.error()` to halt your program if the user provides a bad argument. By relying on `argparse` to handle so much busy work, you are saving yourself loads of time as well as ensuring that you have good data to work with. Let's move on to the new stuff!

11.3.1   *Counting down*

You know how to count down from the given `--num`, and you know you can use a `for` loop to iterate:

```
>>> for n in range(3, 0, -1):
...     print(f'{n} bottles of beer')
...
3 bottles of beer
2 bottles of beer
1 bottles of beer
```

Instead of directly creating each verse inside the `for` loop, I suggested that you could create a function called `verse()` to create any given verse and use that with the `range()` of numbers. Up to this point, we've been doing all our work in the `main()` function. As you grow as a programmer, though, your programs will become longer—hundreds to even thousands of lines of code (LOC). Long programs and functions can get very difficult to test and maintain, so you should try to break ideas into small, functional units that you can understand and test. Ideally, functions should do *one* thing. If you understand and trust your small, simple *functions*, then you know you can safely compose them into longer, more complicated *programs*.

11.3.2   *Test-driven development*

I wanted you to add a `test_verse()` function to your program to use with Pytest to create a working `verse()` function. This idea follows the principles described by Kent Beck in his book, *Test-Driven Development* (Addison-Wesley Professional, 2002):

1   Add a new test for an unimplemented unit of functionality.
2   Run all previously written tests and see the newly added test fails.
3   Write code that implements the new functionality.
4   Run all tests and see them succeed.
5   Refactor (rewrite to improve readability or structure).
6   Start at the beginning (repeat).

For instance, suppose we want a function that adds 1 to any given number. We'll called it `add1()` and define the function body as `pass` to tell Python "nothing to see here":

```
def add1(n):
    pass
```

Now write a `test_add1()` function where you pass some arguments to the function, and use `assert` to verify that you get back the value that you expect:

```
def test_add1():
    assert add1(0) == 1
    assert add1(1) == 2
    assert add1(-1) == 0
```

Run pytest (or whatever testing framework you like) and verify that the function *does not work* (of course it won't, because it just executes `pass`). Then go fill in some function code that *does* work (`return n + 1` instead of `pass`). Pass all manner of arguments you can imagine, including nothing, one thing, and many things.[1]

11.3.3 *The verse() function*

I provided you with a `test_verse()` function that shows you exactly what is expected for the arguments of 1 and 2. What I like about writing my tests first is that it gives me an opportunity to think about how I'd like to use the code, what I'd like to give as arguments, and what I expect to get back in return. For instance, what *should* the function `add1()` return if given

- No arguments
- More than one argument
- The value `None`
- Anything other than a numeric type (`int`, `float`, or `complex`) like a `str` value or a `dict`

You can write tests to pass both good and bad values and decide how you want your code to behave under both favorable and adverse conditions.

Here's the `verse()` function I wrote, which passes the `test_verse()` function:

```
def verse(bottle):
    """Sing a verse"""

    next_bottle = bottle - 1
    s1 = '' if bottle == 1 else 's'
    s2 = '' if next_bottle == 1 else 's'
    num_next = 'No more' if next_bottle == 0 else next_bottle
    return '\n'.join([
        f'{bottle} bottle{s1} of beer on the wall,',
        f'{bottle} bottle{s1} of beer,',
        f'Take one down, pass it around,',
        f'{num_next} bottle{s2} of beer on the wall!',
    ])
```

---

[1] A CS professor once told me in office hours to handle the cases of 0, 1, and *n* (infinity), and that has always stuck with me.

This code is annotated in section 11.2, but I essentially isolate all the parts of the return string that change, and I create variables to substitute into those places. I use bottle and next_bottle to decide if there should be an "s" or not after the "bottle" strings. I also need to figure out whether to print the next bottle as a number, or if I should print the string "No more" (when next_bottle is 0). Choosing the values for s1, s2, and num_next all involve *binary* decisions, meaning they are a choice between *two* values, so I find it best to use an if expression.

This function passes test_verse(), so I can move on to using it to generate the song.

11.3.4 *Iterating through the verses*

I could use a for loop to count down and print() each verse():

```
>>> for n in range(3, 0, -1):
...     print(verse(n))
...
3 bottles of beer on the wall,
3 bottles of beer,
Take one down, pass it around,
2 bottles of beer on the wall!
2 bottles of beer on the wall,
2 bottles of beer,
Take one down, pass it around,
1 bottle of beer on the wall!
1 bottle of beer on the wall,
1 bottle of beer,
Take one down, pass it around,
No more bottles of beer on the wall!
```

That's *almost* correct, but we need two newlines in between all the verses. I could use the end option to print to include two newlines for all values greater than 1:

```
>>> for n in range(3, 0, -1):
...     print(verse(n), end='\n' * (2 if n > 1 else 1))
...
3 bottles of beer on the wall,
3 bottles of beer,
Take one down, pass it around,
2 bottles of beer on the wall!

2 bottles of beer on the wall,
2 bottles of beer,
Take one down, pass it around,
1 bottle of beer on the wall!

1 bottle of beer on the wall,
1 bottle of beer,
Take one down, pass it around,
No more bottles of beer on the wall!
```

I would rather use the `str.join()` method to put two newlines in between items in a `list`. My items are the verses, and I can turn a `for` loop into a list comprehension as shown in figure 11.5.

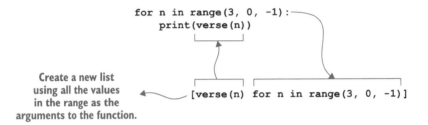

Create a new list using all the values in the range as the arguments to the function.

Figure 11.5   A `for` loop compared to a list comprehension

```
>>> verses = [verse(n) for n in range(3, 0, -1)]
>>> print('\n\n'.join(verses))
3 bottles of beer on the wall,
3 bottles of beer,
Take one down, pass it around,
2 bottles of beer on the wall!

2 bottles of beer on the wall,
2 bottles of beer,
Take one down, pass it around,
1 bottle of beer on the wall!

1 bottle of beer on the wall,
1 bottle of beer,
Take one down, pass it around,
No more bottles of beer on the wall!
```

That is a fine solution, but I would like you to start noticing a pattern we will see repeatedly: applying a function to every element of a sequence, which is exactly what `map()` does! As shown in figure 11.6, our list comprehension can be rewritten very concisely using `map()`.

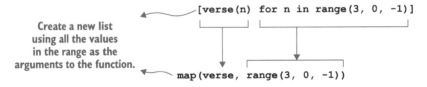

Create a new list using all the values in the range as the arguments to the function.

Figure 11.6   A list comprehension can be replaced with `map()`. They both return a new `list`.

In our case, our sequence is a descending `range()` of numbers, and we want to apply our `verse()` function to each number and collect the resulting verses. It's like the paint booth idea in chapter 8, where the function "painted" the cars "blue" by adding the word "blue" to the start of the string. When we want to apply a function to every element in a sequence, we might consider refactoring the code using `map()`:

```
>>> verses = map(verse, range(3, 0, -1))
>>> print('\n\n'.join(verses))
3 bottles of beer on the wall,
3 bottles of beer,
Take one down, pass it around,
2 bottles of beer on the wall!

2 bottles of beer on the wall,
2 bottles of beer,
Take one down, pass it around,
1 bottle of beer on the wall!

1 bottle of beer on the wall,
1 bottle of beer,
Take one down, pass it around,
No more bottles of beer on the wall!
```

Whenever I need to transform some sequence of items with some function, I like to start off by thinking about how I'll handle just *one* of the items. I find it's much easier to write and test one function with one input rather than some possibly huge list of operations. List comprehensions are often considered more "Pythonic," but I tend to favor `map()` because it usually involves shorter code. If you search the internet for "python list comprehension map," you'll find that some people think list comprehensions are easier to read than `map()`, but `map()` might possibly be somewhat faster. I wouldn't say either approach is better than the other. It really comes down to taste or perhaps a discussion with your teammates.

If you want to use `map()`, remember that it wants a *function* as the first argument and then a sequence of elements that will become arguments to the function. The `verse()` function (which you've tested!) is the first argument, and the `range()` provides the `list`. The `map()` function will pass each element of the `range()` as an argument to the `verse()` function, as shown in figure 11.7. The result is a new `list` with the return values from all those function calls. Many are the `for` loops that can be better written as mapping a function over a list of arguments!

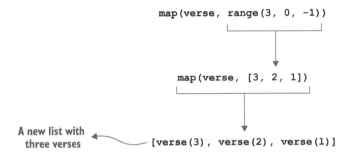

Figure 11.7 The `map()` function will call the `verse()` function with each element produced by the `range()` function. It's functions all the way down.

11.3.5 *1,500 other solutions*

There are literally hundreds of ways to solve this problem. The "99 Bottles of Beer" website (www.99-bottles-of-beer.net) claims to have 1,500 variations in various languages. Compare your solution to others there. Trivial as the program may be, it has allowed us to explore some really interesting ideas in Python, testing, and algorithms.

11.4   *Going further*

- Replace the Arabic numbers (1, 2, 3) with text (one, two, three).
- Add a `--step` option (positive `int`, default `1`) that allows the user to skip numbers, like by twos or fives.
- Add a `--reverse` flag to reverse the order of the verses, counting up instead of down.

Summary

- Test-driven development (TDD) is central to developing dependable, reproducible code. Tests also give you the freedom to refactor your code (reorganize and improve it for speed or clarity), knowing that you can always verify your new version still works properly. As you write your code, always write tests!
- The `range()` function will count backwards if you swap `start` and `stop` and supply the optional third `step` value of `-1`.
- A `for` loop can often be replaced with a list comprehension or a `map()` for shorter, more concise code.

Ransom: Randomly capitalizing text

All this hard work writing code is getting on my nerves. I'm ready to turn to a life of crime! I've kidnapped (cat-napped?) the neighbor's cat, and I want to send them a ransom note. In the good old days, I'd cut letters from magazines and paste them onto a piece of paper to spell out my demands. That sounds like too much work. Instead, I'm going to write a Python program called ransom.py that will encode text into randomly capitalized letters:

```
$ ./ransom.py 'give us 2 million dollars or the cat
    gets it!'
gIVe US 2 milLION DoLlArs or ThE cAt GEts It!
```

As you can see, my diabolical program accepts the heinous input text as a positional argument. Since this program uses the random module, I want to accept an -s or --seed option so I can replicate the vile output:

```
$ ./ransom.py --seed 3 'give us 2 million dollars or the cat gets it!'
giVE uS 2 MILlioN dolLaRS OR tHe cAt GETS It!
```

The dastardly positional argument might name a vicious file, in which case that should be read for the demoniac input text:

```
$ ./ransom.py --seed 2 ../inputs/fox.txt
the qUIck BROWN fOX JUmps ovEr ThE LAZY DOg.
```

If the unlawful program is run with no arguments, it should print a short, infernal usage statement:

```
$ ./ransom.py
usage: ransom.py [-h] [-s int] text
ransom.py: error: the following arguments are required: text
```

If the nefarious program is run with -h or --help flags, it should print a longer, fiendish usage:

```
$ ./ransom.py -h
usage: ransom.py [-h] [-s int] text

Ransom Note

positional arguments:
  text                 Input text or file

optional arguments:
  -h, --help           show this help message and exit
  -s int, --seed int   Random seed (default: None)
```

Figure 12.1 shows a noxious string diagram to visualize the inputs and outputs.

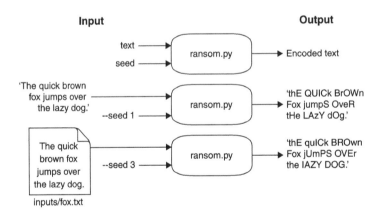

Figure 12.1   The awful program will transform input text into a ransom note by randomly capitalizing letters.

In this chapter, you will

- Learn how to use the random module to figuratively "flip a coin" to decide between two choices
- Explore ways to generate new strings from an existing one, incorporating random decisions
- Study the similarities of for loops, list comprehensions, and the map() function

12.1 Writing ransom.py

I suggest starting with new.py or copying the template/template.py file to create ransom.py in the 12_ransom directory. This program, like several before it, accepts a required, positional string for the text and an optional integer (default None) for the --seed. Also, as in previous exercises, the text argument may name a file that should be read for the text value.

To start out, use this for your main() code:

```
def main():
    args = get_args()        ◁──┐  Get the processed
    random.seed(args.seed)   ◁─┐ │  command-line arguments.
    print(args.text)    ◁──┐  │ │
                           │  │ │  Set the random.seed() with the value
        Start off by echoing  │ │  from the user. The default is None,
             back the input.  │ │  which is the same as not setting it.
```

If you run this program, it should echo the input from the command line:

```
$ ./ransom.py 'your money or your life!'
your money or your life!
```

Or the text from an input file:

```
$ ./ransom.py ../inputs/fox.txt
The quick brown fox jumps over the lazy dog.
```

The important thing when writing a program is to take baby steps. You should run your program *after every change*, checking manually and with the tests to see if you are progressing.

Once you have this working, it's time to think about how to randomly capitalize this awful message.

12.1.1 Mutating the text

You've seen before that you can't directly modify a str value:

```
>>> text = 'your money or your life!'
>>> text[0] = 'Y'
Traceback (most recent call last):
  File "<stdin>", line 1, in <module>
TypeError: 'str' object does not support item assignment
```

So how can we randomly change the case of some of the letters?

I suggest that instead of thinking about how to change many letters, you should think about how to change *one* letter. That is, given a single letter, how can you randomly return the upper- or lowercase version of the letter? Let's create a dummy choose() function that accepts a single character. For now, we'll have the function return the character unchanged:

```
def choose(char):
    return char
```

Here's a test for it:

The state of the random module is global to the program. Any change we make here could affect unknown parts of the program, so we save our current state.

Set the random seed to a known value. This is a global change to our program. Any other calls to functions from the random module will be affected!

```
def test_choose():
    state = random.getstate()
    random.seed(1)
    assert choose('a') == 'a'
    assert choose('b') == 'b'
    assert choose('c') == 'C'
    assert choose('d') == 'd'
    random.setstate(state)
```

The choose() function is given a series of letters, and we use the assert statement to test if the value returned by the function is the expected letter.

Reset the global state to the original value.

Random seeds

Have you wondered how I knew what would be the result of choose() for a given random seed? Well, I confess that I wrote the function, then set the seed, and ran it with the given inputs. I recorded the results as the assertions you see. In the future, these results should still be the same. If they are not, I've changed something and probably broken my program.

12.1.2 Flipping a coin

We need to choose() between returning the upper- or lowercase version of the character you are given. It's a *binary* choice, meaning we have two options, so we can use the analogy of flipping a coin. Heads or tails? Or, for our purposes, 0 or 1:

```
>>> import random
>>> random.choice([0, 1])
1
```

Or True or False if you prefer:

```
>>> random.choice([False, True])
True
```

Think about using an if expression where you return the uppercase answer when the 0 or False option is selected and the lowercase version otherwise. My entire choose() function is this one line.

12.1.3 Creating a new string

Now we need to apply our choose() function to each character in the input string. I hope this is starting to feel like a familiar tactic. I encourage you to start by mimicking the first approach from chapter 8 where we used a for loop to iterate through each character of the input text and replace all the vowels with a single vowel. In this program, we can iterate through the characters of text and use them as the argument to the `choose()` function. The result will be a new `list` (or `str`) of the transformed characters. Once you can pass the test with a `for` loop, try to rewrite it as a list comprehension, and then a `map()`.

Now off you go! Write the program, pass the tests.

12.2 Solution

We're going to explore many ways to process all the characters in the input text. We'll start off with a `for` loop that builds up a new list, and I hope to convince you that a list comprehension is a better way to do this. Finally, I'll show you how to use `map()` to create a very terse (perhaps even elegant) solution.

```python
#!/usr/bin/env python3
"""Ransom note"""

import argparse
import os
import random


# --------------------------------------------------
def get_args():
    """get command-line arguments"""

    parser = argparse.ArgumentParser(
        description='Ransom Note',
        formatter_class=argparse.ArgumentDefaultsHelpFormatter)

    parser.add_argument('text', metavar='text', help='Input text or file')

    parser.add_argument('-s',
                        '--seed',
                        help='Random seed',
                        metavar='int',
                        type=int,
                        default=None)

    args = parser.parse_args()

    if os.path.isfile(args.text):
        args.text = open(args.text).read().rstrip()

    return args

# --------------------------------------------------
def main():
    """Make a jazz noise here"""

    args = get_args()
    text = args.text
```

The text argument is a positional string value.

The --seed option is an integer that defaults to None.

Process the command-line arguments into the args variable.

If the args.text is a file, use the contents of that as the new args.text value.

Return the arguments to the caller.

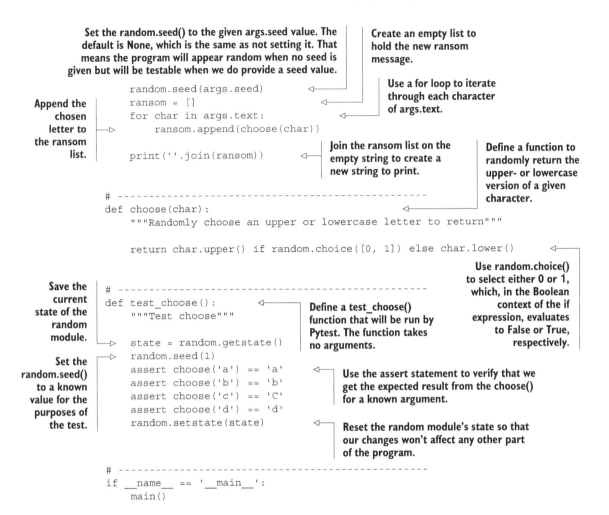

Set the random.seed() to the given args.seed value. The default is None, which is the same as not setting it. That means the program will appear random when no seed is given but will be testable when we do provide a seed value.

Create an empty list to hold the new ransom message.

Use a for loop to iterate through each character of args.text.

Append the chosen letter to the ransom list.

```
random.seed(args.seed)
ransom = []
for char in args.text:
    ransom.append(choose(char))

print(''.join(ransom))
```

Join the ransom list on the empty string to create a new string to print.

Define a function to randomly return the upper- or lowercase version of a given character.

```
# -------------------------------------------------
def choose(char):
    """Randomly choose an upper or lowercase letter to return"""

    return char.upper() if random.choice([0, 1]) else char.lower()
```

Use random.choice() to select either 0 or 1, which, in the Boolean context of the if expression, evaluates to False or True, respectively.

Save the current state of the random module.

Set the random.seed() to a known value for the purposes of the test.

```
# -------------------------------------------------
def test_choose():
    """Test choose"""

    state = random.getstate()
    random.seed(1)
    assert choose('a') == 'a'
    assert choose('b') == 'b'
    assert choose('c') == 'C'
    assert choose('d') == 'd'
    random.setstate(state)
```

Define a test_choose() function that will be run by Pytest. The function takes no arguments.

Use the assert statement to verify that we get the expected result from the choose() for a known argument.

Reset the random module's state so that our changes won't affect any other part of the program.

```
# -------------------------------------------------
if __name__ == '__main__':
    main()
```

12.3 *Discussion*

I like this problem because there are so many interesting ways to solve it. I know, I know, Python likes there to be "one obvious way" to solve it, but let's explore, shall we? There's nothing in get_args() that we haven't seen several times by now, so let's skip that.

12.3.1 *Iterating through elements in a sequence*

Assume that we have the following cruel message:

```
>>> text = '2 million dollars or the cat sleeps with the fishes!'
```

I want to randomly upper- and lowercase the letters. As suggested in the earlier description of the problem, we can use a for loop to iterate over each character.

One way to print an uppercase version of the text is to print an uppercase version *of each letter*:

```
for char in text:
    print(char.upper(), end='')
```

That would give me "2 MILLION DOLLARS OR THE CAT SLEEPS WITH THE FISHES!" Now, instead of always printing `char.upper()`, I can randomly choose between `char.upper()` and `char.lower()`. For that, I'll use `random.choice()` to choose between two values like `True` and `False` or `0` and `1`:

```
>>> import random
>>> random.choice([True, False])
False
>>> random.choice([0, 1])
0
>>> random.choice(['blue', 'green'])
'blue'
```

Following the first solution from chapter 8, I created a new `list` to hold the ransom message and added these random choices:

```
ransom = []
for char in text:
    if random.choice([False, True]):
        ransom.append(char.upper())
    else:
        ransom.append(char.lower())
```

Then I joined the new characters on the empty string to print a new string:

```
print(''.join(ransom))
```

It's far less code to write this with an `if` expression to select whether to take the upper- or lowercase character, as shown in figure 12.2:

```
ransom = []
for char in text:
    ransom.append(char.upper() if random.choice([False, True]) else char.lower())
```

```
ransom.append(char.upper()
    if random.choice([False, True])
    else char.lower())
```

```
if random.choice([False, True]):
    ransom.append(char.upper())
else:
    ransom.append(char.lower())
```

Figure 12.2 A binary if/else branch is more succinctly written using an `if` expression.

You don't have to use actual Boolean values (`False` and `True`). You could use `0` and `1` instead:

```
ransom = []
for char in text:
    ransom.append(char.upper() if random.choice([0, 1]) else char.lower())
```

When numbers are evaluated *in a Boolean context* (that is, in a place where Python expects to see a Boolean value), `0` is considered `False`, and every other number is `True`.

12.3.2 *Writing a function to choose the letter*

The `if` expression is a bit of code that could be put into a function. I find it hard to read inside the `ransom.append()`.

By putting it into a function, I can give it a descriptive name and write a test for it:

```
def choose(char):
    """Randomly choose an upper or lowercase letter to return"""

    return char.upper() if random.choice([0, 1]) else char.lower()
```

Now I can run the `test_choose()` function to test that my function does what I think. This code is much easier to read:

```
ransom = []
for char in text:
    ransom.append(choose(char))
```

12.3.3 *Another way to write list.append()*

The solution in section 12.2 creates an empty `list`, to which I `list.append()` the return from `choose()`. Another way to write `list.append()` is to use the `+=` operator to add the right-hand value (the element to add) to the left-hand side (the list), as in figure 12.3.

```
def main():
    args = get_args()
    random.seed(args.seed)

    ransom = []
    for char in args.text:
        ransom += choose(char)

    print(''.join(ransom))
```

ransom.append(choose(char))

ransom += choose(char)

Add the result
of the function
to ransom.

Figure 12.3 The `+=` operator is another way to write `list.append()`.

This is the same syntax for concatenating a character to a string or adding a number to another number.

12.3.4 *Using a str instead of a list*

The two previous solutions require that the lists be joined on the empty string to make a new string to print. We could, instead, start off with an empty string and build that up, one character at a time, using the += operator:

```
def main():
    args = get_args()
    random.seed(args.seed)

    ransom = ''
    for char in args.text:
        ransom += choose(char)

    print(ransom)
```

As we just noted, the += operator is another way to append an element to a list. Python often treats strings and lists interchangeably, often implicitly, for better or worse.

12.3.5 *Using a list comprehension*

The previous patterns all initialize an empty str or list and then build it up with a for loop. I'd like to convince you that it's almost always better to express this using a list comprehension, because its entire raison d'être is to return a new list. We can condense our three lines of code to just one:

```
def main():
    args = get_args()
    random.seed(args.seed)
    ransom = [choose(char) for char in args.text]
    print(''.join(ransom))
```

Or you can skip creating the ransom variable altogether. As a general rule, I only assign a value to a variable if I use it more than once or if I feel it makes my code more readable:

```
def main():
    args = get_args()
    random.seed(args.seed)
    print(''.join([choose(char) for char in args.text]))
```

A for loop is really for iterating through some sequence and producing *side effects*, like printing values or handling lines in a file. If your goal is to create a new list, a list comprehension is probably the best tool. Any code that would go into the body of the for loop to process an element is better placed in a function with a test.

12.3.6 *Using a map() function*

I've mentioned before that map() is just like a list comprehension, though usually with less typing. Both approaches generate a new list from some iterable, as shown in figure 12.4. In this case, the resulting list from map() is created by applying the choose() function to each character of args.text:

```
def main():
    args = get_args()
    random.seed(args.seed)
    ransom = map(choose, args.text)
    print(''.join(ransom))
```

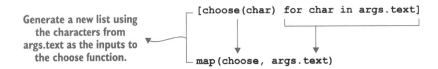

Generate a new list using the characters from args.text as the inputs to the choose function.

Figure 12.4 The ideas of the list comprehension can be expressed more succinctly with map().

Or, again, you could leave out the ransom assignment and use the list that comes back from map() directly:

```
def main():
    args = get_args()
    random.seed(args.seed)
    print(''.join(map(choose, args.text)))
```

12.4 *Comparing methods*

It may seem silly to spend so much time working through so many ways to solve what is essentially a trivial problem, but one of the goals of this book is to explore the various ideas available in Python. The first solution in section 12.2 is a very imperative solution that a C or Java programmer would probably write. The version using a list comprehension is very idiomatic to Python—it is "Pythonic," as Pythonistas would say. The map() solution would look very familiar to someone coming from a purely functional language like Haskell.

All these approaches accomplish the same goal, but they embody different aesthetics and programming paradigms. My preferred solution would be the last one, using map(), but you should choose an approach that makes the most sense to you.

MapReduce

In 2004, Google released a paper on their "MapReduce" algorithm. The "map" phase applies some transformation to all the elements in a collection, such as all the pages of the internet that need to be indexed for searching. These operations can happen in *parallel*, meaning you can use many machines to process the pages separately from each other and in any order. The "reduce" phase then brings all the processed elements back together, maybe to put the results into a unified database.

In our ransom.py program, the "map" part selected a randomized case for the given letter, and the "reduce" part was putting all those bits back together into a new string. Conceivably, map() could make use of multiple processors to run the functions *in parallel* as opposed to *sequentially* (like with a for loop), possibly cutting the time to produce the results.

The ideas of map/reduce can be found in many places, from indexing the internet to our ransom program.

Learning about MapReduce was, to me, a bit like learning the name of a new bird. I never even noticed that bird before, but, once I was told its name, I saw it everywhere. Once you understand this pattern, you'll begin to see it in many places.

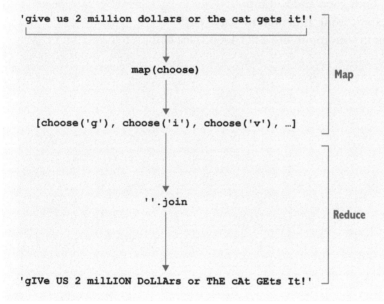

12.5 Going further

Write a version of ransom.py that represents letters in other ways by combining ASCII characters, such as the following. Feel free to make up your own substitutions. Be sure to update your tests.

```
A   4        K   |<
B   |3       L   |_
```

```
C   (        M    |\/|
D   |)       N    |\|
E   3        P    |`
F   |=       S    5
G   (-       T    +
H   |-|      V    \/
I   1        W    \/\/
J   _|
```

Summary

- Whenever you have lots of things to process, try to think about how you'd process just one of them.
- Write a test that helps you imagine how you'd like to use the function to process one item. What will you pass in, and what do you expect back?
- Write your function to pass your test. Be sure to think about what you'll do with both good and bad input.
- To apply your function to each element in your input, use a `for` loop, a list comprehension, or a `map()`.

Twelve Days of Christmas: Algorithm design

Perhaps one of the worst songs of all time, and the one that is sure to ruin my Christmas spirit, is "The Twelve Days of Christmas." WILL IT EVER STOP!? AND WHAT IS WITH ALL THE BIRDS?! Still, it's pretty interesting to write an algorithm to generate the song starting from any given day because you have to count *up* as you add each verse (day) and then count *down* inside the verses (recapitulating the previous days' gifts). You'll be able to build on what you learned writing the program for "99 Bottles of Beer."

Our program in this chapter will be called twelve_days.py, and it will generate the "Twelve Days of Christmas" song up to a given day, specified by the -n or --num argument (default 12). Note that there should be two newlines between verses but only one at the end:

```
$ ./twelve_days.py -n 3
On the first day of Christmas,
My true love gave to me,
A partridge in a pear tree.

On the second day of Christmas,
My true love gave to me,
Two turtle doves,
And a partridge in a pear tree.
```

```
On the third day of Christmas,
My true love gave to me,
Three French hens,
Two turtle doves,
And a partridge in a pear tree.
```

The text will be printed to STDOUT unless there is an -o or --outfile argument, in which case the text should be placed inside a file with the given name. Note that there should be 113 lines of text for the entire song:

```
$ ./twelve_days.py -o song.txt
$ wc -l song.txt
     113 song.txt
```

In this exercise, you will

- Create an algorithm to generate "The Twelve Days of Christmas" from any given day in the range 1–12
- Reverse a list
- Use the range() function
- Write text to a file or to STDOUT

13.1 Writing twelve_days.py

As always, I suggest you create your program by running new.py or by copying the template/template.py file. This one must be called twelve_days.py and live in the 13_twelve_days directory.

Your program should take two options:

- -n or --num—An int with a default of 12
- -o or --outfile—An optional filename for writing the output

For the second option, you can go back to chapter 5 to see how we handled this in the Howler solution. That program writes its blistering output to the given filename if one is supplied, and otherwise writes to sys.stdout. For this program, I suggest you declare the --outfile using type=argparse.FileType('wt') to indicate that argparse will require an argument to name a *writable text* file. If the user supplies a valid argument, args.outfile will be an *open, writable file handle*. If you also use a default of sys.stdout, you'll have quickly handled both options of writing to a text file or STDOUT!

The only downside to this approach is that the usage statement for the program looks a little funny in describing the default for the --outfile parameter:

```
$ ./twelve_days.py -h
usage: twelve_days.py [-h] [-n days] [-o FILE]

Twelve Days of Christmas

optional arguments:
  -h, --help             show this help message and exit
```

```
-n days, --num days    Number of days to sing (default: 12)
-o FILE, --outfile FILE
                       Outfile (default: <_io.TextIOWrapper name='<stdout>'
                       mode='w' encoding='utf-8'>)
```

Once you've completed the usage, your program should pass the first two tests.

Figure 13.1 shows a holly, jolly string diagram to get you in the mood for writing the rest of the program.

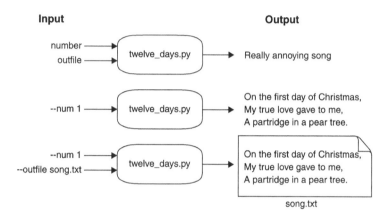

Figure 13.1   The twelve_days.py program takes options for which day to start on and an output file to write.

The program should complain if the --num value is not in the range 1–12. I suggest you check this inside the get_args() function and use parser.error() to halt with an error and usage message:

```
$ ./twelve_days.py -n 21
usage: twelve_days.py [-h] [-n days] [-o FILE]
twelve_days.py: error: --num "21" must be between 1 and 12
```

Once you've handled the bad --num, you should pass the first three tests.

13.1.1 *Counting*

In the "99 Bottles of Beer" song, we needed to count down from a given number. Here we need to count up to --num and then count back down through the gifts. The range() function will give us what we need, but we must remember to start at 1 because we don't start singing "On the zeroth day of Christmas." Keep in mind that the upper bound is not included:

```
>>> num = 3
>>> list(range(1, num))
[1, 2]
```

You'll need to add 1 to whatever you're given for `--num`:

```
>>> list(range(1, num + 1))
[1, 2, 3]
```

Let's start by printing something like the first line of each verse:

```
>>> for day in range(1, num + 1):
...     print(f'On the {day} day of Christmas,')
...
On the 1 day of Christmas,
On the 2 day of Christmas,
On the 3 day of Christmas,
```

At this point, I'm starting to think about how we wrote "99 Bottles of Beer." There we ended up creating a `verse()` function that would generate any *one* verse. Then we used `str.join()` to put them all together with two newlines. I suggest we try the same approach here, so I'll move the code inside the `for` loop into its own function:

```
def verse(day):
    """Create a verse"""
    return f'On the {day} day of Christmas,'
```

Notice that the function will not `print()` the string but will `return` the verse, so that we can test it:

```
>>> assert verse(1) == 'On the 1 day of Christmas,'
```

Let's see how we can use this `verse()` function:

```
>>> for day in range(1, num + 1):
...     print(verse(day))
...
On the 1 day of Christmas,
On the 2 day of Christmas,
On the 3 day of Christmas,
```

Here's a simple `test_verse()` function we could start off with:

```
def test_verse():
    """ Test verse """
    assert verse(1) == 'On the 1 day of Christmas,'
    assert verse(2) == 'On the 2 day of Christmas,'
```

This is incorrect, of course, because it should say "On the *first* day" or the "*second* day," not "1 day" or "2 day." Still, it's a place to start. Add the `verse()` and `test_verse()` functions to your twelve_days.py program, and then run `pytest twelve_days.py` to verify this much works.

13.1.2 *Creating the ordinal value*

Maybe the first thing to do is to change the numeric value to its ordinal position, that is "1" to "first," "2" to "second." You could use a dictionary like we used in "Jump The Five" to associate each int value 1–12 with its str value. That is, you might create a new dict called ordinal:

```
>>> ordinal = {} # what goes here?
```

Then you could do this:

```
>>> ordinal[1]
'first'
>>> ordinal[2]
'second'
```

You could also use a list, if you think about how you could use each day in the range() to index into a list of ordinal strings.

```
>>> ordinal = [] # what goes here?
```

Your verse() function might look something like this now:

```
def verse(day):
    """Create a verse"""
    ordinal = [] # something here!
    return f'On the {ordinal[day]} of Christmas,'
```

You can update your test with your expectations:

```
def test_verse():
    """ Test verse """
    assert verse(1) == 'On the first day of Christmas,'
    assert verse(2) == 'On the second day of Christmas,'
```

Once you have this working, you should be able to replicate something like this:

```
>>> for day in range(1, num + 1):
...     print(verse(day))
...
On the day first day of Christmas,
On the day second day of Christmas,
On the day third day of Christmas,
```

If you put the test_verse() function inside your twelve_days.py program, you can verify that your verse() function works by running pytest twelve_days.py. The pytest module will run any function that has a name starting with test_.

Shadowing

You might be tempted to use the variable name `ord`, and you would be allowed by Python to do this. The problem is that Python has a function called `ord()` that returns "the Unicode code point for a one-character string":

```
>>> ord('a')
97
```

Python will not complain if you define a variable or another function with the name `ord`,

```
>>> ord = {}
```

such that you could do this:

```
>>> ord[1]
'first'
```

But that overwrites the actual `ord` function and so breaks a function call:

```
>>> ord('a')
Traceback (most recent call last):
  File "<stdin>", line 1, in <module>
TypeError: 'dict' object is not callable
```

This is called "shadowing," and it's quite dangerous. Any code in the scope of the shadowing would be affected by the change.

Tools like Pylint can help you find problems like this in your programs. Assume you have the following code:

```
$ cat shadow.py
#!/usr/bin/env python3

ord = {}
print(ord('a'))
```

Here is what Pylint has to say:

```
$ pylint shadow.py
************* Module shadow
shadow.py:3:0: W0622: Redefining built-in 'ord' (redefined-builtin)
shadow.py:1:0: C0111: Missing module docstring (missing-docstring)
shadow.py:4:6: E1102: ord is not callable (not-callable)

------------------------------------
Your code has been rated at -25.00/10
```

It's good to double-check your code with tools like Pylint and Flake8!

13.1.3 *Making the verses*

Now that we have the basic structure of the program, let's focus on creating the *correct* output. We'll update test_verse() with the actual values for the first two verses. You can, of course, add more tests, but presumably if we can manage the first two days, we can handle all the other days:

```
def test_verse():
    """Test verse"""

    assert verse(1) == '\n'.join([
        'On the first day of Christmas,', 'My true love gave to me,',
        'A partridge in a pear tree.'
    ])

    assert verse(2) == '\n'.join([
        'On the second day of Christmas,', 'My true love gave to me,',
        'Two turtle doves,', 'And a partridge in a pear tree.'
    ])
```

If you add this to your twelve_days.py program, you can run pytest twelve_days.py to see how your verse() function is failing:

```
=================================== FAILURES ===================================
_____ test_verse _____

        def test_verse():
            """Test verse"""

>           assert verse(1) == '\n'.join([
                'On the first day of Christmas,', 'My true love gave to me,',
                'A partridge in a pear tree.'
            ])
E           AssertionError: assert 'On the first...of Christmas,' == 'On the first
    ... a pear tree.'
E             - On the first day of Christmas,
E             + On the first day of Christmas,
E             ?                              +
E             + My true love gave to me,
E             + A partridge in a pear tree.

twelve_days.py:88: AssertionError
=========================== 1 failed in 0.11 seconds ===========================
```

The leading > shows that this is the code that is creating an exception. We are running verse(1) and asking if it's equal to the expected verse.

This is the text that verse(1) actually produced, which is only the first line of the verse.

The lines following are what was expected.

Now we need to supply the rest of the lines for each verse. They all start off the same:

```
On the {ordinal[day]} day of Christmas,
My true love gave to me,
```

Then we need to add these gifts for each day:

1 A partridge in a pear tree
2 Two turtle doves
3 Three French hens
4 Four calling birds
5 Five gold rings
6 Six geese a laying
7 Seven swans a swimming
8 Eight maids a milking
9 Nine ladies dancing
10 Ten lords a leaping
11 Eleven pipers piping
12 Twelve drummers drumming

Note that for every day greater than 1, the last line changes "*A partridge…*" to "*And a partridge in a pear tree.*"

Each verse needs to count backwards from the given day. For example, if the day is 3, then the verse lists

1 Three French hens
2 Two turtle doves
3 And a partridge in a pear tree

We talked in chapter 3 about how you can reverse a `list`, either with the `list.reverse()` method or the `reversed()` function. We also used these ideas in chapter 11 to get the bottles of beer off the wall, so this code should not be unfamiliar:

```
>>> day = 3
>>> for n in reversed(range(1, day + 1)):
...     print(n)
...
3
2
1
```

Try to make the function return the first two lines and then the countdown of the days:

```
>>> print(verse(3))
On the third day of Christmas,
My true love gave to me,
3
2
1
```

Then, instead of 3 2 1, add the actual gifts:

```
>>> print(verse(3))
On the third day of Christmas,
My true love gave to me,
```

```
Three French hens,
Two turtle doves,
And a partridge in a pear tree.
```

If you can get that to work, you ought to be able to pass the test_verse() test.

13.1.4 Using the verse() function

Once you have that working, think about a final structure that calls your verse(). It could be a for loop:

```
verses = []
for day in range(1, args.num + 1):
    verses.append(verse(day))
```

Since we're trying to create a list of the verses, a list comprehension is a better choice:

```
verses = [verse(day) for day in range(1, args.num + 1)]
```

Or it could be a map():

```
verses = map(verse, range(1, args.num + 1))
```

13.1.5 Printing

Once you have all the verses, you can use the str.join() method to print the output. The default is to print this to "standard out" (STDOUT), but the program will also take an optional --outfile that names a file to write the output to. You can copy exactly what we did in chapter 5, but it's really worth your time to learn how to declare output files using type=argparse.FileType('wt'). You can even set the default to sys.stdout so that you'll never have to open() the output file yourself!

13.1.6 Time to write

It's not at all mandatory that you solve the problem the way that I describe. The "correct" solution is one that you write and understand and that passes the test suite. It's fine if you like the idea of creating a function for verse() and using the provided test. It's also fine if you want to go another way, but do try to think of writing small functions *and tests* to solve small parts of your problem, and then combining them to solve the larger problem.

If you need more than one sitting or even several days to pass the tests, take your time. Sometimes a good walk or a nap can do wonders for solving problems. Don't neglect your hammock[1] or a nice cup of tea.

---

[1] Search the internet for the talk "Hammock Driven Development" by Rich Hickey, the creator of the Clojure language.

13.2   *Solution*

A person would receive almost 200 birds in this song! Anyway, here is a solution that
uses map(). After that you'll see versions that use for and list comprehensions.

```python
#!/usr/bin/env python3
"""Twelve Days of Christmas"""

import argparse
import sys


# --------------------------------------------------
def get_args():
    """Get command-line arguments"""

    parser = argparse.ArgumentParser(
        description='Twelve Days of Christmas',
        formatter_class=argparse.ArgumentDefaultsHelpFormatter)

    parser.add_argument('-n',
                        '--num',
                        help='Number of days to sing',
                        metavar='days',
                        type=int,
                        default=12)

    parser.add_argument('-o',
                        '--outfile',
                        help='Outfile',
                        metavar='FILE',
                        type=argparse.FileType('wt'),
                        default=sys.stdout)

    args = parser.parse_args()

    if args.num not in range(1, 13):
        parser.error(f'--num "{args.num}" must be between 1 and 12')

    return args
```

If args.num is invalid, use
parser.error() to print a
short usage statement and
the error message to STDERR
and exit the program with an
error value. Note that the
error message includes the
bad value for the user and
explicitly states that a good
value should be in the
range 1–12.

The --num option is an
int with a default of 12.

The --outfile option is a
type=argparse.FileType('wt') with a
default of sys.stdout. If the user supplies
a value, it must be the name of a writable
file, in which case argparse will open the
file for writing.

Check that
the given
args.num is
in the
allowed
range1–12,
inclusive.

Capture the results of parsing the command-
line arguments into the args variable.

```python
# --------------------------------------------------
def main():
    """Make a jazz noise here"""

    args = get_args()
    verses = map(verse, range(1, args.num + 1))
    print('\n\n'.join(verses), file=args.outfile)


# --------------------------------------------------
def verse(day):
    """Create a verse"""
```

Generate
the verses
for the
given
args.num
of days.

Get the command-line arguments. Remember that all
argument validation happens inside get_args(). If this
call succeeds, we have good arguments from the user.

Join the verses on two newlines
and print to args.outfile, which is
an open file handle, or sys.stdout.

Define a function to create any one
verse from a given number.

The ordinal values is a list of str values.

```
ordinal = [
    'first', 'second', 'third', 'fourth', 'fifth', 'sixth', 'seventh',
    'eighth', 'ninth', 'tenth', 'eleventh', 'twelfth'
]
```

The gifts for the days is a list of str values.

```
gifts = [
    'A partridge in a pear tree.',
    'Two turtle doves,',
    'Three French hens,',
    'Four calling birds,',
    'Five gold rings,',
    'Six geese a laying,',
    'Seven swans a swimming,',
    'Eight maids a milking,',
    'Nine ladies dancing,',
    'Ten lords a leaping,',
    'Eleven pipers piping,',
    'Twelve drummers drumming,',
]
```

The lines of each verse start off the same, substituting in the ordinal value of the given day.

```
lines = [
    f'On the {ordinal[day - 1]} day of Christmas,',
    'My true love gave to me,'
]
```

Use the list.extend() method to add the gifts, which are a slice from the given day and then reversed().

```
lines.extend(reversed(gifts[:day]))
```

Check if this is for a day greater than 1.

```
if day > 1:
    lines[-1] = 'And ' + lines[-1].lower()
```

Change the last of the lines to add "And " to the beginning, appended to the lowercased version of the line.

Return the lines joined on the newline.

```
return '\n'.join(lines)


# -------------------------------------------------
def test_verse():
    """Test verse"""
```

The unit test for the verse() function

```
    assert verse(1) == '\n'.join([
        'On the first day of Christmas,', 'My true love gave to me,',
        'A partridge in a pear tree.'
    ])

    assert verse(2) == '\n'.join([
        'On the second day of Christmas,', 'My true love gave to me,',
        'Two turtle doves,', 'And a partridge in a pear tree.'
    ])


# -------------------------------------------------
if __name__ == '__main__':
    main()
```

13.3 *Discussion*

Not much in get_args() is new, so we'll throw it a sidelong, cursory glance. The --num option is an int value with a default value of 12, and we use parser.error() to halt the program if the user provides a bad value. The --outfile option is a bit different, though, as we're declaring it with type=argparse.FileType('wt') to indicate the value must be a writable file. This means the value we get from argparse will be an open, writable file. We set the default to sys.stdout, which is also an open, writable file, so we've handled the two output options entirely through argparse, which is a real time saver!

13.3.1 *Making one verse*

I chose to make a function called verse() to create any one verse given an int value of the day:

```
def verse(day):
    """Create a verse"""
```

I decided to use a list to represent the ordinal value of the day:

```
ordinal = [
    'first', 'second', 'third', 'fourth', 'fifth', 'sixth', 'seventh',
    'eighth', 'ninth', 'tenth', 'eleventh', 'twelfth'
]
```

Since the day is based on counting from 1, but Python lists start from 0 (see figure 13.2), I have to subtract 1:

```
>>> day = 3
>>> ordinal[day - 1]
'third'
```

ordinal = [	Index	Day
'first'	0	1
'second'	1	2
'third'	2	3
'fourth'	3	4
'fifth'	4	5
'sixth'	5	6
'seventh'	6	7
'eighth'	7	8
'ninth'	8	9
'tenth'	9	10
'eleventh'	10	11
'twelfth'	11	12
]		

Figure 13.2 Our days start counting from 1, but Python indexes from 0.

I could just as easily have used a `dict`:

```
ordinal = {
    1: 'first', 2: 'second', 3: 'third', 4: 'fourth',
    5: 'fifth', 6: 'sixth', 7: 'seventh', 8: 'eighth',
    9: 'ninth', 10: 'tenth', 11: 'eleventh', 12: 'twelfth',
}
```

In this case you don't have to subtract 1. Whatever works for you:

```
>>> ordinal[3]
'third'
```

I also used a `list` for the `gifts`:

```
gifts = [
    'A partridge in a pear tree.',
    'Two turtle doves,',
    'Three French hens,',
    'Four calling birds,',
    'Five gold rings,',
    'Six geese a laying,',
    'Seven swans a swimming,',
    'Eight maids a milking,',
    'Nine ladies dancing,',
    'Ten lords a leaping,',
    'Eleven pipers piping,',
    'Twelve drummers drumming,',
]
```

This makes a bit more sense, as I can use a list slice to get the `gifts` for a given day (see figure 13.3):

```
>>> gifts[:3]
['A partridge in a pear tree.',
 'Two turtle doves,',
 'Three French hens,']
```

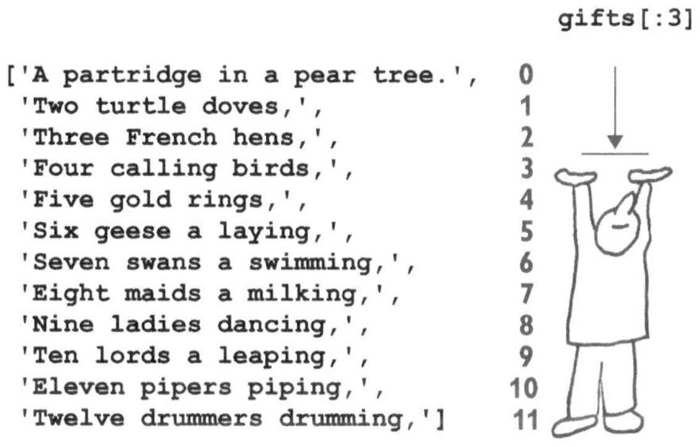

Figure 13.3 The gifts are listed by their days in ascending order.

But I want them in reverse order. The `reversed()` function is lazy, so I need to use the `list()` function in the REPL to coerce the values:

```
>>> list(reversed(gifts[:3]))
['Three French hens,',
 'Two turtle doves,',
 'A partridge in a pear tree.']
```

The first two lines of any verse are the same, substituting in the `ordinal` value for the day:

```
lines = [
    f'On the {ordinal[day - 1]} day of Christmas,',
    'My true love gave to me,'
]
```

I need to put these two `lines` together with the `gifts`. Since each verse is made of some number of lines, I think it will make sense to use a `list` to represent the entire verse.

I need to add the `gifts` to the `lines`, and I can use the `list.extend()` method to do that:

```
>>> lines.extend(reversed(gifts[:day]))
```

Now there are five `lines`:

```
>>> lines
['On the third day of Christmas,',
 'My true love gave to me,',
 'Three French hens,',
 'Two turtle doves,',
 'A partridge in a pear tree.']
>>> assert len(lines) == 5
```

Note that I cannot use the `list.append()` method. It's easy to confuse it with the `list.extend()` method, which takes another `list` as its argument, expands it, and adds all of the individual elements to the original `list`. The `list.append()` method is meant to add *just one* element to a `list`, so if you give it a `list`, it will tack that entire `list` onto the end of the original list!

Here the `reversed()` iterator will be added to the end of `lines`, such that it would have three elements rather than the desired five:

```
>>> lines.append(reversed(gifts[:day]))
>>> lines
['On the third day of Christmas,',
 'My true love gave to me,',
 <list_reverseiterator object at 0x105bc8588>]
```

Maybe you're thinking you could coerce `reversed()` with the `list()` function? Thinking you are, young Jedi, but, alas, that will still add a new `list` to the end:

```
>>> lines.append(list(reversed(gifts[:day])))
>>> lines
```

```
['On the third day of Christmas,',
 'My true love gave to me,',
 ['Three French hens,', 'Two turtle doves,', 'A partridge in a pear tree.']]
```

And we still have three `lines` rather than five:

```
>>> len(lines)
3
```

If day is greater than 1, I need to change the last line to say "And a" instead of "A":

```
if day > 1:
    lines[-1] = 'And ' + lines[-1].lower()
```

Note that this is another good reason to represent the `lines` as a `list`, because the elements of a `list` are *mutable*. I could have represented the `lines` as a `str`, but strings are *immutable*, so it would be much harder to change the last line.

I want to return a single `str` value from the function, so I join the `lines` on a newline:

```
>>> print('\n'.join(lines))
On the third day of Christmas,
My true love gave to me,
Three French hens,
Two turtle doves,
A partridge in a pear tree.
```

My function returns the joined `lines` and will pass the `test_verse()` function I provided.

13.3.2 *Generating the verses*

Given the `verse()` function, I can create all the needed verses by iterating from 1 to the given --num. I could collect them in a `list` of verses:

```
day = 3
verses = []
for n in range(1, day + 1):
    verses.append(verse(n))
```

I can test that I have the right number of verses:

```
>>> assert len(verses) == day
```

Whenever you see this pattern of creating an empty `str` or `list` and then using a `for` loop to add to it, consider instead using a list comprehension:

```
>>> verses = [verse(n) for n in range(1, day + 1)]
>>> assert len(verses) == day
```

I personally prefer using map() over list comprehensions. See figure 13.4 to review how the three methods fit together. I need to use the list() function to coerce the lazy map() function in the REPL, but it's not necessary in the program code:

```
>>> verses = list(map(verse, range(1, day + 1)))
>>> assert len(verses) == day
```

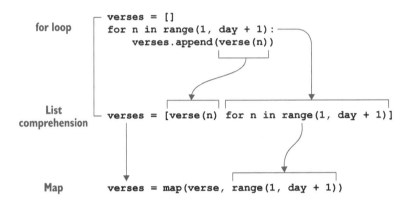

Figure 13.4   Building a list using a for loop, a list comprehension, and map().

All of these methods will produce the correct number of verses. Choose whichever one makes the most sense to you.

13.3.3 Printing the verses

Just like with "99 Bottles of Beer" in chapter 11, I want to print() the verses with two newlines in between. The str.join() method is a good choice:

```
>>> print('\n\n'.join(verses))
On the first day of Christmas,
My true love gave to me,
A partridge in a pear tree.

On the second day of Christmas,
My true love gave to me,
Two turtle doves,
And a partridge in a pear tree.

On the third day of Christmas,
My true love gave to me,
Three French hens,
Two turtle doves,
And a partridge in a pear tree.
```

You can use the `print()` function with the optional `file` argument to put the text into an open file handle. The `args.outfile` value will be either the file indicated by the user or `sys.stdout`:

```
print('\n\n'.join(verses), file=args.outfile)
```

Or you can use the `fh.write()` method, but you need to remember to add the trailing newline that `print()` adds for you:

```
args.outfile.write('\n\n'.join(verses) + '\n')
```

There are dozens to hundreds of ways to write this algorithm, just as there are for "99 Bottles of Beer." If you came up with an entirely different approach that passed the test, that's terrific! Please share it with me. I wanted to stress the idea of how to write, test, and use a single `verse()` function, but I'd love to see other approaches!

13.4 Going further

Install the `emoji` module (https://pypi.org/project/emoji/) and print various emojis for the gifts rather than text. For instance, you could use `':bird:'` to print 🕊 for every bird, like a hen or dove. I also used `':man:'`, `':woman:'`, and `':drum:'`, but you can use whatever you like:

```
On the twelfth day of Christmas,
My true love gave to me,
Twelve 🥁s drumming,
Eleven 👨s piping,
Ten 👨s a leaping,
Nine 👩s dancing,
Eight 👩s a milking,
Seven 🕊s a swimming,
Six 🕊s a laying,
Five gold ♂s,
Four calling 🕊s,
Three French 🕊s,
Two turtle 🕊s,
And a 🕊 in a pear tree.
```

Summary

- There are many ways to encode algorithms to perform repetitive tasks. In my version, I wrote and tested a function to handle one task and then mapped a range of input values over that.
- The `range()` function will return `int` values between given start and stop values, the latter of which is not included.
- You can use the `reversed()` function to reverse the values returned by `range()`.

- If you use `type=argparse.FileType('wt')` to define an argument with `argparse`, you get a file handle that is open for writing text.

- The `sys.stdout` file handle is always open and available for writing.

- Modeling `gifts` as a `list` allowed me to use a list slice to get all the gifts for a given day. I used the `reversed()` function to put them into the right order for the song.

- I modeled `lines` as a `list` because a `list` is mutable, which I needed in order to change the last line when the day is greater than 1.

- Shadowing a variable or function is reusing an existing variable or function name. If, for instance, you create a variable with the name of an existing function, that function is effectively hidden because of the shadow. Avoid shadowing by using tools like Pylint to find these and many other common coding problems.

Rhymer: Using regular expressions to create rhyming words

In the movie *The Princess Bride*, the characters Inigo and Fezzik have a rhyming game they like to play, especially when their cruel boss, Vizzini, yells at them:

Inigo: That Vizzini, he can fuss.
Fezzik: I think he likes to scream at us.
Inigo: Probably he means no harm.
Fezzik: He's really very short on charm.

When I was writing the alternate.txt for chapter 7, I would come up with a word like "cyanide" and wonder what I could rhyme with that. Mentally I started with the first consonant sound of the alphabet and substituted "b" for "byanide," skipped "c" because that's already the first character, then "d" for "dyanide," and so forth. This is effective but tedious, so I decided to write a program to do this for me, as one does.

This is basically another find-and-replace type of program, like swapping all the numbers in a string in chapter 4 or all the vowels in a string in chapter 8. We wrote those programs using very manual, *imperative* methods, like iterating through all the characters of a string, comparing them to some wanted value, and possibly returning a new value.

In the final solution for chapter 8, we briefly touched on "regular expressions" (also called "regexes"—pronounced with a soft "g" like in "George"), which give us a *declarative* way to describe patterns of text. The material here may seem a bit of a reach, but I really want to help you dig into regexes to see what they can do.

In this chapter, we're going to take a given word and create "words" that rhyme. For instance, the word "bake" rhymes with words like "cake," "make," and "thrake," the last of which isn't actually a dictionary word but just a new string I created by replacing the "b" in "bake" with "thr."

The algorithm we'll use will split a word into any initial consonants and the rest of the word, so "bake" is split into "b" and "ake." We'll replace the "b" with all the other consonants from the alphabet plus these consonant clusters:

```
bl br ch cl cr dr fl fr gl gr pl pr sc sh sk sl sm sn sp st
sw th tr tw thw wh wr sch scr shr sph spl spr squ str thr
```

These are the first three words our program will produce for "cake":

```
$ ./rhymer.py cake | head -3
bake
blake
brake
```

And these are the last three:

```
$ ./rhymer.py cake | tail -3
xake
yake
zake
```

Make sure your output is sorted alphabetically as this is important for the tests.

We'll replace any leading consonants with a list of other consonant sounds to create a total of 56 words:

```
$ ./rhymer.py cake | wc -l
      56
```

Note that we'll replace *all* the leading consonants, not just the first one. For instance, with the word "chair" we need to replace "ch":

```
$ ./rhymer.py chair | tail -3
xair
yair
zair
```

If a word like "apple" does not start with a consonant, we'll append all the consonant sounds to the beginning to create words like "bapple" and "shrapple."

```
$ ./rhymer.py apple | head -3
bapple
blapple
brapple
```

Because there is no consonant to *replace*, words that start with a vowel will produce 57 rhyming words:

```
$ ./rhymer.py apple | wc -l
      57
```

To make this a bit easier, the output should always be all lowercase, even if the input has uppercase letters:

```
$ ./rhymer.py GUITAR | tail -3
xuitar
yuitar
zuitar
```

If a word contains nothing but consonants, we'll print a message stating that the word cannot be rhymed:

```
$ ./rhymer.py RDNZL
Cannot rhyme "RDNZL"
```

The task of finding the initial consonants is made significantly easier with regexes.

In this program, you will

- Learn to write and use regular expressions
- Use a guard with a list comprehension
- Explore the similarities of list comprehension with a guard to the `filter()` function
- Entertain ideas of "truthiness" when evaluating Python types in a Boolean context

14.1 Writing rhymer.py

The program takes a single, positional argument, which is the string to rhyme. Figure 14.1 shows a snazzy, jazzy, frazzy, thwazzy string diagram.

If given no arguments or the -h or --help flags, it should print a usage statement:

```
$ ./rhymer.py -h
usage: rhymer.py [-h] word

Make rhyming "words"

positional arguments:
  word        A word to rhyme

optional arguments:
  -h, --help  show this help message and exit
```

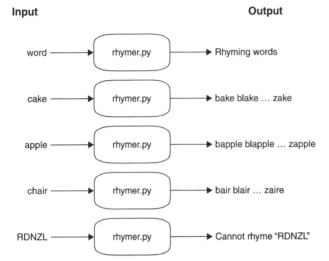

Figure 14.1   The input for our rhymer program should be a word, and the output will be a list of rhyming words or an error.

14.1.1 Breaking a word

To my mind, the main problem of the program is breaking the given word into the leading consonant sounds and the rest—something like the "stem" of the word.

To start out, we can define a placeholder for a function I call `stemmer()` that does nothing right now:

```
def stemmer():
    """Return leading consonants (if any), and 'stem' of word"""
    pass
```

The pass statement will do nothing at all. Since the function does not return a value, Python will return None by default.

Then we can define a `test_stemmer()` function to help us think about the values we might give the function and what we expect it to return. We want a test with good values like "cake" and "apple" that can be rhymed as well as values like the empty string or a number, which cannot:

```
def test_stemmer():
    """ Test stemmer """
    assert stemmer('') == ('', '')           ❶
    assert stemmer('cake') == ('c', 'ake')   ❷
    assert stemmer('chair') == ('ch', 'air') ❸
    assert stemmer('APPLE') == ('', 'apple') ❹
    assert stemmer('RDNZL') == ('rdnzl', '') ❺
    assert stemmer('123') == ('123', '')     ❻
```

The tests cover the following good and bad inputs:

❶ The empty string

❷ A word with a single leading consonant

❸ A word with a leading consonant cluster

❹ A word with no initial consonants; also an uppercase word, so this checks that lowercase is returned

❺ A word with no vowels

❻ Something that isn't a word at all

I decided that my `stemmer()` function will always returns a 2-tuple of the `(start, rest)` of the word. (You can write a function that does something different, but be sure to change the test to match.) It's the second part of that `tuple`—the `rest`—that we can use to create rhyming words. For instance, the word "cake" produces a `tuple` with (`'c'`, `'ake'`), and "chair" is split into (`'ch'`, `'air'`). The argument "`APPLE`" has no `start` and only the `rest` of the word, which is lowercase.

When I'm writing tests, I usually try to provide both good and bad data to my functions and programs. Three of the test values cannot be rhymed: the empty string (`''`), a string with no vowels (`'RDNZL'`), and a string with no letters (`'123'`). The `stemmer()` function will still return a `tuple` containing the lowercased word in the first position of the tuples and the empty string in the second position for the `rest` of the word. It is up to the calling code to deal with a word that has no part that can be used to rhyme.

14.1.2 *Using regular expressions*

It's certainly *possible* to write this program without regular expressions, but I hope you'll see how radically different using regexes can be from manually writing your own search-and-replace code.

To start off, we need to bring in the `re` module:

```
>>> import re
```

I encourage you to read `help(re)` to get a feel for all that you can do with regexes. They are a deep subject with many books and whole branches of academia devoted to them (*Mastering Regular Expressions* by Jeffrey Friedl (O'Reilly, 2006) is one book I would recommend). There are many helpful websites that can further explain regexes, and some can help you write them (such as https://regexr.com/). We will only scratch the surface of what you can do with regexes.

Our goal in this program is to write a regex that will find consonants at the beginning of a string. We can define consonants as the characters of the English alphabet that are not vowels ("a," "e," "i," "o," and "u"). Our `stemmer()` function will only return lowercase letters, so there are only 21 consonants we need to define. You could write them out, but I'd rather write a bit of code!

We can start with `string.ascii_lowercase`:

```
>>> import string
>>> string.ascii_lowercase
'abcdefghijklmnopqrstuvwxyz'
```

Next, we can use a list comprehension with a "guard" clause to filter out the vowels. As we want a str of consonants and not a list, we can use str.join() to make a new str value:

```
>>> import string as s
>>> s.ascii_lowercase
'abcdefghijklmnopqrstuvwxyz'
>>> consonants = ''.join([c for c in s.ascii_lowercase if c not in 'aeiou'])
>>> consonants
'bcdfghjklmnpqrstvwxyz'
```

The longer way to write this with a for loop and an if statement is as follows (see figure 14.2):

```
consonants = ''
for c in string.ascii_lowercase:
    if c not in 'aeiou':
        consonants += c
```

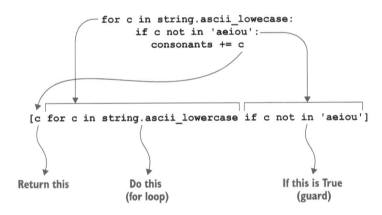

Figure 14.2 The for loop (top) can be written as a list comprehension (bottom). This list comprehension includes a guard so that only consonants are selected, which is like the if statement at the top.

In chapter 8 we created a "character class" for matching the vowels by listing them in square brackets, like '[aeiou]'. We can do the same here with our consonants, like so:

```
>>> pattern = '[' + consonants + ']'
>>> pattern
'[bcdfghjklmnpqrstvwxyz]'
```

The re module has two search-like functions called re.match() and re.search(), and I always get them confused. They both look for a pattern (the first argument) in some text, but the re.match() functions starts *from the beginning* of the text, whereas the re.search() function will match starting *anywhere* in the text.

As it happens, `re.match()` is just fine because we are looking for consonants at the beginning of a string (see figure 14.3).

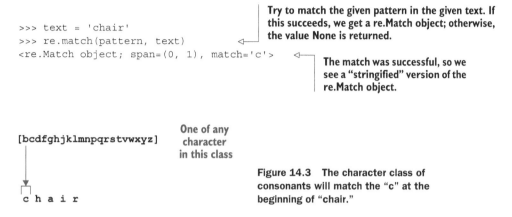

```
>>> text = 'chair'
>>> re.match(pattern, text)
<re.Match object; span=(0, 1), match='c'>
```

Try to match the given pattern in the given text. If this succeeds, we get a re.Match object; otherwise, the value None is returned.

The match was successful, so we see a "stringified" version of the re.Match object.

[bcdfghjklmnpqrstvwxyz]

One of any character in this class

c h a i r

Figure 14.3 The character class of consonants will match the "c" at the beginning of "chair."

The `match='c'` shows us that the regular expression found the string `'c'` at the beginning. Both the `re.match()` and `re.search()` functions will return a `re.Match` object on success. You can read `help(re.Match)` to learn more about all the cool things you can do with them:

```
>>> match = re.match(pattern, text)
>>> type(match)
<class 're.Match'>
```

How do we get our regex to match the letters `'ch'`? We can put a `'+'` sign after the character class to say we want *one or more* (see figure 14.4). (Does this sound a bit like `nargs='+'` to say one or more arguments?) I will use an f-string here to create the pattern:

```
>>> re.match(f'[{consonants}]+', 'chair')
<re.Match object; span=(0, 2), match='ch'>
```

[bcdfghjklmnpqrstvwxyz]+

One or more of any character in this class

c h a i r

Figure 14.4 Adding a plus sign to the class will match one or more characters.

What does it give us for a string with no leading consonants like "apple," as in figure 14.5?

```
>>> re.match(f'[{consonants}]+', 'apple')
```

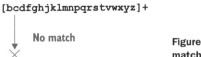

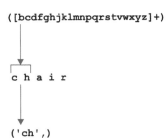

Figure 14.5   **This regex fails to match a word that does not start with a consonant.**

It seems we got nothing back from that. What is the `type()` of that return value?

```
>>> type(re.match(f'[{consonants}]+', 'apple'))
<class 'NoneType'>
```

Both the `re.match()` and `re.search()` functions return `None` to indicate a failure to match any text. We know that only some words will have a leading consonant sound, so this is not surprising. We'll see in a moment how to make this an optional match.

14.1.3 Using capture groups

It's all well and good to have found (or not) the leading consonants, but the goal here is to split the `text` into two parts: the consonants (if any) and the rest of the word.

We can wrap parts of the regex in parentheses to create "capture groups." If the regex matches successfully, we can recover the parts using the `re.Match.groups()` method (see figure 14.6):

```
>>> match = re.match(f'([{consonants}]+)', 'chair')
>>> match.groups()
('ch',)
```

([bcdfghjklmnpqrstvwxyz]+)

c h a i r

('ch',)

Figure 14.6   **Adding parentheses around a pattern causes the matching text to be available as a capture group.**

To capture everything that comes after the `consonants`, we can use a period (`.`) to match anything, and add a plus sign (`+`) to mean one or more. We can put that into parentheses to capture it (see figure 14.7):

```
>>> match = re.match(f'([{consonants}]+)(.+)', 'chair')
>>> match.groups()
('ch', 'air')
```

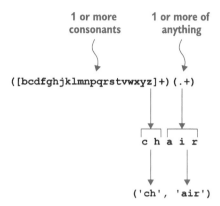

Figure 14.7 We define two capture groups to access the leading consonant sound and whatever follows.

What happens when we try to use this on "apple"? It fails to make the first match on the consonants, so *the whole match fails* and returns None (see figure 14.8):

```
>>> match = re.match(f'([{consonants}]+)(.+)', 'apple')
>>> match.groups()
Traceback (most recent call last):
  File "<stdin>", line 1, in <module>
AttributeError: 'NoneType' object has no attribute 'groups'
```

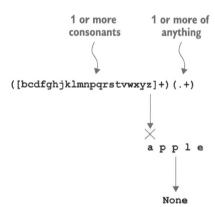

Figure 14.8 The pattern still fails when the text starts with a vowel.

Remember that re.match() returns None when it fails to find the pattern. We can add a question mark (?) at the end of the consonants pattern to make it optional (see figure 14.9):

```
>>> match = re.match(f'([{consonants}]+)?(.+)', 'apple')
>>> match.groups()
(None, 'apple')
```

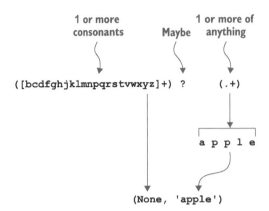

Figure 14.9   A question mark after a pattern makes it optional.

The `match.groups()` function returns a `tuple` containing the matches for each grouping created by the parentheses. You can also use `match.group()` (singular) with a group number to get a specific group. Note that these start numbering from 1:

```
>>> match.group(1)          ◁──┐ There was no match for the first
                                 group on "apple," so this is a None.
>>> match.group(2)          ◁──
'apple'                          The second group captured
                                 the entire word.
```

If you match on "chair," there are values for both groups:

```
>>> match = re.match(f'([{consonants}]+)?(.+)', 'chair')
>>> match.group(1)
'ch'
>>> match.group(2)
'air'
```

So far we've only dealt with lowercase text because our program will always emit lowercase values. Still, let's explore what happens when we try to match uppercase text:

```
>>> match = re.match(f'([{consonants}]+)?(.+)', 'CHAIR')
>>> match.groups()
(None, 'CHAIR')
```

Not surprisingly, that fails. Our pattern only defines lowercase characters. We could add all the uppercase consonants, but it's a bit easier to use a third optional argument to `re.match()` to specify case-insensitive searching:

```
>>> match = re.match(f'([{consonants}]+)?(.+)', 'CHAIR', re.IGNORECASE)
>>> match.groups()
('CH', 'AIR')
```

Or you can force the text you are searching to lowercase:

```
>>> match = re.match(f'([{consonants}]+)?(.+)', 'CHAIR'.lower())
>>> match.groups()
('ch', 'air')
```

What do you get when you search on text that has nothing but consonants?

```
>>> match = re.match(f'([{consonants}]+)?(.+)', 'rdnzl')
>>> match.groups()
('rdnz', 'l')
```

Were you expecting the first group to include *all* the consonants and the second group to have nothing? It might seem a bit odd that it decided to split off the "l" into the last group, as shown in figure 14.10, but we have to think *extremely literally* about how the regex engine is working. We described an optional group of one or more consonants that *must be followed* by one or more of anything else. The "l" counts as one or more of anything else, so the regex matched exactly what we requested.

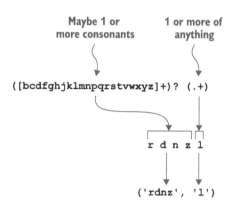

Figure 14.10 The regex does exactly what we ask, but perhaps not what we wanted.

If we change the (.+) to (.*) to make it *zero or more*, it works as expected:

```
>>> match = re.match(f'([{consonants}]+)?(.*)', 'rdnzl')
>>> match.groups()
('rdnzl', '')
```

Our regex is not quite complete, as it doesn't handle matching on something like 123. That is, it matches too well because the period (.) will match the digits, which we don't want:

```
>>> re.match(f'([{consonants}]+)?(.*)?', '123')
<re.Match object; span=(0, 3), match='123'>
```

We need to indicate that there should be *at least one vowel* after the consonants, which may be followed by anything else. We can use another character class to describe any vowel. Since we need to capture this, we'll put it in parentheses, so ([aeiou]). That may be followed by *zero or more* of anything, which also needs to be captured, so (.*), as shown in figure 14.11.

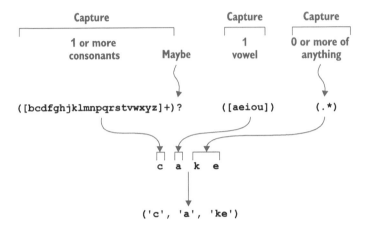

Figure 14.11   The regex now requires the presence of a vowel.

Let's go back and try this on values we expect to work:

```
>>> re.match(f'([{consonants}]+)?([aeiou])(.*)', 'cake').groups()
('c', 'a', 'ke')
>>> re.match(f'([{consonants}]+)?([aeiou])(.*)', 'chair').groups()
('ch', 'a', 'ir')
>>> re.match(f'([{consonants}]+)?([aeiou])(.*)', 'apple').groups()
(None, 'a', 'pple')
```

As you can see, this fails to match when the string contains no vowels or letters:

```
>>> type(re.match(f'([{consonants}]+)?([aeiou])(.*)', 'rdnzl'))
<class 'NoneType'>
>>> type(re.match(f'([{consonants}]+)?([aeiou])(.*)', '123'))
<class 'NoneType'>
```

14.1.4 *Truthiness*

We know that our program will receive some inputs that cannot be rhymed, so what should the stemmer() function do with these? Some people like to use exceptions in cases like this. We've encountered exceptions like asking for a list index or a dictionary key that does not exist. If exceptions are not caught and handled, they cause our programs to crash!

I try to avoid writing code that creates exceptions. I decided that my stemmer() function would always return a 2-tuple of (start, rest), and that I would always use the empty string to denote a missing value rather than a None. Here is one way I could write the code for returning those tuples:

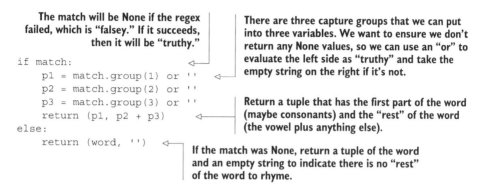

The match will be None if the regex failed, which is "falsey." If it succeeds, then it will be "truthy."

```
if match:
    p1 = match.group(1) or ''
    p2 = match.group(2) or ''
    p3 = match.group(3) or ''
    return (p1, p2 + p3)
else:
    return (word, '')
```

There are three capture groups that we can put into three variables. We want to ensure we don't return any None values, so we can use an "or" to evaluate the left side as "truthy" and take the empty string on the right if it's not.

Return a tuple that has the first part of the word (maybe consonants) and the "rest" of the word (the vowel plus anything else).

If the match was None, return a tuple of the word and an empty string to indicate there is no "rest" of the word to rhyme.

Let's take a moment to think about the or operator, which we're using to decide between something on the left *or* something on the right. The or will return the first "truthy" value, the one that—sort of, kind of—evaluates to True in a Boolean context:

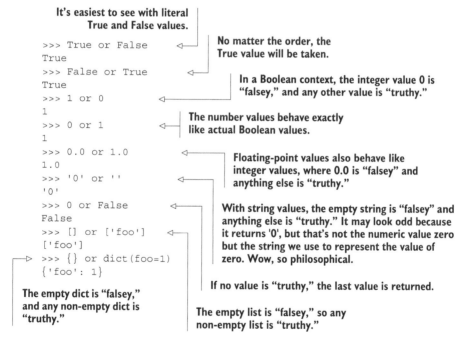

It's easiest to see with literal True and False values.

```
>>> True or False
True
>>> False or True
True
>>> 1 or 0
1
>>> 0 or 1
1
>>> 0.0 or 1.0
1.0
>>> '0' or ''
'0'
>>> 0 or False
False
>>> [] or ['foo']
['foo']
>>> {} or dict(foo=1)
{'foo': 1}
```

No matter the order, the True value will be taken.

In a Boolean context, the integer value 0 is "falsey," and any other value is "truthy."

The number values behave exactly like actual Boolean values.

Floating-point values also behave like integer values, where 0.0 is "falsey" and anything else is "truthy."

With string values, the empty string is "falsey" and anything else is "truthy." It may look odd because it returns '0', but that's not the numeric value zero but the string we use to represent the value of zero. Wow, so philosophical.

If no value is "truthy," the last value is returned.

The empty list is "falsey," so any non-empty list is "truthy."

The empty dict is "falsey," and any non-empty dict is "truthy."

You should be able to use these ideas to write a stemmer() function that will pass the test_stemmer() function. Remember, if both of these functions are in your rhymer.py program, you can run the test_ functions like so:

```
$ pytest -xv rhymer.py
```

14.1.5 Creating the output

Let's review what the program should do:

1 Take a positional string argument.
2 Try to split it into two parts: any leading consonants and the rest of the word.
3 If the split is successful, combine the "rest" of the word (which might actually be the entire word if there are no leading consonants) with all the other consonant sounds. Be sure to *not* include the original consonant sound and to sort the rhyming strings.
4 If you are unable to split the word, print the message Cannot rhyme "<word>".

Now it's time to write the program. Have fun storming the castle!

14.2 Solution

"No more rhymes now, I mean it!"
"Anybody want a peanut?"

Let's take a look at one way to solve this problem. How different was your solution?

```python
#!/usr/bin/env python3
"""Make rhyming words"""

import argparse
import re                    The re module is for
import string                regular expressions.


# -------------------------------------------------
def get_args():
    """get command-line arguments"""

    parser = argparse.ArgumentParser(
        description='Make rhyming "words"',
        formatter_class=argparse.ArgumentDefaultsHelpFormatter)

    parser.add_argument('word', metavar='word', help='A word to rhyme')

    return parser.parse_args()
```

Get the command-line arguments.

```python
# -------------------------------------------------
def main():
    """Make a jazz noise here"""

    args = get_args()
    prefixes = list('bcdfghjklmnpqrstvwxyz') + (
        'bl br ch cl cr dr fl fr gl gr pl pr sc '
        'sh sk sl sm sn sp st sw th tr tw thw wh wr '
        'sch scr shr sph spl spr squ str thr').split()

    start, rest = stemmer(args.word)
    if rest:
```

Define all the prefixes that will be added to create rhyming words.

Split the word argument into two possible parts. Because the stemmer() function always returns a 2-tuple, we can unpack the values into two variables.

Check if there is a part of the word that we can use to create rhyming strings.

If there is, use a list comprehension to iterate through all the prefixes and add them to the stem of the word. Use a guard to ensure that any given prefix is not the same as the beginning of the word. Sort all the values and print them, joined on newlines.

```
            print('\n'.join(sorted([p + rest for p in prefixes if p != start])))
        else:
            print(f'Cannot rhyme "{args.word}"')
```

If there is nothing for the "rest" of the word that can be used to create rhymes, let the user know.

```
# ------------------------------------------------
def stemmer(word):
    """Return leading consonants (if any), and 'stem' of word"""

    word = word.lower()
    vowels = 'aeiou'
    consonants = ''.join(
        [c for c in string.ascii_lowercase if c not in vowels])
    pattern = (
        '([' + consonants + ']+)?'  # capture one or more, optional
        '([' + vowels     + '])'    # capture at least one vowel
        '(.*)'                      # capture zero or more of anything
    )

    match = re.match(pattern, word)
    if match:
        p1 = match.group(1) or ''
        p2 = match.group(2) or ''
        p3 = match.group(3) or ''
        return (p1, p2 + p3)
    else:
        return (word, '')
```

Lowercase the word.

Since we will use the vowels more than once, assign them to a variable.

The consonants are the letters that are not vowels. We will only match to lowercase letters.

The pattern is defined using consecutive literal strings that Python will join together into one string. By breaking up the pieces onto separate lines, we can comment on each part of the regular expression.

Use the re.match() function to start matching at the beginning of the word.

The re.match() function will return None if the pattern failed to match, so check if the match is "truthy" (not None).

Put each group into a variable, always ensuring that we use the empty string rather than None.

```
# ------------------------------------------------
def test_stemmer():
    """test the stemmer"""

    assert stemmer('') == ('', '')
    assert stemmer('cake') == ('c', 'ake')
    assert stemmer('chair') == ('ch', 'air')
    assert stemmer('APPLE') == ('', 'apple')
    assert stemmer('RDNZL') == ('rdnzl', '')
    assert stemmer('123') == ('', '')
```

The tests for e stemmer() function. I usually like put my unit tests directly after the functions they test.

Return a new tuple that has the "first" part of the word (possible leading consonants) and the "rest" of the word (the vowel plus anything else).

If the match failed, return the word and an empty string for the "rest" of the word to indicate there is nothing to rhyme.

```
# ------------------------------------------------
if __name__ == '__main__':
    main()
```

14.3   Discussion

There are many ways you could have written this, but, as always, I wanted to break the problem down into units I could write and test. For me, this came down to splitting the word into a possible leading consonant sound and the rest of the word. If I can manage that, I can create rhyming strings; if I cannot, then I need to alert the user.

14.3.1   Stemming a word

For the purposes of this program, the "stem" of a word is the part after any initial consonants, which I define using a list comprehension with a guard to take only the letters that are not vowels:

```
>>> vowels = 'aeiou'
>>> consonants = ''.join([c for c in string.ascii_lowercase if c not in vowels])
```

Throughout the chapters, I have shown how a list comprehension is a concise way to generate a list and is preferable to using a `for` loop to append to an existing list. Here we have added an `if` statement to only include some characters if they are not vowels. This is called a *guard* statement, and only those elements that evaluate as "truthy" will be included in the resulting `list`.

We've looked at `map()` several times now and talked about how it is a *higher-order function* (HOF) because it takes *another function* as the first argument and will apply it to all the elements from some *iterable* (something that can be *iterated*, like a `list`). Here I'd like to introduce another HOF called `filter()`, which also takes a function and an iterable (see figure 14.12). As with the list comprehension with the guard, only those elements that return a "truthy" value from the function are allowed in the resulting `list`.

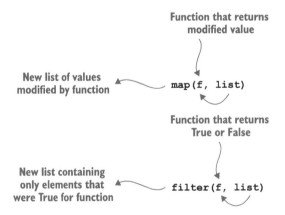

Function that returns
modified value

New list of values
modified by function   ←   map(f, list)

Function that returns
True or False

New list containing
only elements that   ←   filter(f, list)
were True for function

Figure 14.12   The `map()` **and** `filter()` **functions both take a function and an iterable, and both produce a new list.**

Here is another way to write the idea of the list comprehension using `filter()`:

```
>>> consonants = ''.join(filter(lambda c: c not in vowels,
      string.ascii_lowercase))
```

Just as with `map()`, I use the `lambda` keyword to create an *anonymous function.* The `c` is the variable that will hold the argument, which, in this case, will be each character from `string.ascii_lowercase`. The entire body of the function is the evaluation `c` not in vowels. Each of the vowels will return `False` for this:

```
>>> 'a' not in vowels
False
```

And each of the consonants will return `True`:

```
>>> 'b' not in vowels
True
```

Therefore, only the consonants will be allowed to pass through `filter()`. Think back to our "blue" cars; let's write a `filter()` that only accepts cars that start with the string "blue":

```
>>> cars = ['blue Honda', 'red Chevy', 'blue Ford']
>>> list(filter(lambda car: car.startswith('blue '), cars))
['blue Honda', 'blue Ford']
```

When the `car` variable has the value "red Chevy," the `lambda` returns `False`, and that value is rejected:

```
>>> car = 'red Chevy'
>>> car.startswith('blue ')
False
```

Note that if none of the elements from the original iterable are accepted, `filter()` will produce an empty `list` (`[]`). For example, I could `filter()` for numbers greater than 10. Note that `filter()` is another *lazy* function that I must coerce using the `list` function in the REPL:

```
>>> list(filter(lambda n: n > 10, range(0, 5)))
[]
```

A list comprehension would also return an empty list:

```
>>> [n for n in range(0, 5) if n > 10]
[]
```

Figure 14.13 shows the relationship between creating a new `list` called `consonants` using an imperative `for`-loop approach, an idiomatic list comprehension with a guard, and a purely functional approach using `filter()`. All of these are perfectly acceptable, though the most Pythonic technique is probably the list comprehension. The `for` loop would be very familiar to a C or Java programmer, while the `filter()` approach would be immediately recognizable to the Haskeller or even someone from a Lisp-like language. The `filter()` might be slower than the list comprehension, especially if the iterable were large. Choose whichever way makes more sense for your style and application.

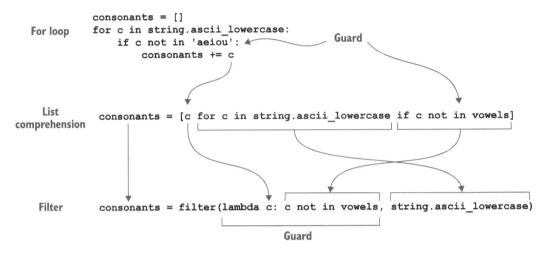

Figure 14.13   Three ways to create a list of consonants: using a `for` loop with an `if` statement, a list comprehension with a guard, and a `filter()`

14.3.2   *Formatting and commenting the regular expression*

We talked in the introduction about the individual parts of the regular expression I ended up using. I'd like to take a moment to mention the way I formatted the regex in the code. I used an interesting trick of the Python interpreter that will implicitly concatenate adjacent string literals. See how these four strings become one:

```
>>> this_is_just_to_say = ('I have eaten '
... 'the plums '
... 'that were in '
... 'the icebox')
>>> this_is_just_to_say
'I have eaten the plums that were in the icebox'
```

Note that there are no commas after each string, as that would create a `tuple` with four individual strings:

```
>>> this_is_just_to_say = ('I have eaten ',
... 'the plums ',
... 'that were in ',
... 'the icebox')
>>> this_is_just_to_say
('I have eaten ', 'the plums ', 'that were in ', 'the icebox')
```

The advantage of writing out the regular expression on separates lines is that you can add comments to help your reader understand each part:

```
pattern = (
    '([' + consonants + ']+)?' # capture one or more, optional
    '([' + vowels     + '])'   # capture at least one vowel
    '(.*)'                     # capture zero or more of anything
)
```

The individual strings will be concatenated by Python into a single string:

```
>>> pattern
'([bcdfghjklmnpqrstvwxyz]+)?([aeiou])(.*)'
```

I could have written the entire regex on one line, but ask yourself which version would you rather read and maintain, the preceding version or the following:[1]

```
pattern = f'([{consonants}]+)?([{vowels}])(.*)'
```

14.3.3 *Using the stemmer() function outside your program*

One of the very interesting things about Python code is that your rhymer.py program is also—kind of, sort of—a sharable *module* of code. That is, you haven't explicitly written it to be a container of reusable (and tested!) functions, but it is. You can even run the functions from inside the REPL.

For this to work, be sure you run `python3` inside the same directory as the rhymer.py code:

```
>>> from rhymer import stemmer
```

Now you can run and test your `stemmer()` function manually:

```
>>> stemmer('apple')
('', 'apple')
>>> stemmer('banana')
('b', 'anana')
>>> import string
>>> stemmer(string.punctuation)
('!"#$%&\'()*+,-./:;<=>?@[\\]^_`{|}~', '')
```

The deeper meaning of `if __name__ == '__main__':`
Note that if you were to change the last two lines of rhymer.py from this,

```
if __name__ == '__main__':
    main()
```

to this,

```
main()
```

the `main()` function would be run when you try to import the module:

```
>>> from rhymer import stemmer
usage: [-h] str
: error: the following arguments are required: str
```

---

[1] "Looking at code you wrote more than two weeks ago is like looking at code you are seeing for the first time."—Dan Hurvitz

(continued)

This is because `import rhymer` causes Python to execute the rhymer.py file to the end. If the last line of the module calls `main()`, then `main()` will run!

The `__name__` variable is set to '`__main__`' when rhymer.py is being *run as a program*. That is the only time `main()` is executed. When the module is being imported by another module, then `__name__` is equal to `rhymer`.

If you don't explicitly `import` a function, you can use the fully qualified function name by adding the module name to the front:

```
>>> import rhymer
>>> rhymer.stemmer('cake')
('c', 'ake')
>>> rhymer.stemmer('chair')
('ch', 'air')
```

There are many advantages to writing many small functions rather than long, sprawling programs. One is that small functions are much easier to write, understand, and test. Another is that you can put your tidy, tested functions into modules and share them across different programs you write.

As you write more and more programs, you will find yourself solving some of the same problems repeatedly. It's far better to create modules with reusable code than to copy pieces from one program to another. If you ever find a bug in a shared function, you can fix it once, and all the programs sharing the function get the fix. The alternative is to find the duplicated code in every program and change it (hoping that this doesn't introduce even more problems because the code is entangled with other code).

14.3.4 Creating rhyming strings

I decided that my `stemmer()` function would always return a 2-tuple of the (`start,` `rest`) for any given word. As such, I can unpack the two values into two variables:

```
>>> start, rest = stemmer('cat')
>>> start
'c'
>>> rest
'at'
```

If there is a value for `rest`, I can add all my `prefixes` to the beginning:

```
>>> prefixes = list('bcdfghjklmnpqrstvwxyz') + (
...      'bl br ch cl cr dr fl fr gl gr pl pr sc '
```

```
...        'sh sk sl sm sn sp st sw th tr tw wh wr'
...        'sch scr shr sph spl spr squ str thr').split()
```

I decided to use another list comprehension with a guard to skip any prefix that is the same as the `start` of the word. The result will be a new `list` that I pass to the `sorted()` function to get the correctly ordered strings:

```
>>> sorted([p + rest for p in prefixes if p != start])
['bat', 'blat', 'brat', 'chat', 'clat', 'crat', 'dat', 'drat', 'fat',
 'flat', 'frat', 'gat', 'glat', 'grat', 'hat', 'jat', 'kat', 'lat',
 'mat', 'nat', 'pat', 'plat', 'prat', 'qat', 'rat', 'sat', 'scat',
 'schat', 'scrat', 'shat', 'shrat', 'skat', 'slat', 'smat', 'snat',
 'spat', 'sphat', 'splat', 'sprat', 'squat', 'stat', 'strat', 'swat',
 'tat', 'that', 'thrat', 'thwat', 'trat', 'twat', 'vat', 'wat',
 'what', 'wrat', 'xat', 'yat', 'zat']
```

I then `print()` that `list`, joined on newlines. If there is no `rest` of the given word, I `print()` a message that the word cannot be rhymed:

```
if rest:
    print('\n'.join(sorted([p + rest for p in prefixes if p != start])))
else:
    print(f'Cannot rhyme "{args.word}"')
```

14.3.5 *Writing stemmer() without regular expressions*

It is certainly possible to write a solution that does not use regular expressions. We could start by finding the first position of a vowel in the given string. If one is present, we could use a list slice to return the portion of the string up to that position and the portion starting at that position:

Lowercase the given word to avoid dealing with uppercase letters.

Filter the vowels 'aeiou' to find those in word, and then map the present vowels to word.index to find their positions. This is one of the rare instances when we need to use the list() function to coerce Python into evaluating the lazy map() function because the next if statement needs a concrete value.

```
def stemmer(word):
    """Return leading consonants (if any), and 'stem' of word"""
    word = word.lower()
    vowel_pos = list(map(word.index, filter(lambda v: v in word, 'aeiou')))
    if vowel_pos:
        first_vowel = min(vowel_pos)
        return (word[:first_vowel], word[first_vowel:])
    else:
        return (word, '')
```

Check if there are any vowels present in the word.

Find the index of the first vowel by taking the minimum (min) value from the positions.

Return a tuple of a slice of the word up to the first vowel, and another starting at the first vowel.

Otherwise, no vowels were found in the word.

Return a 2-tuple of the word and the empty string to indicate there is no rest of the word to use for rhyming.

This function will also pass the `test_stemmer()` function. By writing a test just for the idea of this one function, and exercising it with all the different values I would expect, I'm free to *refactor* my code. In my mind, the `stemmer()` function is a black box. What goes on inside the function is of no concern to the code that calls it. As long as the function passes the tests, it is "correct" (for certain values of "correct").

Small functions and their *tests* will set you free to improve your programs. First make something work, and make it beautiful. Then try to make it better, using your tests to ensure it keeps working as expected.

14.4 Going further

- Add an `--output` option to write the words to a given file. The default should be to write to `STDOUT`.

- Read an input file and create rhyming words for all the words in the file. You can borrow from the program in chapter 6 to read a file and break it into words, then iterate each word, and create an output file for each word with the rhyming words.

- Write a new program that finds all unique consonant sounds in a dictionary of English words. (I have included inputs/words.txt.zip, which is a compressed version of the dictionary from my machine. Unzip the file to use inputs/words.txt.) Print the output in alphabetical order and use those to expand this program's consonants.

- Alter your program to only emit words that are found in the system dictionary (for example, inputs/words.txt).

- Write a program to create Pig Latin, where you move the initial consonant sound from the beginning of the word to the end and add "-ay," so that "cat" becomes "at-cay." If a word starts with a vowel, add "-yay" to the end so that "apple" becomes "apple-yay."

- Write a program to create spoonerisms, where the initial consonant sounds of adjacent words are switched, so you get "blushing crow" instead of "crushing blow."

Summary

- Regular expressions allow you to declare a pattern that you wish to find. The regex *engine* will sort out whether the pattern is found or not. This is a *declarative* approach to programming, in contrast to the *imperative* method of manually seeking out patterns by writing code ourselves.

- You can wrap parts of the pattern in parentheses to "capture" them into groups that you can fetch from the result of `re.match()` or `re.search()`.

- You can add a guard to a list comprehension to avoid taking some elements from an iterable.

- The `filter()` function is another way to write a list comprehension with a guard. Like `map()`, it is a lazy, higher-order function that takes a function that will be applied to every element of an iterable. Only those elements that are deemed "truthy" by the function are returned.

- Python can evaluate many types—including strings, numbers, lists, and dictionaries—in a Boolean context to arrive at a sense of "truthiness." That is, you are not restricted to just `True` and `False` in `if` expressions. The empty string `''`, the `int` 0, the `float` 0.0, the empty `list []`, and the empty `dict{}` are all considered "falsey," so any non-falsey value from those types, like the non-empty `str`, `list`, or `dict`, or any numeric value not zero-ish, will be considered "truthy."

- You can break long string literals into shorter adjacent strings in your code to have Python join them into one long string. It's advisable to break long regexes into shorter strings and add comments on each line to document the function of each pattern.

- Write small functions and tests, and share them in modules. Every .py file can be a module from which you can `import` functions. Sharing small, tested functions is better than writing long programs and copying/pasting code as needed.

The Kentucky Friar:
More regular expressions

I grew up in the American Deep South where we tend to drop the final "g" of words ending in "ing," like "cookin'" instead of "cooking." We also tend to say "y'all" for the second-person plural pronoun, which makes sense because Standard English is missing a distinctive word for this. In this exercise, we'll write a program called friar.py that will accept some input as a single positional argument and transform the text by replacing the final "g" with an apostrophe (') for two-syllable words ending in "ing" and changing "you" to "y'all." Granted, we have no way to know if we're changing the first- or second-person "you," but it makes for a fun challenge nonetheless.

Figure 15.1 is a string diagram that will help you see the inputs and outputs. When run with no arguments or with the -h or --help flags, your program should present the following usage statement:

```
$ ./friar.py -h
usage: friar.py [-h] text

Southern fry text

positional arguments:
  text         Input text or file

optional arguments:
  -h, --help   show this help message and exit
```

Input   **Output**

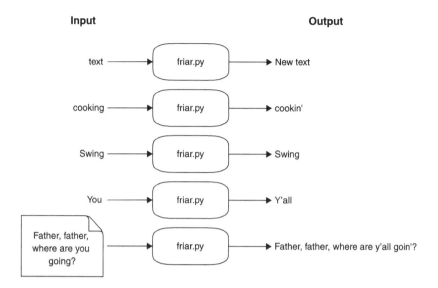

Figure 15.1   Our program will modify the input text to give it a Southern lilt.

We will only change "-ing" words with *two syllables*, so "cooking" becomes "cookin'" but "swing" will stay the same. Our heuristic for identifying two-syllable "-ing" words is to inspect the part of the word before the "-ing" ending to see if it contains a vowel, which in this case will include "y." We can split "cooking" into "cook" and "ing," and because there is an "o" in "cook," we should drop the final "g":

```
$ ./friar.py Cooking
Cookin'
```

When we remove "ing" from "swing," though, we're left with "sw," which contains no vowel, so it will remain the same:

```
$ ./friar.py swing
swing
```

When changing "you" to "y'all," be mindful to keep the case the same on the first letter. For example, "You" should become "Y'all":

```
$ ./friar.py you
y'all
$ ./friar.py You
Y'all
```

As in several previous exercises, the input may name a file, in which case you should read the file for the input text. To pass the tests, you will need to preserve the line structure of the input, so I recommend you read the file line by line. Given this input,

```
$ head -2 inputs/banner.txt
O! Say, can you see, by the dawn's early light,
What so proudly we hailed at the twilight's last gleaming -
```

the output should have the same line breaks:

```
$ ./friar.py inputs/banner.txt | head -2
O! Say, can y'all see, by the dawn's early light,
What so proudly we hailed at the twilight's last gleamin' -
```

To me, it's quite amusing to transform texts this way, but maybe I'm just weird:

```
$ ./friar.py inputs/raven.txt
Presently my soul grew stronger; hesitatin' then no longer,
"Sir," said I, "or Madam, truly your forgiveness I implore;
But the fact is I was nappin', and so gently y'all came rappin',
And so faintly y'all came tappin', tappin' at my chamber door,
That I scarce was sure I heard y'all" - here I opened wide the door: -
Darkness there and nothin' more.
```

In this exercise you will

- Learn more about using regular expressions
- Use both re.match() and re.search() to find patterns anchored to the beginning of a string or anywhere in the string, respectively
- Learn how the $ symbol in a regex anchors a pattern to the *end* of a string
- Learn how to use re.split() to split a string
- Explore how to write a manual solution for finding two-syllable "-ing" words or the word "you"

15.1   Writing friar.py

As usual, I recommend you start with new.py friar.py or copy the template/template.py file to 15_friar/friar.py. I suggest you start with a simple version of the program that echoes back the input from the command line:

```
$ ./friar.py cooking
cooking
```

Or from a file:

```
$ ./friar.py inputs/blake.txt
Father, father, where are you going?
 Oh do not walk so fast!
Speak, father, speak to your little boy,
 Or else I shall be lost.
```

We need to process the input line by line, and then word by word. You can use the `str.splitlines()` method to get each line of the input, and then use the `str.split()` method to break the line on spaces into word-like units. This code,

```
for line in args.text.splitlines():
    print(line.split())
```

should create this output:

```
$ ./friar.py inputs/blake.txt
['Father,', 'father,', 'where', 'are', 'you', 'going?']
['Oh', 'do', 'not', 'walk', 'so', 'fast!']
['Speak,', 'father,', 'speak', 'to', 'your', 'little', 'boy,']
['Or', 'else', 'I', 'shall', 'be', 'lost.']
```

If you look closely, it's going to be difficult to handle some of these word-like units because the adjacent punctuation is still attached to the words, as in `'Father,'` and `'going?'` Splitting the text on spaces is not sufficient, so I'll show you how to split the text *using a regular expression.*

15.1.1 *Splitting text using regular expressions*

As in chapter 14, we need to `import re` to use regexes:

```
>>> import re
```

For demonstration purposes, I'm going to set `text` to the first line:

```
>>> text = 'Father, father, where are you going?'
```

By default, `str.split()` breaks text on spaces. Note that whatever text is used for splitting will be missing from the result, so here there are no spaces:

```
>>> text.split()
['Father,', 'father,', 'where', 'are', 'you', 'going?']
```

You can pass an optional value to `str.split()` to indicate the string you want to use for splitting. If we choose the comma, we'll end up with three strings instead of six. Note that there are no commas in the resulting list, as that is the argument to `str.split()`:

```
>>> text.split(',')
['Father', ' father', ' where are you going?']
```

The `re` module has a function called `re.split()` that works similarly. I recommend you read `help(re.split)`, as this is a very powerful and flexible function. Like `re.match()`, which we used in chapter 14, this function wants at least a `pattern` and a `string`. We can use `re.split()` with a comma to get the same output as `str.split()`, and, as before, the commas are missing from the result:

```
>>> re.split(',', text)
['Father', ' father', ' where are you going?']
```

15.1.2 *Shorthand classes*

We are after the things that look like "words," in that they are composed of the characters that normally occur in words. The characters that *don't* normally occur in words (things like punctuation) are what we want to use for splitting. You've seen before that we can create a *character class* by putting literal values inside square brackets, like `'[aeiou]'` for the vowels. What if we create a character class where we enumerate all the non-letter characters? We could do something like this:

```
>>> import string
>>> ''.join([c for c in string.printable if c not in string.ascii_letters])
'0123456789!"#$%&\'()*+,-./:;<=>?@[\\]^_`{|}~ \t\n\r\x0b\x0c'
```

That won't be necessary, because almost every implementation of regular expression engines define shorthand character classes. Table 15.1 lists some of the most common shorthand classes and how they can be written longhand.

Table 15.1   Regex shorthand classes

Character class	Shorthand	Other ways to write the class
Digits	\d	`[0123456789]`, `[0-9]`
Whitespace	\s	`[ \t\n\r\x0b\x0c]`, same as `string.whitespace`
Word characters	\w	`[a-zA-Z0-9_-]`

NOTE   There is a basic flavor of regular expression syntax that is recognized by everything from Unix command-line tools like `awk` to regex support inside of languages like Perl, Python, and Java. Some tools add extensions to their regexes that may not be understood by other tools. For example, there was a time when Perl's regex engine added many new ideas that eventually became a dialect known as "PCRE" (Perl-Compatible Regular Expressions). Not every tool that understands regexes will understand every flavor of regex, but in all my years of writing and using regexes, I've rarely found this to be a problem.

The shorthand \d means any *digit* and is equivalent to `'[0123456789]'`. I can use the `re.search()` method to look anywhere in a string for any digit. In the following example, it will find the character `'1'` in the string `'abc123!'` because this is the first digit in the string (see figure 15.2):

```
>>> re.search('\d', 'abc123!')
<re.Match object; span=(3, 4), match='1'>
```

\d

abc123!   **Figure 15.2   The digit shorthand will match any single digit.**

That is the same as using the longhand version (see figure 15.3):

```
>>> re.search('[0123456789]', 'abc123!')
<re.Match object; span=(3, 4), match='1'>
```

[0123456789]

abc123!

Figure 15.3   We can also create a character class enumerating all the digits.

It's also the same as the version that uses the range of characters '[0-9]' (see figure 15.4):

```
>>> re.search('[0-9]', 'abc123!')
<re.Match object; span=(3, 4), match='1'>
```

[0-9]

abc123!

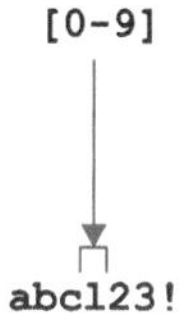

Figure 15.4   Character classes can use a range of contiguous values, like 0–9.

To have it find *one or more digits in a row*, add the + (see figure 15.5):

```
>>> re.search('\d+', 'abc123!')
<re.Match object; span=(3, 6), match='123'>
```

\d+

abc123!

Figure 15.5   The plus signs means to match one or more of the preceding expression.

The \w shorthand means "any word-like character." It includes all the Arabic numbers, the letters of the English alphabet, the dash ('-'), and the underscore ('_'). The first match in the string is 'a' (see figure 15.6):

```
>>> re.search('\w', 'abc123!')
<re.Match object; span=(0, 1), match='a'>
```

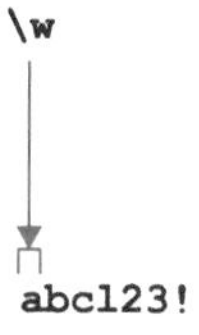

\w

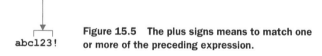

abc123!   **Figure 15.6   The shorthand for word characters is \w.**

If you add the + as in figure 15.7, it matches one or more word characters in a row, which includes abc123 but not the exclamation mark (!):

```
>>> re.search('\w+', 'abc123!')
<re.Match object; span=(0, 6), match='abc123'>
```

Figure 15.7   Add the plus sign to match one or more word characters.

15.1.3 Negated shorthand classes

You can complement or "negate" a character class by putting the caret (^) *immediately inside* the character class as in figure 15.8. One or more of any character *not* a digit is '[^0-9]+'. With it, 'abc' is found:

```
>>> re.search('[^0-9]+', 'abc123!')
<re.Match object; span=(0, 3), match='abc'>
```

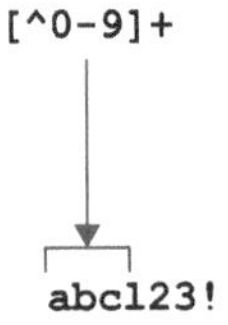

Figure 15.8   A caret just inside a character class will negate or complement the characters. This regex matches non-digits.

The shorthand class of non-digits [^0-9]+ can also be written as \D+ as in figure 15.9:

```
>>> re.search('\D+', 'abc123!')
<re.Match object; span=(0, 3), match='abc'>
```

\D+

abc123!

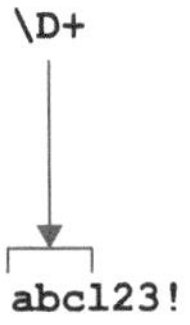

Figure 15.9   The shorthand \D+ matches one or more non-digits.

The shorthand for non-word characters is \W, which will match the exclamation point (see figure 15.10):

```
>>> re.search('\W', 'abc123!')
<re.Match object; span=(6, 7), match='!'>
```

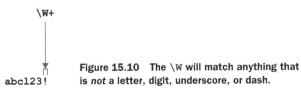

Figure 15.10   The \W will match anything that is *not* a letter, digit, underscore, or dash.

Table 15.2 summarizes these shorthand classes and how they can be expanded.

Table 15.2 Negated regex shorthand classes

Character class	Shorthand	Other ways to write the class
Not a digit	`\D`	`[^0123456789]`, `[^0-9]`
Not whitespace	`\S`	`[^ \t\n\r\x0b\x0c]`
Not word characters	`\W`	`[^a-zA-Z0-9_-]`

15.1.4 *Using re.split() with a captured regex*

We can use `\W` as the argument to `re.split()`:

```
>>> re.split('\W', 'abc123!')
['abc123', '']
```

> **NOTE** Pylint will complain if we use `'\W'` in a regular expression in our program, returning the message "Anomalous backslash in string: `'\W'`. String constant might be missing an r prefix." We can use the r prefix to create a "raw" string, one where Python does not try to interpret the `\W` as it will, for instance, interpret `\n` to mean a newline or `\r` to mean a carriage return. From this point on, I will use the r-string syntax to create a raw string.

There is a problem, though, because the result of `re.split()` *omits those strings matching the pattern.* Here we've lost the exclamation point! If we read `help(re.split)` closely, we can find the solution:

> *If **capturing parentheses are used in [the] pattern**, then the text of all groups in the pattern are also returned as part of the resulting list.*

We used capturing parentheses in chapter 14 to tell the regex engine to "remember" certain patterns, like the consonant(s), vowel, and the rest of a word. When the regex matched, we were able to use `match.groups()` to retrieve strings that were found by the patterns. Here we will use the parentheses around the pattern to `re.split()` so that the strings matching the pattern will also be returned:

```
>>> re.split(r'(\W)', 'abc123!')
['abc123', '!', '']
```

If we try that on our `text`, the result is a `list` of strings that match and do not match the regular expression:

```
>>> re.split(r'(\W)', text)
['Father', ',', '', ' ', 'father', ',', '', ' ', 'where', ' ', 'are', ' ',
    'you', ' ', 'going', '?', '']
```

I'd like to group all the non-word characters together by adding + to the regex (see figure 15.11):

```
>>> re.split(r'(\W+)', text)
['Father', ', ', 'father', ', ', 'where', ' ', 'are', ' ', 'you', ' ', 'going
    ', '?', '']
```

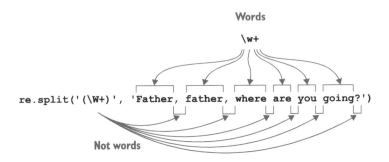

Figure 15.11   The re.split() function can use a captured regex to return both the parts that match the regex and those that do not.

That is so cool! Now we have a way to process each *actual* word and the bits in between them.

15.1.5   *Writing the fry() function*

Our next step is to write a function that will decide whether and how to modify *just one word*. That is, rather than thinking about how to handle all the text at once, we'll think about how to handle one word at a time. We can call this function fry().

To help us think about how this function should work, let's start off by writing the test_fry() function and a stub for the actual fry() function that contains just the single command pass, which tells Python to do nothing. To get started on this, you can paste this into your program:

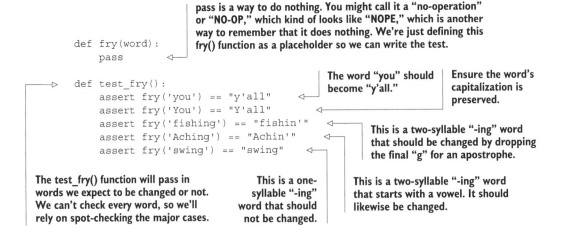

Now run `pytest friar.py` to see that, as expected, the test will fail:

```
================================ FAILURES ================================
_____ test_fry _____

    def test_fry():
>       assert fry('you') == "y'all"            ⊲─┐    The first test is failing.
E       assert None == "y'all"                  ⊲─
E         + where None = fry('you')                    The result of fry('you') was None,
                                                       which does not equal "y'all."

friar.py:47: AssertionError
========================= 1 failed in 0.08 seconds =========================
```

Let's change our `fry()` function to handle that string:

```python
def fry(word):
    if word == 'you':
        return "y'all"
```

Now let's run our tests again:

```
================================ FAILURES ================================
_____ test_fry _____

    def test_fry():
        assert fry('you') == "y'all"            ⊲─┐    Now the first test passes.
>       assert fry('You') == "Y'all"            ⊲─┤    The second test fails because
E       assert None == "Y'all"                  ⊲─     the "You" is capitalized.
E         + where None = fry('You')
                                                       The function returned None but
                                                       should have returned "Y'all."

friar.py:49: AssertionError
========================= 1 failed in 0.16 seconds =========================
```

Let's handle those:

```python
def fry(word):
    if word == 'you':
        return "y'all"
    elif word == 'You':
        return "Y'all"
```

If you run the tests now, you'll see that the first two tests pass; however, I'm definitely not happy with that solution. There is already a good bit of duplicated code. Can we find a more elegant way to match both "you" and "You" and still return the correctly capitalized answer? Yes, we can!

```python
def fry(word):
    if word.lower() == 'you':
        return word[0] + "'all"
```

Better still, we can write a regular expression! There is one difference between "you" and "You"—the "y" or "Y"—that we can represent using the character class `'[yY]'` (see figure 15.12). This will match the lowercase version:

```
>>> re.match('[yY]ou', 'you')
<re.Match object; span=(0, 3), match='you'>
```

Either "y" or "Y"

[yY]

y   Y

Figure 15.12   We can use a character class to match lower- and uppercase Y.

It will also match the capitalized version (see figure 15.13):

```
>>> re.match('[yY]ou', 'You')
<re.Match object; span=(0, 3), match='You'>
```

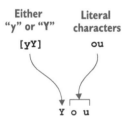

Either "y" or "Y"   **Literal characters**

[yY]   ou

Y o u

Figure 15.13   This regex will match "you" and "You."

Now we want to reuse the initial character (either "y" or "Y") in the return value. We could *capture* it by placing it into parentheses. Try to rewrite your `fry()` function using this idea, and getting it to pass the first two tests again, before moving on:

```
>>> match = re.match('([yY])ou', 'You')
>>> match.group(1) + "'all"
"Y'all"
```

The next step is to handle a word like "fishing":

```
================================= FAILURES =================================
_____ test_fry _____

    def test_fry():
        assert fry('you') == "y'all"
        assert fry('You') == "Y'all"
>       assert fry('fishing') == "fishin'"
E       assert None == "fishin'"
E         +  where None = fry('fishing')
```

The third test fails.

The return from fry('fishing') was None, but the value "fishin'" was expected.

```
friar.py:52: AssertionError
=========================== 1 failed in 0.10 seconds ===========================
```

How can we identify a word that ends with "ing"? With the `str.endswith()` function:

```
>>> 'fishing'.endswith('ing')
True
```

A regular expression to find "ing" at the end of a string would use `$` (pronounced "dollar") at the end of the expression to *anchor* the expression to the end of the string (see figure 15.14):

```
>>> re.search('ing$', 'fishing')
<re.Match object; span=(4, 7), match='ing'>
```

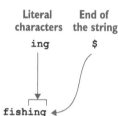

Figure 15.14 The dollar sign indicates the end of the word.

As shown in figure 15.15, we can use a string slice to get all the characters up to the last at index `-1` and then append an apostrophe.

```
f i s h i n g
─────────────▶│-1

word[:-1] + "'"  ─────────▶ fishin'
```

Figure 15.15 Use a string slice to get all the letters up to the last one and add an apostrophe.

Add this to your `fry()` function and see how many tests you pass:

```
if word.endswith('ing'):
    return word[:-1] + "'"
```

Or you could use a group within the regex to capture the first part of the word (see figure 15.16):

```
>>> match = re.search('(.+)ing$', 'fishing')
>>> match.group(1) + "in'"
"fishin'"
```

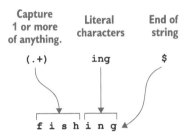

Figure 15.16   Using a capture group so we can access the matching string

You should be able to get results like this:

```
=================================== FAILURES ===================================
_____ test_fry _____

    def test_fry():
        assert fry('you') == "y'all"
        assert fry('You') == "Y'all"
        assert fry('fishing') == "fishin'"
        assert fry('Aching') == "Achin'"
>       assert fry('swing') == "swing"
E       assert "swin'" == 'swing'
E         - swin'
E         ?    ^
E         + swing
E         ?    ^

friar.py:59: AssertionError
============================ 1 failed in 0.10 seconds ===========================
```

This test failed.

The result of fry('swing') was "swin'," but it should have been "swing."

Sometimes the test results will be able to highlight the exact point of failure. Here you are being shown that there is an apostrophe (') where there should be a "g."

We need a way to identify words that have two syllables. I mentioned before that we'll use a heuristic that looks for a vowel, '[aeiouy]', in the part of the word *before* the "ing" ending, as shown in figure 15.17. Another regex could do the trick:

Here we know there will be a match value, so we can use match.group(1) to get the first capture group, which will be anything immediately before "ing." In actual code, we should check that match is not None or we'd trigger an exception by trying to execute the group method on a None.

The (.+) will match and capture one or more of anything followed by the characters "ing." The return from re.search() will either be a re.Match object if the pattern was found or None to indicate it was not.

```
>>> match = re.search('(.+)ing$', 'fishing')
>>> first = match.group(1)
>>> re.search('[aeiouy]', first)
<re.Match object; span=(1, 2), match='i'>
```

As the return from re.search() is a re.Match object, we know there is a vowel in the first part, so the word looks to have two syllables.

We can use re.search() on the first part of the string to look for a vowel.

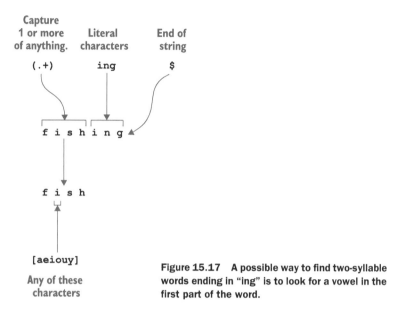

Figure 15.17 A possible way to find two-syllable words ending in "ing" is to look for a vowel in the first part of the word.

If the word matches this test, return the word with the final "g" replaced with an apostrophe; otherwise, return the word unchanged. I suggest you not proceed until you are passing all of `test_fry()`.

15.1.6 *Using the fry() function*

Now your program should be able to

1 Read input from the command line or a file
2 Read the input line by line
3 Split each line into words and non-words
4 `fry()` any individual word

The next step is to apply the `fry()` function to all the word-like units. I hope you can see a familiar pattern emerging—applying a function to all elements of a list! You can use a `for` loop:

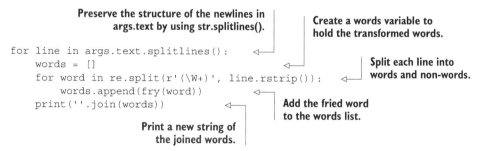

That (or something like it) should work well enough to pass the tests. Once you have a version that works, see if you can rewrite the `for` loop as a list comprehension and a `map()`.

Alrighty! Time to bear down and write this.

15.2   Solution

This reminds me of when Robin Hood's mate Friar Tuck was captured by the Sheriff of Nottingham. The Friar was sentenced to be boiled in oil, to which he replied "You can't boil me, I'm a friar!"

```python
#!/usr/bin/env python3
"""Kentucky Friar"""

import argparse
import os
import re


# --------------------------------------------------
def get_args():
    """get command-line arguments"""
    parser = argparse.ArgumentParser(
        description='Southern fry text',
        formatter_class=argparse.ArgumentDefaultsHelpFormatter)

    parser.add_argument('text', metavar='text', help='Input text or file')

    args = parser.parse_args()

    if os.path.isfile(args.text):
        args.text = open(args.text).read()

    return args
```

If the argument is a file, replace the text value with the contents from the file.

Use the `str.splitlines()` method to preserve the line breaks in the input text.

```python
# --------------------------------------------------
def main():
    """Make a jazz noise here"""

    args = get_args()

    for line in args.text.splitlines():
        print(''.join(map(fry, re.split(r'(\W+)', line.rstrip()))))
```

Get the command-line arguments. The text value will either be the command-line text or the contents of a file by this point.

Define a fry() function that will handle one word.

```python
# --------------------------------------------------
def fry(word):
    """Drop the `g` from `-ing` words, change `you` to `y'all`"""
```

Map the pieces of text split by the regular expression through the fry() function, which will return the words modified as needed. Use str.join() to turn that resulting list back into a string to print.

```
    ing_word = re.search('(.+)ing$', word)
    you = re.match('([Yy])ou$', word)

    if ing_word:
        prefix = ing_word.group(1)
        if re.search('[aeiouy]', prefix, re.IGNORECASE):
            return prefix + "in'"
    elif you:
        return you.group(1) + "'all"

    return word
```

Check if the search for "ing" returned a match.

Get the prefix (the bit before the "ing"), which is in group number 1.

Return the captured first character plus "'all."

Otherwise, return the word unaltered.

```
# --------------------------------------------------
def test_fry():
    """Test fry"""

    assert fry('you') == "y'all"
    assert fry('You') == "Y'all"
    assert fry('fishing') == "fishin'"
    assert fry('Aching') == "Achin'"
    assert fry('swing') == "swing"



# --------------------------------------------------
if __name__ == '__main__':
    main()
```

The tests for the fry() function

Check if the match for "you" succeeded.

Append "in'" to the prefix and return it to the caller.

Search for "you" or "You" starting from the beginning of word. Capture the [yY] alternation in a group.

Perform a case-insensitive search for a vowel (plus "y") in the prefix. If nothing is found, None will be returned, which evaluates to False in this Boolean context. If a match is returned, the not-None value will evaluate to True.

Search for "ing" anchored to the end of word. Use a capture group to remember the part of the string before the "ing."

15.3   Discussion

Again, there is nothing new in get_args(), so let's just move to breaking the text into lines. In several previous exercises, I used a technique of reading an input file into the args.text value. If the input is coming from a file, there will be newlines separating each line of text. I suggested using a for loop to handle each line of input text returned by str.splitlines() to preserve the newlines in the output. I also suggested you start with a second for loop to handle each word-like unit returned by the re.split():

```
for line in args.text.splitlines():
    words = []
    for word in re.split(r'(\W+)', line.rstrip()):
        words.append(fry(word))
    print(''.join(words))
```

That's five lines of code that could be written in two if we replace the second `for` with a list comprehension:

```
for line in args.text.splitlines():
    print(''.join([fry(w) for w in re.split(r'(\W+)', line.rstrip())]))
```

Or it could be slightly shorter using a `map()`:

```
for line in args.text.splitlines():
    print(''.join(map(fry, re.split(r'(\W+)', line.rstrip()))))
```

One other way to slightly improve readability is to use the `re.compile()` function to compile the regular expression. When you use the `re.split()` function inside the `for` loop, the regex must be compiled anew each iteration. By compiling the regex first, the compilation happens just once, so your code is (maybe just slightly) faster. More importantly, though, I think this is slightly easier to read, and the benefits are greater when the regex is more complicated:

```
splitter = re.compile(r'(\W+)')
for line in args.text.splitlines():
    print(''.join(map(fry, splitter.split(line.rstrip()))))
```

15.3.1 Writing the fry() function manually

You were not required, of course, to write a `fry()` function. However you wrote your solution, I hope you wrote tests for it!

The following version is fairly close to some of the suggestions I made earlier in the chapter. This version uses no regular expressions:

Force the word to lowercase and see if it matches "you."

```
def fry(word):
    """Drop the `g` from `-ing` words, change `you` to `y'all`"""

    if word.lower() == 'you':
        return word[0] + "'all"

    if word.endswith('ing'):
        if any(map(lambda c: c.lower() in 'aeiouy', word[:-3])):
            return word[:-1] + "'"
        else:
            return word

    return word
```

If so, return the first character (to preserve the case) plus "'all."

Check if it's True that any of the vowels are in the word up to the "ing" suffix.

Check if the word ends with "ing."

If so, return the word up to the last index plus the apostrophe.

Otherwise, return the word unchanged.

If the word is neither an "ing" or "you" word, return it unchanged.

Let's take a moment to appreciate the any() function as it's one of my favorites. The preceding code uses a map() to check if each of the vowels exists in the portion of the word before the "ing" ending:

```
>>> word = "cooking"
>>> list(map(lambda c: (c, c.lower() in 'aeiouy'), word[:-3]))
[('c', False), ('o', True), ('o', True), ('k', False)]
```

The first character of "cooking" is "c," and it does not appear in the string of vowels. The next two characters ("o") do appear in the vowels, but "k" does not.

Let's reduce this to just the True/False values:

```
>>> list(map(lambda c: c.lower() in 'aeiouy', word[:-3]))
[False, True, True, False]
```

Now we can use any to tell us if *any* of the values are True:

```
>>> any([False, True, True, False])
True
```

It's the same as joining the values with or:

```
>>> False or True or True or False
True
```

The all() function returns True only if *all* the values are true:

```
>>> all([False, True, True, False])
False
```

That's the same as joining those values on and:

```
>>> False and True and True and False
False
```

If it's True that one of the vowels appears in the first part of the word, we have determined that this is (probably) a two-syllable word, and we can return the word with the final "g" replaced with an apostrophe. Otherwise, we return the unaltered word:

```
if any(map(lambda c: c.lower() in 'aeiouy', word[:-3])):
    return word[:-1] + "'"
else:
    return word
```

This approach works fine, but it's quite manual as we have to write quite a bit of code to find our patterns.

15.3.2 *Writing the fry() function with regular expressions*

Let's revisit the version of the fry() function that uses regular expressions:

The re.match() starts matching at the beginning of the given word, and it is looking for either an upper- or lowercase "y" followed by "ou" and then the end of the string ($).

We use re.search() to look anywhere in the prefix for any of the vowels (plus "y") in a case-insensitive fashion. Remember that re.match() would start at the beginning of word, which is not what we want.

The pattern '(.+)ing$' matches one or more of anything followed by "ing." The dollar sign anchors the pattern to the end of the string, so this is looking for a string that ends in "ing," but the string cannot just be "ing" as it has to have at least one of something before it. The parentheses capture the part before the "ing."

```
def fry(word):
    """Drop the `g` from `-ing` words, change `you` to `y'all`"""

    ing_word = re.search('(.+)ing$', word)
    you = re.match('([Yy])ou$', word)

    if ing_word:
        prefix = ing_word.group(1)
        if re.search('[aeiouy]', prefix, re.IGNORECASE):
            return prefix + "in'"
    elif you:
        return you.group(1) + "'all"

    return word
```

The prefix is the bit before the "ing" that we wrapped in parentheses. Because it is the first set of parentheses, we can fetch it with ing_word.group(1).

If ing_word is None, that means it failed to match. If it is not None (so it is "truthy"), that means it is a re.Match object we can use.

Return the prefix plus the string "in'" so as to drop the final "g."

If re.match() for the "you" pattern fails, then "you" will be None. If it is not None, then it matched, and "you" is a re.Match object.

We used parentheses to capture the first character so as to maintain the case. That is, if the word was "You," we want to return "Y'all." Here we return that first group plus the string "'all."

If the word matched neither a two-syllable "ing" pattern or the word "you," we return the word unchanged.

I've been using regexes for maybe 20 years, so this version seems much simpler to me than the manual version. You may feel differently. If you are completely new to regexes, trust me that they are so very worth the effort to learn. I absolutely would not be able to do much of my work without them.

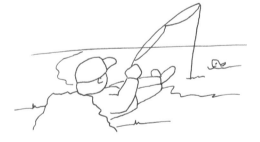

15.4   *Going further*

- You could also replace "your" with "y'all's." For instance, "Where are your britches?" could become "Where are y'all's britches?"
- Change "getting ready" or "preparing" to "fixin'," as in "I'm getting ready to eat" to "I'm fixin' to eat." Also change the string "think" to "reckon," as in "I

think this is funny" to "I reckon this is funny." You should also change "thinking" to "reckoning," which then should become "reckonin'." That means you either need to make two passes for the changes or find both "think" and "thinking" in the one pass.

- Make a version of the program for another regional dialect. I lived in Boston for a while and really enjoyed saying "wicked" all the time instead of "very," as in "IT'S WICKED COLD OUT!"

Summary

- Regular expressions can be used to find patterns in text. The patterns can be quite complicated, like a grouping of non-word characters in between groupings of word characters.

- The re module has seriously handy functions like re.match() to find a pattern at the beginning of some text, re.search() to find a pattern anywhere inside some text, re.split() to break text on a pattern, and re.compile() to compile a regex so you can use it repeatedly.

- If you use capturing parentheses on the pattern for re.split(), the captured split pattern will be included in the returned values. This allows you to reconstruct the original string with the strings that are described by the pattern.

The scrambler: Randomly reordering the middles of words

Yuor brian is an azinamg cmiobiaontn of hdarware and sftraowe. Yoru'e rdineag tihs rhgit now eevn thgouh the wrdos are a mses, but yuor biran can mkae snese of it bceause the frsit and lsat ltrtees of ecah wrod hvae saeytd the smae. Yuor biran de'onst atlaulcy raed ecah lteetr of ecah wrod but rades wlohe wdors. The scamrbeld wrdos difteienly solw you dwon, but y'roue not rlleay eevn tyinrg to ulsrmbance the lrttees, are you? It jsut hnaepps!

In this chapter, you will write a program called scrambler.py that will scramble each word of the text given as an argument. The scrambling should only work on words with four characters or more, and it should only scramble the letters in the middle of the word, leaving the first and last characters unchanged. The program should take an -s or --seed option (an int with default None) to pass to random.seed().

It should handle text on the command line:

```
$ ./scrambler.py --seed 1 "foobar bazquux"
faobor buuzaqx
```

Or text from a file:

```
$ cat ../inputs/spiders.txt
Don't worry, spiders,
I keep house
casually.
$ ./scrambler.py ../inputs/spiders.txt
```

```
D'not wrory, sdireps,
I keep hsuoe
csalluay.
```

Figure 16.1 shows a string diagram to help you think about it.

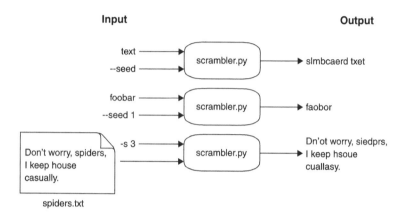

Input   **Output**

Figure 16.1   **Our program will take input text from the command line or a file and will scramble the letters in words with four or more characters.**

In this chapter you will

- Use a regular expression to split text into words
- Use the random.shuffle() function to shuffle a list
- Create scrambled versions of words by shuffling the middle letters while leaving the first and last letters unchanged

16.1   *Writing scrambler.py*

I recommend you start by using new.py scrambler.py to create the program in the 16_scrambler directory. Alternatively, you can copy template/template.py to 16_scrambler/scrambler.py. You can refer to previous exercises, like the one in chapter 5, to remember how to handle a positional argument that might be text or might be a text file to read.

When run with no arguments or the flags -h or --help, scrambler.py should present a usage statement:

```
$ ./scrambler.py -h
usage: scrambler.py [-h] [-s seed] text

Scramble the letters of words

positional arguments:
  text                 Input text or file
```

```
optional arguments:
  -h, --help              show this help message and exit
  -s seed, --seed seed  Random seed (default: None)
```

Once your program's usage statement matches this, change your `main()` definition as follows:

```
def main():
    args = get_args()
    print(args.text)
```

Then verify that your program can echo text from the command line:

```
$ ./scrambler.py hello
hello
```

Or from an input file:

```
$ ./scrambler.py ../inputs/spiders.txt
Don't worry, spiders,
I keep house
casually.
```

16.1.1 *Breaking the text into lines and words*

As in chapter 15, we want to preserve the line breaks of the input text by using `str.splitlines()`:

```
for line in args.text.splitlines():
    print(line)
```

If we are reading the spiders.txt haiku, this is the first line:

```
>>> line = "Don't worry, spiders,"
```

We need to break the `line` into words. In chapter 6 we used `str.split()`, but that approach leaves punctuation stuck to our words—both `worry` and `spiders` have commas:

```
>>> line.split()
["Don't", 'worry,', 'spiders,']
```

In chapter 15 we used the `re.split()` function with the regular expression `(\W+)` to split text on one or more non-word characters. Let's try that:

```
>>> re.split('(\W+)', line)
['Don', "'", 't', ' ', 'worry', ', ', 'spiders', ',', '']
```

That won't work because it splits `Don't` into three parts: `Don`, `'`, and `t`.

Perhaps we could use `\b` to break on *word boundaries*. Note that we'd have to put an `r''` in front of the first quote, `r'\b'`, to denote that it is a "raw" string.

This still won't work because \b thinks the apostrophe is a word boundary and so splits the contracted word:

```
>>> re.split(r'\b', "Don't worry, spiders,")
['', 'Don', "'", 't', ' ', 'worry', ', ', 'spiders', ',']
```

While searching the internet for a regex to split this text properly, I found the following pattern on a Java discussion board. It perfectly separates *words* from *non-words*:[1]

```
>>> re.split("([a-zA-Z](?:[a-zA-Z']*[a-zA-Z])?)", "Don't worry, spiders,")
['', "Don't", ' ', 'worry', ', ', 'spiders', ',']
```

The beautiful thing about regular expressions is that they are their own language— one that is used inside many other languages from Perl to Haskell. Let's dig into this pattern, shown in figure 16.2.

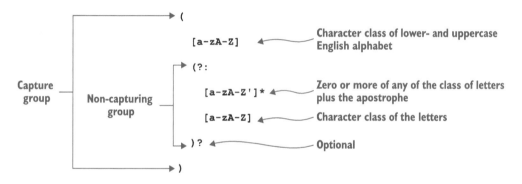

Figure 16.2   A regular expression that will find words that include an apostrophe

16.1.2 *Capturing, non-capturing, and optional groups*

In figure 16.2 you can see that groups can contain other groups. For instance, here is a regex that can capture the entire string "foobarbaz" as well as the substring "bar":

```
>>> match = re.match('(foo(bar)baz)', 'foobarbaz')
```

Capture groups are numbered by the position of their left parenthesis. Since the first left parenthesis starts the capture starting at "f" and going to "z," that is group 1:

```
>>> match.group(1)
'foobarbaz'
```

---

[1]   I would like to stress that a significant part of my job is spent looking for answers both in the books I own but also on the internet!

The second left parenthesis starts just before the "b" and goes to the "r":

```
>>> match.group(2)
'bar'
```

We can also make a group *non-capturing* by using the starting sequence (?:. If we use this sequence on the second group, we no longer capture the substring "bar":

```
>>> match = re.match('(foo(?:bar)baz)', 'foobarbaz')
>>> match.groups()
('foobarbaz',)
```

Non-capturing groups are commonly used when you are grouping primarily for the purpose of making it optional by placing a ? after the closing parenthesis. For instance, we can make the "bar" optional and then match both "foobarbaz,"

```
>>> re.match('(foo(?:bar)?baz)', 'foobarbaz')
<re.Match object; span=(0, 9), match='foobarbaz'>
```

as well as "foobaz":

```
>>> re.match('(foo(?:bar)?baz)', 'foobaz')
<re.Match object; span=(0, 6), match='foobaz'>
```

16.1.3 *Compiling a regex*

I mentioned the re.compile() function in chapter 15 as a way to incur the cost of compiling a regular expression just once. Whenever you use something like re.search() or re.split(), the regex engine must parse the str value you provide for the regex into something it understands and can use. This parsing step must happen *each time* you call the function. When you compile the regex and assign it to a variable, the parsing step is done before you call the function, which improves performance.

I especially like to use re.compile() to assign a regex to a meaningful variable name and/or reuse the regex in multiple places in my code. Because this regex is quite long and complicated, I think it makes the code more readable to assign it to a variable called splitter, which will help me to remember how it will be used:

```
>>> splitter = re.compile("([a-zA-Z](?:[a-zA-Z']*[a-zA-Z])?)")
>>> splitter.split("Don't worry, spiders,")
['', "Don't", ' ', 'worry', ', ', 'spiders', ',']
```

16.1.4 *Scrambling a word*

Now that we have a way to process the *lines* and then *words* of the text, let's think about how we'll scramble the words by starting with just *one word*. You and I will need to use the same algorithm for scrambling the words in order to pass the tests, so here are the rules:

- If the word is three characters or shorter, return the word unchanged.
- Use a string slice to copy the characters, not including the first and last.
- Use the `random.shuffle()` method to mix up the letters in the middle.
- Return the new "word" by combining the first, middle, and last parts.

I recommend you create a function called `scramble()` that will do all this, and also create a test for it. Feel free to add this to your program:

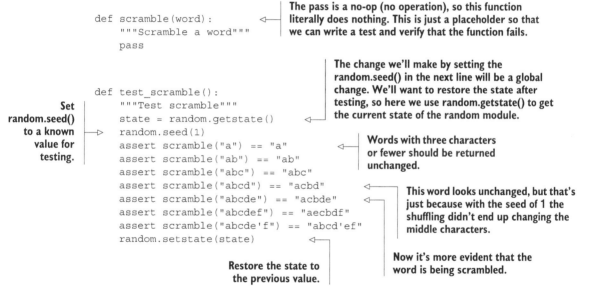

```
def scramble(word):
    """Scramble a word"""
    pass
```
The pass is a no-op (no operation), so this function literally does nothing. This is just a placeholder so that we can write a test and verify that the function fails.

Set random.seed() to a known value for testing.

```
def test_scramble():
    """Test scramble"""
    state = random.getstate()
    random.seed(1)
    assert scramble("a") == "a"
    assert scramble("ab") == "ab"
    assert scramble("abc") == "abc"
    assert scramble("abcd") == "acbd"
    assert scramble("abcde") == "acbde"
    assert scramble("abcdef") == "aecbdf"
    assert scramble("abcde'f") == "abcd'ef"
    random.setstate(state)
```

The change we'll make by setting the random.seed() in the next line will be a global change. We'll want to restore the state after testing, so here we use random.getstate() to get the current state of the random module.

Words with three characters or fewer should be returned unchanged.

This word looks unchanged, but that's just because with the seed of 1 the shuffling didn't end up changing the middle characters.

Now it's more evident that the word is being scrambled.

Restore the state to the previous value.

Inside the `scramble()` function, we will have a word like "worry." We can use list slices to extract part of a string. Since Python starts numbering at 0, we use 1 to indicate the *second* character:

```
>>> word = 'worry'
>>> word[1]
'o'
```

The last index of any string is -1:

```
>>> word[-1]
'y'
```

To get a slice, we use the list[start:stop] syntax. Since the stop position is not included, we can get the middle like so:

```
>>> middle = word[1:-1]
>>> middle
'orr'
```

We can import random to get access to the random.shuffle() function. As with the list.sort() and list.reverse() methods, the argument will be shuffled *in place*, and the function will return None. That is, you might be tempted to write code like this:

```
>>> import random
>>> x = [1, 2, 3]
>>> shuffled = random.shuffle(x)
```

What is the value of shuffled? Is it something like [3, 1, 2], or is it None?

```
>>> type(shuffled)
<class 'NoneType'>
```

The shuffled value now holds None, while the x list has been shuffled *in place* (see figure 16.3):

```
>>> x
[2, 3, 1]
```

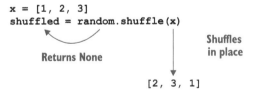

Shuffles in place

Returns None

[2, 3, 1]

Figure 16.3 The return from random.shuffle() was None, so shuffled was assigned None.

If you've been following along, it turns out that we cannot shuffle the middle like this:

```
>>> random.shuffle(middle)
Traceback (most recent call last):
  File "<stdin>", line 1, in <module>
  File "/Users/kyclark/anaconda3/lib/python3.7/random.py", line 278, in shuffle
    x[i], x[j] = x[j], x[i]
TypeError: 'str' object does not support item assignment
```

The `middle` variable is a `str`:

```
>>> type(middle)
<class 'str'>
```

The `random.shuffle()` function is trying to directly modify a `str` value in place, but `str` values in Python are *immutable*. One workaround is to make `middle` into a new `list` of the characters from `word`:

```
>>> middle = list(word[1:-1])
>>> middle
['o', 'r', 'r']
```

That is something we can shuffle:

```
>>> random.shuffle(middle)
>>> middle
['r', 'o', 'r']
```

Then it's a matter of creating a new string with the original first letter, the shuffled middle, and the last letter. I'll leave that for you to work out.

Use `pytest scrambler.py` to have Pytest execute the `test_scramble()` function to see if it works correctly. Run this command *after every change to your program*. Ensure that your program always compiles and runs properly. Only make one change at a time, and then save your program and run the tests.

16.1.5 *Scrambling all the words*

As in several previous exercises, we're now down to applying the `scramble()` function to all the words. Can you see a familiar pattern?

```
splitter = re.compile("([a-zA-Z](?:[a-zA-Z']*[a-zA-Z])?)")
for line in args.text.splitlines():
    for word in splitter.split(line):
        # what goes here?
```

We've talked about how to apply a function to each element in a sequence. You might try a `for` loop, a list comprehension, or maybe a `map()`. Think about how you can split the text into words, feed them to the `scramble()` function, and then join them back together to reconstruct the text.

Note that this approach will pass both the words and the non-words (the bits in between each word) to the `scramble()` function. You don't want to modify the non-words, so you'll need a way to check that the argument looks like a word. Maybe a regular expression?

That should be enough to go on. Write your solution and use the included tests to check your program.

16.2 Solution

To me, the program comes down to properly splitting the words and then figuring out the `scramble()` function. Then it's a matter of applying the function and reconstructing the text.

```python
#!/usr/bin/env python3
"""Scramble the letters of words"""

import argparse
import os
import re
import random


# --------------------------------------------------
def get_args():
    """Get command-line arguments"""

    parser = argparse.ArgumentParser(
        description='Scramble the letters of words',
        formatter_class=argparse.ArgumentDefaultsHelpFormatter)

    parser.add_argument('text', metavar='text', help='Input text or file')

    parser.add_argument('-s',
                        '--seed',
                        help='Random seed',
                        metavar='seed',
                        type=int,
                        default=None)

    args = parser.parse_args()

    if os.path.isfile(args.text):
        args.text = open(args.text).read().rstrip()

    return args


# --------------------------------------------------
def main():
    """Make a jazz noise here"""

    args = get_args()
    random.seed(args.seed)
    splitter = re.compile("([a-zA-Z](?:[a-zA-Z']*[a-zA-Z])?)")

    for line in args.text.splitlines():
        print(''.join(map(scramble, splitter.split(line))))
```

The text argument may be plain text on the command line or the name of a file to read.

The seed option is an int that defaults to None.

Get the arguments so we can check the text value.

If args.text names an existing file, replace the value of args.text with the result of opening and reading the file's contents.

Return the arguments to the caller.

Get the command-line arguments.

Use args.seed to set the random.seed() value. If args.seed is the default None, this is the same as not setting the seed.

Save the compiled regex into a variable.

Use str.splitlines() to preserve the line breaks in the input text.

Use the splitter to break the line into a new list that map() will feed into the scramble() function. Join the resulting list on the empty string to create a new str to print.

Define a function to scramble() a single word.

```
# --------------------------------------------------
def scramble(word):
    """For words over 3 characters, shuffle the letters in the middle"""

    if len(word) > 3 and re.match(r'\w+', word):
        middle = list(word[1:-1])
        random.shuffle(middle)
        word = word[0] + ''.join(middle) + word[-1]

    return word
```

Shuffle the middle letters.

Only scramble words with four or more characters if they contain word characters.

Return the word, which may have been altered if it met the criteria.

Copy the second through the second-to-last characters of the word into a new list called middle.

Set the word equal to the first character, plus the middle, plus the last character.

```
# --------------------------------------------------
def test_scramble():
    """Test scramble"""

    random.seed(1)
    assert scramble("a") == "a"
    assert scramble("ab") == "ab"
    assert scramble("abc") == "abc"
    assert scramble("abcd") == "acbd"
    assert scramble("abcde") == "acbde"
    assert scramble("abcdef") == "aecbdf"
    assert scramble("abcde'f") == "abcd'ef"
    random.seed(None)
```

The test for the scramble() function

```
# --------------------------------------------------
if __name__ == '__main__':
    main()
```

16.3 Discussion

There is nothing new in get_args(), so I trust you'll understand that code. Refer to chapter 5 if you want to revisit how to handle the args.text coming from the command line or from a file.

16.3.1 Processing the text

As mentioned earlier in the chapter, I often assign a *compiled* regex to a variable. Here I did it with the splitter:

```
splitter = re.compile("([a-zA-Z](?:[a-zA-Z']*[a-zA-Z])?)")
```

The other reason I like to use re.compile() is because I feel it can make my code more readable. Without it, I would have to write this:

```
for line in args.text.splitlines():
    print(''.join(map(scramble, re.split("([a-zA-Z](?:[a-zA-Z']*[a-zA-
        Z])?)", line))))
```

That ends up creating a line of code that is 86 characters wide, and the PEP 8 style guide (www.python.org/dev/peps/pep-0008/) recommends we "limit all lines to a maximum of 79 characters." I find the following version much easier to read:

```
splitter = re.compile("([a-zA-Z](?:[a-zA-Z']*[a-zA-Z])?)")
for line in args.text.splitlines():
    print(''.join(map(scramble, splitter.split(line))))
```

You may still find that code somewhat confusing. Figure 16.4 shows the flow of the data:

1   First Python will split the string `"Don't worry, spiders,"`.
2   The splitter creates a new list composed of words (that matched our regex) and non-words (the bits in between).
3   The `map()` function will apply the `scramble()` function to each element of the list.
4   The result of `map()` is a new list with the results of each application of the `scramble()` function.
5   The result of `str.join()` is a new string, which is the argument to `print()`.

Figure 16.4   A visualization of how data moves through the map() function

A longer way to write this with a `for` loop might look like this:

Use str.splitlines() to preserve the original line breaks.

For each line of input, create an empty list to hold the scrambled words.

```
for line in args.text.splitlines():
    words = []
    for word in splitter.split(line):
        words.append(scramble(word))
    print(''.join(words))
```

Use the splitter to split the line.

Add the result of scramble(word) to the words list.

Join the words on the empty string and pass the result to print().

Because the goal is to create a new `list`, this is better written as a list comprehension:

```
for line in args.text.splitlines():
    words = [scramble(word) for word in splitter.split(line)]
    print(''.join(words))
```

Or you could go in quite the opposite direction and replace all the `for` loops with `map()`:

```
print('\n'.join(
    map(lambda line: ''.join(map(scramble, splitter.split(line))),
        args.text.splitlines())))
```

This last solution reminds me of a programmer I used to work with who would jokingly say, "If it was hard to write, it should be hard to read!" It becomes somewhat clearer if you rearrange the code. Note that Pylint will complain about assigning a `lambda`, but I really don't agree with that criticism:

```
scrambler = lambda line: ''.join(map(scramble, splitter.split(line)))
print('\n'.join(map(scrambler, args.text.splitlines())))
```

Writing code that is correct, tested, and understandable is as much an art as it is a craft. Choose the version that you (and your teammates!) believe is the most readable.

16.3.2 Scrambling a word

Let's take a closer look at my `scramble()` function. I wrote it in a way that would make it easy to incorporate into `map()`:

Check if the given word is one I ought to scramble. First, it must be longer than three characters. Second, it must contain one or more word characters because the function will be passed both "word" and "nonword" strings. If either check returns False, I will return the word unchanged. The r'\w+' is used to create a "raw" string. Note that the regex works fine with or without it being a raw string, but Pylint complains about an "invalid escape character" unless it is a raw string.

Copy the middle of the word to a new list called middle.

```
def scramble(word):
    """For words over 3 characters, shuffle the letters in the middle"""
    if len(word) > 3 and re.match(r'\w+', word):
        middle = list(word[1:-1])
```

```
random.shuffle(middle)
word = word[0] + ''.join(middle) + word[-1]

return word
```

Shuffle the middle in place. Remember that this function returns None.

Reconstruct the word by joining together the first character, the shuffled middle, and the last character.

Return the word, which may or may not have been shuffled.

16.4 Going further

- Write a version of the program where the `scramble()` function sorts the middle letters into alphabetical order rather than shuffling them.

- Write a version that reverses each word rather than scrambles them.

- Write a program to *unscramble* the text. For this, you need to have a dictionary of English words, which I have provided as inputs/words.txt.zip. You will need to split the scrambled text into words and non-words, and then compare each "word" to the words in your dictionary. I recommend you start by comparing the words as anagrams (that is, they have the same composition/frequency of letters) and then using the first and last letters to positively identify the unscrambled word.

Summary

- The regex we used to split the text into words was quite complex, but it also gave us exactly what we needed. Writing the program without this piece would have been significantly more difficult. Regexes, while complex and deep, are wildly powerful black magic that can make your programs incredibly flexible and useful.

- The `random.shuffle()` function accepts a `list`, which is mutated in place.

- List comprehensions and `map()` can often lead to more compact code, but going too far can reduce readability. Choose wisely.

Mad Libs:
Using regular expressions

When I was a wee lad, we used to play at Mad Libs for hours and hours. This was before computers, mind you, before televisions or radio or even paper! No, scratch that, we had paper. Anyway, point is we only had Mad Libs to play, and we loved it! And now you must play!

In this chapter, we'll write a program called mad.py that will read a file given as a positional argument and find all the placeholders in angle brackets, like <verb> or <adjective>. For each placeholder, we'll prompt the user for the part of speech being requested, like "Give me a verb" and "Give me an adjective." (Notice that you'll

need to use the correct article, just as in chapter 2.) Each value from the user will then replace the placeholder in the text, so if the user says "drive" for the verb, then <verb> in the text will be replaced with drive. When all the placeholders have been replaced with inputs from the user, we'll print out the new text.

There is a 17_mad_libs/inputs directory with some sample files you can use, but I also encourage you to create your own. For instance, here is a version of the "fox" text:

```
$ cd 17_mad_libs
$ cat inputs/fox.txt
The quick <adjective> <noun> jumps <preposition> the lazy <noun>.
```

When the program is run with this file as the input, it will ask for each of the place-holders and then print the silliness:

```
$ ./mad.py inputs/fox.txt
Give me an adjective: surly
Give me a noun: car
Give me a preposition: under
Give me a noun: bicycle
The quick surly car jumps under the lazy bicycle.
```

By default, this is an interactive program that will use the input() prompt to ask the user for their answers, but for testing purposes we will have an -i or --inputs option so the test suite can pass in all the answers and bypass the interactive input() calls:

```
$ ./mad.py inputs/fox.txt -i surly car under bicycle
The quick surly car jumps under the lazy bicycle.
```

In this exercise, you will

- Learn to use sys.exit() to halt your program and indicate an error status
- Learn about greedy matching with regular expressions
- Use re.findall() to find all matches for a regex
- Use re.sub() to replace found patterns with new text
- Explore ways to write the solution without using regular expressions

17.1 *Writing mad.py*

To start off, create the program mad.py in the 17_mad_libs directory using new.py or by copying template/template.py to 17_mad_libs/mad.py. You would also do well to define the positional file argument as a readable text file using type=argparse.FileType('rt'). The -i or --inputs option should use nargs='*' to define a list of zero or more str values.

After this, your program should be able to produce a usage statement when given no arguments or the -h or --help flag:

```
$ ./mad.py -h
usage: mad.py [-h] [-i [input [input ...]]] FILE

Mad Libs

positional arguments:
  FILE                  Input file

optional arguments:
  -h, --help            show this help message and exit
  -i [input [input ...]], --inputs [input [input ...]]
                        Inputs (for testing) (default: None)
```

If the given `file` argument does not exist, the program should error out:

```
$ ./mad.py blargh
usage: mad.py [-h] [-i [str [str ...]]] FILE
mad.py: error: argument FILE: can't open 'blargh': \
[Errno 2] No such file or directory: 'blargh'
```

If the text of the file contains no `<>` placeholders, the program should print a message and exit with an error value (something other than 0). Note that this error does not need to print a usage statement, so you don't have to use `parser.error()` as in previous exercises:

```
$ cat no_blanks.txt
This text has no placeholders.
$ ./mad.py no_blanks.txt
"no_blanks.txt" has no placeholders.
```

Figure 17.1 shows a string diagram to help you visualize the program.

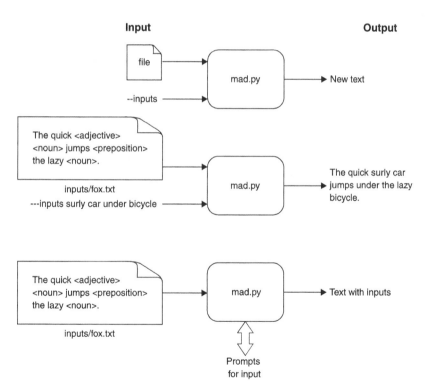

Figure 17.1 The Mad Libs program must have an input file. It may also have a list of strings for the substitutions or it will interactively ask the user for the values.

17.1.1   *Using regular expressions to find the pointy bits*

We've talked before about the possible dangers of reading an entire file into memory. Because we'll be parsing the text to find all the <...> bits in this program, we'll really need to read the whole file at once. We can do this by chaining the appropriate functions like so:

```
>>> text = open('inputs/fox.txt').read().rstrip()
>>> text
'The quick <adjective> <noun> jumps <preposition> the lazy <noun>.'
```

We're looking for patterns of text inside angle brackets, so let's use a regular expression. We can find a literal < character like so (see figure 17.2):

```
>>> import re
>>> re.search('<', text)
<re.Match object; span=(10, 11), match='<'>
```

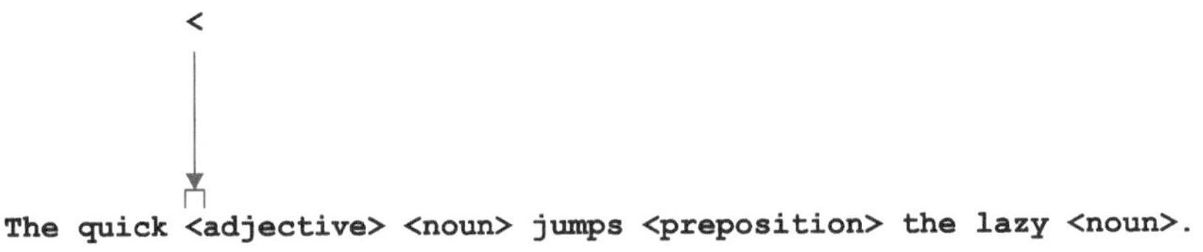

<

The quick **<adjective> <noun>** jumps **<preposition>** the lazy **<noun>**.

Figure 17.2   Matching a literal less-than sign

Now let's find that bracket's mate. The . in a regular expression means "anything," and we can add a + after it to mean "one or more." I'll capture the match so it's easier to see:

```
>>> match = re.search('(<.+>)', text)
>>> match.group(1)
'<adjective> <noun> jumps <preposition> the lazy <noun>'
```

As shown in figure 17.3, that matched all the way to the end of the string instead of stopping at the first available >. It's common when you use * or + for zero, one, or more for the regex engine to be "greedy" on the *or more* part. The pattern matches beyond where we wanted, but it is technically matching exactly what we described. Remember that . means *anything*, and a right angle bracket (or greater-than sign) is

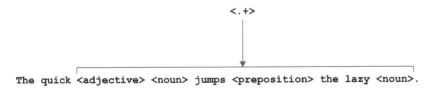

<.+>

The quick **<adjective> <noun>** jumps **<preposition>** the lazy **<noun>**.

Figure 17.3   The plus sign to match one or more is a greedy match, matching as many characters as possible.

"anything." It matches as many characters as possible until it finds the last right angle bracket stop at, which is why this pattern is called "greedy."

We can make the regex "non-greedy" by changing + to +? so that it matches the shortest possible string (see figure 17.4):

```
>>> re.search('<.+?>', text)
<re.Match object; span=(10, 21), match='<adjective>'>
```

The quick <adjective> <noun> jumps <preposition> the lazy <noun>.

Figure 17.4 **The question mark after the plus sign makes the regex stop at the shortest possible match.**

Rather than using . for "anything," it would be more accurate to say that we want to match one or more of anything *that is not either of the angle brackets*. The character class [<>] would match either bracket. We can negate (or complement) the class by putting a caret (^) as the first character, so we have [^<>] (see figure 17.5). That will match anything that is not a left or right angle bracket:

```
>>> re.search('<[^<>]+>', text)
<re.Match object; span=(10, 21), match='<adjective>'>
```

The quick <adjective> <noun> jumps <preposition> the lazy <noun>.

Figure 17.5 **A negated character class to match anything other than the angle brackets**

Why do we have both brackets inside the negated class? Wouldn't the right bracket be enough? Well, I'm guarding against *unbalanced* brackets. With only the right bracket, it would match this text (see figure 17.6):

```
>>> re.search('<[^>]+>', 'foo <<bar> baz')
<re.Match object; span=(4, 10), match='<<bar>'>
```

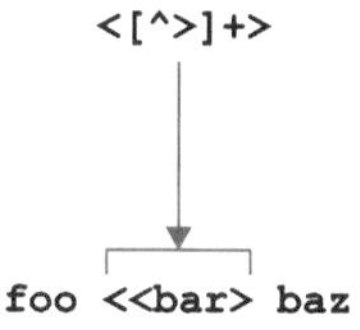

foo <<bar> baz

Figure 17.6 **This regex leaves open the possibility of matching unbalanced brackets.**

But with *both* brackets in the negated class, it finds the correct, balanced pair (see figure 17.7):

```
>>> re.search('<[^<>]+>', 'foo <<bar> baz')
<re.Match object; span=(5, 10), match='<bar>'>
```

Figure 17.7   This regex finds the correctly balanced brackets and contained text.

We'll add two sets of parentheses (). The first will capture the *entire* placeholder pattern (see figure 17.8):

```
>>> match = re.search('(<([^<>]+)>)', text)
>>> match.groups()
('<adjective>', 'adjective')
```

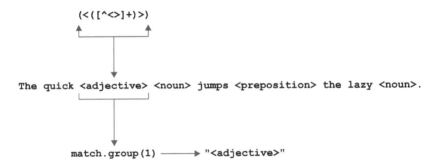

Figure 17.8   The outer parentheses capture the brackets and text.

The other is for the string *inside* the <> (see figure 17.9):

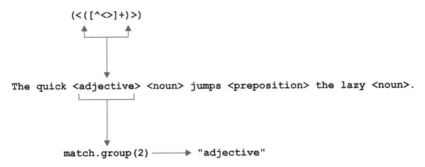

Figure 17.9   The inner parentheses capture just the text.

There is a very handy function called `re.findall()` that will return all matching text groups as a `list` of `tuple` values:

```
>>> from pprint import pprint
>>> matches = re.findall('(<([^<>]+)>)', text)
>>> pprint(matches)
[('<adjective>', 'adjective'),
 ('<noun>', 'noun'),
 ('<preposition>', 'preposition'),
 ('<noun>', 'noun')]
```

Note that the capture groups are returned in the order of their opening parentheses, so the entire placeholder is the first member of each `tuple`, and the contained text is the second. We can iterate over this `list`, *unpacking* each `tuple` into variables (see figure 17.10):

```
>>> for placeholder, name in matches:
...     print(f'Give me {name}')
...
Give me adjective
Give me noun
Give me preposition
Give me noun
```

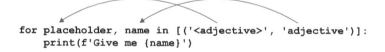

```
for placeholder, name in [('<adjective>', 'adjective')]:
    print(f'Give me {name}')
```

Figure 17.10   Since the list contains 2-tuples, we can unpack them into two variables in the `for` loop.

You should insert the correct article ("a" or "an," as you did in chapter 2) to use as the prompt for `input()`.

17.1.2 *Halting and printing errors*

If we find there are no placeholders in the text, we need to print an error message. It's common to print error messages to STDERR (standard error), and the `print()` function allows us to specify a `file` argument. We'll use `sys.stderr`, just as we did in chapter 9. To do that, we need to import that module:

```
import sys
```

You may recall that `sys.stderr` is like an already open file handle, so there's no need to `open()` it:

```
print('This is an error!', file=sys.stderr)
```

If there really are no placeholders, we should exit the program with an error value to indicate to the operating system that the program failed to run properly. The normal exit value for a program is 0, as in "zero errors," so we need to exit with some int value that is *not* 0. I always use 1:

```
sys.exit(1)
```

One of the tests checks whether your program can detect missing placeholders and if your program exits correctly.

You can also call sys.exit() with a string value, in which case the string will be printed to sys.stderr and the program will exit with the value 1:

```
sys.exit('This will kill your program and print an error message!')
```

17.1.3 Getting the values

For each one of the parts of speech in the text, we need a value that will come either from the --inputs argument or directly from the user. If we have nothing for --inputs, we can use the input() function to get an answer from the user.

The input() function takes a str value to use as a prompt:

```
>>> value = input('Give me an adjective: ')
Give me an adjective: blue
```

And it returns a str value of whatever the user typed before pressing the Return key:

```
>>> value
'blue'
```

If, however, we have values for the inputs, we can use those and not bother with the input() function. I'm only making you handle the --inputs option for testing purposes. You can safely assume that you will always have the same number of inputs as you have placeholders (see figure 17.11).

Figure 17.11   If given inputs from the command line, they will match up with the placeholders in the text.

For instance, you might have the following as the --inputs option to your program for the fox.txt example:

```
>>> inputs = ['surly', 'car', 'under', 'bicycle']
```

You need to remove and return the first string, "surly," from inputs. The list.pop() method is what you need, but it wants to remove the *last* element by default:

```
>>> inputs.pop()
'bicycle'
```

The list.pop() method takes an optional argument to indicate the index of the element you want to remove. Can you figure out how to make that work? Be sure to read help(list.pop) if you're stuck.

17.1.4 Substituting the text

When you have values for each of the placeholders, you will need to substitute them into the text. I suggest you look into the re.sub() (substitute) function, which will replace any text matching a given regular expression with some other value. I definitely recommend you read help(re.sub):

```
sub(pattern, repl, string, count=0, flags=0)
    Return the string obtained by replacing the leftmost
    non-overlapping occurrences of the pattern in string by the
    replacement repl.
```

I don't want to give away the ending, but you will need to use a pattern similar to the preceding to replace each <placeholder> with each value.

Note that it's not a requirement that you use the re.sub() function to solve this. I challenge you, in fact, to try writing a solution that does not use the re module at all. Now go write the program, and use the tests to guide you!

17.2 Solution

Are you getting more comfortable with regular expressions? I know they are complicated, but really understanding them will help you more than you might expect.

```
#!/usr/bin/env python3
"""Mad Libs"""

import argparse
import re
import sys


# --------------------------------------------------
def get_args():
    """Get command-line arguments"""

    parser = argparse.ArgumentParser(
        description='Mad Libs',
        formatter_class=argparse.ArgumentDefaultsHelpFormatter)

    parser.add_argument('file',                          ⊲──┤ The file argument should
                        metavar='FILE',                      │ be a readable text file.
```

```
                                        type=argparse.FileType('rt'),
                                        help='Input file')

        parser.add_argument('-i',                    ◁──┐ The --inputs option may
                             '--inputs',                 │ have zero or more strings.
                             help='Inputs (for testing)',
                             metavar='input',
                             type=str,
                             nargs='*')

        return parser.parse_args()


    # --------------------------------------------------
    def main():
        """Make a jazz noise here"""

        args = get_args()
        inputs = args.inputs
        text = args.file.read().rstrip()   ◁──
        blanks = re.findall('(<([^<>]+)>)', text)      ◁───

        if not blanks:
            sys.exit(f'"{args.file.name}" has no placeholders.')

        tmpl = 'Give me {} {}: '                                    ◁──
        for placeholder, pos in blanks:                            ◁──
            article = 'an' if pos.lower()[0] in 'aeiou' else 'a'   ◁──
            answer = inputs.pop(0) if inputs else input(tmpl.format(article, pos))
            text = re.sub(placeholder, answer, text, count=1)

        print(text)     ◁──┐ Print the resulting
                           │ text to STDOUT.

    # --------------------------------------------------
    if __name__ == '__main__':
        main()
```

Use a regex to find all matches for a left angle bracket, followed by one or more of anything that is not a left or right angle bracket, followed by a right angle bracket. Use two capture groups to capture the entire expression and the text inside the brackets.

Open and read the input file, stripping off the trailing newline.

Check if there are no placeholders.

Choose the correct article based on the first letter of the name of the part of speech (pos): "an" for those starting with a vowel and "a" otherwise.

Iterate through the blanks, unpacking each tuple into variables.

Create a string template for the prompt to ask for input() from the user.

Replace the current placeholder text with the answer from the user. Use count=1 to ensure that only the first value is replaced. Overwrite the existing value of text so that all the placeholders will be replaced by the end of the loop.

If there are inputs, remove the first one for the answer; otherwise, use input() to prompt the user for a value.

Print a message to STDERR that the specified file contains no placeholders, and exit the program with a non-zero status to indicate an error to the operating system.

17.3   *Discussion*

We start off by defining our arguments well. The input file should be declared using type=argparse.FileType('rt') so that argparse will verify that the argument is a readable text file. The --inputs are optional, so we can use nargs='*' to indicate zero or more strings. If no inputs are provided, the default value will be None, so be sure you don't assume it's a list and try doing list operations on a None.

17.3.1 *Substituting with regular expressions*

There is a subtle bug waiting for you in using re.sub(). Suppose we have replaced the first <adjective> with "blue" so that we have this:

```
>>> text = 'The quick blue <noun> jumps <preposition> the lazy <noun>.'
```

Now we want to replace <noun> with "dog," so we try this:

```
>>> text = re.sub('<noun>', 'dog', text)
```

Let's check on the value of text now:

```
>>> text
'The quick blue dog jumps <preposition> the lazy dog.'
```

Since there were two instances of the string <noun>, both got replaced with "dog," as shown in figure 17.12.

```
re.sub('<noun>', 'dog', 'The quick blue <noun> jumps <preposition> the lazy <noun>.')
```

Figure 17.12 The re.sub() function will replace all matches.

We must use count=1 to ensure that only the first occurrence is changed (see figure 17.13):

```
>>> text = 'The quick blue <noun> jumps <preposition> the lazy <noun>.'
>>> text = re.sub('<noun>', 'dog', text, count=1)
>>> text
'The quick blue dog jumps <preposition> the lazy <noun>.'
```

```
re.sub('<noun>', 'dog', 'The quick blue <noun> jumps <prepositlon> the lazy <noun>.', count=1)
```

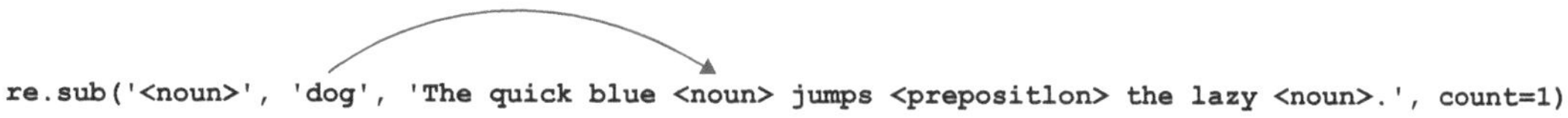

Figure 17.13 Use the count option to re.sub() to limit the number of replacements.

Now we can keep moving on to replace the other placeholders.

17.3.2 *Finding the placeholders without regular expressions*

I trust the explanation of the regex solution earlier in the chapter was sufficient. I find that solution fairly elegant, but it is certainly possible to solve this without using regexes. Here is how I might solve it manually.

First I need a way to search the text for <...>. I start off by writing a test that helps me imagine what I might give to my function and what I might expect in return for both good and bad values.

I decide to return None when the pattern is missing and to return a tuple of (start, stop) indices when the pattern is present:

There is no text, so it should return None.

There are angle brackets, but they lack any text inside, so this should return None.

```
def test_find_brackets():
    """Test for finding angle brackets"""
    assert find_brackets('') is None
    assert find_brackets('<>') is None
    assert find_brackets('<x>') == (0, 2)
    assert find_brackets('foo <bar> baz') == (4, 8)
```

The pattern should be found at the beginning of a string.

The pattern should be found further into the string.

Now I need to write the code that will satisfy that test. Here is what I wrote:

Find the index of the left bracket if one is found in the text.

Find the index of the right bracket if one is found starting two positions after the left.

```
def find_brackets(text):
    """Find angle brackets"""
    start = text.index('<') if '<' in text else -1
    stop = text.index('>') if start >= 0 and '>' in text[start + 2:] else -1
    return (start, stop) if start >= 0 and stop >= 0 else None
```

If both brackets were found, return a tuple of their start and stop positions; otherwise, return None.

This function works well enough to pass the given tests, but it is not quite correct because it will return a region that contains unbalanced brackets:

```
>>> text = 'foo <<bar> baz'
>>> find_brackets(text)
[4, 9]
>>> text[4:10]
'<<bar>'
```

That may seem unlikely, but I chose angle brackets to make you think of HTML tags like <head> and <img>. HTML is notorious for being incorrect, maybe because it was hand generated by a human who messed up a tag or because some tool that generated the HTML had a bug. The point is that most web browsers have to be fairly relaxed in parsing HTML, and it would not be unexpected to see a malformed tag like <<head> instead of the correct <head>.

The regex version, on the other hand, specifically guards against matching unbalanced brackets by using the class [^<>] to define text that cannot contain any angle brackets. I could write a version of find_brackets() that finds only balanced brackets, but, honestly, it's just not worth it. This function points out that one of the strengths of the regex engine is that it can find a partial match (the first left bracket), see that it's unable to make a complete match, and start over (at the next left bracket). Writing this myself would be tedious and, frankly, not that interesting.

Still, this function works for all the given test inputs. Note that it only returns one set of brackets at a time. I will alter the text after I find each set of brackets, which will likely change the start and stop positions of any following brackets, so it's best to handle one set at a time.

Here is how I would incorporate it into the `main()` function:

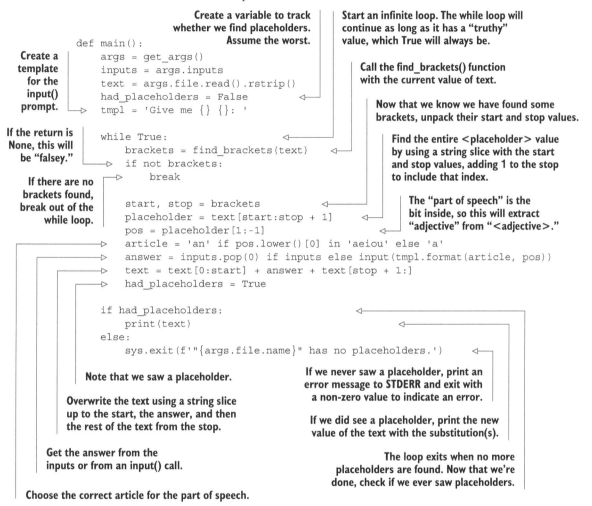

Create a variable to track whether we find placeholders. Assume the worst.

Start an infinite loop. The while loop will continue as long as it has a "truthy" value, which True will always be.

Create a template for the input() prompt.

Call the find_brackets() function with the current value of text.

Now that we know we have found some brackets, unpack their start and stop values.

If the return is None, this will be "falsey."

Find the entire <placeholder> value by using a string slice with the start and stop values, adding 1 to the stop to include that index.

If there are no brackets found, break out of the while loop.

The "part of speech" is the bit inside, so this will extract "adjective" from "<adjective>."

```python
def main():
    args = get_args()
    inputs = args.inputs
    text = args.file.read().rstrip()
    had_placeholders = False
    tmpl = 'Give me {} {}: '

    while True:
        brackets = find_brackets(text)
        if not brackets:
            break

        start, stop = brackets
        placeholder = text[start:stop + 1]
        pos = placeholder[1:-1]
        article = 'an' if pos.lower()[0] in 'aeiou' else 'a'
        answer = inputs.pop(0) if inputs else input(tmpl.format(article, pos))
        text = text[0:start] + answer + text[stop + 1:]
        had_placeholders = True

    if had_placeholders:
        print(text)
    else:
        sys.exit(f'"{args.file.name}" has no placeholders.')
```

Note that we saw a placeholder.

Overwrite the text using a string slice up to the start, the answer, and then the rest of the text from the stop.

Get the answer from the inputs or from an input() call.

Choose the correct article for the part of speech.

If we never saw a placeholder, print an error message to STDERR and exit with a non-zero value to indicate an error.

If we did see a placeholder, print the new value of the text with the substitution(s).

The loop exits when no more placeholders are found. Now that we're done, check if we ever saw placeholders.

17.4 Going further

- Extend your code to find all the HTML tags enclosed in <...> and </...> in a web page you download from the internet.
- Write a program that will look for unbalanced open/close pairs for parentheses (), square brackets [], and curly brackets {}. Create input files that have balanced and unbalanced text, and write tests that verify your program identifies both.

Summary

- Regular expressions are almost like functions where we *describe* the patterns we want to find. The regex engine will do the work of trying to find the patterns, handling mismatches and starting over to find the pattern in the text.

- Regex patterns with * or + are "greedy" in that they match as many characters as possible. Adding a ? after them makes them "non-greedy" so that they match as *few* characters as possible.

- The re.findall() function will return a list of all the matching strings or capture groups for a given pattern.

- The re.sub() function will substitute a pattern in some text with new text.

- You can halt your program at any time using the sys.exit() function. If it's given no arguments, the default exit value will be 0 to indicate no errors. If you wish to indicate there was an error, use any non-zero value such as 1. Or use a string value, which will be printed to STDERR, and a non-zero exit value will be used automatically.

Gematria: Numeric encoding of text using ASCII values

Gematria is a system for assigning a number to a word by summing the numeric values of each of the characters (https://en.wikipedia.org/wiki/Gematria). In the standard encoding (*Mispar hechrechi*), each character of the Hebrew alphabet is assigned a numeric value ranging from 1 to 400, but there are more than a dozen other methods for calculating the numeric value for the letters. To encode a word, these values are added together. Revelation 13:18 from the Christian Bible says, "Let the one who has insight calculate the number of the wild beast, for it is a man's number, and its number is 666." Some scholars believe that number is derived from the encoding of the characters representing Nero Caesar's name and title and that it was used as a way of writing about the Roman emperor without naming him.

We will write a program called gematria.py that will numerically encode each word in a given text by similarly adding numeric values for the characters in each word. There are many ways we could assign these values. For instance, we could start by giving "a" the value 1, "b" the value 2, and so forth. Instead, we will use the ASCII table (https://en.wikipedia.org/wiki/ASCII) to derive a numeric value for English alphabet characters. For non-English characters, we could consider using a Unicode value, but this exercise will stick to ASCII letters.

The input text may be entered on the command line:

```
$ ./gematria.py 'foo bar baz'
324 309 317
```

Or it could be in a file:

```
$ ./gematria.py ../inputs/fox.txt
289 541 552 333 559 444 321 448 314
```

Figure 18.1 shows a string diagram showing how the program should work.

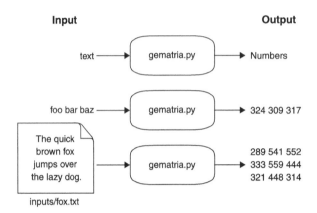

Figure 18.1   The gematria program will accept input text and will produce a numeric encoding for each word.

In this exercise, you will

- Learn about the ord() and chr() functions
- Explore how characters are organized in the ASCII table
- Understand character ranges used in regular expressions
- Use the re.sub() function
- Learn how map() can be written without lambda
- Use the sum() function and see how that relates to using reduce()
- Learn how to perform case-insensitive string sorting

18.1   *Writing gematria.py*

I will always recommend you start your programs in some way that avoids having to type all the boilerplate text. Either copy template/template.py to 18_gematria/gematria.py or use new.py gematria.py in the 18_gematria directory to create a starting point.

Modify the program until it prints the following usage statement if it's given no arguments or the -h or --help flag:

```
$ ./gematria.py -h
usage: gematria.py [-h] text

Gematria

positional arguments:
  text        Input text or file
```

```
optional arguments:
  -h, --help  show this help message and exit
```

As in previous exercises, the input may come from the command line or from a file. I suggest you copy the code you used in chapter 5 to handle this, and then modify your `main()` function as follows:

```
def main():
    args = get_args()
    print(args.text)
```

Verify that your program will print text from the command line,

```
$ ./gematria.py 'Death smiles at us all, but all a man can do is smile back.'
Death smiles at us all, but all a man can do is smile back.
```

or from a file:

```
$ ./gematria.py ../inputs/spiders.txt
Don't worry, spiders,
I keep house
casually.
```

18.1.1 Cleaning a word

Let's discuss how a single word will be encoded, as it will affect how we will break the text in the next section. In order to be absolutely sure we are only dealing with ASCII values, let's remove anything that is not an upper- or lowercase English alphabet character or any of the Arabic numerals 0–9. We can define that class of characters using the regular expression `[A-Za-z0-9]`.

We can use the `re.findall()` function we used in chapter 17 to find all the characters in `word` that match this class. For instance, we should expect to find everything except the apostrophe in the word "Don't" (see figure 18.2):

```
>>> re.findall('[A-Za-z0-9]', "Don't")
['D', 'o', 'n', 't']
```

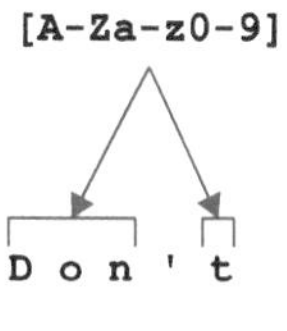

[A-Za-z0-9]

Figure 18.2   **This character class only matches alphanumeric values.**

If we put a caret (^) as the first character inside the class, like `[^A-Za-z0-9]`, we'll find anything that is *not* one of those characters. Now we would expect to match *only* the apostrophe (see figure 18.3):

```
>>> import re
>>> re.findall('[^A-Za-z0-9]', "Don't")
["'"]
```

Figure 18.3   The caret will find the complement of the character class, so any non-alphanumeric character.

We can use the re.sub() function to replace any characters in that second class with the empty string. As you learned in chapter 17, this will replace *all* occurrences of the pattern unless we use the count=n option:

```
>>> word = re.sub('[^A-Za-z0-9]', '', "Don't")
>>> word
'Dont'
```

We will want to use this operation to clean each word that we'll encode, as shown in figure 18.4.

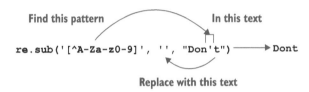

Figure 18.4   The re.sub() function will replace any text matching a pattern with another value.

18.1.2   *Ordinal character values and ranges*

We will encode a string like "Dont" by converting *each character* to a numeric value and then adding them together, so let's first figure out how to encode a single character.

Python has a function called ord() that will convert a character to its "ordinal" value. For all alphanumeric values that we are using, this will be equal to the character's position in the American Standard Code for Information Interchange (ASCII, pronounced like "as-kee") table:

```
>>> ord('D')
68
>>> ord('o')
111
```

The chr() function works in reverse to convert a number to a character:

```
>>> chr(68)
'D'
>>> chr(111)
'o'
```

Following is the ASCII table. For simplicity's sake, I show "NA" ("not available") for the values up to index 31 as they are not printable.

```
$ ./asciitbl.py
 0 NA      16 NA      32 SPACE   48 0      64 @      80 P       96 `      112 p
 1 NA      17 NA      33 !       49 1      65 A      81 Q       97 a      113 q
 2 NA      18 NA      34 "       50 2      66 B      82 R       98 b      114 r
 3 NA      19 NA      35 #       51 3      67 C      83 S       99 c      115 s
 4 NA      20 NA      36 $       52 4      68 D      84 T      100 d      116 t
 5 NA      21 NA      37 %       53 5      69 E      85 U      101 e      117 u
 6 NA      22 NA      38 &       54 6      70 F      86 V      102 f      118 v
 7 NA      23 NA      39 '       55 7      71 G      87 W      103 g      119 w
 8 NA      24 NA      40 (       56 8      72 H      88 X      104 h      120 x
 9 NA      25 NA      41 )       57 9      73 I      89 Y      105 i      121 y
10 NA      26 NA      42 *       58 :      74 J      90 Z      106 j      122 z
11 NA      27 NA      43 +       59 ;      75 K      91 [      107 k      123 {
12 NA      28 NA      44 ,       60 <      76 L      92 \      108 l      124 |
13 NA      29 NA      45 -       61 =      77 M      93 ]      109 m      125 }
14 NA      30 NA      46 .       62 >      78 N      94 ^      110 n      126 ~
15 NA      31 NA      47 /       63 ?      79 O      95 _      111 o      127 DEL
```

> **NOTE** I have included the asciitbl.py program in the 18_gematria directory of the source code repository.

We can use a `for` loop to cycle through all the characters in a string:

```
>>> word = "Dont"
>>> for char in word:
...     print(char, ord(char))
...
D 68
o 111
n 110
t 116
```

Note that upper- and lowercase letters have different `ord()` values. This makes sense because they are two different letters:

```
>>> ord('D')
68
>>> ord('d')
100
```

We can iterate over the values from "a" to "z" by finding their `ord()` values:

```
>>> [chr(n) for n in range(ord('a'), ord('z') + 1)]
['a', 'b', 'c', 'd', 'e', 'f', 'g', 'h', 'i', 'j', 'k', 'l', 'm',
 'n', 'o', 'p', 'q', 'r', 's', 't', 'u', 'v', 'w', 'x', 'y', 'z']
```

As you can see in the previous ASCII table, the letters "a" through "z" lie contiguously. The same is true for "A" to "Z" and "0" to "9," which is why we can use `[A-Za-z0-9]` as a regex.

Note that the uppercase letters have *lower* ordinal values than their lowercase versions, which is why you cannot use the range [a-Z]. Try this in the REPL and note the error you get:

```
>>> re.findall('[a-Z]', word)
```

If I execute the preceding function in the REPL, the last line of the error I see is this:

```
re.error: bad character range a-Z at position 1
```

You *can*, however, use the range [A-z]:

```
>>> re.findall('[A-z]', word)
['D', 'o', 'n', 't']
```

But note that "Z" and "a" are not contiguous:

```
>>> ord('Z'), ord('a')
(90, 97)
```

There are other characters in between them:

```
>>> [chr(n) for n in range(ord('Z') + 1, ord('a'))]
['[', '\\', ']', '^', '_', '`']
```

If we try to use that range on all the printable characters, you'll see that it matches characters that are not letters:

```
>>> import string
>>> re.findall('[A-z]', string.printable)
['a', 'b', 'c', 'd', 'e', 'f', 'g', 'h', 'i', 'j', 'k', 'l', 'm',
 'n', 'o', 'p', 'q', 'r', 's', 't', 'u', 'v', 'w', 'x', 'y', 'z',
 'A', 'B', 'C', 'D', 'E', 'F', 'G', 'H', 'I', 'J', 'K', 'L', 'M',
 'N', 'O', 'P', 'Q', 'R', 'S', 'T', 'U', 'V', 'W', 'X', 'Y', 'Z',
 '[', '\\', ']', '^', '_', '`']
```

That is why it is safest to specify the characters we want as the three separate ranges, [A-Za-z0-9], which you may sometimes hear pronounced as "A to Z, a to z, zero to nine," as it assumes you understand that there are two "a to z" ranges that are distinct according to their case.

18.1.3 *Summing and reducing*

Let's keep reminding ourselves what the goal is here: convert all the characters in a word, and then sum those values. There is a handy Python function called sum() that will add a list of numbers:

```
>>> sum([1, 2, 3])
6
```

We can manually encode the string "Dont" by calling `ord()` on each letter and passing the results as a `list` to `sum()`:

```
>>> sum([ord('D'), ord('o'), ord('n'), ord('t')])
405
```

The question is how to apply the function `ord()` to all the characters in a `str` and pass a `list` to `sum()`. You've seen this pattern many times now. What's the first tool you'll reach for? We can always start with our handy `for` loop:

```
>>> word = 'Dont'
>>> vals = []
>>> for char in word:
...     vals.append(ord(char))
...
>>> vals
[68, 111, 110, 116]
```

Can you see how to make that into a single line using a list comprehension?

```
>>> vals = [ord(char) for char in word]
>>> vals
[68, 111, 110, 116]
```

From there, we can move to a `map()`:

```
>>> vals = map(lambda char: ord(char), word)
>>> list(vals)
[68, 111, 110, 116]
```

Here I'd like to show that the `map()` version doesn't need the `lambda` declaration because the `ord()` function expects a single value, which is exactly what it will get from `map()`. Here is a nicer way to write it:

```
>>> vals = map(ord, word)
>>> list(vals)
[68, 111, 110, 116]
```

To my eye, that is a really beautiful piece of code!

Now we can `sum()` that to get a final value for our `word`:

```
>>> sum(map(ord, word))
405
```

That is correct:

```
>>> sum([68, 111, 110, 116])
405
```

18.1.4 *Using functools.reduce*

If Python has a sum() function, you might suspect it also has a product() function to multiply a list of numbers together. Alas, this is not a built-in function, but it does represent a common idea of *reducing* a list of values into a single value.

The reduce() function from the functools module provides a generic way to reduce a list. Let's consult the documentation for how to use it:

```
>>> from functools import reduce
>>> help(reduce)
reduce(...)
    reduce(function, sequence[, initial]) -> value

    Apply a function of two arguments cumulatively to the items of a sequence,
    from left to right, so as to reduce the sequence to a single value.
    For example, reduce(lambda x, y: x+y, [1, 2, 3, 4, 5]) calculates
    (((((1+2)+3)+4)+5).  If initial is present, it is placed before the items
    of the sequence in the calculation, and serves as a default when the
    sequence is empty.
```

This is another higher-order function that wants *another function* as the first argument, just like map() and filter(). The documentation shows us how to write our own sum() function:

```
>>> reduce(lambda x, y: x + y, [1, 2, 3, 4, 5])
15
```

If we change the + operator to *, we have a product:

```
>>> reduce(lambda x, y: x * y, [1, 2, 3, 4, 5])
120
```

Here is how you might write a function for this:

```
def product(vals):
    return reduce(lambda x, y: x * y, vals)
```

And now you can call it:

```
>>> product(range(1,6))
120
```

Instead of writing our own lambda, we can use any function that expects two arguments. The operator.mul function fits this bill:

```
>>> import operator
>>> help(operator.mul)
mul(a, b, /)
    Same as a * b.
```

So it would be easier to write this:

```
def product(vals):
    return reduce(operator.mul, vals)
```

Fortunately, the math module also contains a prod() function you can use:

```
>>> import math
>>> math.prod(range(1,6))
120
```

If you think about it, the str.join() method also reduces a list of strings to a single str value. Here's how we can write our own:

```
def join(sep, vals):
    return reduce(lambda x, y: x + sep + y, vals)
```

I much prefer the syntax of calling this join over the str.join() function:

```
>>> join(', ', ['Hey', 'Nonny', 'Nonny'])
'Hey, Nonny, Nonny'
```

Whenever you have a list of values that you want to combine to produce a single value, consider using the reduce() function.

18.1.5 *Encoding the words*

That was a lot of work just to get to summing the ordinal values of the characters, but wasn't it fascinating to explore? Let's get back on track, though.

We can create a function to encapsulate the idea of converting a word into a numeric value derived from summing the ordinal values of the characters. I call mine word2num(), and here is my test:

```
def test_word2num():
    """Test word2num"""
    assert word2num("a") == "97"
    assert word2num("abc") == "294"
    assert word2num("ab'c") == "294"
    assert word2num("4a-b'c,") == "346"
```

Notice that my function returns a str value, not an int. This is because I want to use the result with the str.join() function that only accepts str values—so '405' instead of 405:

```
>>> from gematria import word2num
>>> word2num("Don't")
'405'
```

To summarize, the word2num() function accepts a word, removes unwanted characters, converts the remaining characters to ord() values, and returns a str representation of the sum() of those values.

18.1.6 Breaking the text

The tests expect you to maintain the same line breaks as the original text, so I recommend you use `str.splitlines()` as in other exercises. In chapters 15 and 16, we used different regexes to split each line into "words," a process sometimes called "tokenization" in programs that deal with natural language processing (NLP). If you write a `word2num()` function that passes the tests I've provided, then you can use `str.split()` to break a line on spaces because the function will ignore anything that is not a character or number. You are, of course, welcome to break the line into words using whatever means you like.

The following code will maintain the line breaks and reconstruct the text. Can you modify it to add the `word2num()` function so that it instead prints out encoded words as shown in figure 18.5?

```
def main():
    args = get_args()
    for line in args.text.splitlines():
        for word in line.split():
            # what goes here?
            print(' '.join(line.split()))
```

Figure 18.5   Each word of the text will be cleaned and encoded into a number.

The output will be one number for each word:

```
$ ./gematria.py ../inputs/fox.txt
289 541 552 333 559 444 321 448 314
```

Time to finish writing the solution. Be sure to use the tests! See you on the flip side.

18.2 Solution

I do enjoy the ideas of cryptography and encoding messages, and this program is (sort of) encrypting the input text, albeit in a way that cannot be reversed. Still, it's fun to think of other ways you might process some text and transmogrify it to some other value.

```
#!/usr/bin/env python3
"""Gematria"""

import argparse
import os
import re
```

```
# -------------------------------------------------
def get_args():
    """Get command-line arguments"""

    parser = argparse.ArgumentParser(
        description='Gematria',
        formatter_class=argparse.ArgumentDefaultsHelpFormatter)

    parser.add_argument('text', metavar='text', help='Input text or file')

    args = parser.parse_args()

    if os.path.isfile(args.text):
        args.text = open(args.text).read().rstrip()

    return args
```

Get the parsed command-line arguments.

The text argument is a string that might be a filename.

Check if the text argument is an existing file.

Overwrite the args.text with the contents of the file.

Return the arguments.

```
# -------------------------------------------------
def main():
    """Make a jazz noise here"""

    args = get_args()

    for line in args.text.splitlines():
        print(' '.join(map(word2num, line.split())))
```

Get the parsed arguments.

Split args.text on newlines to retain line breaks.

Split the line on spaces, map the result through word2num(), and then join that result on spaces.

Define a function to convert a word to a number.

```
# -------------------------------------------------
def word2num(word):
    """Sum the ordinal values of all the characters"""

    return str(sum(map(ord, re.sub('[^A-Za-z0-9]', '', word))))
```

Define a function to test the word2num() function.

```
# -------------------------------------------------
def test_word2num():
    """Test word2num"""

    assert word2num("a") == "97"
    assert word2num("abc") == "294"
    assert word2num("ab'c") == "294"
    assert word2num("4a-b'c,") == "346"
```

Use re.sub() to remove anything that's not an alphanumeric character. Map the resulting string through the ord() function, sum the ordinal values of the characters, and return a str representation of the sum.

```
# -------------------------------------------------
if __name__ == '__main__':
    main()
```

18.3 Discussion

I trust you understand get_args(), as we've used this exact code several times now. Let's jump to the word2num() function.

18.3.1 *Writing word2num()*

I could have written the function like this:

```
def word2num(word):
    vals = []                                          ◁──── Initialize an empty list to
                                                             hold the ordinal values.
    for char in re.sub('[^A-Za-z0-9]', '', word):      ◁──── Iterate all the
        vals.append(ord(char))        ◁────                  characters returned
                                                             from re.sub().
    return str(sum(vals))             ◁─
                                                     Convert the character to
          Sum the values and return a              an ordinal value and
              string representation.               append that to the
                                                   values.
```

That's four lines of code instead of the one I wrote. I would at least rather use a list comprehension, which collapses three lines of code into one:

```
def word2num(word):
    vals = [ord(char) for char in re.sub('[^A-Za-z0-9]', '', word)]
    return str(sum(vals))
```

That could be written in one line, though it could be argued that readability suffers:

```
def word2num(word):
    return str(sum([ord(char) for char in re.sub('[^A-Za-z0-9]', '', word)]))
```

I still think the map() version is the most readable and concise:

```
def word2num(word):
    return str(sum(map(ord, re.sub('[^A-Za-z0-9]', '', word))))
```

Figure 18.6 shows how the three methods relate to each other.

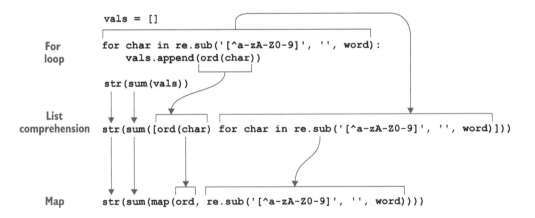

Figure 18.6   How the for loop, a list comprehension, and a map() relate to each other

Figure 18.7 will help you see how the data moves through the map() version with the string "Don't."

1 The re.sub() function will replace any character not in the character class with the empty string. This will turn a word like "Don't" into "Dont" (without the apostrophe).

2 The map() will apply the given function ord() to each element of a sequence. Here that "sequence" is a str, so it will use each character of the word.

3 The result of map() is a new list, where each character from "Dont" is given to the ord() function.

4 The results of the calls to ord() will be a list of int values, one for each letter.

5 The sum() function will reduce a list of numbers to a single value by adding them together.

6 The final value from our function needs to be a str, so we use the str() function to turn the return from sum() into a string representation of the number.

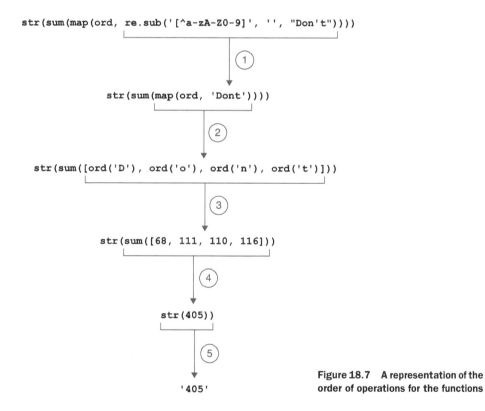

Figure 18.7 A representation of the order of operations for the functions

18.3.2 Sorting

The point of this exercise was less about the ord() and chr() functions and more about exploring regular expressions, function application, and how characters are represented inside programming languages like Python.

For instance, the sorting of strings is case sensitive because of the relative order of the ord() values of the characters (because the uppercase letters are defined earlier in the ASCII table than the lowercase values). Note that the words that begin with uppercase letters are sorted before those with lowercase letters:

```
>>> words = 'banana Apple Cherry anchovies cabbage Beets'
>>> sorted(words)
['Apple', 'Beets', 'Cherry', 'anchovies', 'banana', 'cabbage']
```

This is because all the uppercase ordinal values are lower than those of the lowercase letters. In order to perform a case sensitive sorting of strings, you can use key=str.casefold. The str.casefold() function will return "a version of the string suitable for caseless comparisons." We are using the function's name *without parentheses* here because we are passing *the function itself* as the argument for key:

```
>>> sorted(words, key=str.casefold)
['anchovies', 'Apple', 'banana', 'Beets', 'cabbage', 'Cherry']
```

If you add the parentheses, it will cause an exception. This is exactly the same way we pass functions as arguments to map() and filter():

```
>>> sorted(words, key=str.casefold())
Traceback (most recent call last):
  File "<stdin>", line 1, in <module>
TypeError: descriptor 'casefold' of 'str' object needs an argument
```

The option is the same with list.sort() if you prefer to sort the list in place:

```
>>> words.sort(key=str.casefold)
>>> words
['anchovies', 'Apple', 'banana', 'Beets', 'cabbage', 'Cherry']
```

Command-line tools like the sort program behave in the same way due to the same representation of characters. Given a file of these same words,

```
$ cat words.txt
banana
Apple
Cherry
anchovies
cabbage
Beets
```

the sort program on my Mac[1] will first sort the uppercase words and then the lower-case:

```
$ sort words
Apple
Beets
Cherry
anchovies
banana
cabbage
```

I have to read the sort manual page (via man sort) to find the -f flag to perform a case-insensitive sort:

```
$ sort -f words
anchovies
Apple
banana
Beets
cabbage
Cherry
```

18.3.3 Testing

I would like to take a moment to point out how often I use my own tests. Every time I write an alternative version of a function or program, I run my own tests to verify that I'm not accidentally showing you buggy code. Having a test suite gives me the freedom and confidence to extensively refactor my programs because I know I can check my work. If I ever find a bug in my code, I add a test to verify that the bug exists. Then I fix the bug and verify that it's handled. I know if I accidentally reintroduce that bug, my tests will catch it.

For the purposes of this book, I've tried to never write a program over 100 lines. It's common for programs to grow to thousands of lines of code spread over dozens of modules. I recommend you start writing and using tests, no matter how small you start. It's a good habit to establish early on, and it will only help you as you write longer code.

18.4 Going further

- Analyze text files to find other words that sum to the value 666. Are these particularly scary words?
- Given some text input, find the most frequently occurring value from word2num() and all the words that reduce to that value.
- Create a version using your own numeric values for each character. For instance, each letter could be encoded as its position in the alphabet so that "A"

---

[1] The GNU coreutils 8.30 version on one of my Linux machines will perform a case-insensitive sort by default. How does your sort work?

and "a" are 1, "B" and "b" are 2, and so on. Or you might decide to weigh each consonant as 1 and each vowel as –1. Create your own scheme, and write tests to ensure your program performs as you expect.

Summary

- The `ord()` function will return the Unicode code point of a character. For our alphanumeric values, the ordinal values correspond to their position in the ASCII table.
- The `chr()` function will return the character for a given ordinal value.
- You can use character ranges like `a-z` in regular expressions when ordinal values of the characters lie contiguously, such as in the ASCII table.
- The `re.sub()` function will replace matching patterns of text in a string with new values, such as replacing all non-characters with the empty string to remove punctuation and whitespace.
- A `map()` can be written using a function reference instead of a `lambda` if the function expects a single positional argument.
- The `sum()` function reduces a list of numbers using addition. You can manually write a version of this using the `functools.reduce()` function.
- To perform a case-insensitive sort of string values, use the `key=str.casefold` option with both the `sorted()` and `list.sort()` functions.

Workout of the Day: Parsing CSV files, creating text table output

Several years ago, I joined a workout group. We meet several times a week in our coach's unpaved driveway. We pick up and drop heavy things and run around trying to keep Death at bay for another day. I'm no paragon of strength and fitness, but it's been a nice way to exercise and visit with friends. One of my favorite parts of going is that our coach will write a "Workout of the Day" or "WOD" on the board. Whatever it says is what I do. It doesn't matter if I actually want to do 200 push-ups that day, I just get them done no matter how long it takes.[1]

In that spirit, we'll write a program called wod.py to help us create a random daily workout that we have to do, no questions asked:

```
$ ./wod.py
Exercise           Reps
------------------ ------
Pushups              40
```

---

[1] See "More Isn't Always Better" by Barry Schwartz (https://hbr.org/2006/06/more-isnt-always-better). He notes that increasing the number of choices given to people actually creates more distress and feelings of dissatisfaction, whatever choice is made. Imagine an ice cream shop with three flavors: chocolate, vanilla, and strawberry. If you choose chocolate, you'll likely be happy with that choice. Now imagine that the shop has 60 flavors of ice cream, including 20 different fruit creams and sorbets and 12 different chocolate varieties from Rocky Road to Fudgetastic Caramel Tiramisu Ripple. Now when you choose a "chocolate" variety, you may leave with remorse about the 11 other kinds you could have chosen. Sometimes having no choice at all provides a sense of calm. Call it fatalism or whatnot.

```
Plank                  38
Situps                 99
Hand-stand pushups      5
```

NOTE Each time you run the program, you are required to perform all the exercises *immediately*. Heck, even just *reading* them means you have to do them. Like *NOW*. Sorry, I don't make the rules. Better get going on those sit-ups!

We'll choose from a list of exercises stored in a *delimited text file*. In this case, the "delimiter" is the comma, and it will separate each field value. Data files that use commas as delimiters are often described as *comma-separated values* or CSV files. Usually the first line of the file names the columns, and each subsequent line represents a row in the table:

```
$ head -3 inputs/exercises.csv
exercise,reps
Burpees,20-50
Situps,40-100
```

In this exercise, you will

- Parse delimited text files using the `csv` module
- Coerce text values to numbers
- Print tabular data using the `tabulate` module
- Handle missing and malformed data

This chapter and the next are meant to be a step up in how challenging they are. You will be applying many of the skills you've learned in previous chapters, so get ready!

19.1   *Writing wod.py*

You will be creating a program called wod.py in the 19_wod directory. Let's start by taking a look at the usage that should print when it's run with -h or --help. Modify your program's parameters until it produces this:

```
$ ./wod.py -h
usage: wod.py [-h] [-f FILE] [-s seed] [-n exercises] [-e]

Create Workout Of (the) Day (WOD)

optional arguments:
  -h, --help            show this help message and exit
  -f FILE, --file FILE  CSV input file of exercises (default:
                        inputs/exercises.csv)
  -s seed, --seed seed  Random seed (default: None)
  -n exercises, --num exercises
                        Number of exercises (default: 4)
  -e, --easy            Halve the reps (default: False)
```

Our program will read an input -f or --file, which should be a readable text file (default, inputs/exercises.csv). The output will be some -n or --num number of exercises (default, 4). There might be an -e or --easy flag to indicate that the repetitions of each exercise should be cut in half. Since we'll be using the random module to choose the exercises, we'll need to accept an -s or --seed option (int with a default of None) to pass to random.seed() for testing purposes.

19.1.1 Reading delimited text files

We're going to use the csv module to parse the input file. This is a standard module that should already be installed on your system. You can verify that by opening a python3 REPL and trying to import it. If this works, you're all set:

```
>>> import csv
```

We'll also look at two other modules that you probably will need to install:

- Tools from the csvkit module to look at the input file on the command line
- The tabulate module to format the output table

Run this command to install these modules:

```
$ python3 -m pip install csvkit tabulate
```

There is also a requirements.txt file, which is a common way to document the dependencies for a program. Instead of the previous command, you can install all the modules with this one:

```
$ python3 -m pip install -r requirements.txt
```

Despite having "csv" in the name, the csvkit module can handle just about any delimited text file. For instance, it's typical to use the tab (\t) character as a delimiter, too. The module includes many tools that you can read about in its documentation (https://csvkit.readthedocs.io/en/1.0.3/). I've included several delimited files in the 19_wod/inputs directory that you can use to test your program.

After installing csvkit, you should be able to use csvlook to parse the inputs/exercises.csv file into a table structure showing the columns:

```
$ csvlook --max-rows 3 inputs/exercises.csv
| exercise | reps   |
| -------- | ------ |
| Burpees  | 20-50  |
| Situps   | 40-100 |
| Pushups  | 25-75  |
| ...      | ...    |
```

The "reps" column of the input file will have two numbers separated by a dash, like 10-20 meaning "from 10 to 20 reps." To select the final value for the reps, you will use the `random.randint()` function to select an integer value between the low and high values. When run with a seed, your output should exactly match this:

```
$ ./wod.py --seed 1 --num 3
Exercise        Reps
----------      ------
Pushups           32
Situps            71
Crunches          27
```

When run with the `--easy` flag, the reps should be halved:

```
$ ./wod.py --seed 1 --num 3 --easy
Exercise        Reps
----------      ------
Pushups           16
Situps            35
Crunches          13
```

The `--file` option should default to the inputs/exercises.csv file, or we can indicate a different input file:

```
$ ./wod.py --file inputs/silly-exercises.csv
Exercise            Reps
----------------    ------
Hanging Chads         46
Squatting Chinups     46
Rock Squats           38
Red Barchettas        32
```

Figure 19.1 shows our trusty string diagram to help you think about it.

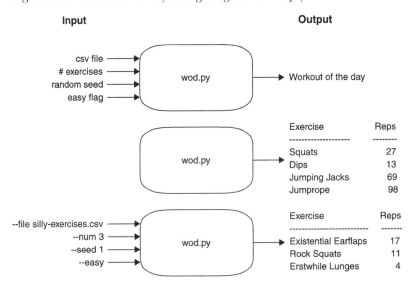

Figure 19.1   The WOD program will randomly select exercises and reps from a CSV file to create a table listing the workout of the day.

19.1.2 *Manually reading a CSV file*

First I'm going to show you how to manually parse each record from a CSV file into a list of dictionaries, and then I'll show you how to use the csv module to do this more quickly. The reason we want to make a dictionary from each record is so that we can get at the values for each exercise and the number of reps (repetitions, or how many times to repeat a given exercise). We're going to need to split the reps into low and high values so that we can get a range of numbers from which we'll randomly select the number of reps. Finally, we'll randomly select some exercises along with their reps to make a workout. Whew, just describing that was a workout!

Notice that reps is given as a range from a low number to a high number, separated by a dash:

```
$ head -3 inputs/exercises.csv
exercise,reps
Burpees,20-50
Situps,40-100
```

It would be convenient to read this as a list of dictionaries where the column names in the first line are combined with each line of data, like this:

```
$ ./manual1.py
[{'exercise': 'Burpees', 'reps': '20-50'},
 {'exercise': 'Situps', 'reps': '40-100'},
 {'exercise': 'Pushups', 'reps': '25-75'},
 {'exercise': 'Squats', 'reps': '20-50'},
 {'exercise': 'Pullups', 'reps': '10-30'},
 {'exercise': 'Hand-stand pushups', 'reps': '5-20'},
 {'exercise': 'Lunges', 'reps': '20-40'},
 {'exercise': 'Plank', 'reps': '30-60'},
 {'exercise': 'Crunches', 'reps': '20-30'}]
```

It may seem like overkill to use a dictionary for records that contain just two columns, but I regularly deal with records that contain dozens to *hundreds* of columns, and then field names are essential. A dictionary is really the only sane way to handle most delimited text files, so it's good to learn with a small example like this.

Let's look at the manual1.py code that will do this:

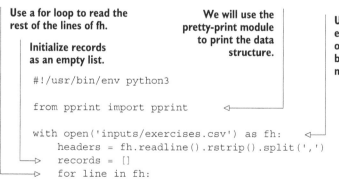

Use a for loop to read the rest of the lines of fh.

Initialize records as an empty list.

We will use the pretty-print module to print the data structure.

Use the "with" construct to open the exercises as the fh variable. One advantage of using "with" is that the file handle will be closed automatically when the code moves beyond the block.

Use fh.readline() to read only the first line of the file. Remove the whitespace from the right side (str.rstrip()), and then use str.split() to split the resulting string on commas to create a list of strings, which are the column headers.

```
#!/usr/bin/env python3

from pprint import pprint

with open('inputs/exercises.csv') as fh:
    headers = fh.readline().rstrip().split(',')
    records = []
    for line in fh:
```

```
                    rec = dict(zip(headers, line.rstrip().split(',')))
                    records.append(rec)
```

Append the resulting dictionary to the records.

```
pprint(records)
```

Pretty-print the records.

Strip and split the line of text into a list of field values. Use the zip() function to create a new list of tuples containing each of the headers paired with each of the values. Use the dict() function to turn this list of tuples into a dictionary.

Let's break this down a bit more. First we'll open() the file and read the first line:

```
>>> fh = open('exercises.csv')
>>> fh.readline()
'exercise,reps\n'
```

The line still has a newline stuck to it, so we can use the str.rstrip() function to remove that:

```
>>> fh = open('exercises.csv')
>>> fh.readline().rstrip()
'exercise,reps'
```

NOTE   Note that I need to keep reopening this file for this demonstration, or each subsequent call to fh.readline() would read the next line of text.

Now let's use str.split() to split that line on the comma to get a list of strings:

```
>>> fh = open('exercises.csv')
>>> headers = fh.readline().rstrip().split(',')
>>> headers
['exercise', 'reps']
```

We can likewise read the next line of the file to get a list of the field values:

```
>>> line = fh.readline().rstrip().split(',')
>>> line
['Burpees', '20-50']
```

Next we use the zip() function to merge the two lists into one list where the elements of each list have been mated with their counterparts in the same positions. That might seem complicated, but think about the end of a wedding ceremony when the bride and groom turn around to face the assembled crowd. Usually they will hold hands and start walking down the aisle to leave the ceremony. Imagine three groomsmen ('G') and three bridesmaids ('B') left standing on their respective sides facing each other:

```
>>> groomsmen = 'G' * 3
>>> bridesmaids = 'B' * 3
```

If there are two lines each containing three people, then we end up with a single line containing three pairs:

```
>>> pairs = list(zip(groomsmen, bridesmaids))
>>> pairs
[('G', 'B'), ('G', 'B'), ('G', 'B')]
>>> len(pairs)
3
```

Or think of two lines of cars merging to exit a parking lot. It's customary for one car from one lane (say, "A") to merge into traffic, then a car from the other lane (say, "B"). The cars are combining like the teeth of a zipper, and the result is "A," "B," "A," "B," and so forth.

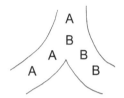

The zip() function will group the elements of the lists into tuples, grouping all the elements in the first position together, then the second position, and so on, as shown in figure 19.2. Note that this is another *lazy* function, so I will use list to coerce this in the REPL:

```
>>> list(zip('abc', '123'))
[('a', '1'), ('b', '2'), ('c', '3')]
```

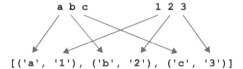

Figure 19.2   Zipping two lists creates a new list with pairs of elements.

The zip() function can handle more than two lists. Note that it will only create groupings for the shortest list. In the following example, the first two lists have four elements ("abcd" and "1234"), but the last has only three ("xyz"), so only three tuples are created:

```
>>> list(zip('abcd', '1234', 'xyz'))
[('a', '1', 'x'), ('b', '2', 'y'), ('c', '3', 'z')]
```

In our data, zip() will combine the header "exercise" with the value "Burpees" and then the header "reps" with the value "20–50" (see figure 19.3):

```
>>> list(zip(headers, line))
[('exercise', 'Burpees'), ('reps', '20-50')]
```

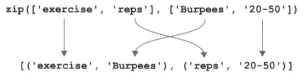

Figure 19.3   Zipping the headers and values together to create a list of tuples

That created a `list` of `tuple` values. Instead of `list()`, we can use `dict()` to create a dictionary:

```
>>> rec = dict(zip(headers, line))
>>> rec
{'exercise': 'Burpees', 'reps': '20-50'}
```

Recall that the `dict.items()` function will turn a `dict` into a `list` of `tuple` (key/value) pairs, so you can think of these two data structures as being fairly interchangeable:

```
>>> rec.items()
dict_items([('exercise', 'Burpees'), ('reps', '20-50')])
```

We can drastically shorten our code by replacing the `for` loop with a list comprehension:

```
with open('inputs/exercises.csv') as fh:
    headers = fh.readline().rstrip().split(',')        ◁──┐  We still need to break out
                                                          the headers separately by
                                                          reading the first line.
    records = [dict(zip(headers, line.rstrip().split(','))) for line in fh]   ◁──┐
    pprint(records)
                                            This combines the three lines of the for loop
                                            into a single list comprehension.
```

We can use `map()` to write equivalent code:

```
with open('inputs/exercises.csv') as fh:
    headers = fh.readline().rstrip().split(',')
    mk_rec = lambda line: dict(zip(headers, line.rstrip().split(',')))   ◁──┐
    records = map(mk_rec, fh)
    pprint(list(records))
```

Flake8 will complain about assigning this lambda expression. I generally write my code so as to produce no warnings, but I do tend to disagree with this suggestion. I quite like writing one-line functions using a lambda assignment.

In the next section, I'm going to show you how to use the `csv` module to handle much of this code, which may lead you to wonder why I bothered showing you how to handle this yourself. Unfortunately, I often have to handle data that is terribly formatted, such that the first line is not the header, or there are other rows of information between the header row and the actual data. When you've seen as many badly formatted Excel files as I have, you'll come to appreciate that you sometimes have no choice but to parse the file yourself.

19.1.3 *Parsing with the csv module*

Parsing delimited text files in this way is extremely common, and it would not make sense to write or copy this code every time you needed to parse a file. Luckily, the `csv` module is a standard module installed with Python, and it can handle all of this very gracefully.

Let's look at how our code can change if we use `csv.DictReader()` (see using_csv1.py in the repo):

```
#!/usr/bin/env python3

import csv
from pprint import pprint

with open('inputs/exercises.csv') as fh:
    reader = csv.DictReader(fh, delimiter=',')
    records = []
    for rec in reader:
        records.append(rec)

    pprint(records)
```

Import the csv module.

Create a csv.DictReader() that will create a dictionary for each record in the file. It zips the headers in the first line with the data values in the subsequent lines. It uses the delimiter to indicate the string value for splitting the columns of text.

Initialize an empty list to hold the records.

Use a for loop to iterate through each record returned by the reader.

The records will be a dictionary that is appended to the list of records.

The following code creates the same `list` of `dict` values as before, but with far less code. Note that each record is shown as an `OrderedDict`, which is a type of dictionary where the keys are maintained in their insertion order:

```
$ ./using_csv1.py
[OrderedDict([('exercise', 'Burpees'), ('reps', '20-50')]),
 OrderedDict([('exercise', 'Situps'), ('reps', '40-100')]),
 OrderedDict([('exercise', 'Pushups'), ('reps', '25-75')]),
 OrderedDict([('exercise', 'Squats'), ('reps', '20-50')]),
 OrderedDict([('exercise', 'Pullups'), ('reps', '10-30')]),
 OrderedDict([('exercise', 'Hand-stand pushups'), ('reps', '5-20')]),
 OrderedDict([('exercise', 'Lunges'), ('reps', '20-40')]),
 OrderedDict([('exercise', 'Plank'), ('reps', '30-60')]),
 OrderedDict([('exercise', 'Crunches'), ('reps', '20-30')])]
```

We can remove the entire `for` loop and use the `list()` function to coerce the `reader` to give us that same `list`. This code (in using_csv2.py) will print the same output:

Open the file.

Create a csv.DictReader() to read fh, using the comma for the delimiter.

```
with open('inputs/exercises.csv') as fh:
    reader = csv.DictReader(fh, delimiter=',')
    records = list(reader)
    pprint(records)
```

Use the list() function to coerce all the values from the reader.

Pretty-print the records.

19.1.4   *Creating a function to read a CSV file*

Let's try to imagine how we could write and test a function we might call read_csv() to read in our data. Let's start with a placeholder for our function and the test_read _csv() definition:

```
def read_csv(fh):
    """Read the CSV input"""
    pass

def test_read_csv():
    """Test read_csv"""
    text = io.StringIO('exercise,reps\nBurpees,20-50\nSitups,40-100')
    assert read_csv(text) == [('Burpees', 20, 50), ('Situps', 40, 100)]
```

Use io.StringIO() to create a mock file handle to wrap around a valid text that we might read from a file. The \n represents the newlines that break each line in the input data, and each line uses commas to separate the fields. We previously used io.StringIO() in the low-memory version of chapter 5's program.

Affirm that our imaginary read_csv() file would turn this text into a list of tuple values with the name of the exercise and the reps, which have been split into low and high values. Note that these values have been converted to integers.

Hey, we just did all that work to make a list of dict values, so why am I suggesting that we now create a list of tuple values? I'm looking ahead here to how we might use the tabulate module to print out the result, so just trust me here. This is a good way to go!

Let's go back to using csv.DictReader() to parse our file and think about how we can break the reps value into int values for the low and high:

```
reader = csv.DictReader(fh, delimiter=',')
exercises = []
for rec in reader:
    name, reps = rec['exercise'], rec['reps']
    low, high = 0, 0 # what goes here?
    exercises.append((name, low, high))
```

You have a couple of tools at your disposal. Imagine reps is this:

```
>>> reps = '20-50'
```

The str.split() function could break that into two strings, "20" and "50":

```
>>> reps.split('-')
['20', '50']
```

How could you turn each of the str values into integers?

Another way you could go is to use a regular expression. Remember that \d will match a digit, so \d+ will match one or more digits. (Refer back to chapter 15 to refresh your memory on \d as a shortcut to the character class of digits.) You can wrap that expression in parentheses to capture the "low" and "high" values:

```
>>> match = re.match('(\d+)-(\d+)', reps)
>>> match.groups()
('20', '50')
```

Can you write a read_csv() function that passes the previous test_read_csv()?

19.1.5 *Selecting the exercises*

By this point, I'm hoping you've got get_args() straight and your read_csv() passes the given test. Now we can start in main() with printing out the data structure:

Get the command-line arguments.

**Set the random.seed()
with the args.seed value.**

```
def main():
    args = get_args()
    random.seed(args.seed)
    pprint(read_csv(args.file))
```

**Read the args.file (which will be an open file
handle) using the read_csv() function and print the
resulting data structure. Note that I've imported
the pprint() function for demonstration purposes.**

If you run the preceding code, you should see this:

```
$ ./wod.py
[('Burpees', 20, 50),
 ('Situps', 40, 100),
 ('Pushups', 25, 75),
 ('Squats', 20, 50),
 ('Pullups', 10, 30),
 ('Hand-stand pushups', 5, 20),
 ('Lunges', 20, 40),
 ('Plank', 30, 60),
 ('Crunches', 20, 30)]
```

We will use the random.sample() function to select the --num of exercises indicated by the user. Add import random to your program and modify your main to match this:

```
def main():
    args = get_args()
    random.seed(args.seed)
    exercises = read_csv(args.file)
    pprint(random.sample(exercises, k=args.num))
```

**Always set your random
seed before calling
random functions.**

Read the input file.

**Randomly select the given
number of exercises.**

Now instead of printing all the exercises, it should print a random sample of the correct number of exercises. In addition, your sampling should exactly match this output if you set the random.seed() value:

```
$ ./wod.py -s 1
[('Pushups', 25, 75),
 ('Situps', 40, 100),
 ('Crunches', 20, 30),
 ('Burpees', 20, 50)]
```

We need to iterate through the sample and select a single "reps" value using the random.randint() function. The first exercise is push-ups, and the range is between 25 and 75 reps:

```
>>> import random
>>> random.seed(1)
```

```
>>> random.randint(25, 75)
33
```

If `args.easy` is `True`, you will need to halve that value. Unfortunately, we cannot have a fraction of a rep:

```
>>> 33/2
16.5
```

You can use the `int()` function to truncate the number to the integer component:

```
>>> int(33/2)
16
```

19.1.6 *Formatting the output*

Modify your program until it can reproduce this output:

```
$ ./wod.py -s 1
[('Pushups', 56), ('Situps', 88), ('Crunches', 27), ('Burpees', 35)]
```

We will use the `tabulate()` function from the `tabulate` module to format this `list` of tuple values into a text table:

```
>>> from tabulate import tabulate
>>> wod = [('Pushups', 56), ('Situps', 88), ('Crunches', 27), ('Burpees', 35)]
>>> print(tabulate(wod))
--------  --
Pushups   56
Situps    88
Crunches  27
Burpees   35
--------  --
```

If you read `help(tabulate)`, you will see that there is a `headers` option where you can specify a `list` of strings to use for the headers:

```
>>> print(tabulate(wod, headers=('Exercise', 'Reps')))
Exercise      Reps
----------  ------
Pushups         56
Situps          88
Crunches        27
Burpees         35
```

If you synthesize all these ideas, you should be able to pass the provided tests.

19.1.7 *Handling bad data*

None of the tests will give your program bad data, but I have provided several "bad" CSV files in the 19_wod/inputs directory that you might be interested in figuring out how to handle:

- bad-headers-only.csv is well-formed but has no data. It only has headers.
- bad-empty.csv is empty. That is, it is a zero-length file that I created with `touch bad-empty.csv`, and it has no data at all.
- bad-headers.csv has headers that are capitalized, so "Exercise" instead of "exercise," "Reps" instead of "reps."
- bad-delimiter.tab uses the tab character (`\t`) instead of the comma (`,`) as the field delimiter.
- bad-reps.csv contains reps that are not in the format x-y or which are not numeric or integer values.

Once your program passes the given tests, trying running it on the "bad" files to see how your program breaks. What should your program do when there is no usable data? Should your program print error messages when it encounters bad or missing values, or should it quietly ignore errors and only print the usable data? These are all real-world concerns that you will encounter, and it's up to you to decide what your program will do. After the solution, I will show you ways I might deal with these files.

19.1.8 Time to write

OK, enough lollygagging. Time to write this program. You must do 10 push-ups every time you find a bug!

Here are a few hints:

- Use `csv.DictReader()` to parse the input CSV files.
- Break the `reps` field on the `-` character, coerce the low/high values to `int` values, and then use `random.randint()` to choose a random integer in that range.
- Use `random.sample()` to select the correct number of exercises.
- Use the `tabulate` module to format the output into a text table.

19.2 Solution

How did that go for you? Did you manage to modify your program to gracefully handle all the bad input files?

```
#!/usr/bin/env python3
"""Create Workout Of (the) Day (WOD)"""

import argparse
import csv
import io
import random
from tabulate import tabulate
```

Import the tabulate function we will use to format the output table.

```
# -------------------------------------------------
def get_args():
    """Get command-line arguments"""
```

```
parser = argparse.ArgumentParser(
    description='Create Workout Of (the) Day (WOD)',
    formatter_class=argparse.ArgumentDefaultsHelpFormatter)

parser.add_argument('-f',
                    '--file',
                    help='CSV input file of exercises',
                    metavar='FILE',
                    type=argparse.FileType('rt'),
                    default='exercises.csv')

parser.add_argument('-s',
                    '--seed',
                    help='Random seed',
                    metavar='seed',
                    type=int,
                    default=None)

parser.add_argument('-n',
                    '--num',
                    help='Number of exercises',
                    metavar='exercises',
                    type=int,
                    default=4)

parser.add_argument('-e',
                    '--easy',
                    help='Halve the reps',
                    action='store_true')

args = parser.parse_args()

if args.num < 1:
    parser.error(f'--num "{args.num}" must be greater than 0')

return args


# -------------------------------------------------
def main():
    """Make a jazz noise here"""

    args = get_args()
    random.seed(args.seed)
    wod = []
    exercises = read_csv(args.file)

    for name, low, high in random.sample(exercises, k=args.num):
        reps = random.randint(low, high)
        if args.easy:
            reps = int(reps / 2)
        wod.append((name, reps))
```

The --file option, if provided, must be a readable text file.

Ensure that args.num is a positive value.

Randomly sample the given number of exercises. The result will be a list of tuples that each contain three values, which can be unpacked directly into the variables name and low and high values.

Initialize wod as an empty list.

Read the input file into a list of exercises.

Randomly select a value for reps that is in the provided range.

If args.easy is "truthy," cut the reps in half.

Append a tuple containing the name of the exercise and the reps to the wod.

Define a function to read an open CSV file handle.

```
            print(tabulate(wod, headers=('Exercise', 'Reps')))
```

Use the tabulate() function to format the wod into
a text table using the appropriate headers.

```
    # --------------------------------------------------
    def read_csv(fh):
        """Read the CSV input"""
```

Initialize exercises
to an empty list.

```
        exercises = []
        for row in csv.DictReader(fh, delimiter=','):
            low, high = map(int, row['reps'].split('-'))
            exercises.append((row['exercise'], low, high))
```

Return the list of exercises to the caller.

```
        return exercises
```

Append a tuple containing the
name of the exercise with the
low and high values.

```
    # --------------------------------------------------
    def test_read_csv():
        """Test read_csv"""
```

Define a function that Pytest will
use to test the read_csv() function.

```
        text = io.StringIO('exercise,reps\nBurpees,20-50\nSitups,40-100')
        assert read_csv(text) == [('Burpees', 20, 50), ('Situps', 40, 100)]
```

```
    # --------------------------------------------------
    if __name__ == '__main__':
        main()
```

Split the "reps" column on the dash,
turn those values into integers, and
assign to low and high variables.

Verify that read_csv() can handle valid input data.

Iterate through the file handle using the csv.DictReader()
to create a dictionary combining the column names from
the first row with the field values from the rest of the file.
Use the comma as the field delimiter.

Create a mock file handle containing valid sample data.

19.3   Discussion

Almost half the lines of the program are found within the get_args() function! Even though there's nothing new to discuss, I really want to point out how much work is being done to validate the inputs, provide defaults, create the usage statement, and so forth. Let's dig into the program, starting with the read_csv() function.

19.3.1 Reading a CSV file

Earlier in the chapter, I left you with one line where you needed to split the reps column and convert the values to integers. Here is one way:

```
def read_csv(fh):
    exercises = []
    for row in csv.DictReader(fh, delimiter=','):
        low, high = map(int, row['reps'].split('-'))
        exercises.append((row['exercise'], low, high))

    return exercises
```

Split the reps field on
the dash, map the
values through the int()
function, and assign to
low and high.

The annotated line works as follows. Assume a reps value like so:

```
>>> '20-50'.split('-')
['20', '50']
```

We need to turn each of those into an `int` value, which is what the `int()` function will do. We could use a list comprehension:

```
>>> [int(x) for x in '20-50'.split('-')]
[20, 50]
```

But the `map()` is much shorter and easier to read, in my opinion:

```
>>> list(map(int, '20-50'.split('-')))
[20, 50]
```

Since that produces exactly two values, we can assign them to two variables:

```
>>> low, high = map(int, '20-50'.split('-'))
>>> low, high
(20, 50)
```

19.3.2 *Potential runtime errors*

This code makes many, many assumptions that will cause it to fail miserably when the data doesn't match the expectations. For instance, what happens if the `reps` field contains no dash? It will produce one value:

```
>>> list(map(int, '20'.split('-')))
[20]
```

That will cause a *runtime* exception when we try to assign one value to two variables:

```
>>> low, high = map(int, '20'.split('-'))
Traceback (most recent call last):
  File "<stdin>", line 1, in <module>
ValueError: not enough values to unpack (expected 2, got 1)
```

What if one or more of the values cannot be coerced to an `int`? It will cause an exception, and, again, you won't discover this until you run the program with bad data:

```
>>> list(map(int, 'twenty-thirty'.split('-')))
Traceback (most recent call last):
  File "<stdin>", line 1, in <module>
ValueError: invalid literal for int() with base 10: 'twenty'
```

What happens if there is no `reps` field in the record, as is the case when the field names are capitalized?

```
>>> rec = {'Exercise': 'Pushups', 'Reps': '20-50'}
```

Then the dictionary access `rec['reps']` will cause an exception:

```
>>> list(map(int, rec['reps'].split('-')))
Traceback (most recent call last):
  File "<stdin>", line 1, in <module>
KeyError: 'reps'
```

The `read_csv()` function seems to work just fine as long as we pass it well-formed data, but the real world does not always give us clean datasets. An unfortunately large part of my job, in fact, is finding and correcting errors like this.

Earlier in the chapter, I suggested you might use a regular expression to extract the low and high values from the `reps` field. A regex has the advantage of inspecting the entire field, ensuring that it looks correct. Here is a more robust way to implement `read_csv()`:

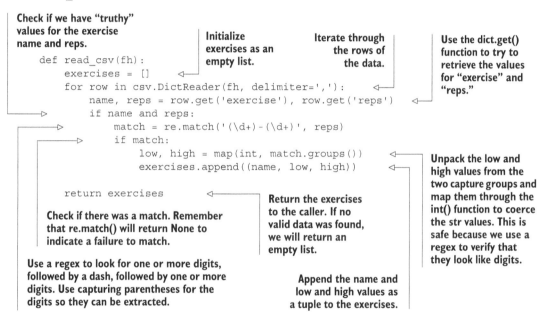

Check if we have "truthy" values for the exercise name and reps.

Initialize exercises as an empty list.

Iterate through the rows of the data.

Use the dict.get() function to try to retrieve the values for "exercise" and "reps."

```
def read_csv(fh):
    exercises = []
    for row in csv.DictReader(fh, delimiter=','):
        name, reps = row.get('exercise'), row.get('reps')
        if name and reps:
            match = re.match('(\d+)-(\d+)', reps)
            if match:
                low, high = map(int, match.groups())
                exercises.append((name, low, high))

    return exercises
```

Unpack the low and high values from the two capture groups and map them through the int() function to coerce the str values. This is safe because we use a regex to verify that they look like digits.

Check if there was a match. Remember that re.match() will return None to indicate a failure to match.

Return the exercises to the caller. If no valid data was found, we will return an empty list.

Use a regex to look for one or more digits, followed by a dash, followed by one or more digits. Use capturing parentheses for the digits so they can be extracted.

Append the name and low and high values as a tuple to the exercises.

19.3.3 Using pandas.read_csv() to parse the file

Many people familiar with statistics and data science will likely know the Python module called `pandas`, which mimics many ideas from the R programming language. I specifically chose the function name `read_csv()` because this is similar to a built-in function in R called `read.csv`, which was in turn used as the model for the `pandas.read_csv()` function. Both R and `pandas` tend to think of the data in delimited/CSV files in terms of a "data frame"—a two-dimensional object that allows you to deal with columns and rows of data.

To run the using_pandas.py version, you'll need to install `pandas` like so:

```
$ python3 -m pip install pandas
```

Now you can try running this program:

```
import pandas as pd

df = pd.read_csv('inputs/exercises.csv')
print(df)
```

You'll see this output:

```
$ ./using_pandas.py
              exercise     reps
0              Burpees    20-50
1               Situps   40-100
2              Pushups    25-75
3               Squats    20-50
4               Pullups   10-30
5   Hand-stand pushups     5-20
6               Lunges    20-40
7                Plank    30-60
8             Crunches    20-30
```

Learning how to use pandas is far beyond the scope of this book. Mostly I just want you to be aware that this is a very popular way to parse delimited text files, especially if you intend to run statistical analyses over various columns of the data.

19.3.4 *Formatting the table*

Let's look at the main() function I included in the solution. You may notice a runtime exception waiting to happen:

```
def main():
    args = get_args()                          This line will fail if args.num is
    random.seed(args.seed)               greater than the number of elements
    wod = []                                  in exercises, such as if read_csv()
    exercises = read_csv(args.file)          returns None or an empty list.

    for name, low, high in random.sample(exercises, k=args.num):  ←┐
        reps = random.randint(low, high)
        if args.easy:
            reps = int(reps / 2)
        wod.append((name, reps))

    print(tabulate(wod, headers=('Exercise', 'Reps')))
```

If you test the given solution with the bad-headers-only.csv file, you will see this error:

```
$ ./wod.py -f inputs/bad-headers-only.csv
Traceback (most recent call last):
  File "./wod.py", line 93, in <module>
    main()
  File "./wod.py", line 62, in main
    for name, low, high in random.sample(exercises, k=args.num):
  File "/Library/Frameworks/Python.framework/Versions/3.8/lib/python3.8/rando
    m.py", line 363, in sample
```

```
        raise ValueError("Sample larger than population or is negative")
ValueError: Sample larger than population or is negative
```

A safer way to handle this is to check that `read_csv()` returns enough data to pass to `random.sample()`. We have a couple of possible errors:

- No usable data was found in the input file.
- We are trying to sample too many records from the file.

Here is a possible way to handle these problems. Remember that calling `sys.exit()` with a string value will cause the program to print the message to `sys.stderr` and exit with a value of `1` (which is an error value):

```
def main():
    """Make a jazz noise here"""                    Read the input file into exercises.
                                                     The function should only return a
                                                     list, possibly empty.
    args = get_args()
    random.seed(args.seed)
    exercises = read_csv(args.file)    ◄──┐         Check if exercises is "falsey,"
                                                     such as an empty list.
    if not exercises:                   ◄──
        sys.exit(f'No usable data in --file "{args.file.name}"')
                                                     Check if we are trying to
    num_exercises = len(exercises)                   sample too many records.
    if args.num > num_exercises:        ◄──┘
        sys.exit(f'--num "{args.num}" > exercises "{num_exercises}"')

    wod = []                                                          ◄──┐
    for name, low, high in random.sample(exercises, k=args.num):
        reps = random.randint(low, high)
        if args.easy:                              Continue after we
            reps = int(reps / 2)                   verify that we have
        wod.append((name, reps))                   enough valid data.

    print(tabulate(wod, headers=('Exercise', 'Reps')))
```

The version in solution2.py has these updated functions and gracefully handles all the bad input files. Note that I moved the `test_read_csv()` function to the unit.py file because it became much longer as I tested with various bad inputs.

You can run `pytest -xv unit.py` to run the unit tests. Let's inspect unit.py to see a more rigorous testing scheme:

```
import io
from wod import read_csv    ◄──      Remember that you can import your own functions from
                                      your own modules into other programs. Here we are
                                      bringing in our read_csv() function. If we had instead used
         def test_read_csv():         import wod, we could call wod.read_csv().
The           """Test read_csv"""
original,
valid input
         └──► good = io.StringIO('exercise,reps\nBurpees,20-50\nSitups,40-100')
              assert read_csv(good) == [('Burpees', 20, 50), ('Situps', 40, 100)]
```

Testing with no data at all

```
no_data = io.StringIO('')
assert read_csv(no_data) == []

headers_only = io.StringIO('exercise,reps\n')
assert read_csv(headers_only) == []

bad_headers = io.StringIO('Exercise,Reps\nBurpees,20-50\nSitups,40-100')
assert read_csv(bad_headers) == []

bad_numbers = io.StringIO('exercise,reps\nBurpees,20-50\nSitups,forty-100')
assert read_csv(bad_numbers) == [('Burpees', 20, 50)]

no_dash = io.StringIO('exercise,reps\nBurpees,20\nSitups,40-100')
assert read_csv(no_dash) == [('Situps', 40, 100)]

tabs = io.StringIO('exercise\treps\nBurpees\t20-40\nSitups\t40-100')
assert read_csv(tabs) == []
```

Well-formed file (correct headers and delimiter), but no data

Well-formed data with correct headers, but using a tab for the delimiter

A "reps" value ("20") missing a dash

A string ("forty") that cannot be coerced by int() to a numeric value

The headers are capitalized, but only lowercase headers are expected.

19.4   Going further

- Add an option to use a different delimiter, or guess that the delimiter is a tab if the input file extension is ".tab" as in the bad-delimiter.tab file.
- The `tabulate` module supports many table formats, including plain, simple, grid, pipe, orgtbl, rst, media-wiki, latex, latex_raw, and latex_booktabs. Add an option to choose a different `tabulate` format using these as the valid choices. Choose a reasonable default value.

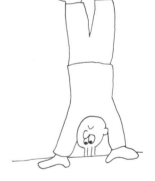

Summary

- The `csv` module is useful for parsing delimited text data such as CSV and tab-delimited files.
- Text values representing numbers must be coerced to numeric values using `int()` or `float()` in order to be used as numbers inside your program.
- The `tabulate` module can be used to create text tables to format tabular output.
- Great care must be taken to anticipate and handle bad and missing data values. Tests can help you imagine all the ways in which your code might fail.

Password strength: Generating a secure and memorable password

It's not easy to create passwords that are both difficult to guess and easy to remember. An XKCD comic describes an algorithm that provides both security and recall by suggesting that a password be composed of "four random common words" (https://xkcd.com/936/). For instance, the comic suggests that the password composed of the words "correct," "horse," "battery," and "staple" would provide "~44 bits of entropy" which would require around 550 years for a computer to guess, given 1,000 guesses per second.

We're going to write a program called password.py that will create passwords by randomly combining words from some input files. Many computers have a file that lists thousands of English words, each on a separate line. On most of my systems, I can find this at /usr/share/dict/words, and it contains over 235,000 words! As the file can vary by system, I've added a version to the repo so that we can use the same file. This file is a little large, so I've compressed to inputs/words.txt.zip. You should unzip it before using it:

```
$ unzip inputs/words.txt.zip
```

Now we should both have the same inputs/words.txt file so that this is reproducible for you:

```
$ ./password.py ../inputs/words.txt --seed 14
CrotalLeavesMeeredLogy
NatalBurrelTizzyOddman
UnbornSignerShodDehort
```

Hmm, maybe those aren't going to be the easiest to remember! Perhaps instead we should be a bit more judicious about the source of our words? We're drawing from

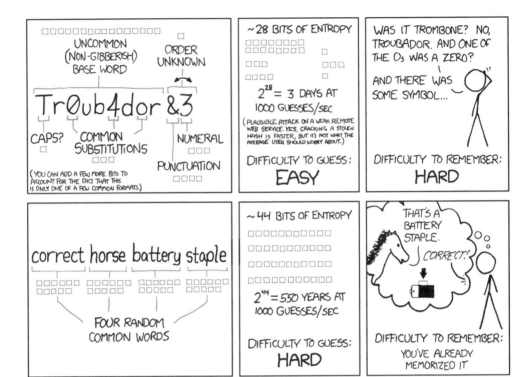

THROUGH 20 YEARS OF EFFORT, WE'VE SUCCESSFULLY TRAINED
EVERYONE TO USE PASSWORDS THAT ARE HARD FOR HUMANS
TO REMEMBER, BUT EASY FOR COMPUTERS TO GUESS.

(Image used with permission from xkcd.com.)

a pool of over 200,000 words, but the average speaker tends to use somewhere
between 20,000 and 40,000 words.

We can generate more memorable passwords by drawing from an actual piece of
English text, such as the US Constitution. Note that to use a piece of input text in this
way, we will need to remove any punctuation, as we have done in previous exercises:

```
$ ./password.py --seed 8 ../inputs/const.txt
DulyHasHeadsCases
DebtSevenAnswerBest
ChosenEmitTitleMost
```

Another strategy for generating memorable words could be to limit the pool of words
to the more interesting parts of speech, like nouns, verbs, and adjectives taken from
texts like novels or poetry. I've included a program I wrote called harvest.py that uses
a natural language processing library in Python called spaCy (https://spacy.io) that
will extract those parts of speech into files that we can use as input to our program. If

you want to use this program on your own input files, you'll need to be sure you first install the module:

```
$ python3 -m pip install spacy
```

I ran the harvest.py program on some texts and placed the outputs into directories in the 20_password directory of the source repo. For instance, here is the output drawing from nouns found in the US Constitution:

```
$ ./password.py --seed 5 const/nouns.txt
TaxFourthYearList
TrialYearThingPerson
AidOrdainFifthThing
```

And here we have passwords generated using only verbs found in *The Scarlet Letter* by Nathaniel Hawthorne:

```
$ ./password.py --seed 1 scarlet/verbs.txt
CrySpeakBringHold
CouldSeeReplyRun
WearMeanGazeCast
```

And here are some generated from adjectives extracted from William Shakespeare's sonnets:

```
$ ./password.py --seed 2 sonnets/adjs.txt
BoldCostlyColdPale
FineMaskedKeenGreen
BarrenWiltFemaleSeldom
```

Just in case that does not result in a strong enough password, we will also provide a --133t flag to further obfuscate the text by

1 Passing the generated password through the ransom.py algorithm from chapter 12
2 Substituting various characters with a given table, as we did in jump_the_five.py from chapter 4
3 Adding a randomly selected punctuation character to the end

Here is what the Shakespearean passwords look like with this encoding:

```
$ ./password.py --seed 2 sonnets/adjs.txt --133t
B0LDco5TLYColdp@13,
f1n3M45K3dK3eNGR33N[
B4rReNW1LTFeM413seldoM/
```

In this exercise, you will

- Take a list of one or more input files as positional arguments
- Use a regular expression to remove non-word characters
- Filter words by some minimum length requirement
- Use sets to create unique lists

- Generate a given number of passwords by combining some given number of randomly selected words
- Optionally encode text using a combination of algorithms we've previously written

20.1 *Writing password.py*

Our program should be written in the 20_password directory and will be called password.py. It will create some --num number of passwords (default, 3) each by randomly choosing some --num_words number of words (default, 4) from a unique set of words from one or more input files. As it will use the random module, the program will also accept a random --seed argument, which should be an integer value with a default of None. The words from the input files will need to be a --min_word_len minimum length (default, 3) up to a --max_word_len maximum length (default, 6) after removing any non-characters.

As always, our first priority is to sort out the inputs to the program. Do not move ahead until your program can produce this usage with the -h or --help flags and can pass the first eight tests:

```
$ ./password.py -h
usage: password.py [-h] [-n num_passwords] [-w num_words] [-m minimum]
                   [-x maximum] [-s seed] [-l]
                   FILE [FILE ...]

Password maker

positional arguments:
  FILE                  Input file(s)

optional arguments:
  -h, --help            show this help message and exit
  -n num_passwords, --num num_passwords
                        Number of passwords to generate (default: 3)
  -w num_words, --num_words num_words
                        Number of words to use for password (default: 4)
  -m minimum, --min_word_len minimum
                        Minimum word length (default: 3)
  -x maximum, --max_word_len maximum
                        Maximum word length (default: 6)
  -s seed, --seed seed  Random seed (default: None)
  -l, --l33t            Obfuscate letters (default: False)
```

The words from the input files will be title cased (first letter uppercase, the rest lowercase), which we can achieve using the str.title() method. This makes it easier to see and remember the individual words in the output. Note that we can vary the number of words included in each password as well as the number of passwords generated:

```
$ ./password.py --num 2 --num_words 3 --seed 9 sonnets/*
QueenThenceMasked
GullDeemdEven
```

The `--min_word_len` argument helps to filter out shorter, less interesting words like "a," "I," "an," "of," and so on, while the `--max_word_len` argument prevents the passwords from becoming unbearably long. If you increase these values, the passwords change quite drastically:

```
$ ./password.py -n 2 -w 3 -s 9 -m 10 -x 20 sonnets/*
PerspectiveSuccessionIntelligence
DistillationConscienceCountenance
```

The `--l33t` flag is a nod to "leet"-speak, where `31337 H4X0R` means "ELITE HACKER".[1] When this flag is present, we'll encode each of the passwords in two ways. First, we'll pass the word through the `ransom()` algorithm we wrote in chapter 12:

```
$ ./ransom.py MessengerRevolutionImportune
MesSENGeRReVolUtIonImpoRtune
```

Then, we'll use the following substitution table to substitute characters in the same way we did in chapter 4:

```
a => @
A => 4
O => 0
t => +
E => 3
I => 1
S => 5
```

To cap it off, we'll use `random.choice()` to select one character from `string.punctuation` to add to the end:

```
$ ./password.py --num 2 --num_words 3 --seed 9 --min_word_len 10 --max_word_len
    20 sonnets/* --l33t
p3RsPeC+1Vesucces5i0niN+3lL1Genc3$
D1s+iLl@+ioNconsc1eNc3coun+eN@Nce^
```

Figure 20.1 shows a string diagram that summarizes the inputs.

20.1.1 Creating a unique list of words

Let's start off by making our program print the name of each input file:

```
def main():
    args = get_args()
    random.seed(args.seed)      ◁──┘  Always set random.seed() right
                                      away as it will globally affect all
                                      actions by the random module.

    for fh in args.file:        ◁──┘  Iterate through the file arguments.
        print(fh.name)          ◁──┘  Print the name of the file.
```

---

[1] See the "Leet" Wikipedia page (https://en.wikipedia.org/wiki/Leet) or the Cryptii translator https://cryptii.com/.

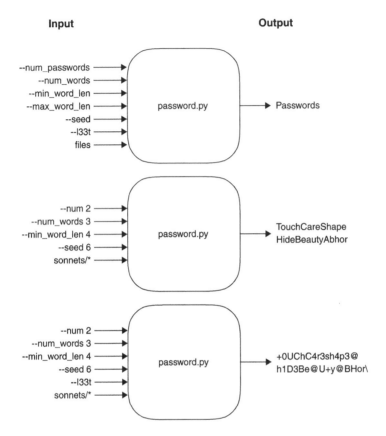

Figure 20.1 Our program has many possible options but requires only one or more input files. The output will be unbreakable passwords.

Let's test it with the words.txt file:

```
$ ./password.py ../inputs/words.txt
../inputs/words.txt
```

Now let's try it with some of the other inputs:

```
$ ./password.py scarlet/*
scarlet/adjs.txt
scarlet/nouns.txt
scarlet/verbs.txt
```

Our first goal is to create a unique list of words we can use for sampling. So far we've used lists to keep ordered collections of things like strings and numbers. The elements in a list do not have to be *unique*, though. We've also used dictionaries to create key/value pairs, and the keys of a dictionary *are* unique. Since we don't care about the values, we could set each key of a dictionary equal to some arbitrary value, like 1:

```
def main():
    args = get_args()
    random.seed(args.seed)
    words = {}

    for fh in args.file:
        for line in fh:
            for word in line.lower().split():
                words[word] = 1

    print(words)
```

Create an empty dict to hold the unique words.

Iterate through the files.

Iterate through the lines of the file.

Lowercase the line and split it on spaces into words.

Set the key words[word] equal to 1 to indicate we saw it. We're only using a dict to get the unique keys. We don't care about the values, so you could use whatever value you like.

If you run this on the US Constitution, you should see a fairly large list of words (some output elided here):

```
$ ./password.py ../inputs/const.txt
{'we': 1, 'the': 1, 'people': 1, 'of': 1, 'united': 1, 'states,': 1, ...}
```

I can spot one problem, in that the word `'states,'` has a comma attached to it. If we try in the REPL with the first bit of text from the Constitution, we can see the problem:

```
>>> 'We the People of the United States,'.lower().split()
['we', 'the', 'people', 'of', 'the', 'united', 'states,']
```

How can we get rid of the punctuation?

20.1.2 Cleaning the text

We've seen several times that splitting on spaces leaves punctuation, but splitting on non-word characters can break contracted words like "Don't" in two. We'd like a function that will `clean()` a word.

First let's imagine the test for it. Note that in this exercise, I'll put all my unit tests into a file called unit.py, which I can run with `pytest -xv unit.py`.

Here is the test for our `clean()` function:

```
def test_clean():
    assert clean('') == ''
    assert clean("states,") == 'states'
    assert clean("Don't") == 'Dont'
```

It's always good to test your functions on nothing, just to make sure it does something sane.

The function should remove punctuation at the end of a string.

The function should not split a contracted word in two.

I would like to apply this to all the elements returned by splitting each line into words, and `map()` is a fine way to do that. We often use a `lambda` when writing `map()`, as in figure 20.2.

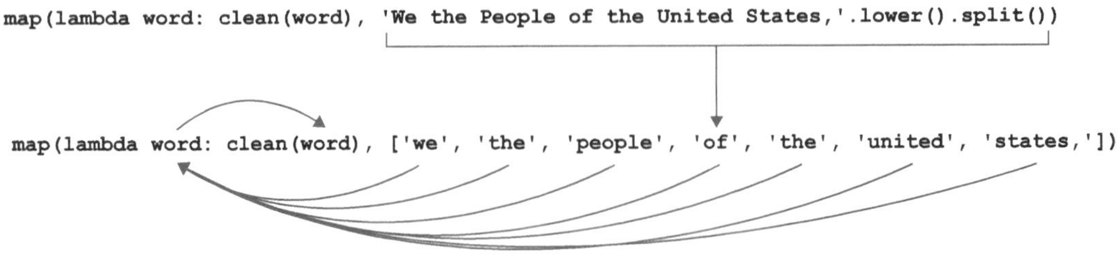

```
map(lambda word: clean(word), 'We the People of the United States,'.lower().split())
```

```
map(lambda word: clean(word), ['we', 'the', 'people', 'of', 'the', 'united', 'states,'])
```

Figure 20.2   Writing `map()` **using a** `lambda` **to accept each word from splitting a string**

We don't actually need to write a `lambda` for `map()` here because the `clean()` function expects a single argument, as shown in figure 20.3.

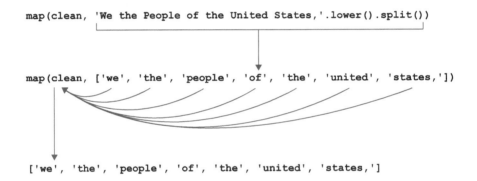

```
map(clean, 'We the People of the United States,'.lower().split())
```

```
map(clean, ['we', 'the', 'people', 'of', 'the', 'united', 'states,'])
```

```
['we', 'the', 'people', 'of', 'the', 'united', 'states,']
```

Figure 20.3   Writing the `map()` **without the** `lambda` **because the function expects a single value**

See how it integrates with the code:

```
def main():
    args = get_args()
    random.seed(args.seed)                  Use map() to apply the clean() function to
    words = {}                              the results of splitting the line on spaces.
                                            No lambda is required because clean()
    for fh in args.file:                    expects a single argument.
        for line in fh:
            for word in map(clean, line.lower().split()):   ◁─┘
                words[word] = 1

    print(words)
```

If we run that on the US Constitution again, we can see that `'states'` has been fixed:

```
$ ./password.py ../inputs/const.txt
{'we': 1, 'the': 1, 'people': 1, 'of': 1, 'united': 1, 'states': 1, ...}
```

I'll leave it to you to write a `clean()` function that will satisfy that test. You might use a list comprehension, a `filter()`, or maybe a regular expression. The choice is yours, so long as it passes the test.

20.1.3 Using a set

There is a better data structure than a `dict` to use for our purposes here. It's called a `set`, and you can think of it as being like a unique `list` or just the keys of a `dict`. Here is how we could change our code to use a `set` to keep track of *unique* words:

```
def main():
    args = get_args()
    random.seed(args.seed)          Use the set() function to
    words = set()            ◄──┘   create an empty set.

    for fh in args.file:
        for line in fh:
            for word in map(clean, line.lower().split()):
                words.add(word)  ◄──┐
    print(words)                    │  Use set.add() to
                                    └─ add a value to a set.
```

If you run this code now, you will see slightly different output, where Python shows you a data structure in curly brackets ({}) that will make you think of a `dict`, but you'll notice that the contents look more like a `list` (as pointed out in figure 20.4):

```
$ ./password.py ../inputs/const.txt
{'', 'impartial', 'imposed', 'jared', 'levying', ...}
```

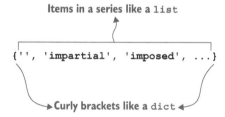

Figure 20.4   A set looks like a cross between a dictionary and a list.

We're using sets here because they so easily allow us to keep a unique list of words, but sets are much more powerful than this. For instance, you can find the shared values between two lists by using `set.intersection()`:

```
>>> nums1 = set(range(1, 10))
>>> nums2 = set(range(5, 15))
>>> nums1.intersection(nums2)
{5, 6, 7, 8, 9}
```

You can read `help(set)` in the REPL or in the documentation online to learn about all the amazing things you can do with sets.

20.1.4   *Filtering the words*

If we look again at the output we have, we'll see that the empty string is the first element:

```
$ ./password.py ../inputs/const.txt
{'', 'impartial', 'imposed', 'jared', 'levying', ...}
```

We need a way to filter out unwanted values like strings that are too short. In chapter 14 we looked at the `filter()` function, which is a higher-order function that takes two arguments:

- A function that accepts one element and returns `True` if the element should be kept or `False` if the element should be excluded
- Some "iterable" (like a `list` or `map()`) that produces a sequence of elements to be filtered

In our case, we want to accept only words that have a length greater than or equal to the `--min_word_len` argument, and less than or equal to `--max_word_len`. In the REPL, we can use a `lambda` to create an anonymous function that accepts a `word` and makes these comparisons. The result of that comparison is either `True` or `False`. Only words with a length from 3 to 6 are allowed, so this has the effect of removing short, uninteresting words. Remember that `filter()` is lazy, so I have to coerce it using the `list` function in the REPL to see the output:

```
>>> shorter = ['', 'a', 'an', 'the', 'this']
>>> min_word_len = 3
>>> max_word_len = 6
>>> list(filter(lambda word: min_word_len <= len(word) <= max_word_len, shorter))
['the', 'this']
```

This `filter()` will also remove longer words that would make our passwords cumbersome:

```
>>> longer = ['that', 'other', 'egalitarian', 'disequilibrium']
>>> list(filter(lambda word: min_word_len <= len(word) <= max_word_len, longer))
['that', 'other']
```

One way we could incorporate the `filter()` is to create a `word_len()` function that encapsulates the preceding `lambda`. Note that I defined it inside `main()` in order to create a *closure*, because I want to reference the values of `args.min_word_len` and `args.max_word_len`:

```
def main():
    args = get_args()
    random.seed(args.seed)          This function will return True
    words = set()                   if the length of the given word
                                    is in the allowed range.
    def word_len(word):        ◁─┘
        return args.min_word_len <= len(word) <= args.max_word_len
```

```
for fh in args.file:
    for line in fh:
        for word in filter(word_len, map(clean, line.lower().split())):
            words.add(word)
print(words)
```

**We can use word_len (without the parentheses!)
as the function argument to filter().**

We can again try our program to see what it produces:

```
$ ./password.py ../inputs/const.txt
{'measures', 'richard', 'deprived', 'equal', ...}
```

Try it on multiple inputs, such as all the nouns, adjectives,
and verbs from *The Scarlet Letter*:

```
$ ./password.py scarlet/*
{'walk', 'lose', 'could', 'law', ...}
```

20.1.5 *Titlecasing the words*

We used the `line.lower()` function to lowercase all the input, but the passwords we
generate will need each word to be in "Title Case," where the first letter is uppercase
and the rest of the word is lowercase. Can you figure out how to change the program
to produce this output?

```
$ ./password.py scarlet/*
{'Dark', 'Sinful', 'Life', 'Native', ...}
```

Now we have a way to process any number of files to produce a unique list of title-cased
words that have non-word characters removed and have been filtered to remove the ones
that are too short or long. That's quite a lot of power packed into a few lines of code!

20.1.6 *Sampling and making a password*

We're going to use the `random.sample()` function to randomly choose `--num` number
of words from our `set` to create an unbreakable, yet memorable, password. We've
talked before about the importance of using a random seed to test that our "random"
selections are reproducible. It's also quite important that the items from which we
sample always be ordered in the same way so that the same selections are made. If we
use the `sorted()` function on a `set`, we get back a sorted `list`, which is perfect for
using with `random.sample()`.

We can add this line to the code from before:

```
words = sorted(words)
print(random.sample(words, args.num_words))
```

Now when I run the program with *The Scarlet Letter* input, I will get a list of words that
might make an interesting password:

```
$ ./password.py scarlet/*
['Lose', 'Figure', 'Heart', 'Bad']
```

The result of random.sample() is a list that you can join on the empty string in order to make a new password:

```
>>> ''.join(random.sample(words, num_words))
'TokenBeholdMarketBegin'
```

You will need to create the number of passwords indicated by the user, similar to how we created some number of insults in chapter 9. How will you do that?

20.1.7 l33t-ify

The last piece of our program involves creating an l33t() function that will obfuscate the password. The first step is to convert the password with the same algorithm we wrote for ransom.py. I'm going to create a ransom() function for this, and here is the test that is in unit.py:

```
def test_ransom():
    state = random.getstate()        ← Save the current global state.
    random.seed(1)                   ← Set random.seed()
    assert ransom('Money') == 'moNeY'   to a known value
    assert ransom('Dollars') == 'DOLlaRs'  for the test.
    random.setstate(state)           ← Restore the state.
```

I'll leave it to you to create the function that satisfies this test.

> **NOTE** You can run pytest -xv unit.py to run the unit tests. The program will import the various functions from your password.py file to test. Open unit.py and inspect it to understand how this happens.

Next I will replace some of the characters according to the following table. I recommend you revisit chapter 4 to see how you did that:

```
a => @
A => 4
O => 0
t => +
E => 3
I => 1
S => 5
```

I wrote an l33t() function that combines ransom() with the preceding substitution and then adds a punctuation character by appending random.choice(string.punctuation).

Here is the test_l33t() function you can use to write your function. It works almost identically to the previous test, so I shall eschew commentary:

```
def test_l33t():
    state = random.getstate()
    random.seed(1)
    assert l33t('Money') == 'moNeY{'
    assert l33t('Dollars') == 'D0ll4r5`'
    random.setstate(state)
```

20.1.8 *Putting it all together*

Without giving away the ending, I'd like to say that you need to be *really careful* about the order of operations that include the `random` module. My first implementation would print different passwords given the same seed when I used the `--l33t` flag. Here was the output for plain passwords:

```
$ ./password.py -s 1 -w 2 sonnets/*
EagerCarcanet
LilyDial
WantTempest
```

I would have expected the *exact same passwords*, only encoded. Here is what my program produced instead:

```
$ ./password.py -s 1 -w 2 sonnets/* --l33t
3@G3RC@rC@N3+{
m4dnes5iNcoN5+4n+|
MouTh45s15T4nCe^
```

The first password looks OK, but what are those other two? I modified my code to print both the original password and the l33ted one:

```
$ ./password.py -s 1 -w 2 sonnets/* --l33t
3@G3RC@rC@N3+{ (EagerCarcanet)
m4dnes5iNcoN5+4n+| (MadnessInconstant)
MouTh45s15T4nCe^ (MouthAssistance)
```

The `random` module uses a global state to make each of its "random" choices. In my first implementation, I was modifying this state after choosing the first password by immediately modifying the new password with the `l33t()` function. Because the `l33t()` function also uses `random` functions, the state was altered for the next password. My solution was to first generate *all* the passwords and then alter them using the `l33t()` function, if necessary.

Those are all the pieces you should need to write your program. You have the unit tests to help you verify the functions, and you have the integration tests to ensure your program works as a whole.

20.2 *Solution*

I hope you will use your program to generate your passwords. Be sure to share them with your author, especially the ones to your bank account and favorite shopping sites!

```
#!/usr/bin/env python3
"""Password maker, https://xkcd.com/936/"""

import argparse
import random
import re
import string
```

```python
# ------------------------------------------------
def get_args():
    """Get command-line arguments"""

    parser = argparse.ArgumentParser(
        description='Password maker',
        formatter_class=argparse.ArgumentDefaultsHelpFormatter)

    parser.add_argument('file',
                        metavar='FILE',
                        type=argparse.FileType('rt'),
                        nargs='+',
                        help='Input file(s)')

    parser.add_argument('-n',
                        '--num',
                        metavar='num_passwords',
                        type=int,
                        default=3,
                        help='Number of passwords to generate')

    parser.add_argument('-w',
                        '--num_words',
                        metavar='num_words',
                        type=int,
                        default=4,
                        help='Number of words to use for password')

    parser.add_argument('-m',
                        '--min_word_len',
                        metavar='minimum',
                        type=int,
                        default=3,
                        help='Minimum word length')

    parser.add_argument('-x',
                        '--max_word_len',
                        metavar='maximum',
                        type=int,
                        default=6,
                        help='Maximum word length')

    parser.add_argument('-s',
                        '--seed',
                        metavar='seed',
                        type=int,
                        help='Random seed')

    parser.add_argument('-l',
                        '--l33t',
                        action='store_true',
                        help='Obfuscate letters')

    return parser.parse_args()
```

Set the random.seed() to the given value or the default None, which is the same as not setting the seed.

Iterate through each word generated by splitting the lowercased line on spaces, removing non-word characters with the clean() function, and filtering for words of an acceptable length.

```
# --------------------------------------------------
def main():
    args = get_args()
    random.seed(args.seed)
    words = set()

    def word_len(word):
        return args.min_word_len <= len(word) <= args.max_word_len

    for fh in args.file:
        for line in fh:
            for word in filter(word_len, map(clean, line.lower().split())):
                words.add(word.title())

    words = sorted(words)
    passwords = [
        ''.join(random.sample(words, args.num_words)) for _ in range(args.num)
    ]

    if args.l33t:
        passwords = map(l33t, passwords)

    print('\n'.join(passwords))
```

Create an empty set to hold all the unique words we'll extract from the texts.

Create a word_len() function for filter() that returns True if the word's length is in the allowed range and False otherwise.

Iterate through each open file handle.

Iterate through each line of text in the file handle.

Title-case the word before adding it to the set.

See if the args.l33t flag is True.

Use map() to run all the passwords through the l33t() function to produce a new list of passwords. It's safe to call the l33t() function here. If we had used the function in the list comprehension, it would have altered the global state of the random module, thereby altering the following passwords.

Use a list comprehension with a range to create the correct number of passwords. Since I don't need the actual value from range, I can use _ to ignore the value.

Print the passwords joined on newlines.

Use the sorted() function to order words into a new list.

```
# --------------------------------------------------
def clean(word):
    """Remove non-word characters from word"""

    return re.sub('[^a-zA-Z]', '', word)
```

Define a function to clean() a word.

Use a regular expression to substitute the empty string for anything that is not an English alphabet character.

Define a function to l33t() a word.

```
# --------------------------------------------------
def l33t(text):
    """l33t"""

    text = ransom(text)
    xform = str.maketrans({
        'a': '@', 'A': '4', 'O': '0', 't': '+', 'E': '3', 'I': '1', 'S': '5'
    })
    return text.translate(xform) + random.choice(string.punctuation)
```

Use the ransom() function to randomly capitalize letters.

Make a translation table/dict for character substitutions.

Use the str.translate() function to perform the substitutions and append a random piece of punctuation.

```
# --------------------------------------------------
def ransom(text):
    """Randomly choose an upper or lowercase letter to return"""

    return ''.join(
        map(lambda c: c.upper() if random.choice([0, 1]) else c.lower(), text))


# --------------------------------------------------
if __name__ == '__main__':
    main()
```

Define a function for the ransom() algorithm from chapter 12.

Return a new string created by randomly upper- or lowercasing each letter in a word.

20.3 Discussion

I hope you found this program challenging and interesting. There wasn't anything new in get_args(), but, again, about half the lines of code are found just in this function. I feel this is indicative of just how important it is to correctly define and validate the inputs to a program!

Now, let's get on with talking about the auxiliary functions.

20.3.1 Cleaning the text

I chose to use a regular expression to remove any characters that are outside the set of lower- and uppercase English characters:

```
def clean(word):
    """Remove non-word characters from word"""
    return re.sub('[^a-zA-Z]', '', word)
```

The re.sub() function will substitute any text matching the pattern (the first argument) found in the given text (the third argument) with the value given by the second argument.

Recall from chapter 18 that we can write the character class [a-zA-Z] to define the characters in the ASCII table bounded by those two ranges. We can then *negate* or complement that class by placing a caret (^) as the *first character* inside that class, so [^a-zA-Z] can be read as "any character not matching a to z or A to Z."

It's perhaps easier to see it in action in the REPL. In the following example, only the letters "AbCd" will be left from the text "A1b*C!d4":

```
>>> import re
>>> re.sub('[^a-zA-Z]', '', 'A1b*C!d4')
'AbCd'
```

If the only goal were to match ASCII letters, it would be possible to solve it by looking for membership in string.ascii_letters:

```
>>> import string
>>> text = 'A1b*C!d4'
>>> [c for c in text if c in string.ascii_letters]
['A', 'b', 'C', 'd']
```

A list comprehension with a guard can also be written using `filter()`:

```
>>> list(filter(lambda c: c in string.ascii_letters, text))
['A', 'b', 'C', 'd']
```

Both of the non-regex versions seem like more effort to me. Additionally, if the function ever needed to be changed to allow, say, numbers and a few specific pieces of punctuation, the regular expression version becomes significantly easier to write and maintain.

20.3.2 *A king's ransom*

The `ransom()` function was taken straight from the ransom.py program in chapter 12, so there isn't too much to say about it except, hey, look how far we've come! What was the idea for an entire chapter is now a single line in a much longer and more complicated program:

```
def ransom(text):
    """Randomly choose an upper or lowercase letter to return"""
    return ''.join(
        map(lambda c: c.upper() if random.choice([0, 1]) else c.lower(), text))
```

Join the resulting list from the map() on the empty string to create a new string.

Use map() to iterate through each character in the text and select either the upper- or lowercase version of the character based on a "coin toss," using random.choice() to select between a "truthy" value (1) or a "falsey" value (0).

20.3.3 *How to l33t()*

The `l33t()` function builds on `ransom()` and then adds a text substitution that is straight out of chapter 4. I like the `str.translate()` version of that program, so I used it again here:

```
def l33t(text):
    """l33t"""
    text = ransom(text)
    xform = str.maketrans({
        'a': '@', 'A': '4', 'O': '0', 't': '+', 'E': '3', 'I': '1', 'S': '5'
    })
    return text.translate(xform) + random.choice(string.punctuation)
```

Randomly capitalize the given text.

Make a translation table from the given dict that describes how to modify one character to another. Any characters not listed in the keys of this dict will be ignored.

Use the str.translate() method to make all the character substitutions. Use random.choice() to select one additional character from string.punctuation to append to the end.

20.3.4 *Processing the files*

To use these functions, we need to create a unique set of all the words in our input files. I wrote this bit of code with an eye both on performance and on style:

```
words = set()
for fh in args.file:
    for line in fh:
```

Iterate through each open file handle.

Read the file handle line by line with a for loop, not with a method like fh.read(), which will read the entire contents of the file at once.

```
                  for word in filter(word_len, map(clean, line.lower().split())):  ◁─┐
          ┌─▷         words.add(word.title())
```

Title-case the word before adding it to the set.

Reading this code requires starting at the end where I split line.lower() on spaces. Each word from str.split() goes into clean(), which then must pass through the filter() function.

Figure 20.5 shows a diagram of that `for` line.

1 `line.lower()` will return a lowercase version of `line`.
2 The `str.split()` method will break the text on whitespace to return words.
3 Each word is fed into the `clean()` function to remove any character that is not in the English alphabet.
4 The cleaned words are filtered by the `word_len()` function.
5 The resulting `word` has been transformed, cleaned, and filtered.

Figure 20.5   A visualization of the order of operations for the various functions

If you don't like the `map()` and `filter()` functions, you might rewrite the code like so:

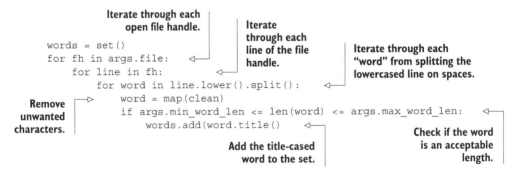

However you choose to process the files, at this point you should have a complete `set` of all the unique, title-cased words from the input files.

20.3.5 *Sampling and creating the passwords*

As noted earlier, it's vital to sort the `words` for our tests so that we can verify that we are making consistent choices. If you only wanted random choices and didn't care about testing, you would not need to worry about sorting—but then you'd also be a morally deficient person for not testing, so perish the thought! I chose to use the `sorted()` function, as there is no other way to sort a `set`:

```
words = sorted(words)
```

> There is no set.sort() function. Sets are
> ordered internally by Python. Calling sorted()
> on a set will create a new, sorted list.

We need to create a given number of passwords, and I thought it might be easiest to use a `for` loop with a `range()`. In my code, I used `for _ in range(…)` just as in chapter 9 because I don't need to know the value each time through the loop. The underscore (_) is a way to indicate that you are ignoring the value. It's fine to say `for i in range(…)` if you want, but some linters might complain if they see that your code declares the variable `i` but never uses it. That could legitimately be a bug, so it's best to use the _ to show that you mean to ignore this value.

Here is the first way I wrote the code that led to the bug I mentioned earlier, where different passwords would be chosen even when I used the same random seed. Can you spot the bug?

> Iterate through the args.num
> of passwords to create.

> Each password will be based on a random sampling from
> words, and I will choose the value given in args.num_words.
> The random.sample() function returns a list of words that I
> str.join() on the empty string to create a new string.

```
for _ in range(args.num):
    password = ''.join(random.sample(words, args.num_words))
    print(l33t(password) if args.l33t else password)
```

> If the args.l33t flag is True, we'll print the l33t version of the password; otherwise, I'll print
> the password as is. This is the bug! Calling l33t() here modifies the global state used by the
> random module, so the next time I call random.sample(), I get a different sample.

The solution is to separate the concerns of generating the passwords and possibly modifying them:

> Use a list comprehension to iterate through
> range(args.num) to generate the correct
> number of passwords.

```
passwords = [
    ''.join(random.sample(words, args.num_words)) for _ in range(args.num)
]

if args.l33t:
    passwords = map(l33t, passwords)

print('\n'.join(passwords))
```

> If the args.leet flag is True, use the l33t()
> function to modify the passwords.

> Print the passwords
> joined on newlines.

20.4 Going further

- The substitution part of the `l33t()` function changes every available character, which perhaps makes the password too difficult to remember. It would be better to modify only maybe 10% of the password, much like how we changed the input strings in chapter 10's Telephone exercise.

- Create programs that combine other skills you've learned. Like maybe a lyrics generator that randomly selects lines from files of songs by your favorite bands, then encodes the text as in chapter 15, then changes all the vowels to one vowel as in chapter 8, and then SHOUTS IT OUT as in chapter 5?

Summary

- A `set` is a unique collection of values. Sets can interact with other sets to create differences, intersections, unions, and more.
- Changing the order of operations using the `random` module can change the output of a program because the global state of the `random` module may be affected.
- Short, tested functions can be composed to create more complicated, tested programs. Here we combined many ideas from previous exercises in concise, powerful expressions.

Tic-Tac-Toe: Exploring state

One of my favorite movies is the 1983 release *War Games* starring Matthew Broderick, whose character, David, plays a young hacker who enjoys cracking into computer systems ranging from his school's grade book to a Pentagon server that has the potential to launch intercontinental ballistic missiles. Central to the plot is the game of Tic-Tac-Toe, a game so simple that it usually ends in a draw between the two players.

In the movie, David engages Joshua, an artificial intelligence (AI) agent, who is capable of playing lots of nice games like chess. David would rather play the game Global Thermonuclear War with Joshua. Eventually David realizes that Joshua is using the simulation of a war game to trick the US military into initiating a nuclear first strike against the Soviet Union. Understanding the mutually assured destruction (MAD) doctrine, David asks Joshua to play himself at Tic-Tac-Toe so that he can explore the futility of games that can never result in victory. After hundreds or thousands of rounds all ending in draws, Joshua concludes that "the only winning move is not to play," at which point Joshua stops trying to destroy the Earth and suggests instead that they could play "a nice game of chess."

I assume you already know the game of Tic-Tac-Toe, but we'll review briefly in case your childhood missed countless games of this with your friends. The game starts out with a 3-by-3 square grid. There are two players who take turns marking first X and then O in the cells. A player wins by placing their mark in any three squares in a straight line, horizontally, vertically, or diagonally. This is usually impossible, as each player will generally use their moves to block a potential win by their opponent.

We will spend the last two chapters writing Tic-Tac-Toe. We will explore ideas for representing and tracking program *state*, which is a way of thinking about how the pieces of a program change over time. For instance, we'll start off with a blank board, and the first player to go is X. Play alternates between the X and O, and after each round two cells on the board will have been taken by the two players. We'll need to keep track of these moves and more, so that, at any moment, we always know the state of the game.

If you recall, the hidden state of the `random` module proved to be a problem in chapter 20, where an early solution we explored produced inconsistent results depending on the order of the operations that used the module. In this exercise, we're going to think about ways to make the state of our game, and any changes to it, explicit.

In this chapter, we'll write a program that plays just one turn of the game; then in the next chapter we'll expand the program to handle a full game. This version of the program will be given a string that represents the state of the playing board at any time during a game. The default is the empty board at the beginning of the game, before either player has made a move. The program may also be given one move to add to that board. It will print a picture of the board and report if there is a winner after making the move.

For this program, we need to track at least two ideas in our state:

- The board, identifying which player has marked which squares of the grid
- The winner, if there is one

For the next version, we'll write an interactive version of the game where we will need to track and update several more items in the state through a complete game of Tic-Tac-Toe.

In this exercise, you will

- Consider how to use elements like strings and lists to represent aspects of a program's state
- Enforce the rules of a game in code, such as preventing a player from playing in a cell that has already been taken
- Use a regular expression to validate the initial board
- Use and and or to reduce combinations of Boolean values to a single value
- Use lists of lists to find a winning board
- Use the `enumerate()` function to iterate a `list` with the index and value

21.1 *Writing tictactoe.py*

You will create a program called tictactoe.py in the 21_tictactoe directory. As usual, I would recommend you start the program using new.py or template.py. Let's discuss the parameters for the program.

The initial state of the board will come from a -b or --board option that describes which cells are occupied by which players. Since there are nine cells, we'll use a string that is nine characters long, composed only of the characters X and O, or the period (.) to indicate that the cell is open. The default board will be a string of nine dots. When you display the board, you will either display the player's mark in a cell or the cell's number, from one to nine. In the next version of the game, this number will be used by the player to identify a cell for their move. As there is no winner for the default board, the program should print "No winner":

```
$ ./tictactoe.py
-------------
| 1 | 2 | 3 |
-------------
| 4 | 5 | 6 |
-------------
| 7 | 8 | 9 |
-------------
No winner.
```

The --board option will describe which cells should be marked for which player, where the positions in the string describe the different cells, ascending from 1 to 9. In the string X.O..O..X, the positions 1 and 9 are occupied by "X" and positions 3 and 6 by "O" (see figure 21.1).

Here is how that grid would be rendered by the program:

```
$ ./tictactoe.py -b X.O..O..X
-------------
| X | 2 | O |
-------------
| 4 | 5 | O |
-------------
| 7 | 8 | X |
-------------
No winner.
```

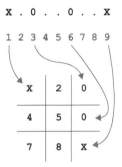

Figure 21.1   The board is nine characters describing the nine cells of the board.

We can additionally modify the given --board by passing a -c or --cell option of 1–9 *and* a -p or --player option of "X" or "O." For instance, we can mark the first cell as "X" like so:

```
$ ./tictactoe.py --cell 1 --player X
-------------
| X | 2 | 3 |
-------------
```

```
| 4 | 5 | 6 |
-------------
| 7 | 8 | 9 |
-------------
No winner.
```

The winner, if any, should be declared with gusto:

```
$ ./tictactoe.py -b XXXOO....
-------------
| X | X | X |
-------------
| O | O | 6 |
-------------
| 7 | 8 | 9 |
-------------
X has won!
```

As usual, we'll use a test suite to ensure that our program works properly. Figure 21.2 shows the string diagram.

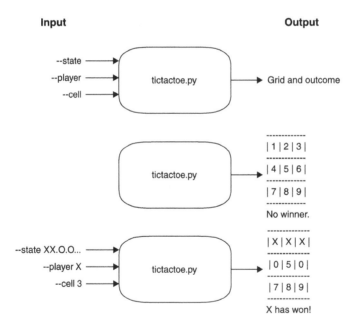

Figure 21.2   Our Tic-Tac-Toe program will play one turn of the game using a board, player, and cell. It should print the board and winner.

21.1.1 *Validating user input*

There's a fair bit of input validation that needs to happen. The `--board` needs to ensure that any argument is exactly 9 characters and is composed only of X, O, and .:

```
$ ./tictactoe.py --board XXXOOO..
usage: tictactoe.py [-h] [-b board] [-p player] [-c cell]
tictactoe.py: error: --board "XXXOOO.." must be 9 characters of ., X, O
```

Likewise, the `--player` can only be X or O:

```
$ ./tictactoe.py --player A --cell 1
usage: tictactoe.py [-h] [-b board] [-p player] [-c cell]
tictactoe.py: error: argument -p/--player: \
invalid choice: 'A' (choose from 'X', 'O')
```

And the `--cell` can only be an integer value from 1 to 9:

```
$ ./tictactoe.py --player X --cell 10
usage: tictactoe.py [-h] [-b board] [-p player] [-c cell]
tictactoe.py: error: argument -c/--cell: \
invalid choice: 10 (choose from 1, 2, 3, 4, 5, 6, 7, 8, 9)
```

Both `--player` and `--cell` must be present together, or neither can be present:

```
$ ./tictactoe.py --player X
usage: tictactoe.py [-h] [-b board] [-p player] [-c cell]
tictactoe.py: error: Must provide both --player and --cell
```

Lastly, if the `--cell` specified is already occupied by an X or an O, the program should error out:

```
$ ./tictactoe.py --player X --cell 1 --board X..O.....
usage: tictactoe.py [-h] [-b board] [-p player] [-c cell]
tictactoe.py: error: --cell "1" already taken
```

I would recommend you put all this error checking into `get_args()` so that you can use `parser.error()` to throw the errors and halt the program.

21.1.2 *Altering the board*

The initial board, once validated, describes which cells are occupied by which player. This board can be altered by adding the `--player` and `--cell` arguments. It may seem silly to not just pass in the already altered `--board`, but this is necessary practice for writing the interactive version.

If I represent `board` as a `str` value, like `'XX.O.O..X'`, and you need to change cell 3 to an X, for instance, how will you do that? For one thing, cell 3 is not found at *index* 3 in the given `board`—the index is *one less* than the cell number. The other issue is that a `str` is immutable. Just as in chapter 10's Telephone program, you'll need to figure out a way to modify one character in the board value.

21.1.3 *Printing the board*

Once you have a board, you'll need to format it with ASCII characters to create a grid. I recommend you make a function called `format_board()` that takes the `board` string as an argument and returns a `str` that uses dashes (`-`) and vertical pipes (`|`) to create a table. I have provided a unit.py file that contains the following test for the default, unoccupied grid:

```
def test_board_no_board():
    """makes default board"""

    board = """
-------------
| 1 | 2 | 3 |
-------------
| 4 | 5 | 6 |
-------------
| 7 | 8 | 9 |
-------------
""".strip()

    assert format_board('.' * 9) == board
```

Use triple quotes because the string has embedded newlines. The final str.strip() call will remove the trailing newline used to format the code.

If you multiply a string by an integer value, Python will repeat the given string that number of times. Here we create a string of nine dots as the input to format_board(). We expect the return should be an empty board as formatted here.

Now try formatting a board with some other combination. Here's another test I wrote that you might like to use, but feel free to write your own:

```
def test_board_with_board():
    """makes board"""

    board = """
-------------
| 1 | 2 | 3 |
-------------
| O | X | X |
-------------
| 7 | 8 | 9 |
-------------
""".strip()

    assert format_board('...OXX...') == board
```

The given board should have the first and third rows open and the second row with "OXX."

It would be impractical to test every possible combination for the board. When you're writing tests, you'll often have to rely on spot-checking your code. Here I am checking the empty board and a non-empty board. Presumably if the function can handle these two arguments, it can handle any others.

21.1.4 *Determining a winner*

Once you have validated the input and printed the board, your last task is to declare a winner if there is one. I chose to write a function called `find_winner()` that returns either X or O if one of those is the winner, or returns `None` if there is no winner. To test this, I wrote out every possible winning board, to test my function with values for both players. You are welcome to use this test:

```
def test_winning():
    """test winning boards"""

    wins = [('PPP......'), ('...PPP...'), ('......PPP'), ('P..P..P..'),
            ('.P..P..P.'), ('..P..P..P'), ('P...P...P'), ('..P.P.P..')]

    for player in 'XO':
        other_player = 'O' if player == 'X' else 'X'

        for board in wins:
            board = board.replace('P', player)
            dots = [i for i in range(len(board)) if board[i] == '.']
            mut = random.sample(dots, k=2)
            test_board = ''.join([
                other_player if i in mut else board[i]
                for i in range(len(board))
            ])
            assert find_winner(test_board) == player
```

This is a list of the board indexes that, if occupied by the same player, would win.

Check for both players, X and O.

Determine which is the opposite player from X or O.

Iterate through each of the winning combinations.

Change all the P (for "player") values in the given board to the player that we're checking.

Randomly sample two open cells. We will mutate these, so I call them mut.

Alter the board to change the two selected mut cells to other_player.

Find the indexes of the open cells (indicated by a dot).

Assert that find_winner() will determine that this board wins for the given player.

I also wanted to be sure I would not falsely claim that a losing board is winning, so I also wrote the following test to ensure that None is returned when there is no winner:

```
def test_losing():
    """test losing boards"""

    losing_board = list('XXOO.....')

    for _ in range(10):
        random.shuffle(losing_board)
        assert find_winner(''.join(losing_board)) is None
```

No matter how this board is arranged, it cannot win, as there are only two marks for each player.

Run 10 tests.

Shuffle the losing board into another configuration.

Assert that, no matter how the board is arranged, we will still find no winner.

If you choose the same function names as I did, you can run pytest -xv unit.py to run the unit tests I wrote. If you wish to write different functions, you can create your own unit tests either inside your tictactoe.py file or in another unit file.

After printing the board, be sure to print "{Winner} has won!" or "No winner" depending on the outcome. All righty, you have your orders, so get marching!

21.2 Solution

We're taking baby steps towards the full, interactive game in the next chapter. Right now we need to cement some basics on how just one turn will be played. It's good to make iterations of difficult programs, where you start as simply as possible and slowly add features to build a more complex idea.

```
#!/usr/bin/env python3
"""Tic-Tac-Toe"""

import argparse
import re


# -------------------------------------------------
def get_args():
    """Get command-line arguments"""

    parser = argparse.ArgumentParser(
        description='Tic-Tac-Toe',
        formatter_class=argparse.ArgumentDefaultsHelpFormatter)

    parser.add_argument('-b',
                        '--board',
                        help='The state of the board',
                        metavar='board',
                        type=str,
                        default='.' * 9)

    parser.add_argument('-p',
                        '--player',
                        help='Player',
                        choices='XO',
                        metavar='player',
                        type=str,
                        default=None)

    parser.add_argument('-c',
                        '--cell',
                        help='Cell 1-9',
                        metavar='cell',
                        type=int,
                        choices=range(1, 10),
                        default=None)

    args = parser.parse_args()

    if any([args.player, args.cell]) and not all([args.player, args.cell]):
        parser.error('Must provide both --player and --cell')

    if not re.search('^[.XO]{9}$', args.board):
        parser.error (f'--board "{args.board}" must be 9 characters of ., X, O')

    if args.player and args.cell and args.board[args.cell - 1] in 'XO':
        parser.error(f'--cell "{args.cell}" already taken')

    return args
```

The --board will default to nine dots. If you use the multiplication operator (*) with a string value and an integer (in any order), the result is the string value repeated that many times. So ".' * 9" will produce '.........'.

The --player must be either X or O, which can be validated using choices.

The --cell must be an integer from 1 to 9, which can be validated with type=int and choices=range(1, 10), remembering that the upper bound (10) is not included.

The combination of any() and all() is a way to test that both arguments are present or neither is.

Use a regular expression to check that --board is comprised of exactly nine valid characters.

If both --player and --cell are present and valid, verify that the cell in the board is not currently occupied.

Modify the board if both cell and player are "truthy." Since the arguments are validated in get_args(), it's safe to use them here. That is, I won't accidentally assign an index value that is out of range because I have taken the time to check that the cell value is acceptable.

```python
# -------------------------------------------------
def main():
    """Make a jazz noise here"""

    args = get_args()
    board = list(args.board)

    if args.player and args.cell:
        board[args.cell - 1] = args.player

    print(format_board(board))
    winner = find_winner(board)
    print(f'{winner} has won!' if winner else 'No winner.')
```

Since we may need to alter the board, it's easiest to convert it to a list.

Since the cells start numbering at 1, subtract 1 from the cell to change the correct index in board.

Look for a winner in the board.

Print the board.

Define a function to format the board. The function does not print() the board because that would make it hard to test. The function returns a new string value that can be printed or tested.

Print the outcome of the game. The find_winner() function returns either X or O if one of the players has won, or None to no indicate no winner.

```python
# -------------------------------------------------
def format_board(board):
    """Format the board"""

    cells = [str(i) if c == '.' else c for i, c in enumerate(board, 1)]
    bar = '-------------'
    cells_tmpl = '| {} | {} | {} |'
    return '\n'.join([
        bar,
        cells_tmpl.format(*cells[:3]), bar,
        cells_tmpl.format(*cells[3:6]), bar,
        cells_tmpl.format(*cells[6:]), bar
    ])
```

Iterate through the cells in the board and decide whether to print the player, if the cell is occupied, or the cell number, if it is not.

The return from the function is a new string created by joining all the lines of the grid on newlines.

Define a function that returns a winner or the value None if there is no winner. Again, the function does not print() the winner but only returns an answer that can be printed or tested.

```python
# -------------------------------------------------
def find_winner(board):
    """Return the winner"""

    winning = [[0, 1, 2], [3, 4, 5], [6, 7, 8], [0, 3, 6], [1, 4, 7],
               [2, 5, 8], [0, 4, 8], [2, 4, 6]]

    for player in ['X', 'O']:
        for i, j, k in winning:
```

Iterate through both players, X and O.

Iterate through each winning combination of cells, unpacking them into the variables i, j, and k.

There are eight winning boards, which are defined as eight lists of the cells that need to be occupied by the same player. Note that I chose here to represent the actual zero-offset index values and not the 1-based values I expect from the user.

```
            combo = [board[i], board[j], board[k]]
            if combo == [player, player, player]:
                return player
```

> ◁ Create a combo that is the value of the board for each of i, j, and k.
>
> Check if the combo is the same player in every position.

```
#  -------------------------------------------------
if __name__ == '__main__':
    main()
```

> If that is True, return the player. If this is never True for any of the combinations, we exit the function without returning a value, and so None is returned by default.

21.2.1 Validating the arguments and mutating the board

Most of the validation can be handled by using argparse effectively. Both the --player and --cell options can be handled by the choices option. It's worth taking time to appreciate the use of any() and all() in this code:

```
if any([args.player, args.cell]) and not all([args.player, args.cell]):
    parser.error('Must provide both --player and --cell')
```

We can play with these functions in the REPL. The any() function is the same as using or in between Boolean values:

```
>>> True or False or True
True
```

If *any* of the items in a given list is "truthy," the whole expression will evaluate to True:

```
>>> any([True, False, True])
True
```

If cell is a non-zero value, and player is not the empty string, they are both "truthy":

```
>>> cell = 1
>>> player = 'X'
>>> any([cell, player])
True
```

The all() function is the same as using and in between all the elements in a list, so *all* of the elements need to be "truthy" in order for the whole expression to be True:

```
>>> cell and player
'X'
```

Why does that return X? It returns the last "truthy" value, which is the player value, so if we reverse the arguments, we'll get the cell value:

```
>>> player and cell
1
```

If we use `all()`, it evaluates the truthiness of anding the values, which will be `True`:

```
>>> all([cell, player])
True
```

We are trying to figure out if the user has provided only *one* of the arguments for `--player` and `--cell`, because we need both or we want neither. So we pretend `cell` is None (the default) but `player` is X. It's true that `any()` of those values is "truthy":

```
>>> cell = None
>>> player = 'X'
>>> any([cell, player])
True
```

But it's not true that they *both* are:

```
>>> all([cell, player])
False
```

So when we and those two expressions, they return `False`,

```
>>> any([cell, player]) and all([cell, player])
False
```

because that is the same as saying this:

```
>>> True and False
False
```

The default for `--board` is provided as nine dots, and we can use a regular expression to verify that it's correct:

```
>>> board = '.' * 9
>>> import re
>>> re.search('^[.XO]{9}$', board)
<re.Match object; span=(0, 9), match='.........'>
```

Our regular expression creates a character class composed of the dot (.), "X," and "O" by using `[.XO]`. The `{9}` indicates that there must be exactly 9 characters, and the `^` and `$` characters anchor the expression to the beginning and end of the string, respectively (see figure 21.3).

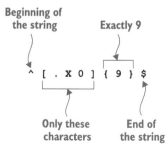

Figure 21.3   We can use a regular expression to exactly describe a valid `--board`.

You could manually validate this using the magic of all() again:

- Is the length of board exactly 9 characters?
- Is it true that each of the characters is one of those allowed?

Here is one way to write it:

```
>>> board = '...XXXOOO'
>>> len(board) == 9 and all([c in '.XO' for c in board])
True
```

The all() part is checking this:

```
>>> [c in '.XO' for c in board]
[True, True, True, True, True, True, True, True, True]
```

Since each character c ("cell") in board is in the allowed set of characters, all the comparisons are True. If we change one of the characters, a False will show up:

```
>>> board = '...XXXOOA'
>>> [c in '.XO' for c in board]
[True, True, True, True, True, True, True, True, False]
```

Any False value in an all() expression will return False:

```
>>> all([c in '.XO' for c in board])
False
```

The last piece of validation checks if the --cell being set to --player is already occupied:

```
if args.player and args.cell and args.board[args.cell - 1] in 'XO':
    parser.error(f'--cell "{args.cell}" already taken')
```

Because --cell starts counting from 1 instead of 0, we must subtract 1 when we use it as an index into the --board argument. Given the following inputs, the first cell has been set to X, and now O wants the same cell:

```
>>> board = 'X........'
>>> cell = 1
>>> player = 'O'
```

We can ask if the value in board at cell - 1 has already been set:

```
>>> board[cell - 1] in 'XO'
True
```

Or you could instead check if that position is *not* a dot:

```
>>> boards[cell - 1] != '.'
True
```

It's rather exhausting to validate all the inputs, but this is the only way to ensure that the game is played properly.

In the `main()` function, we might need to alter the `board` of the game if there are arguments for both cell and player. I decided to make `board` into a `list` precisely because I might need to alter it in this way:

```
if player and cell:
    board[cell - 1] = player
```

21.2.2 Formatting the board

Now it's time to create the grid. I chose to create a function that returns a string value that I could test rather than directly printing the grid. Here is my version:

```
def format_board(board):
    """Format the board"""

    cells = [str(i) if c == '.' else c for i, c in enumerate(board, start=1)]
    bar = '-------------'
    cells_tmpl = '| {} | {} | {} |'
    return '\n'.join([
        bar,
        cells_tmpl.format(*cells[:3]), bar,
        cells_tmpl.format(*cells[3:6]), bar,
        cells_tmpl.format(*cells[6:]), bar
    ])
```

I used a list comprehension to iterate through each position and character of board using the enumerate() function. Because I would rather start counting from index position 1 than 0, I used the start=1 option. If the character is a dot, I want to print the position as the cell number; otherwise, I print the character, which will be X or O.

The asterisk, or "splat" (*), is shorthand to expand the list returned by the list slice operation into values that the str.format() function can use.

The "splat" syntax of `*cell[:3]` is a shorter way of writing the code, like so:

```
return '\n'.join([
    bar,
    cells_tmpl.format(cells[0], cells[1], cells[2]), bar,
    cells_tmpl.format(cells[3], cells[4], cells[5]), bar,
    cells_tmpl.format(cells[6], cells[7], cells[8]), bar
])
```

The `enumerate()` function returns a `list` of tuples that include the index and value of each element in a `list` (see figure 21.4). Since it's a lazy function, I must use the `list()` function in the REPL to view the values:

```
>>> board = 'XX.O.O...'
>>> list(enumerate(board))
[(0, 'X'), (1, 'X'), (2, '.'), (3, 'O'), (4, '.'), (5, 'O'), (6, '.'), (7, '.'),
    (8, '.')]
```

In this instance, I would rather start counting at 1, so I can use the `start=1` option:

```
>>> list(enumerate(board, start=1))
[(1, 'X'), (2, 'X'), (3, '.'), (4, 'O'), (5, '.'), (6, 'O'), (7, '.'), (8, '.'),
    (9, '.')]
```

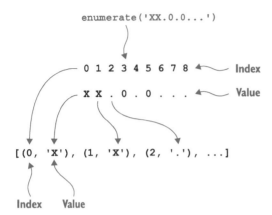

Figure 21.4   The `enumerate()` function will return the index and value of items in a series. By default, the initial index is 0.

This list comprehension could alternatively be written as a `for` loop:

Initialize an empty list to hold the cells.

Unpack each tuple of the index (starting at 1) and value of each character in board into the variables i (for "integer") and char.

```
cells = []
for i, char in enumerate(board, start=1):
    cells.append(str(i) if char == '.' else char)
```

If the char is a dot, use the string version of the i value; otherwise, use the char value.

Figure 21.5 illustrates how `enumerate()` is unpacked into i and char.

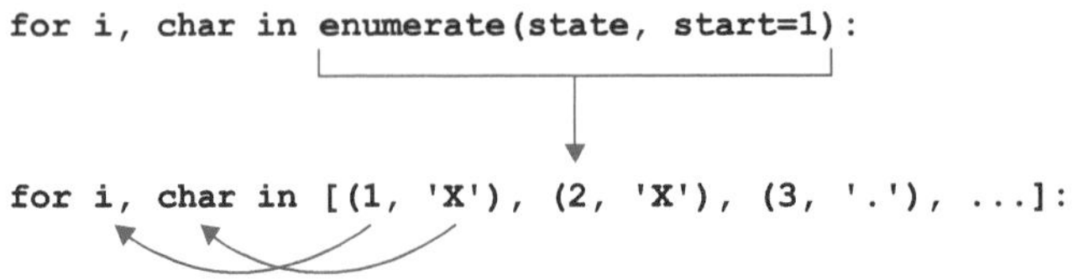

```
for i, char in enumerate(state, start=1):

for i, char in [(1, 'X'), (2, 'X'), (3, '.'), ...]:
```

Figure 21.5   The tuples containing the indexes and values returned by `enumerate()` can be assigned to two variables in the `for` loop.

This version of `format_board()` passes all the tests found in unit.py.

21.2.3   *Finding the winner*

The last major piece to this program is determining if either player has won by placing three of their marks in a row horizontally, vertically, or diagonally.

There are eight winning positions—the three horizontal rows, the three vertical columns, and the two diagonals—so I decided to create a list where each element is also a list that contains the three cells in a winning configuration.

```
def find_winner(board):
    """Return the winner"""

    winning = [[0, 1, 2], [3, 4, 5], [6, 7, 8], [0, 3, 6], [1, 4, 7],
               [2, 5, 8], [0, 4, 8], [2, 4, 6]]
```

```
    for player in ['X', 'O']:
        for i, j, k in winning:
            combo = [board[i], board[j], board[k]]
            if combo == [player, player, player]:
                return player
```

It's typical to use i as a variable name for "integer" values, especially when their life is rather brief, as here. When more similar names are needed in the same scope, it's also common to use j, k, l, etc. You may prefer to use names like cell1, cell2, and cell3, which are more descriptive but also longer to type. The unpacking of the cell values is exactly the same as the unpacking of the tuples in the previous enumerate() code (see figure 21.6).

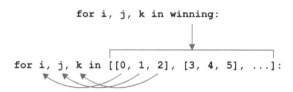

Figure 21.6 As with the unpacking of the enumerate() **tuples, each list of three elements can be unpacked into three variables in the** for **loop.**

The rest of the code checks if either X or O is the only character at each of the three positions. I worked out half a dozen ways to write this, but I'll just share this one alternate version that uses two of my favorite functions, all() and map():

```
                                                                Use map() to get the value
    Iterate through each combination                            of board at each position in
                of cells in winning.                                    the combination.                 Check for
                                                                                                          each player,
for combo in winning:                    ←                                                               X and O.
    group = list(map(lambda i: board[i], combo))    ←
    for player in ['X', 'O']:                       ←
        if all(x == player for x in group):         ←
            return player    ←                      See if all the values in the
                             If so, return           group are equal to the
                             that player.            given player.
```

If a function has no explicit return or never executes a return, as would be the case here when there is no winner, Python will use the None value as the default return. We'll interpret None to mean there is no winner when we print the outcome of the game:

```
winner = find_winner(board)
print(f'{winner} has won!' if winner else 'No winner.')
```

That covers this version of the game that plays just one turn of Tic-Tac-Toe. In the next chapter, we'll expand these ideas into an interactive version that starts with a blank board and dynamically requests user input to play the game.

21.3   *Going further*

- Write a game that will play one hand of a card game like Blackjack (Twenty-one) or War.

Summary

- This program uses a `str` value to represent the Tic-Tac-Toe board with nine characters representing X, O, or . to indicate a taken or empty cell. We sometimes convert that to a `list` to make it easier to modify.

- A regular expression is a handy way to validate the initial board. We can declaratively describe that it should be a string exactly nine characters long composed only of the characters ., X, and O.

- The `any()` function is like chaining `or` between multiple Boolean values. It will return `True` if *any* of the values is "truthy."

- The `all()` function is like using `and` between multiple Boolean values. It will return `True` only if every one of the values is "truthy."

- The `enumerate()` function will return the list index and value for each element in an iterable like a `list`.

Tic-Tac-Toe redux:
An interactive version with type hints

In this last exercise, we're going to revisit the Tic-Tac-Toe game from the previous chapter. That version played one turn of the game by accepting an initial --board and then modifying it if there were also valid options for --player and --cell. It printed the one board and the winner, if any. We're going to extend those ideas into a version that will always start from an empty board and will play as many turns as needed to complete a game, ending with a winner or a draw.

This program will be different from all the other programs in this book because it will accept no command-line arguments. The game will always start with a blank "board" and with the X player going first. It will use the input() function to interactively ask each player, X and then O, for a move. Any invalid move, such as choosing an occupied or non-existing cell, will be rejected. At the end of each turn, the game will decide to stop if it determines there is a win or a draw.

In this chapter you will

- Use and break out of an infinite loop
- Add type hints to your code
- Explore tuples, named tuples, and typed dictionaries
- Use mypy to analyze code for errors, especially misuse of types

367

22.1   *Writing itictactoe.py*

This is the one program where I won't provide an integration test. The program doesn't take any arguments, and I can't easily write tests that will interact dynamically with the program. This also makes it difficult to show a string diagram, because the output of the program will be different depending on the moves you make. Still, figure 22.1 is an approximation of how you could think of the program starting with no inputs and then looping until some outcome is determined, or the player quits.

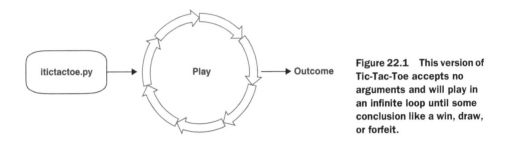

Figure 22.1   This version of Tic-Tac-Toe accepts no arguments and will play in an infinite loop until some conclusion like a win, draw, or forfeit.

I encourage you to start off by running the solution1.py program to play a few rounds of the game. The first thing you may notice is that the program clears the screen of any text and shows you an empty board, along with a prompt for the X player's move. I'll type 1 and press Enter:

```
-------------
| 1 | 2 | 3 |
-------------
| 4 | 5 | 6 |
-------------
| 7 | 8 | 9 |
-------------
Player X, what is your move? [q to quit]: 1
```

Then you will see that cell 1 is now occupied by X, and the player has switched to O:

```
-------------
| X | 2 | 3 |
-------------
| 4 | 5 | 6 |
-------------
| 7 | 8 | 9 |
-------------
Player O, what is your move? [q to quit]:
```

If I choose 1 again, I am told that cell is already taken:

```
-------------
| X | 2 | 3 |
-------------
| 4 | 5 | 6 |
```

```
-------------
| 7 | 8 | 9 |
-------------
Cell "1" already taken
Player O, what is your move? [q to quit]:
```

Note that the player is still O because the previous move was invalid. The same happens if I put in some value that cannot be converted to an integer:

```
-------------
| X | 2 | 3 |
-------------
| 4 | 5 | 6 |
-------------
| 7 | 8 | 9 |
-------------
Invalid cell "biscuit", please use 1-9
Player O, what is your move? [q to quit]:
```

Or if I enter an integer that is out of range:

```
-------------
| X | 2 | 3 |
-------------
| 4 | 5 | 6 |
-------------
| 7 | 8 | 9 |
-------------
Invalid cell "10", please use 1-9
Player O, what is your move? [q to quit]:
```

You should be able to reuse many of the ideas from chapter 21's version of the game to validate the user input.

If I play the game to a conclusion where one player gets three in a row, it prints the winning board and proclaims the victor:

```
-------------
| X | O | 3 |
-------------
| 4 | X | 6 |
-------------
| 7 | O | X |
-------------
X has won!
```

22.1.1 *Tuple talk*

In this version, we'll write an interactive game that always starts with an empty grid and plays as many rounds as necessary to reach a conclusion with a win or a draw. The idea of "state" in the last game was limited to the board—which players were in which cells. This version requires us to track quite a few more variables in our game state:

- The cells of the board, like ..XO..X.O
- The current player, either X or O
- Any error, such as the player entering a cell that is occupied or that does not exist or a value that cannot be converted to a number
- Whether the user wishes to quit the game early
- Whether the game is a draw, which happens when all the cells of the grid are occupied but there is no winner
- The winner, if any, so we know when the game is over

You don't need to write your program exactly the way I wrote mine, but you still may find yourself needing to keep track of many items. A dict is a natural data structure for that, but I'd like to introduce a new data structure called a "named tuple," as it plays nicely with Python's type hints, which will figure prominently in my solution.

We've encountered tuples throughout the exercises. They've been returned by something like match.groups() when a regular expression contains capturing parentheses, like in chapters 14 and 17; when using zip to combine two lists, like in chapter 19; or when using enumerate() to get a list of index values and elements from a list. A tuple is an immutable list, and we'll explore how that immutability can prevent us from introducing subtle bugs into our programs.

You create a tuple whenever you put commas between values:

```
>>> cell, player
(1, 'X')
```

It's most common to put parentheses around them to make it more explicit:

```
>>> (cell, player)
(1, 'X')
```

We could assign this to a variable called state:

```
>>> state = (cell, player)
>>> type(state)
<class 'tuple'>
```

We index into a tuple using list index values:

```
>>> state[0]
1
>>> state[1]
'X'
```

Unlike with a list, we cannot change any of the values inside the tuple:

```
>>> state[1] = 'O'
Traceback (most recent call last):
  File "<stdin>", line 1, in <module>
TypeError: 'tuple' object does not support item assignment
```

It's going to be inconvenient remembering that the first position is the `cell` and the second position is the `player`, and it will get much worse when we add all the other fields. We could switch to using a `dict` so that we can use strings to access the values of `state`, but dictionaries are mutable, and it's also easy to misspell a key name.

22.1.2 *Named tuples*

It would be nice to combine the safety of an immutable `tuple` with named fields, which is exactly what we get with the `namedtuple()` function. First, you must import it from the `collections` module:

```
>>> from collections import namedtuple
```

The `namedtuple()` function allows us to describe a new `class` for values. Let's say we want to create a class that describes the idea of `State`. A class is a group of variables, data, and functions that together can be used to represent some idea. The Python language itself, for example, has the `str` class, which represents the idea of a sequence of characters that can be contained in a variable that has some `len` (length), and which can be converted to uppercase with `str.upper()`, can be iterated with a `for` loop, and so forth. All these ideas are grouped into the `str` class, and we've used `help(str)` to read the documentation for that class inside the REPL.

The class name is the first argument we pass to `namedtuple()`, and the second argument is a `list` of the field names in the class. It's common practice to capitalize class names:

```
>>> State = namedtuple('State', ['cell', 'player'])
```

We've just created a new type called `State`!

```
>>> type(State)
<class 'type'>
```

Just as there is a function called `list()` to create a `list` type, we can now use the `State()` function to create a named tuple of the type `State` that has two named fields, `cell` and `player`:

```
>>> state = State(1, 'X')
>>> type(state)
<class '__main__.State'>
```

We can still access the fields with index values, like any `list` or `tuple`:

```
>>> state[0]
1
>>> state[1]
'X'
```

But we can also use their names, which is much nicer. Notice that there are no parentheses at the end, as we are accessing a field, not calling a method:

```
>>> state.cell
1
>>> state.player
'X'
```

Because `state` is a `tuple`, we cannot mutate the value once it has been created:

```
>>> state.cell = 1
Traceback (most recent call last):
  File "<stdin>", line 1, in <module>
AttributeError: can't set attribute
```

This is actually *good* in many instances. It's often quite dangerous to change your data values once your program has started. You should use tuples or named tuples whenever you want a list- or dictionary-like structure that cannot be accidentally modified.

There is a problem, however, in that there's nothing to prevent us from instantiating a `state` with the fields out of order *and of the wrong types*—`cell` should be an `int`, and `player` should be a `str`!

```
>>> state2 = State('O', 2)
>>> state2
State(cell='O', player=2)
```

In order to avoid that, you can use the field names, so that their order no longer matters:

```
>>> state2 = State(player='O', cell=2)
>>> state2
State(cell=2, player='O')
```

Now you have a data structure that looks like a `dict` but has the immutability of a tuple!

22.1.3 *Adding type hints*

We still have a big problem in that there's nothing preventing us from assigning a `str` to the `cell`, which ought to be an `int`, and vice versa for `int` and `player`:

```
>>> state3 = State(player=3, cell='X')
>>> state3
State(cell='X', player=3)
```

Starting in Python 3.6, the `typing` module allows you to add *type hints* to describe the data types for variables. You should read PEP 484 (www.python.org/dev/peps/pep-0484/) for more information, but the basic idea is that we can use this module to describe the appropriate types for variables and type signatures for functions.

I'm going to improve our `State` class by using the `NamedTuple` class from the `typing` module as the base class. First we need to import from the `typing` module the classes we'll need, such as `NamedTuple`, `List`, and `Optional`, the last of which describes a type that could be `None` or some other class like a `str`:

```
from typing import List, NamedTuple, Optional
```

Now we can specify a `State` class with named fields, types, and even default values to represent the initial state of the game where the board is empty (all dots) and player X goes first. Note that I decided to store the `board` as a `list` of characters rather than a `str`:

```
class State(NamedTuple):
    board: List[str] = list('.' * 9)
    player: str = 'X'
    quit: bool = False
    draw: bool = False
    error: Optional[str] = None
    winner: Optional[str] = None
```

We can use the `State()` function to create a new value that's set to the initial state:

```
>>> state = State()
>>> state.board
['.', '.', '.', '.', '.', '.', '.', '.', '.']
>>> state.player
'X'
```

You can override any default value by providing the field name and a value. For instance, we could start the game off with player O by specifying `player='O'`. Any field we don't specify will use the default:

```
>>> state = State(player='O')
>>> state.board
['.', '.', '.', '.', '.', '.', '.', '.', '.']
>>> state.player
'O'
```

We get an exception if we misspell a field name, like `playre` instead of `player`:

```
>>> state = State(playre='O')
Traceback (most recent call last):
  File "<stdin>", line 1, in <module>
TypeError: __new__() got an unexpected keyword argument 'playre'
```

22.1.4 *Type verification with Mypy*

As nice as all the above is, *Python will not generate a runtime error if we assign an incorrect type.* For instance, I can assign `quit` a `str` value of `'True'` instead of the `bool` value `True`, and nothing at all happens:

```
>>> state = State(quit='True')
>>> state.quit
'True'
```

The benefit of type hints comes from using a program like Mypy to check our code. Let's place all this code into a small program called typehints.py in the repo:

```
#!/usr/bin/env python3
""" Demonstrating type hints """

from typing import List, NamedTuple, Optional


class State(NamedTuple):
    board: List[str] = list('.' * 9)
    player: str = 'X'
    quit: bool = False          ◁──────────
    draw: bool = False
    error: Optional[str] = None
    winner: Optional[str] = None
```

quit is defined as a bool, which means it should only allow values of True and False.

```
state = State(quit='False')     ◁──────

print(state)
```

We are assigning the str value 'True' instead of the bool value True, which might be an easy mistake to make, especially in a very large program. We'd like to know this type of error will be caught!

The program will execute *with no errors*:

```
$ ./typehints.py
State(board=['.', '.', '.', '.', '.', '.', '.', '.', '.'], player='X', \
quit='False', draw=False, error=None, winner=None)
```

But the Mypy program will report the error of our ways:

```
$ mypy typehints.py
typehints.py:16: error: Argument "quit" to "State" has incompatible type
    "str"; expected "bool"
Found 1 error in 1 file (checked 1 source file)
```

If I correct the program like so,

```
#!/usr/bin/env python3
""" Demonstrating type hints """

from typing import List, NamedTuple, Optional


class State(NamedTuple):
    board: List[str] = list('.' * 9)
    player: str = 'X'
    quit: bool = False          ◁──┐  Again, quit is a bool value.
    draw: bool = False
    error: Optional[str] = None
    winner: Optional[str] = None
```

```
state = State(quit=True)        ←——  We have to assign an actual
                                      bool value in order to pass
print(state)                          muster with Mypy.
```

now Mypy will be satisfied:

```
$ mypy typehints2.py
Success: no issues found in 1 source file
```

22.1.5 *Updating immutable structures*

If one of the advantages of using `NamedTuples` is their *immutability*, how will we keep track of changes to our program? Consider our initial state of an empty grid with the player X going first:

```
>>> state = State()
```

Imagine X takes cell 1, so we need to change `board` to `X........` and the `player` to `O`. We can't directly modify `state`:

```
>>> state.board=list('X.........')
Traceback (most recent call last):
  File "<stdin>", line 1, in <module>
AttributeError: can't set attribute
```

We could use the `State()` function to create a new value to overwrite the existing `state`. That is, since we can't change anything *inside* the `state` variable, we could instead point `state` to an entirely new value. We did this in the second solution in chapter 8, where we needed to change a `str` value, because they are also immutable in Python.

To do this, we can copy all the current values that haven't changed and combine them with the changed values:

```
>>> state = State(board=list('X.........'), player='O', quit=state.quit, \
    draw=state.draw, error=state.error, winner=state.winner)
```

The `namedtuple._replace()` method, however, provides a much simpler way to do this. Only the values we provide are changed, and the result is a new `State`:

```
>>> state = state._replace(board=list('X.........'), player='O')
```

We overwrite our `state` variable with the return from `state._replace()`, just as we have repeatedly overwritten string variables with new values:

```
>>> state
State(board=['X', '.', '.', '.', '.', '.', '.', '.', '.', '.'], player='O', \
      quit=False, draw=False, error=None, winner=None)
```

This is much more convenient than having to list all the fields—we only need to specify the fields that have changed. We are also prevented from accidentally modifying any of the other fields, and we are likewise prevented from forgetting or misspelling any fields or setting them to the wrong types.

22.1.6 Adding type hints to function definitions

Now let's look at how we can add type hints to our function definitions. For an example, we can modify our `format_board()` function to indicate that it takes a parameter called `board`, which is a list of string values, by adding `board: List[str]`. Additionally, the function returns a `str` value, so we can add `-> str` after the colon on the `def` to indicate this, as in figure 22.2.

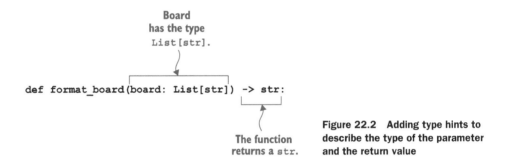

Board
has the type
`List[str]`.

`def format_board(board: List[str]) -> str:`

The function
returns a `str`.

Figure 22.2   Adding type hints to describe the type of the parameter and the return value

The annotation for `main()` indicates that the `None` value is returned, as shown in figure 22.3.

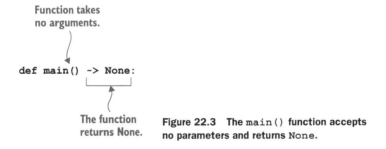

Function takes
no arguments.

`def main() -> None:`

The function
returns None.

Figure 22.3   The `main()` function accepts no parameters and returns `None`.

What's really terrific is that we can define a function that takes a value of the type `State`, and Mypy will check that this kind of value is actually being passed (see figure 22.4).

Try playing my version of the game and then writing your own that behaves similarly. Then take a look at how I wrote an interactive solution that incorporates these ideas of data immutability and type safety.

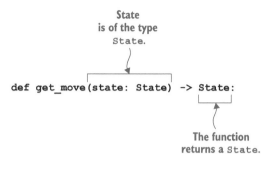

State
is of the type
`State`.

```
def get_move(state: State) -> State:
```

The function
returns a `State`.

Figure 22.4 We can use custom types in type hints. This function takes and returns a value of the type `State`.

22.2 Solution

This is the last program! I hope that writing the simpler version in the previous chapter gave you ideas for making this work. Did the type hints and unit tests also help?

```python
#!/usr/bin/env python3
""" Interactive Tic-Tac-Toe using NamedTuple """

from typing import List, NamedTuple, Optional
```

Import the classes we'll need from the typing module.

```python
class State(NamedTuple):
    board: List[str] = list('.' * 9)
    player: str = 'X'
    quit: bool = False
    draw: bool = False
    error: Optional[str] = None
    winner: Optional[str] = None
```

Declare a class that is based on the NamedTuple class. Define field names, types, and defaults for the values this class can hold.

Start an infinite loop. When we have a reason to stop, we can break out of the loop.

Print a special sequence that most terminals will interpret as a command to clear the screen.

```python
# --------------------------------------------------
def main() -> None:
    """Make a jazz noise here"""

    state = State()
```

Instantiate the initial state as an empty grid and the first player as X.

```python
    while True:
        print("\033[H\033[J")
        print(format_board(state.board))

        if state.error:
            print(state.error)
        elif state.winner:
            print(f'{state.winner} has won!')
            break

        state = get_move(state)
```

Print the current state of the board.

Print any errors, such as the user not choosing a valid cell.

If there is a winner, proclaim the victor and break out of the loop.

Get the next move from the player. The get_move() function accepts a State type and returns one too. We overwrite the existing state variable each time through the loop.

```
        if state.quit:
            print('You lose, loser!')
            break
        elif state.draw:
            print("All right, we'll call it a draw.")
            break
```

If the game has reached a stalemate where all cells are occupied but there is no winner, declare a draw and break from the loop.

If the user has decided to withdraw from the game prematurely, insult them, and break from the loop.

If so, replace the quit value of the state with True and return with the new state. Note that no other values in the state are modified.

Check if the user entered a value that can be converted to a digit using str.isdigit() and if the integer version of the value is in the valid range.

Copy the player from the state, since we'll refer to it several times in the function body.

Define a get_move() function that takes and returns a State type.

Use the input() function to ask the player for their next move. Tell them how to quit the game early so they don't have to use Ctrl-C to interrupt the program.

```
# -------------------------------------------------
def get_move(state: State) -> State:
    """Get the player's move"""

    player = state.player
    cell = input(f'Player {player}, what is your move? [q to quit]: ')

    if cell == 'q':
        return state._replace(quit=True)

    if not (cell.isdigit() and int(cell) in range(1, 10)):
        return state._replace(error=f'Invalid cell "{cell}", please use 1-9')

    cell_num = int(cell)
    if state.board[cell_num - 1] in 'XO':
        return state._replace(error=f'Cell "{cell}" already taken')

    board = state.board
    board[cell_num - 1] = player
    return state._replace(board=board,
                          player='O' if player == 'X' else 'X',
                          winner=find_winner(board),
                          draw='.' not in board,
                          error=None)
```

First check if the user wants to quit.

See if the board is open at the indicated cell.

Return a new state value with the new board value, the current player switched to the other player, and if there is a winner or a draw.

After we have verified that cell is a valid integer value, convert it to an integer.

Use the cell value to update the board with the current player.

If not, return an updated state that has an error. Note that the current state and player remain unchanged so that the same player has a retry with the same board until they provide valid input.

Copy the current board because we need to modify it and state.board is immutable.

If not, return an updated state with an error. Again, nothing else about the state is changed, so we retry the round with the same player and state.

```
# --------------------------------------------------
def format_board(board: List[str]) -> str:
    """Format the board"""

    cells = [str(i) if c == '.' else c for i, c in enumerate(board, 1)]
    bar = '-------------'
    cells_tmpl = '| {} | {} | {} |'
    return '\n'.join([
        bar,
        cells_tmpl.format(*cells[:3]), bar,
        cells_tmpl.format(*cells[3:6]), bar,
        cells_tmpl.format(*cells[6:]), bar
    ])
```

◄── **The only change from the previous version of this function is the addition of type hints. The function accepts a list of string values (the current board) and returns a formatted grid of the board state.**

```
# --------------------------------------------------
def find_winner(board: List[str]) -> Optional[str]:
    """Return the winner"""

    winning = [[0, 1, 2], [3, 4, 5], [6, 7, 8], [0, 3, 6], [1, 4, 7],
               [2, 5, 8], [0, 4, 8], [2, 4, 6]]

    for player in ['X', 'O']:
        for i, j, k in winning:
            combo = [board[i], board[j], board[k]]
            if combo == [player, player, player]:
                return player

    return None
```

◄── **This is also the same function as before, but with type hints. The function accepts the board as a list of strings and returns an optional string value, which means it could also return None.**

```
# --------------------------------------------------
if __name__ == '__main__':
    main()
```

22.2.1 A version using TypedDict

New to Python 3.8 is the TypedDict class, which looks very similar to a NamedTuple. Let's look at how using this as the base class changes parts of our program. One crucial difference is that you cannot (yet) set default values for the fields:

```
#!/usr/bin/env python3
""" Interactive Tic-Tac-Toe using TypedDict """

from typing import List, Optional, TypedDict
```

◄── **Import TypedDict instead of NamedTuple.**

```
class State(TypedDict):
```
◄── **Base State on a TypedDict.**
```
    board: str
    player: str
    quit: bool
    draw: bool
    error: Optional[str]
    winner: Optional[str]
```

We have to set our initial values when we instantiate a new state:

```
def main() -> None:
    """Make a jazz noise here"""

    state = State(board='.' * 9,
                  player='X',
                  quit=False,
                  draw=False,
                  error=None,
                  winner=None)
```

Syntactically, I prefer using state.board with the named tuple rather than the dictionary access of state['board']:

```
while True:
    print("\033[H\033[J")
    print(format_board(state['board']))

    if state['error']:
        print(state['error'])
    elif state['winner']:
        print(f"{state['winner']} has won!")
        break

    state = get_move(state)

    if state['quit']:
        print('You lose, loser!')
        break
    elif state['draw']:
        print('No winner.')
        break
```

Beyond the convenience of accessing the fields, I prefer the read-only nature of the NamedTuple to the mutable TypedDict. Note how in the get_move() function, we can change the state:

```
def get_move(state: State) -> State:
    """Get the player's move"""

    player = state['player']
    cell = input(f'Player {player}, what is your move? [q to quit]: ')

    if cell == 'q':
        state['quit'] = True          ◁──  Here we are directly modifying the TypedDict, whereas
        return state                        the NamedTuple version used state._replace() to return
                                            an entirely new state value.

    if not (cell.isdigit() and int(cell) in range(1, 10)):
        state['error'] = f'Invalid cell "{cell}", please use 1-9'   ◁──┐
        return state                                                   │
                                            Another place where the state
    cell_num = int(cell)                    is directly modifiable. You may
    if state['board'][cell_num - 1] in 'XO':    prefer this approach.  ──┘
```

```
    state['error'] = f'Cell "{cell}" already taken'
    return state

board = list(state['board'])
board[cell_num - 1] = player

return State(
    board=''.join(board),
    player='O' if player == 'X' else 'X',
    winner=find_winner(board),
    draw='.' not in board,
    error=None,
    quit=False,
)
```

In my opinion, a `NamedTuple` has nicer syntax, default values, and immutability over the `TypedDict` version, so I prefer it. Regardless of which you choose, the greater lesson I hope to impart is that we should try to be explicit about the "state" of the program and when and how it changes.

22.2.2 *Thinking about state*

The idea of program state is that a program can remember changes to variables over time. In the previous chapter, our program accepted a given `--board` and possible values for `--cell` and `--player` that might alter the board. Then the game printed a representation of the board. In this chapter's interactive version, the board always begins as an empty grid and changes with each turn, which we modeled as an infinite loop.

It is common in programs like this to see programmers use *global variables* that are declared at the top of the program outside of any function definitions so that they are *globally* visible throughout the program. While common, it's not considered a best practice, and I would discourage you from ever using globals unless you can see no other way. I would suggest, instead, that you stick to using small functions that accept all the values required and return a single type of value. I would also suggest you use data structures like typed, named tuples to represent program state, and that you guard the changes to state very carefully.

22.3 *Going further*

- Incorporate spicier insults. Maybe bring in the Shakespearean generator?
- Write a version that allows the user to start a new game without quitting and restarting the program.
- Write other games like Hangman.

Summary

- Type hints allow you to annotate variables as well as function parameters and return values with the types of the values.
- Python itself will ignore type hints at runtime, but Mypy can use type hints to find errors in your code before you ever run it.
- A NamedTuple behaves a bit like a dictionary and a bit like an object but retains the immutability of tuples.
- Both NamedTuple and TypedDict allow you to create a novel type with defined fields and types that you can use as type hints to your own functions.
- Our program used a NamedTuple to create a complex data structure to represent the state of our program. The state included many variables, such as the current board, the current player, any errors, the winner, and so on, each of which was described using type hints.
- While it is difficult to write integration tests for an interactive program, we can still break a program into small functions (such as format_board() or get_winner()) for which we write and run unit tests.

Epilogue

Well, that's the whole book. We came a long way, from writing the crow's nest program in chapter 2 to chapter 22's interactive Tic-Tac-Toe game, incorporating a custom class based on named tuples and using type hints. I hope you can see now how much you can do with Python's strings, lists, tuples, dictionaries, sets, and functions. I especially hope I've convinced you that, above all, you should always write programs that are

- *Flexible*, by taking command-line arguments
- *Documented*, by using something like `argparse` to parse your arguments and produce usage statements
- *Tested*, by writing both *unit* tests for your functions and *integration* tests for your program as a whole

The people using your programs will really appreciate knowing how to use your program and how to make it behave differently. They'll also appreciate that you took the time to verify that your program is correct. Let's be honest, though. The person most likely to be using and modifying your programs will be you, several months from now. I've heard it said that "documentation is a love letter to your future self." All this work you put into making your programs good will be very appreciated by you when you come back to your code.

Now that you've worked through all the exercises and seen how to use the tests I've written, I challenge you to go back to the beginning and read the test.py programs. If you intend to adopt test-driven development, you may find that you can steal many ideas and techniques from those programs.

Further, each chapter included suggestions for how to extend the ideas and exercises presented. Go back and think about how you can use ideas you learned later in the book to improve or extend earlier programs. Here are some ideas:

- Chapter 2 (The crow's nest)—Add an option to randomly select a greeting other than "Hello" from a list like "Hello," "Hola," "Salut," and "Ciao."
- Chapter 3 (Going on a picnic)—Allow the program to take one or more options and incorporate those into the output with the correct articles for each item joined on the Oxford comma.
- Chapter 7 (Gashlycrumb)—Download *The Devil's Dictionary* by Ambrose Bierce from Project Gutenberg. Write a program that will look up a word's definition if it appears in the text.
- Chapter 16 (The scrambler)—Use the scrambled text as the basis for encrypting messages. Force the scrambled words to uppercase, remove all the punctuation and spaces, and then format the text into "words" of five characters followed by a space, with no more than five per line. Pad the end so that the text completely fills the last line. Can you make sense of the output?
- new.py—I first wrote a program to create a new program when I was a greenhorn Perl hacker. My new-pl program would add a random quote from the poetry of William Blake (yes, really—I also went through phases with the Brontes and Dickinson). Alter your version of new.py to add a random quote or joke or to customize it in some way for your programs.

I hope you've had as much fun writing the programs as I've had creating and teaching them. I want you to feel you now have dozens of programs and tests with ideas and functions you can steal to create even more programs.

All the best to you in your coding adventures!

appendix
Using argparse

Often, getting the right data into your program is a real chore. The `argparse` module makes it much easier to validate arguments from users and to generate useful error messages when they provide bad input. It's like your program's "bouncer," only allowing the right kinds of values into the program. Defining the arguments properly with `argparse` is the crucial first step to making the programs in this book work.

For instance, chapter 1 discusses a very flexible program that can extend warm salutations to an optionally named entity, such as the "World" or "Universe":

```
$ ./hello.py
Hello, World!
$ ./hello.py --name Universe
Hello, Universe!
```

When the program runs with no input values, it will use "World" for the entity to greet.

The program can take an optional --name value to override the default.

The program will respond to the -h and --help flags with helpful documentation:

```
$ ./hello.py -h
usage: hello.py [-h] [-n str]
```

The argument to the program is -h, which is the "short" flag to ask for help.

This line shows a summary of all the options the program accepts. The square brackets [] around the arguments show that they are optional.

```
Say hello
```
This is the description
of the program.

```
optional arguments:
  -h, --help            show this help message and exit
  -n str, --name str    The name to greet (default: World)
```

We can use either the "short" name -h or the "long" name --help to ask the program for help on how to run it.

The optional "name" parameter also has short and long names of -n and --name.

All of this is created by just two lines of code in the hello.py program:

The parser will parse the arguments for us. If the user provides unknown arguments or the wrong number of arguments, the program will halt with a usage statement.

```
parser = argparse.ArgumentParser(description='Say hello')
parser.add_argument('-n', '--name', default='World', help='Name to greet')
```

The only argument to this program is an optional --name value.

NOTE You do not need to define the -h or --help flags. Those are generated automatically by argparse. In fact, you should never try to use those for other values because they are almost universal options that most users will expect.

The argparse module helps us define a parser for the arguments and generates help messages, saving us loads of time and making our programs look professional. Every program in this book is tested on different inputs, so you'll really understand how to use this module by the end. I recommend you look over the argparse documentation (https://docs.python.org/3/library/argparse.html).

Now let's dig further into what this module can do for us. In this appendix, you will

- Learn how to use argparse to handle positional parameters, options, and flags
- Set default values for options
- Use type to force the user to provide values like numbers or files
- Use choices to restrict the values for an option

A.1   *Types of arguments*

Command-line arguments can be classified as follows:

- *Positional arguments*—The order and number of the arguments is what determines their meaning. Some programs might expect, for instance, a filename as the first argument and an output directory as the second. Positional arguments are generally required (not optional) arguments. Making them optional is difficult—how would you write a program that accepts two or three arguments where the second and third ones are independent and optional? In the first version of hello.py in chapter 1, the name to greet was provided as a positional argument.

- *Named options*—Most command-line programs define a *short* name like -n (one dash and a single character) and a *long* name like --name (two dashes and a word) followed by some value, like the name in the hello.py program. Named options allow arguments to be provided in any order—their *position* is not relevant. This makes them the right choice when the user is not required to provide them (they are *options*, after all). It's good to provide reasonable default values for options. When we changed the required positional `name` argument of hello.py to the optional `--name` argument, we used "World" for the default so that the program could run with no input from the user. Note that some other languages, like Java, might define long names with a single dash, like `-jar`.

- *Flags*—A Boolean value like "yes"/"no" or True/`False` is indicated by something that starts off looking like a named option, but there is no value after the name; for example, the `-d` or `--debug` flag to turn on debugging. Typically the presence of the flag indicates a `True` value for the argument, and its absence would mean `False`, so `--debug` turns *on* debugging, whereas its absence means it is off.

A.2 *Using a template to start a program*

It's not easy to remember all the syntax for defining parameters using `argparse`, so I've created a way for you to write new programs from a template that includes this plus some other structure that will make your programs easier to read and run.

One way to start a new program is to use the new.py program. From the top level of the repository, you can execute this command:

```
$ bin/new.py foo.py
```

Alternatively, you could copy the template:

```
$ cp template/template.py foo.py
```

The resulting program will be identical no matter how you create it, and it will have examples of how to declare each of the argument types outlined in the previous section. Additionally, you can use `argparse` to validate the input, such as making sure that one argument is a number while another argument is a file.

Let's look at the help generated by our new program:

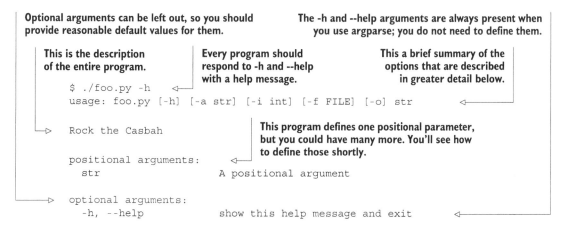

```
-a str, --arg str      A named string argument (default: )
-i int, --int int      A named integer argument (default: 0)
-f FILE, --file FILE   A readable file (default: None)
-o, --on               A boolean flag (default: False)
```

The -f or --file option must be a valid, readable file.

The -i or --int option must be an integer value. If the user provides "one" or "4.2," these will be rejected.

The -o or --on is a flag. Notice how the -f FILE description specifies that a "FILE" value should follow the -f, but for this flag no value follows the option. The flag is either present or absent, and so it's either True or False, respectively.

The -a or --arg option accepts some text, which is often called a "string."

A.3 Using argparse

The code to generate the preceding usage is found in a function, called get_args(), that looks like the following:

```python
def get_args():
    """Get command-line arguments"""

    parser = argparse.ArgumentParser(
        description='Rock the Casbah',
        formatter_class=argparse.ArgumentDefaultsHelpFormatter)

    parser.add_argument('positional',
                        metavar='str',
                        help='A positional argument')

    parser.add_argument('-a',
                        '--arg',
                        help='A named string argument',
                        metavar='str',
                        type=str,
                        default='')

    parser.add_argument('-i',
                        '--int',
                        help='A named integer argument',
                        metavar='int',
                        type=int,
                        default=0)

    parser.add_argument('-f',
                        '--file',
                        help='A readable file',
                        metavar='FILE',
                        type=argparse.FileType('r'),
                        default=None)

    parser.add_argument('-o',
                        '--on',
                        help='A boolean flag',
                        action='store_true')

    return parser.parse_args()
```

You are welcome to put this code wherever you like, but defining and validating the arguments can sometimes get rather long. I like to separate this code out into a function I call `get_args()`, and I always define this function first in my program. That way I can see it immediately when I'm reading the source code.

The `get_args()` function is defined like this:

> **The def keyword defines a new function, and the arguments to the function are listed in the parentheses. Even though the get_args() function takes no arguments, the parentheses are still required.**

```
def get_args():
    """Get command-line arguments"""
```

The triple-quoted line after the function def is the "docstring," which serves as a bit of documentation for the function. Docstrings are not required, but they are good style, and Pylint will complain if you leave them out.

A.3.1 Creating the parser

The following snippet creates a `parser` that will deal with the arguments from the command line. To "parse" here means to derive some meaning from the order and syntax of the bits of text provided as arguments:

> **Call the argparse.ArgumentParser() function to create a new parser.**

> **A short summary of your program's purpose.**

```
parser = argparse.ArgumentParser(
    description='Argparse Python script',
    formatter_class=argparse.ArgumentDefaultsHelpFormatter)
```

The formatter_class argument tells argparse to show the default values in usage.

You should read the documentation for `argparse` to see all the other options you can use to define a `parser` or the parameters. In the REPL, you can start with `help(argparse)`, or you could look up the docs on the internet at https://docs.python.org/3/library/argparse.html.

A.3.2 Creating a positional parameter

The following line will create a new *positional* parameter:

> **The lack of leading dashes makes this a positional parameter, not the name "positional."**

> **Provide a hint to the user about the data type. By default, all arguments are strings.**

```
parser.add_argument('positional',
                    metavar='str',
                    help='A positional argument')
```

A brief description of the parameter for the usage

Remember that the parameter is not positional because the *name* is "positional." That's just there to remind you that it *is* a positional parameter. `argparse` interprets the string `'positional'` as a positional parameter *because the name does not start with any dashes.*

A.3.3   Creating an optional string parameter

The following line creates an *optional* parameter with a short name of -a and a long name of --arg. It will be a str with a default value of ' ' (the empty string).

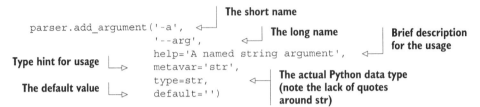

> **NOTE**   You can leave out either the short or long name in your own programs, but it's good form to provide both. Most of the tests in this book will test your programs using both short and long option names.

If you wanted to make this a required, named parameter, you would remove the default and add required=True.

A.3.4   Creating an optional numeric parameter

The following line creates an option called -i or --int that accepts an int (integer) with a default value of 0. If the user provides anything that cannot be interpreted as an integer, the argparse module will stop processing the arguments and will print an error message and a short usage statement.

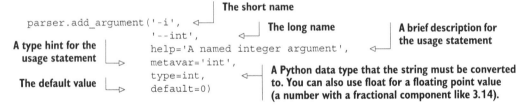

One of the big reasons to define numeric arguments in this way is that argparse will convert the input to the correct type. All values coming from the command are strings, and it's the job of the program to convert each value to an actual numeric value. If you tell argparse that the option should be type=int, it will have already been converted to an actual int value when you ask the parser for the value.

   If the value provided by the user cannot be converted to an int, the value will be rejected. Note that you can also use type=float to accept and convert the input to a floating-point value. That saves you a lot of time and effort.

A.3.5   Creating an optional file parameter

The following line creates an option called -f or --file that will only accept a valid, readable file. This argument alone is worth the price of admission, as it will save you oodles of time validating the input from your user. Note that pretty much every exercise that has a file as input will have tests that pass *invalid* file arguments to ensure that your program rejects them.

```
                              The short name
parser.add_argument('-f', ←
                          '--file', ←    The long name        A brief usage
                          help='A readable file', ←          statement
A type suggestion ┗→      metavar='FILE',
                          type=argparse.FileType('r'), ←     Says that the argument
The default value ┗→      default=None)                      must name a readable
                                                             ('r') file
```

The person running the program is responsible for providing the location of the file. For instance, if you created the foo.py program in the top level of the repository, there will be a README.md file there. We could use that as the input to our program, and it would be accepted as a valid argument:

```
$ ./foo.py -f README.md foo
str_arg = ""
int_arg = "0"
file_arg = "README.md"
flag_arg = "False"
positional = "foo"
```

If we provide a bogus --file argument, like "blargh," we will get an error message:

```
$ ./foo.py -f blargh foo
usage: foo.py [-h] [-a str] [-i int] [-f FILE] [-o] str
foo.py: error: argument -f/--file: can't open 'blargh': \
[Errno 2] No such file or directory: 'blargh'
```

A.3.6 *Creating a flag option*

The flag option is slightly different in that it does not take a value like a string or integer. Flags are either present or not, and they *usually* indicate that some idea is True or False.

You've already seen the -h and --help flags. They are not followed by any values. They either are present, in which case the program should print a "usage" statement, or they are absent, in which case the program should not. For all the exercises in this book, I use flags to indicate a True value when they are present and False otherwise, which we can represent using action='store_true'.

For instance, new.py shows an example of this kind of a flag called -o or --on:

```
                              Short name
parser.add_argument('-o', ←
                          '--on', ←      Long name           Brief usage
                          help='A boolean flag', ←           statement
                          action='store_true') ←
```

What to do when this flag is present. When it is present, we use the value
True for on. The default value will be False when the flag is not present.

It's not always the case that a "flag" like this should be interpreted as True when present. You could instead use action='store_false', in which case on would be False when the flag is present, and the default value would be True. You could also store one or more constant values when the flag is present.

Read the argparse documentation for the various ways you can define this parameter. For the purposes of this book, we will only use a flag to turn "on" some behavior.

A.3.7   *Returning from get_args*

The final statement in get_args() is return, which returns the result of having the parser object parse the arguments. That is, the code that calls get_args() will receive the result of this expression:

```
return parser.parse_args()
```

This expression could fail because argparse finds that the user provided invalid arguments, such as a string value when it expected a float or perhaps a misspelled filename. If the parsing succeeds, we will be able to access all the values the user provided from inside our program.

Additionally, the values of the arguments will be of the *types* that we indicated. That is, if we indicated that the --int argument should be an int, then when we ask for args.int, it will already be an int. If we define a file argument, we'll get an *open file handle.* That may not seem impressive now, but it's really enormously helpful.

If you refer to the foo.py program we generated, you'll see that the main() function calls get_args(), so the return from get_args() goes back to main(). From there, we can access all the values we just defined using the names of the positional parameters or the long names of the optional parameters:

```
def main():
    args = get_args()
    str_arg = args.arg
    int_arg = args.int
    file_arg = args.file
    flag_arg = args.on
    pos_arg = args.positional
```

A.4   *Examples using argparse*

Many of the program tests in this book can be satisfied by learning how to use argparse effectively to validate the arguments to your programs. I think of the command line as the boundary of your program, and you need to be judicious about what you let into your program. You should always expect and defend against every argument being wrong.[1] Our hello.py program in chapter 1 is an example of a single, positional argument and then a single, optional argument. Let's look at some more examples of how you can use argparse.

---

[1]   I always think of the kid who will type "fart" for every input.

A.4.1 A single positional argument

This is the first version of chapter 1's hello.py program, which requires a single argument specifying the name to greet:

```
#!/usr/bin/env python3
"""A single positional argument"""

import argparse


# --------------------------------------------------
def get_args():
    """Get command-line arguments"""

    parser = argparse.ArgumentParser(
        description='A single positional argument',
        formatter_class=argparse.ArgumentDefaultsHelpFormatter)

    parser.add_argument('name', metavar='name', help='The name to greet')   ◁

    return parser.parse_args()


# --------------------------------------------------
def main():
    """Make a jazz noise here"""

    args = get_args()
    print('Hello, ' + args.name + '!')   ◁


# --------------------------------------------------
if __name__ == '__main__':
    main()
```

The name parameter does not start with dashes, so this is a *positional* parameter. The metavar will show up in the help to let the user know what this argument is supposed to be.

Whatever is provided as the first positional argument to the program will be available in the args.name slot.

This program will not print the "Hello" line if it's not provided exactly one argument. If given nothing, it will print a brief usage statement about the proper way to invoke the program:

```
$ ./one_arg.py
usage: one_arg.py [-h] name
one_arg.py: error: the following arguments are required: name
```

If we provide more than one argument, it complains again. Here "Emily" and "Bronte" are two arguments because spaces separate arguments on the command line. The program complains about getting a second argument that has not been defined:

```
$ ./one_arg.py Emily Bronte
usage: one_arg.py [-h] name
one_arg.py: error: unrecognized arguments: Bronte
```

Only when we give the program exactly one argument will it run:

```
$ ./one_arg.py "Emily Bronte"
Hello, Emily Bronte!
```

While it may seem like overkill to use argparse for such a simple program, it shows that argparse can do quite a bit of error checking and validation of arguments for us.

A.4.2   *Two different positional arguments*

Imagine you want two *different* positional arguments, like the *color* and *size* of an item to order. The color should be a str, and the size should be an int value. When you define them positionally, the order in which you declare them is the order in which the user must supply the arguments. Here we define color first, and then size:

```
#!/usr/bin/env python3
"""Two positional arguments"""

import argparse


# --------------------------------------------------
def get_args():
    """get args"""

    parser = argparse.ArgumentParser(
        description='Two positional arguments',
        formatter_class=argparse.ArgumentDefaultsHelpFormatter)

    parser.add_argument('color',
                        metavar='color',
                        type=str,
                        help='The color of the garment')

    parser.add_argument('size',
                        metavar='size',
                        type=int,
                        help='The size of the garment')

    return parser.parse_args()


# --------------------------------------------------
def main():
    """main"""

    args = get_args()
    print('color =', args.color)
    print('size =', args.size)


# --------------------------------------------------
if __name__ == '__main__':
    main()
```

This will be the first of the positional arguments because it is defined first. Notice that metavar has been set to 'color' instead of 'str' as it's more descriptive of the *kind* of string we expect—one that describes the "color" of the garment.

This will be the second of the positional arguments. Here metavar='size', which could be a number like 4 or a string like 'small', so it's still ambiguous.

The "color" argument is accessed via the name of the color parameter.

The "size" argument is accessed via the name of the size parameter.

Again, the user must provide exactly two positional arguments. Entering no arguments triggers a short usage statement:

```
$ ./two_args.py
usage: two_args.py [-h] color size
two_args.py: error: the following arguments are required: color, size
```

Just entering one argument won't cut it either. We are told that "size" is missing:

```
$ ./two_args.py blue
usage: two_args.py [-h] color size
two_args.py: error: the following arguments are required: size
```

If we give it two strings, like "blue" for the color and "small" for the size, the size value will be rejected because it needs to be an integer value:

```
$ ./two_args.py blue small
usage: two_args.py [-h] color size
two_args.py: error: argument size: invalid int value: 'small'
```

If we give it two arguments, the second of which can be interpreted as an `int`, all is well:

```
$ ./two_args.py blue 4
color = blue
size = 4
```

Remember that *all* the arguments coming from the command line are strings. The command line doesn't require quotes around `blue` or the `4` to make them strings the way that Python does. On the command line, everything is a string, and all arguments are passed to Python as strings.

When we tell `argparse` that the second argument needs to be an `int`, `argparse` will attempt to convert the string `'4'` to the integer 4. If you provide 4.1, that will be rejected too:

```
$ ./two_args.py blue 4.1
usage: two_args.py [-h] str int
two_args.py: error: argument int: invalid int value: '4.1'
```

Positional arguments require the user to remember the correct order of the arguments. If we mistakenly switch around `str` and `int` arguments, `argparse` will detect invalid values:

```
$ ./two_args.py 4 blue
usage: two_args.py [-h] COLOR SIZE
two_args.py: error: argument SIZE: invalid int
value: 'blue'
```

Imagine, however, a case of two strings or two numbers that represent two *different* values, like a car's make and model or a person's height and weight. How could you detect that the arguments are reversed?

Generally speaking, I only ever create programs that take exactly one positional argument or one or more *of the same thing*, like a list of files to process.

A.4.3   *Restricting values using the choices option*

In our previous example, there was nothing stopping the user from providing *two integer values*:

```
$ ./two_args.py 1 2
color = 1
size = 2
```

The 1 is a string. It may look like a number to you, but it is actually the *character* '1'. That is a valid string value, so our program accepts it.

Our program would also accept a "size" of -4, which clearly is not a valid size:

```
$ ./two_args.py blue -4
color = blue
size = -4
```

How can we ensure that the user provides both a valid color and size? Let's say we only offer shirts in primary colors. We can pass in a list of valid values using the choices option.

In the following example, we restrict the color to "red," "yellow," or "blue." Additionally, we can use range(1, 11) to generate a list of numbers from 1 to 10 (11 isn't included!) as the valid sizes for our shirts:

```
#!/usr/bin/env python3
"""Choices"""

import argparse


# --------------------------------------------------
def get_args():
    """get args"""

    parser = argparse.ArgumentParser(
        description='Choices',
        formatter_class=argparse.ArgumentDefaultsHelpFormatter)

    parser.add_argument('color',
                        metavar='str',
                        help='Color',
                        choices=['red', 'yellow', 'blue'])      ◁─┐

    parser.add_argument('size',
                        metavar='size',
```

The choices option takes a list of values. argparse stops the program if the user fails to supply one of these.

```
                              type=int,
                              choices=range(1, 11),
                              help='The size of the garment')
```

> The user must choose from the numbers 1–10 or argparse will stop with an error.

```
    return parser.parse_args()
```

```
# --------------------------------------------------
def main():
    """main"""

    args = get_args()
    print('color =', args.color)
    print('size =', args.size)
```

> If our program makes it to this point, we know that args.color will definitely be one of those values and that args.size is an integer value in the range of 1–10. The program will never get to this point unless both arguments are valid.

```
# --------------------------------------------------
if __name__ == '__main__':
    main()
```

Any value not present in the list will be rejected, and the user will be shown the valid choices. Again, no value is rejected:

```
$ ./choices.py
usage: choices.py [-h] color size
choices.py: error: the following arguments are required: color, size
```

If we provide "purple," it will be rejected because it is not in the choices we defined. The error message that argparse produces tells the user the problem ("invalid choice") and even lists the acceptable colors:

```
$ ./choices.py purple 1
usage: choices.py [-h] color size
choices.py: error: argument color: \
invalid choice: 'purple' (choose from 'red', 'yellow', 'blue')
```

Likewise with a negative size argument:

```
$ ./choices.py red -1
usage: choices.py [-h] color size
```

```
choices.py: error: argument size: \
invalid choice: -1 (choose from 1, 2, 3, 4, 5, 6, 7, 8, 9, 10)
```

Only when both arguments are valid may we continue:

```
$ ./choices.py red 4
color = red
size = 4
```

That's really quite a bit of error checking and feedback that you never have to write. The best code is code you don't write!

A.4.4 *Two of the same positional arguments*

If we were writing a program that adds two numbers, we could define them as two positional arguments, like number1 and number2. But since they are the same kinds of arguments (two numbers that we will add), it might make more sense to use the nargs option to tell argparse that you want exactly two of a thing:

```
#!/usr/bin/env python3
"""nargs=2"""

import argparse


# --------------------------------------------------
def get_args():
    """get args"""

    parser = argparse.ArgumentParser(
        description='nargs=2',
        formatter_class=argparse.ArgumentDefaultsHelpFormatter)

    parser.add_argument('numbers',
                        metavar='int',          The nargs=2 will require
                        nargs=2,         ◁───   exactly two values.
                        type=int,        ◁───
                        help='Numbers')         Each value must be parsable
                                                as an integer value, or the
    return parser.parse_args()                  program will error out.


# --------------------------------------------------
def main():
    """main"""                       Since we defined that there are
                                     exactly two values for numbers, we
    args = get_args()                can copy them into two variables.
    n1, n2 = args.numbers     ◁──┘
    print(f'{n1} + {n2} = {n1 + n2}')  ◁───  Because these are actual int values, the
                                             result of + will be numeric addition and
                                             not string concatenation.
# --------------------------------------------------
if __name__ == '__main__':
    main()
```

The help indicates we want two numbers:

```
$ ./nargs2.py
usage: nargs2.py [-h] int int
nargs2.py: error: the following arguments are required: int
```

When we provide two good integer values, we get their sum:

```
$ ./nargs2.py 3 5
3 + 5 = 8
```

Notice that argparse converts the n1 and n2 values to actual integer values. If you change the type=int to type=str, you'll see that the program will print 35 instead of 8 because the + operator in Python both adds numbers and concatenates strings!

```
>>> 3 + 5
8
>>> '3' + '5'
'35'
```

A.4.5 *One or more of the same positional arguments*

You could expand your two-number adding program into one that sums as many numbers as you provide. When you want *one or more* of some argument, you can use nargs='+':

```
#!/usr/bin/env python3
"""nargs=+"""

import argparse


# --------------------------------------------------
def get_args():
    """get args"""

    parser = argparse.ArgumentParser(
        description='nargs=+',
        formatter_class=argparse.ArgumentDefaultsHelpFormatter)

    parser.add_argument('numbers',
                        metavar='int',
                        nargs='+',
                        type=int,
                        help='Numbers')

    return parser.parse_args()
```

> The + will make nargs accept one or more values.

> The int means that all the values must be integer values.

```
# --------------------------------------------------
def main():
    """main"""
```

```
args = get_args()
numbers = args.numbers    ◁──┐
```
numbers will be a list with at least one element.

```
print('{} = {}'.format(' + '.join(map(str, numbers)), sum(numbers)))    ◁──┐
```
Don't worry if you don't understand this line. You will by the end of the book.

```
# --------------------------------------------------
if __name__ == '__main__':
    main()
```

Note that this will mean `args.numbers` is always a `list`. Even if the user provides just one argument, `args.numbers` will be a `list` containing that one value:

```
$ ./nargs+.py 5
5 = 5
$ ./nargs+.py 1 2 3 4
1 + 2 + 3 + 4 = 10
```

You can also use `nargs='*'` to indicate *zero or more* of an argument, and `nargs='?'` means *zero or one* of the argument.

A.4.6   *File arguments*

So far you've seen how you can specify that an argument should be of a `type` like `str` (which is the default), `int`, or `float`. There are also many exercises that require a file as input, and for that you can use the `type` of `argparse.FileType('r')` to indicate that the argument must be a *file* that is *readable* (the `'r'` part).

If, additionally, you want to require that the file be *text* (as opposed to a *binary* file), you would add a `'t'`. These options will make more sense after you've read chapter 5.

Here is an implementation in Python of the command `cat -n`, where `cat` will *concatenate* a readable text file, and the `-n` says to *number* the lines of output:

```
#!/usr/bin/env python3
"""Python version of `cat -n`"""

import argparse


# --------------------------------------------------
def get_args():
    """Get command-line arguments"""

    parser = argparse.ArgumentParser(
        description='Python version of `cat -n`',
        formatter_class=argparse.ArgumentDefaultsHelpFormatter)

    parser.add_argument('file',
                        metavar='FILE',
                        type=argparse.FileType('rt'),    ◁──┐
                        help='Input file')

    return parser.parse_args()
```
The argument will be rejected if it does not name a valid, readable text file.

```
# --------------------------------------------------
def main():
    """Make a jazz noise here"""

    args = get_args()

    for i, line in enumerate(args.file, start=1):
        print(f'{i:6}  {line}', end='')
```

The value of args.file is an open file handle that we can directly read. Again, don't worry if you don't understand this code. We'll talk all about file handles in the chapters.

```
# --------------------------------------------------
if __name__ == '__main__':
    main()
```

When we define an argument as type=int, we get back an actual int value. Here, we define the file argument as a FileType, so we receive an *open file handle*. If we had defined the file argument as a string, we would have to manually check if it were a file and then use open() to get a file handle:

```
#!/usr/bin/env python3
"""Python version of `cat -n`, manually checking file argument"""

import argparse
import os


# --------------------------------------------------
def get_args():
    """Get command-line arguments"""

    parser = argparse.ArgumentParser(
        description='Python version of `cat -n`',
        formatter_class=argparse.ArgumentDefaultsHelpFormatter)

    parser.add_argument('file', metavar='str', type=str, help='Input file')

    args = parser.parse_args()

    if not os.path.isfile(args.file):
        parser.error(f'"{args.file}" is not a file')

    args.file = open(args.file)

    return args
```

Intercept the arguments.

Check if the file argument is *not* a file.

Print an error message and exit the program with a non-zero value.

Replace the file with an open file handle.

```
# --------------------------------------------------
def main():
    """Make a jazz noise here"""

    args = get_args()

    for i, line in enumerate(args.file, start=1):
        print(f'{i:6}  {line}', end='')
```

```
# ----------------------------------------------------
if __name__ == '__main__':
    main()
```

With the `FileType` definition, you don't have to write any of this code.

You can also use `argparse.FileType('w')` to indicate that you want the name of a file that can be opened for *writing* (the `'w'`). You can pass additional arguments specifying how to open the file, like the encoding. See the documentation for more information.

A.4.7   *Manually checking arguments*

It's also possible to manually validate arguments before we `return` from `get_args()`. For instance, we can define that `--int` should be an `int`, but how can we require that it must be between 1 and 10?

One fairly simple way to do this is to manually check the value. If there is a problem, you can use the `parser.error()` function to halt execution of the program, print an error message along with the short usage statement, and then exit with an error value:

```
#!/usr/bin/env python3
"""Manually check an argument"""

import argparse


# ----------------------------------------------------
def get_args():
    """Get command-line arguments"""

    parser = argparse.ArgumentParser(
        description='Manually check an argument',
        formatter_class=argparse.ArgumentDefaultsHelpFormatter)

    parser.add_argument('-v',
                        '--val',
                        help='Integer value between 1 and 10',
                        metavar='int',
                        type=int,
                        default=5)

    args = parser.parse_args()
    if not 1 <= args.val <= 10:
        parser.error(f'--val "{args.val}" must be between 1 and 10')

    return args


# ----------------------------------------------------
def main():
    """Make a jazz noise here"""
```

Parse the arguments.

Check if the args.int value is *not* between 1 and 10.

If we get here, everything was OK, and the program will continue as normal.

Call parser.error() with an error message. The error message and the brief usage statement will be shown to the user, and the program will immediately exit with a non-zero value to indicate an error.

```
    args = get_args()
    print(f'val = "{args.val}"')


# --------------------------------------------------
if __name__ == '__main__':
    main()
```

If we provide a good `--val`, all is well:

```
$ ./manual.py -v 7
val = "7"
```

If we run this program with a value like `20`, we get an error message:

```
$ ./manual.py -v 20
usage: manual.py [-h] [-v int]
manual.py: error: --val "20" must be between 1 and 10
```

It's not possible to tell here, but the `parser.error()` also caused the program to exit with a non-zero status. In the command-line world, an exit status of `0` indicates "zero errors," so anything not `0` is considered an error. You may not realize yet just how wonderful that is, but trust me. It is.

A.4.8 Automatic help

When you define a program's parameters using `argparse`, the `-h` and `--help` flags will be reserved for generating help documentation. You do not need to add these, nor are you allowed to use these flags for other purposes.

I think of this documentation as being like a door into your program. Doors are how we get into buildings and cars and such. Have you ever come across a door that you can't figure out how to open? Or one that requires a "PUSH" sign when clearly the handle is designed to "pull"? The book *The Design of Everyday Things* by Don Norman (Basic Books, 2013) uses the term *affordances* to describe the interfaces that objects present to us that do or do not inherently describe how we should use them.

The usage statement of your program is like the handle of the door. It should let users know exactly how to use it. When I encounter a program I've never used, I either run it with no arguments or with `-h` or `--help`. I *expect* to see some sort of usage statement. The only alternative would be to open the source code itself and study how to make the program run and how I can alter it, and this is a truly unacceptable way to write and distribute software!

When you start creating a new program with `new.py foo.py`, this is the help that will be generated:

```
$ ./foo.py -h
usage: foo.py [-h] [-a str] [-i int] [-f FILE] [-o] str

Rock the Casbah

positional arguments:
  str                   A positional argument

optional arguments:
  -h, --help            show this help message and exit
  -a str, --arg str     A named string argument (default: )
  -i int, --int int     A named integer argument (default: 0)
  -f FILE, --file FILE  A readable file (default: None)
  -o, --on              A boolean flag (default: False)
```

Without writing a single line of code, you have

- An executable Python program
- A variety of command-line arguments
- A standard and useful help message

This is the "handle" to your program, and you don't have to write a single line of code to get it!

Summary

- Positional parameters typically are required parameters. If you have two or more positional parameters representing different ideas, it would be better to make them named options.
- Optional parameters can be named, like `--file fox.txt` where `fox.txt` is the value for the `--file` option. It is recommended that you always define a default value for options.
- `argparse` can enforce many argument types, including numbers like `int` and `float`, or even files.
- Flags like `--help` do not have an associated value. They are (usually) considered `True` if present and `False` if not.
- The `-h` and `--help` flags are reserved for use by `argparse`. If you use `argparse`, your program will automatically respond to these flags with a usage statement.

index

Symbols

$ character 250, 361
: (colon) 113
" (single quotes) 42, 157
"" (double quotes) 42, 157
[] (square brackets) 43, 59, 78,
    80, 89, 125, 293, 385
[<>] character class 285
{} (curly brackets) 48, 52, 78–79,
    113, 124–125, 293, 339
* (asterisk) character 108, 363
* (multiplication operator) 358
. (period) character 235, 284,
    353, 361
^ (caret) character 254, 285,
    297, 346
- (hyphen character) 40
+ operator 176
+= sign 88–89, 203
= (equal sign) 41, 46, 57
>>> prompt 41, 87
| (pipe operator) 108, 356

A

abuse.py (Dial-a-Curse
    program) 150–164
  constructing insults
      162–163
  defining adjectives and
      nouns 155–156
  defining arguments 159
  exit values 160–161
  final program 157–159
  formatting output 156–157
  importing and seeding ran-
      dom module 154–155
  parser.error() function 160
  random.seed() function 161
  range() function 162
  STDERR (standard
      error) 160–161
  taking random samples and
      choices 156
  throwaway variables 162
  validating arguments 153–154
  writing program 151–157
add1() function 145, 189–190
affordances 403
AI (artificial intelligence) 351
algorithm design 207–224
  counting 209–210
  creating ordinal value 211–212
  final program 216–217
  generating verses 221–222
  making verses 213–215,
      218–221
  printing verses 215, 222
  verse() function 215
  writing program 208–215
all() function 358, 360, 365
alpha characters 169
anonymous function 144, 241
any() function 358, 360
append() function 61
apples.py (Apples and Bananas
    program) 128–149
  altering strings 130–132
    str.replace() method 131
    str.translate() method
        131–132
  defining parameters 134–135
  final program 133–134
  refactoring with tests 149
  replacing vowels 135–149
    iterating through every
        character 135–136
    list comprehensions
        140–142
    list comprehensions with
        functions 142–144
    map() function 144–147
    map() function with named
        functions 147
    regular expressions 148–149
    str.replace() method 136
    str.translate() method
        137–139
argparse module 385–404
  creating flag option 391–392
  creating optional file
      parameter 390–391
  creating optional numeric
      parameter 390
  creating optional string
      parameter 390
  creating parser 389
  creating positional
      parameter 389
  returning from get_args()
      function 392
  types of arguments 386–387
  use cases 392–404
    automatic help 403–404
    file arguments 400–402
    manually checking
        arguments 402–403

argparse module *(continued)*
    one or more of the same
      positional arguments
      399–400
    restricting values using
      choices option
      396–398
    single positional
      argument 393–394
    two different positional
      arguments 394–396
    two of the same positional
      arguments 398–399
    using template.py to start
      programs 387–388
argparse.ArgumentParser()
    function 389
arguments
    abuse.py 153–154, 159
    crowsnest.py 39–40, 50–51
    file 400–402
    gashlycrumb.py 123–124
    hello.py 24–25
    howler.py 102
    manually checking
      402–403
    picnic.py 73
    positional
      one or more of the
        same 399–400
      single 393–394
      two different 394–396
      two of the same 398–399
    tictactoe.py 360–363
    types of 386–387
    wc.py 115
artificial intelligence (AI) 351
ASCII values 295–310
    breaking text 304
    cleaning words 297–298
    encoding words 303
    final program 304–305
    functools.reduce()
      function 302–303
    ordinal character values and
      ranges 298–300
    sorting 308–309
    summing and reducing
      300–301
    testing 309
    word2num() function
      306–307
    writing program 296–304
assert statements 60, 83
asterisk (*) character 108, 363

B

binary decisions 191, 198
Black tool 28–29
Boolean values 202
bottles.py (Bottles of Beer
    program) 178–194
    counting down 180–181, 189
    final program 187–188
    iterating through verses
      191–193
    other solutions 194
    test-driven development
      189–190
    verse() function 190–191
      using 186–187
      writing 181–182
      writing tests for 182–186
    writing program 179–187
breaking text 270–271, 304

C

capture groups 232–236
caret (^) character 254, 285,
    297, 346
chmod (change mode)
    command 20
choices option 132, 134, 360,
    386, 396–398
choose() function 197–199,
    202, 204
chr() function 296, 298
class, defined 42
clean() function 337–338, 348
cleaning text 297–298, 337–339,
    346–347
colon (:) 113
comma-separated values files.
    See CSV (comma-separated
    values) files
comment lines 16
    adding shebang line 18–19
    regular expressions 242–243
conditional branching 47–48,
    70–71
consonants pattern 233
copy (cp) command 33
counting down 180–181, 189
cp (copy) command 33
crowsnest.py (Crow's Nest
    program) 35–54
    classifying first character of
      words 51–52
    concatenating strings 41–42

conditional branching 47–48
defining arguments 39–40,
    50–51
final program 49–50
getting individual characters
    of strings 43–44
main() function 51
printing results 52
REPL (Read-Evaluate-Print-
    Loop) 44
starting with new.py 37–38
string comparisons 45–47
string formatting 48
string methods 44–45
test-driven development
    52–53
variable types 42
writing and testing little by
    little 38–39
writing program 49
crowsnest.py file 38
CSV (comma-separated values)
    files 311–330
    final program 323–325
    formatting output 322
    formatting table 328–330
    handling bad data 322–323
    parsing
      with csv module 318–319
      with pandas.read_csv()
        function 327–328
    potential runtime errors
      326–327
    reading 313–314, 325–326
      creating function to
        read 320–321
      manually 315–318
    selecting exercises 321–322
    writing program 312–323
csv module 312, 315, 318–319
csv.DictReader() function
    319–320, 323, 325
csvkit module 313
curly brackets ({}) 48, 52, 78–79,
    113, 124–125, 293, 339

D

declarative programming 149
def (defines) 28, 181
delimited text file 312
deterministic approach 169
Dial-a-Curse program. *See*
    abuse.py (Dial-a-Curse
    program)

dict() function 78–79, 124
dict.get() method 80, 84, 87, 126, 327
dictionaries 77–82
  accessing values 80
  creating 78–79
  defining parameters 85
  dictionary comprehensions 125
  looking up items in 124–126
  methods 81–82
  processing items in series 86–90
    turning for loop into list comprehension 89–90
    using for loop to build new list 89
    using for loop to build new string 88
    using for loop to print() each character 86–88
    using str.translate() function 90
  using for encoding 85
dict.items() method 81, 318
dict.keys() method 81
dict.pop() function 82
dict.values() method 81
domain-specific language (DSL) 148
double quotes ("") 42, 157
double-under methods 60
DSL (domain-specific language) 148
dynamically typed language 48

E

enumerate() function 352, 363–364
env command 18–19
equal sign (=) 46, 57
error checking 287–288
  hello.py 28–29
executability, making programs executable 20
exit values 160–161
extend() function 62

F

fh (file handle) 94–95
fh.read() method 94–95, 103, 111

fh.readline() function 315–316
fh.seek(0) method 95
fh.write() method 223
file arguments 400–402
file handle (fh) 94–95
file parameter (argparse) 390–391
files
  choosing output file handle 104
  printing output 104
  reading 93–97
  reading input from file or command line 103–104
  reading using for loops 115–117
  writing 97–99
FileType 401–402
filter() function 45, 147, 227, 240–241, 339–340, 348
find_brackets() function 292–293
find_winner() function 356–357, 359
flag option 31, 391–392
flags 387
Flake8 program 28
float type 82, 167
floating-point values 237
foo() function 143
foo.py program 391
for loops
  building new lists with 89
  building new strings with 88
  printing each character with 86–88
  reading files using 115–117
  turning into list comprehensions 89–90
format_board() function 356
formatting
  CSV output 322
  game board 363–364
  list items 73–74
  output 156–157
  regular expressions 242–243
  strings 48, 112–114
  text tables 328–330
friar.py (Kentucky Friar program) 248–267
  final program 262–263
  fry() function
    using 261–262
    writing manually 264–265

writing with regular expressions 256–261, 266
  negated shorthand classes 254–255
  re.split() with captured regex 255–256
  shorthand classes 252
  splitting text 251
  writing program 250–262
fry() function
  using 261–262
  writing manually 264–265
  writing with regular expressions 256–261, 266
f-strings 40, 49, 52, 113, 159
functions
  adding type hints to definition 376
  using 186–187
  writing 181–182
  writing tests for 182–186
functools module 302
functools.reduce() function 302–303

G

gashlycrumb.py (Gashlycrumb Tinies program) 118–127
  dictionary comprehensions 125
  dictionary lookups 126
  final program 122–123
  handling arguments 123–124
  reading input file 124–125
  writing program 119–122
gematria.py (Gematria program) 295–310
  breaking text 304
  cleaning words 297–298
  encoding words 303
  final program 304–305
  functools.reduce() function 302–303
  ordinal character values and ranges 298–300
  sorting 308–309
  summing and reducing 300–301
  testing 309
  word2num() function 306–307
  writing program 296–304

get_args() function 39, 49–50, 57, 71, 84–85, 100, 102, 104, 119, 121, 123, 134–135, 154, 157, 167–168, 179, 189, 200, 209, 263, 277, 305, 321, 325, 346, 355, 359, 388–389, 402
  adding 27–29
  defining arguments with 50–51
  returning from 392
getoutput() function 40
global changes 198
guard statement 240

H

hashable values 161
hello.py (Hello, World! program) 15–16
  adding get_args() function 27–29
  adding help messages 22–24
  adding main() function 26–27
  adding parameters 22–24
  comment lines 16
  error checking 28–29
  making argument optional 24–25
  making program executable 20
  $PATH variable 20–22
  shebang line 18–19
  style checking 28–29
  testing 17–18, 26, 29–30
help messages
  adding 22–24
higher-order function. *See* HOF (higher-order function)
HOF (higher-order function) 147, 240, 302
$HOME variable 18, 21
howler.py (Howler program) 92
  defining arguments 102
  files
    choosing output file handle 104
    printing output 104
    reading 93–97
    reading input from file or command line 103–104
    writing 97–99
  final program 101–102
  low-memory version 104–106
  writing program 99–101
hyphen character (-) 40

I

if expressions 47, 52, 142, 202
if/elif/else statements, conditional branching with 70–71
if/else statements 47, 70
immutable strings 130, 165
immutable values 275
imperative methods 225
import statements 154
import sys command 101
in-dels (insertion-deletions) 177
index method 64
indexing 63
indexing lists 63–64
input handles 94
input() function 127, 288
input-output (io) module 105
int type 82, 167
int values 153, 166
int() function 322, 326–327
integer values 153, 365
integration tests 186, 383
io (input-output) module 105
io.StringIO() function 105–106, 320
IPython 41, 59, 78
iterator object 68
itictactoe.py (Interactive Tic-Tac-Toe program) 367–382
  final program 377–381
  state 381
  tuples 369–372
  type hints 372–373
    adding to function definitions 376
    type verification with Mypy 373–375
  updating immutable structures 375–376
  version using TypedDict 379–381
  writing program 368–376

J

joining
  lists 70
  strings 41
jump.py (Jump the Five program) 76–91
  dictionaries 77–82
    accessing values 80
    creating 78–79
    defining parameters 85
    methods 81–82
    processing items in series 86–90
    using for encoding 85
  final program 84–85
  writing program 82–84
Jupyter Notebook 41, 59, 78

K

Kentucky Friar program. *See* friar.py (Kentucky Friar program)

L

l33t() function 342–343, 345, 347, 349
lambda keyword 144, 241
lazy functions 140, 180, 317
len() function 45, 60, 63, 72, 81, 112, 116
lines of code (LOC) 189
line.split() method 114, 116
linters 28
list comprehensions
  replacing vowels 140–142
  turning for loops into 89–90
  with functions 142–144
list context 136
list variable 55
list() function 59, 68, 140, 171, 180, 220, 245, 319, 363
list.append() function 60, 140, 142, 202–203, 220
list.extend() method 62, 217, 220
list.index() method 64
list.insert() method 62
list.pop() method 65, 289
list.remove() method 66
list.reverse() method 67, 69, 214, 274
lists 59–70
  adding many elements to 61–63
  adding one element to 60–61
  building with for loops 89
  finding elements in 64–65
  formatting items 73–74
  indexing 63–64
  iterating 111
  joining 70
  mutability of 69–70

lists *(continued)*
  mutating 176–177
  printing items 74
  removing elements from 65–67
  reversing 67–69
  slicing 64
  sorting items 67–69, 73
list.sort() method 67–69, 274, 308
LOC (lines of code) 189

M

MAD (mutually assured destruction) doctrine 351
mad.py (Mad Libs program) 281–294
  final program 289–290
  finding placeholders 284–287
  finding placeholders without regular expressions 291–293
  getting values 288–289
  halting and printing errors 287–288
  limiting replacements 291
  substituting text 289
  writing program 282–289
main namespace 50
main() function 26–27, 32, 49–51, 72, 85, 104, 120, 136, 143, 158, 160, 168, 181–182, 189, 244, 270, 293, 297, 328
make directory (mkdir) command 21
make program 29
make test command 29, 36, 49, 56, 119, 186
Makefile 29
map() function 45, 144, 146, 179, 186–188, 192, 196, 199, 222, 262, 265, 276, 296, 301, 306, 318, 337, 340, 347, 365
  ransom.py 204
  replacing vowels 144–147
  with named functions 147
MapReduce 205
match.groups() function 234, 255
Mispar hechrechi 295
mkdir (make directory) command 21

multiplication operator (*) 358
mutable elements 221
mutating
  game board 360–363
  lists 69–70, 176–177
  strings 165–177
    calculating number of mutations 168–169
    final program 173–174
    mutation space 169
    selecting characters to mutate 169–172
    writing program 167–173
  text 197–198
  updating immutable structures 375–376
--mutations option 166–167
--mutations parameter 174–175
mutually assured destruction (MAD) doctrine 351
Mypy 373–375

N

--name option 24–25, 31
name parameter 23
--name value 385
named options 386
nargs option 71, 398
natural language processing (NLP) 304
negative index numbers 43
new_char() function 142–144, 147
newline character 98–99
new.py file 30, 38, 56
new.py, starting new program with 30–33, 37–38
NLP (natural language processing) 304
non-capturing groups 272
non-deterministic selection 170
non-greedy regex 285
no-op (no operation) 273
numeric encoding of text 295–310
  breaking text 304
  cleaning words 297–298
  encoding words 303
  final program 304–305
  functools.reduce 302–303
  ordinal character values and ranges 298–300

sorting 308–309
summing and reducing 300–301
testing 309
word2num() function 306–307
writing program 296–304
numeric parameter (argparse) 390

O

open file handles 110, 115, 392
open() method 94, 104–105, 135, 215, 401
operating system (os) module 93
operator.mul function 302
optional arguments 23, 25
optional parameters 25
ord() function 138, 212, 296, 298–299, 301, 307
OrderedDict 319
ordinal value 138
os (operating system) module 93
os.path.basename() method 94
os.path.dirname() method 93
os.path.isfile() function 98, 103, 110, 168
output handles 94
overwritten files 98

P

pandas.read_csv() function 327–328
parallel operations 205
parameters
  apples.py 134–135
  argparse
    file 390–391
    numeric 390
    positional 389
    string 390
  jump.py 85
parser.add_argument() function 50
parser.error() function 151, 154, 157–158, 160, 167, 179, 187, 189, 209, 216, 283, 355, 402–403
pass statement 182

password.py (Secure Password
    Generator program)
    331–350
  cleaning text 337–339,
    346–347
  creating unique list of
    words 335–337
  filtering words 340–341
  final program 343–346
  l33t() function 342, 347
  processing files 347–348
  ransom() function 347
  sampling and creating
    passwords 341–342,
    348–349
  title-casing words 341
  using sets 339
  writing program 334–343
$PATH variable 20–22
PCRE (Perl-Compatible Regular
    Expressions) 252
period (.) character 232, 235,
    284, 353, 361
Perl-Compatible Regular Expres-
    sions (PCRE) 252
picnic.py (Picnic List
    program) 55–75
  defining arguments 73
  final program 71–72
  lists 59–70
    adding many elements
      to 61–63
    adding one element to
      60–61
    conditional branching with
      if/elif/else statements
      70–71
    finding elements in 64–65
    formatting items 73–74
    indexing 63–64
    joining 70
    mutability of 69–70
    printing items 74
    removing elements from
      65–67
    slicing 64
    sorting items 67–69, 73
  starting new program
    56–58
  writing program 58–59
pip module 28
pipe operator (|) 108, 356
placeholders
  finding with regular
    expressions 284–287

finding without regular
    expressions 291–293
positional arguments 23, 25, 32,
    39, 50, 386
  one or more of the same
    399–400
  single 393–394
  two different 394–396
  two of the same 398–399
positional parameters 25, 389
pprint module 124
pprint() function 124–125
pprint.pprint() function 138
print() function 42, 59, 74, 84,
    86, 88, 98, 116, 121, 124,
    140, 157, 159, 210, 222, 278,
    287
printf() function 113
printing
  characters with for loops
    86–88
  errors 287–288
  game board 356
  list items 74
  output 52, 104, 215, 222
  REPL (Read-Evaluate-Print-
    Loop) 44
product() function 302
pseudo-random events 150
PyCharm 15, 29
python3 18–19, 243

R

random events
  capitalizing text 195
    comparing methods
      204–205
    creating new strings
      198–199
    final program 199–200
    flipping coin 198
    iterating through elements
      in sequence 200–202
    list.append() function
      202–203
    map() function 204
    mutating text 197–198
    using list comprehensions
      203
    using strings instead of
      lists 203
    writing function to choose
      letter 202
    writing program 197–199

mutating strings 165–177
  calculating number of
    mutations 168–169
  final program 173–174
  mutation space 169
  selecting characters to
    mutate 169–172
  using lists instead of
    strings 176–177
  writing program 167–173
reordering middles of
    words 268–280
  breaking text into lines and
    words 270–271
  capturing, non-capturing,
    and optional
    groups 271–272
  compiling regexes 272
  final program 276–277
  processing text 277–279
  scrambling all words 275
  scrambling words 273–275,
    279–280
  writing program 269–275
word generation 150–164
  constructing insults 162–163
  defining adjectives and
    nouns 155–156
  defining arguments 159
  exit values 160–161
  final program 157–159
  formatting output 156–157
  importing and seeding ran-
    dom module 154–155
  parser.error() function 160
  random.seed() function 161
  range() function 162
  STDERR (standard
    error) 160–161
  taking random samples and
    choices 156
  throwaway variables 162
  validating arguments
    153–154
  writing program 151–157
random module 161, 166, 313,
    343, 352
random seeds 198
random.choice() function 153,
    156–157, 163, 170, 174–175,
    335
random.choices() function 156
random.getstate() function 273
random.randint() function 314,
    321, 323

random.random() function 170
random.sample() function
    156–157, 159, 163, 171, 174,
    176, 321, 323, 329, 341–342
random.seed() function 154,
    156–158, 161, 168, 175, 197,
    200, 268, 273, 276, 313, 321,
    335, 342, 345
random.shuffle() function 269,
    273–275
range() function 140, 146, 153,
    156–157, 159, 162, 180,
    186–187, 193, 208–209, 211,
    349
ransom() function 335, 342,
    345–347
ransom.py (Ransom Note
    program) 195
    comparing methods 204–205
    creating new strings 198–199
    final program 199–200
    flipping coin 198
    iterating through elements in
        sequence 200–202
    list.append() function 202–203
    map() function 204
    mutating text 197–198
    using list
        comprehensions 203
    using strings instead of
        lists 203
    writing function to choose
        letter 202
    writing program 197–199
Read the Fine Manual
    (RTFM) 44
read() method 94, 96, 135
read_csv() function 320–321,
    325, 327, 329
re.compile() function 264, 272
reduce() function 296, 302–303
refactoring 149
re.findall() function 282, 287,
    297
regular expressions 148–149
    captured 255–256
    compiling 272
    friar.py 248–267
        final program 262–263
        fry() function 256–262,
            264–266
        negated shorthand
            classes 254–255
        re.split() with captured
            regex 255–256

shorthand classes 252
splitting text 251
writing program 250–262
mad.py 281–294
    final program 289–290
    finding placeholders
        284–287
    finding placeholders with-
        out regular
        expressions 291–293
    getting values 288–289
    halting and printing
        errors 287–288
    substituting text 289
    substituting with regular
        expressions 291
    writing program 282–289
rhymer.py 225–247
    commenting 242–243
    creating output 238
    creating rhyming
        strings 244–245
    final program 238–239
    formatting 242–243
    stemmer() function 228–
        229, 240–241, 243, 245
    truthiness 236–237
    using 229–232
    using capture groups 232–
        236
    writing rhymer.py 227–238
re.Match object 260
re.match() function 230, 232,
    234, 239, 250–251, 266, 272,
    327
re.Match.groups() method 232
Repl.it 20, 29
requirements.txt file 313
re.search() function 230, 232,
    250, 252, 260, 266, 272
re.split() function 250, 255–256,
    263–264, 270
re.sub() function 148, 282, 291,
    296, 298, 305, 307, 346
return statement 182
reversed() function 68, 180,
    214, 220
reversing lists 67–69
rhymer.py (Rhymer
    program) 225–247
    commenting 242–243
    creating output 238
    creating rhyming strings
        244–245
    final program 238–239

formatting 242–243
stemmer() function 240–241
    rhymer.py 228–229
    using outside rhymer.py 243
    writing without regular
        expressions 245
truthiness 236–237
using capture groups 232–236
using regular
    expressions 229–232
writing program 227–238
round() function 168
round-tripping 91
rstrip() method 135
RTFM (Read the Fine
    Manual) 44

S

scramble() function 273, 275,
    277–278
scrambler.py (Scrambler
    program) 268–280
    breaking text into lines and
        words 270–271
    capturing, non-capturing, and
        optional groups 271–272
    compiling regexes 272
    final program 276–277
    processing text 277–279
    scrambling all words 275
    scrambling words 273–275,
        279–280
    writing program 269–275
secure password
    generation 331–350
    cleaning text 337–339,
        346–347
    creating unique list of
        words 335–337
    filtering words 340–341
    final program 343–346
    l33t() function 342, 347
    processing files 347–348
    ransom() function 347
    sampling and creating
        passwords 341–342,
        348–349
    title-casing words 341
    using sets 339
    writing program 334–343
Secure Password Generator pro-
    gram. *See* password.py
    (Secure Password Genera-
    tor program)

sep argument 86
set() function 339
set.add() function 339
set.intersection() function 339
sets 339
set.sort() function 349
shebang (#!) line 18–19
shorthand classes 252, 254–255
shuffled value 274
single quotes (") 42, 157
slice notation 43
slices 173
slicing lists 64
SNP (single nucleotide polymorphisms) 177
SNV (single nucleotide variations) 177
sorted() function 68–69, 174, 245, 345, 349
sorting
    list items 67–69, 73
    strings 308–309
spaCy library 332
square brackets ([]) 43, 59, 78, 80, 89, 125, 293, 385
state 351–366, 381
    altering board 355
    determining winner 356–357, 364–365
    final program 357–365
    mutating board 360–363
    printing board 356
    validating arguments 360–363
    validating user input 355
    writing tictactoe.py 353–357
static typing 48
STDERR (standard error) 160–161, 287, 290, 293
STDIN (standard in) 110
STDOUT (standard out) 97, 101, 108, 110, 130, 157, 160, 208, 246, 290
    choosing output file handle 104
    writing files 97–99
stemmer() function 228–229, 236, 238, 244
    rhymer.py 228–229, 240–241
    using outside rhymer.py 243
    writing without regular expressions 245
step value 181
stop value 43, 180, 292

str class 42, 44–45, 60, 63, 85, 90, 96, 134, 172, 183, 197, 303, 320, 394
str.casefold() function 308
str.endswith() function 259
str.format() method 48, 52, 72, 112–113, 157, 363
string module 169
string parameter (argparse) 390
string slices 173
string.ascii_letters 169
string.ascii_lowercase 241
string.punctuation 169, 335
strings
    altering 130–132
        str.replace() method 131
        str.translate() method 131–132
    building with for loops 88
    comparisons of 45–47
    concatenating 41–42
    creating new 198–199
    formatting 48, 112–114
    getting individual characters of strings 43–44
    methods for 44–45
    mutating 172–173, 175–176
    using instead of lists 203
str.isupper() function 45
str.join() method 70, 89, 136, 147, 157, 163, 192, 210, 215, 222, 230, 278, 303, 349
str.lower() method 49
str.maketrans() function 132, 137
str.replace() method 84, 90–91, 131, 171, 175
    altering strings 131
    replacing vowels 136
str.rstrip() method 97, 103, 124, 133, 315–316
str.split() method 112, 155, 157, 162, 251, 270, 316, 348
str.splitlines() function 261, 263, 270, 276
str.splitlines() method 251, 262
str.strip() function 356
str.title() method 334
str.translate() function 90–91, 139, 345, 347
str.translate() method 90
    altering strings 131–132
    replacing vowels 137–139
str.upper() function 44, 49, 97

sum() function 296, 300, 302, 307
sys.exit() function 160, 282, 288, 329
sys.stderr 287
sys.stdout file 101–102, 208

T

tab character 323
tabulate module 312–313, 320, 323, 330
tabulate() function 322, 325
TDD (test-driven development) 53, 182
telephone.py (Telephone program) 165–177
    calculating number of mutations 168–169
    final program 173–174
    mutating strings 172–173, 175–176
    mutation space 169
    selecting characters to mutate 169–172
    non-deterministic selection 170
    randomly sampling characters 170–172
    using lists instead of strings 176–177
    writing program 167–173
template.py, starting new programs with 387–388
test-driven development 52–53, 189–190
testing
    apples.py 149
    gematria.py 309
    hello.py 17–18, 26, 29–30
    writing and testing little by little 38–39
    writing tests for functions 182–186
test.py 17–18, 30
TextIOWrapper class 96
Tic-Tac-Toe program. See itictac-toe.py (Interactive Tic-Tac-Toe program)
tictactoe.py (Tic-Tac-Toe program) 351–366
    altering board 355
    determining winner 356–357, 364–365
    final program 357–365

tictactoe.py (Tic-Tac-Toe program) *(continued)*
  formatting board 363–364
  mutating board 360–363
  printing board 356
  validating arguments 360–363
  validating user input 355
  writing program 353–357
TIMTOWTDI (There Is More Than One Way To Do It) 135
title-casing 341
truthiness 236–237
tuples 369–372
twelve_days.py (Twelve Days of Christmas program) 207–224
  counting 209–210
  creating ordinal value 211–212
  final program 216–217
  generating verses 221–222
  making verses 213–215, 218–221
  printing verses 215, 222
  verse() function 215
  writing program 208–215
two equal signs (==) 46
type hints 372–373
  adding to function definitions 376
  type verification with Mypy 373–375
type() function 42, 45, 60, 78, 80, 97
TypedDict 379–381

U

unbalanced brackets 285
unit tests 183, 186, 383
unit.py file 356
usage statement 23
user input validation 355

V

variables
  $PATH variable 20–22
  throwaway 162
  types of 42
verbose output 17
verse() function 187–189, 193, 210–211, 217, 221
  twelve_days.py 215
  using 186–187
  writing 181–182
  writing tests for 182–186
VS Code 15, 29

W

wc.py (Word Count program) 107–117
  defining arguments 115
  defining file inputs 110
  final program 114–115
  formatting results 112–114
  iterating lists 111
  reading files using for loops 115–117
  what's being counted 111–112
  writing program 109–114
which command 19–20
wildcard 108
wod.py (Workout of the Day program) 311–330
  final program 323–325
  formatting text table output 322, 328–330
  handling bad data 322–323
  parsing delimited text files
    with csv module 318–319
    with pandas.read_csv() function 327–328
  potential runtime errors 326–327
  reading delimited text files 313–314, 325–326
    creating function to read 320–321
    manually 315–318

  selecting exercises 321–322
  writing program 312–323
wod.read_csv() function 329
Word Count program. *See* wc.py (Word Count program)
word variable 41–44, 48, 51, 116
word2num() function 303–307, 309
write() method 96, 98
writing programs 15–34, 353–357
  abuse.py 151–157
  bottles.py 179–187
  crowsnest.py 49
  friar.py 250–262
  gashlycrumb.py 119–122
  gematria.py 296–304
  hello.py 15–30
  howler.py 99–101
  itictactoe.py 368–376
  jump.py 82–84
  mad.py 282–289
  password.py 334–343
  picnic.py 58–59, 71
  ransom.py 197–199
  rhymer.py 227–238
  scrambler.py 269–275
  starting new program with new.py 30–33
  starting new program with template.py 33
  telephone.py 167–173
  twelve_days.py 208–215
  wc.py 109–114
  wod.py 312–323
  writing and testing little by little 38–39
wt (writing text) 104

Y

YAPF 28–29

Z

zero-offset indexing 63
zip() function 316–317